Goodbye, Brazil

Goodbye, Brazil

Émigrés from the Land of Soccer and Samba

Maxine L. Margolis

The University of Wisconsin Press

The University of Wisconsin Press
1930 Monroe Street, 3rd Floor
Madison, Wisconsin 53711-2059
uwpress.wisc.edu

3 Henrietta Street
London WC2E 8LU, England
eurospanbookstore.com

Printed in the United States of America

Library of Congress Cataloging-in-Publication Data

Margolis, Maxine L., 1942–
Goodbye, Brazil : émigrés from the land of soccer and samba /
    Maxine L. Margolis.
        p.   cm.
        Includes bibliographical references and index.
        ISBN 978-0-299-29304-8 (pbk.: alk. paper)
        ISBN 978-0-299-29303-1 (e-book)
    1. Brazilians—Foreign countries.   2. Brazilians—Ethnic identity.
        3. Brazil—Emigration and immigration.   I. Title.
F2510.5.M37   2013
305.800981—dc23
2012032684

The art on the book cover, titled *Migration*, is by Chris Roberts-Antieau (www.chrisroberts-antieau.com). It is owned by Maxine L. Margolis and Jerald T. Milanich.

For
Giacomo and Luca
The most wonderful *netinhos* that a *nonna* could ever have

In exile I was able to feel how difficult it was for a Brazilian to live outside Brazil. Our country has so much singularity as to make it extremely difficult to accept and enjoy life among other peoples. . . . One only has to see a gathering of Brazilians among the half million we are exporting as workers to sense the fanaticism with which they cling to their identity as Brazilians and the rejection of any idea of letting themselves stay where they are.

Darcy Ribeiro (2000, 17)

Contents

Tables

Preface and Acknowledgments

In 1964, the famed Brazilian sociologist Fernando Henrique Cardoso was forced to flee Brazil for Chile and, later, France as military authorities, who had led a coup against the duly elected Brazilian government that year, began breathing down his neck. Fernando Henrique, who later became a two-term president of Brazil, was but one of many distinguished academicians, politicians, musicians, and artists exiled from their homeland in the late 1960s and 1970s as a result of military rule.[1]

Over the past three decades, there has been a new kind of exodus from Brazil, albeit one based on economics, not politics. By 1990, some 1.3 million Brazilians had "gone missing" in the nation's federal census and were presumed to be living outside Brazil, and in 2009, more than 3 million Brazilians were living abroad. They were living in 112 countries, and their numbers ranged in population from about 1.3 million in the United States, 200,000 in Paraguay, and a similar number in Japan to 60 in Vietnam and 32 in Ethiopia.

In 2008, Brazilians living in the United States, Europe, and Japan sent some $7.4 billion back home. But, given the size of the Brazilian economy—today the sixth largest in the world—remittances represented just 1 percent of the nation's gross domestic product. Nevertheless, the money remitted to Brazil by citizens living abroad had a big impact on so-called sending communities, towns, and small cities—such as Governador Valadares in the Brazilian state of Minas Gerais—that have many residents living abroad. Half-built houses and new condominiums line their streets, as do stores with American names like Stop & Shop *Mercearia* (market).

This book is about the Brazilian diaspora, the reality that sizable populations of Brazilians live not only in the United States, Paraguay, and Japan but also in Portugal, Spain, Italy, and England, with smaller concentrations in still other countries. This is true even though, prior to the late

1980s, Brazil as a nation had no history or experience with emigration. Why has this exodus occurred? Who are these émigrés, and why do they choose certain destinations? And how do they fare living in foreign lands?

These topics are covered in this book. How did I come to write it? A word about my own background by way of explanation. I have been researching and writing about Brazilian emigration since the late 1980s, when I first encountered Brazilian immigrants living in New York City. I am a native of Manhattan and an incurable New Yorker—despite having lived in Florida and having taught at the University of Florida for more than thirty years. I am also an anthropologist who speaks Portuguese and specializes in Brazilian culture. During periodic visits to the city in the late 1980s—for what I call my "New York fix"—I began noticing that more and more people there were speaking Portuguese. I heard it not only in the midtown areas usually frequented by tourists but also on city subways—a form of transportation that non-English-speaking tourists often avoid.

There has always been a small Brazilian community in New York City composed of people working for Brazilian companies, airlines, banks, and government agencies. Brazilian artists, writers, musicians, students, and tourists also have long been drawn to the city. And, in 1997, the city officially named a block-long stretch of West Forty-Sixth Street between Fifth Avenue and Avenue of the Americas (almost always referred to by natives as "Sixth Avenue") "Little Brazil Street." The street, with its distinct cluster of Brazilian restaurants and travel and remittance agencies, has long catered to Brazilian residents and tourists alike, and since the mid-1980s has been the site of the annual Brazilian Independence Day Street Fair.

While the soft nasal sounds of Brazilian Portuguese have long been heard on Little Brazil Street, it slowly became apparent to me that the location and extent of the Brazilian presence in the city was of a different order than it had been in the past. A chance conversation became the final catalyst that inspired my original research on Brazilian immigrants in New York City and then, more broadly, on Brazilian emigration in general. During a trip to New York, I met a cousin who lives in Boston. Knowing of my interest in Brazil, she mentioned that she was delighted with the Brazilian woman she had hired as a housekeeper. "A Brazilian?" I asked. "Are you certain that she is Brazilian?" Despite my long familiarity with Brazil and Brazilians, I had never heard of Brazilians being employed as domestic servants in the United States. "Yes," she replied, "a lot of my friends employ Brazilian women as maids and nannies." Now, I thought, I must be on to something.

It soon became apparent that, despite the growing presence of Brazilians in New York, Boston, and other U.S. cities, this newest wave of immigrants was being ignored by researchers. Eager to fill this gap, I began field work on Brazilian immigrants in New York City in the late 1980s, and in 1994 my first book on this new ingredient in the city's intricate ethnic stew, *Little Brazil: An Ethnography of Brazilian Immigrants in New York City*, was published. My New York research has been ongoing. Over the past two decades, in the words of my husband, I have been "trolling for Brazilians" in the city's restaurants, shops, and public spaces.

However, my interest in Brazilian emigration has never been limited to the Brazilian community in New York City. I have always tried to generalize about the Brazilian immigrant experience in the United States by visiting Brazilian communities in Boston and Framingham, Massachusetts; Danbury, Connecticut; and Newark, New Jersey; and by talking with immigrants and community leaders there. On trips to visit friends in South Carolina, I was able to interview a few members of the small Brazilian enclave in Goose Creek, and while on vacation in Portsmouth, New Hampshire, I talked to a number of Brazilians employed at the resort where we were staying. From Philadelphia, Washington, Chicago, and Atlanta to Miami and San Francisco—no matter where I traveled in the United States—I always sought out Brazilian restaurants, stores selling Brazilian products, and locally published Brazilian newspapers, and I spoke with Brazilian immigrants I met along the way.

Emigration was also the focus of my field research in Brazil on two occasions. In the early 1990s, I visited Governador Valadares, the aforementioned "immigrant-sending community," and spent time there interviewing residents about friends and relatives who were living in the United States. I also talked with "well-informed informants," the town's mayor and other city officials, as well as travel agents and the owners of remittance agencies. Some of what I learned during that trip is included in this book. Then, in 1997, I spent a semester in Rio de Janeiro on a Fulbright fellowship. There I interviewed a few dozen returned immigrants, some of whom I had known previously when they lived in New York City. My focus in this research was the impact of the immigrant experience on these individuals and their readjustment to life in Brazil. Some of those findings are also included here.

Soon I was no longer alone in my interest in Brazilian immigration to the United States. As this fresh wave of immigrants grew, more and more researchers—academics as well as journalists—began documenting various aspects of this new migration stream. Books have been published on Brazilian immigrants in Massachusetts and California, and edited volumes report on Brazilian communities elsewhere in the United States.[2] With the explosion of research and researchers interested in Brazilian emigration, a seminal conference on the topic, the first National Congress on Brazilian Immigration to the United States, was held in 2005 at the David Rockefeller Center of Latin American Studies at Harvard University (Jouët-Pastré and Braga 2008). More than fifty scholars, community organizers, and immigrant activists gave presentations at the conference, where I gave the keynote address.

What about Brazilian émigrés in other parts of the world? Scholarly interest also has burgeoned in this instance, and journalistic accounts, academic articles, theses, and dissertations now exist on Brazilian communities in Paraguay, Portugal, Spain, Italy, England, the Republic of Ireland, and Australia. And here, too, a gathering in which I took part, the Conference on the Brazilian Diaspora: Immigration in Times of Globalization, was held in Lisbon in 1997. As yet, however, there are few of the sort of lengthy, detailed studies published on Brazilians in these regions that exist for Brazilian émigrés in the United States.

One country that has received much scholarly attention is Japan. A great deal of research has been done on Brazilian immigrants in Japan, the so-called *dekasseguis*—Brazilians of Japanese descent who began immigrating to the land of their ancestors in the early 1990s. Here, too, there are ethnographies that detail the Brazilian experience in Japan; and a gathering that I attended that touched on the topic—the Conference on Latin American Emigration in North America, Europe and Japan—was held at the National Museum of Ethnology in Osaka, Japan, in 2001 (Yamada 2003).

I have read this vast and growing literature on Brazilian immigration to the United States and elsewhere, and this book incorporates information from all these sources, along with my own field research and relevant news reports from both the North American and the Brazilian media.

I am extremely grateful to those whose research and writings have contributed immeasurably to this book. Ana Cristina Braga Martes has long been an inspiration in our mutual devotion to this topic, and I have relied on her research and analysis in many instances here. Rosana Resende, whose PhD committee I chaired, has done exemplary research on Brazilians in Florida, as have Valéria Barbosa de Magalhães, Adriana Capuano de

Oliveira, Manuel Vasquez, and Elias Pedroso. Other scholars of Brazilian immigration to the southern United States include Alan Marcus and Cassandra White on Brazilians in Atlanta, and Annie Gibson on post-Katrina immigration to New Orleans.

For informing my work on Brazilian immigrants in Massachusetts, I owe much to the research of Teresa Sales, Soraya Fleischer, Sylvia Dantas DeBiaggi, Eduardo Siqueira, Peter Brown, Teresa Roberts, and Linsey Lee. I am particularly indebted to Alexandra Barker of the U.S. Census Bureau in Boston, who has shared her expertise on the Brazilian population in the United States with me. Conversations with Heloisa Galvão and Fausto da Rocha have always been fruitful, and I thank Clémence Jouët-Pastré and Leticia Braga for organizing the Harvard conference on Brazilian immigration.

In my original site of field research—the New York metropolitan area—I value the graduate theses of Valerie Strategier and Theli Lopes, as well as Yamil Avivi's work in Newark and Gustavo Hamilton Menezes's research in Danbury. Here I am deeply indebted to Maria Teresa da Costa, the New York Consulate's former liaison to the Brazilian community, as well as to Ambassador José Alfredo Graça Lima, former Brazilian consul general in New York, who invited me in 2007 to accompany him on a visit to an "itinerant consulate" serving the Brazilian immigrant community in Danbury.[3]

On the west coast, Bernadete Beserra's work and that of Gustavo Lins Ribeiro has been very useful, as has Tania Cypriano's marvelous film *Grandma Has a Video Camera*, a wonderful depiction of Brazilian trans-nationalism between San Francisco and São Paulo.

I also salute Weber Soares and Sueli Siqueira for their exemplary research in Governador Valadares. And I thank Sueli again, along with Alan Marcus and Glaucia de Oliveira Assis, for their work on returned migrants to Brazil, and Judith McDonnell for organizing a panel on the topic at the meetings of the Latin American Studies Association in Rio de Janeiro in 2009. I also appreciate Helen Marrow's analysis of Brazilian ethnic and racial identity, and Cileine de Lourenço's discussion of gender issues, both within the context of emigration.

Then, too, for their interest in and research on Brazilian writers and musicians living in the United States, I thank Luciano Tosta, Darien Davis, and Jason Stanyek.

Scholars in Europe have also been active, and I appreciate the research of Lúcia Maria Machado Bógus, Maria Silvia Beozzo Bassanesi, and Adriana

Piscitelli on the Brazilian community in Italy; Igor José de Renó Machado, Angela Torresan, and Beatriz Padilla for their research in Portugal; and Carlos Vianna, who was instrumental in organizing the Lisbon conference. Others whose research contributed to this volume include Leonardo Cavalcanti, on Brazilians in Spain; Angela Torresan, Yara Evans, Graça Brightwell, and Ana Souza, on Brazilians in England; and Olivia Sheringham and Clare Healy, on Brazilians in the Republic of Ireland.

I have also benefited from the work of Elisa Massae Sasaki, Keiko Yamanaka, Angelo Ishi, Daniel Touro Linger, Takeyuki Tsuda, Joshua Hotaka Roth, and my former student Chieko Koyama on the *dekassegui* in Japan.

Further afield, I also appreciate the writings of Fernanda Duarte, Cristina Rocha, and Sandra Lobo, on Brazilian immigrants in Australia and New Zealand. I thank Márcia Anita Sprandel, Tomás Palau, Carlos Wagner, and José Lindomar C. Albuquerque for their field work on *brasiguaios*, Brazilians living in Paraguay.

Journalistic reports that have been invaluable to me include those of Fabiano Maisonnave, Valquíria Rey, Néli Pereira, Tania Menai, Daniela Gerson, Nina Bernstein, Joseph Berger, James Brooke, Mila Burns, Larry Rohter, Simon Romero, Joel Millman, Liz Mineo, Jennifer Moroz, Jerry Kammer, and my *xará*, Mac Margolis. I also thank Joseph Salvo, director of the Population Division of New York City's Department of City Planning, for discussing the knotty issue of Brazilian numbers with me, and André Portela Souza and Bruno Oliva for their assistance with data on Brazilian salaries. And David Fleischer, professor emeritus of political science at the University of Brasília, has been an absolutely priceless resource for all manner of news reports and clippings from Brazilian and U.S. newspapers on topics related to immigration in general, Brazilian immigrants in particular, and the Brazilian economy. Professor Bryan McCann of Georgetown University was helpful in introducing me to the Brazilian community in the Washington, DC, area. I also thank Charles Perrone, professor of Portuguese at the University of Florida, for his assistance with several translations. Finally, I am grateful to Professor Conrad Phillip Kottak of the University of Michigan and Professor James N. Green of Brown University for their thoughtful reviews of my manuscript.

To the innumerable Brazilian immigrants who shared their life stories with me and who so enriched the present account, I can only say in the most heartfelt way, "*Muitíssima obrigada!*"

And to Nara Milanich and Nicola Cetorelli, my very accomplished daughter and son-in-law and the parents of Giacomo and Luca—my *netinhos muito amado* to whom this work is lovingly dedicated—thank you all for being in my life and keeping me happy throughout this project. And last but certainly not least, I thank Jerry Milanich, the most wonderful husband of many decades a *brazilianista* could have, whose amazing research expertise, unceasing patience, and loving support have been so critical to this venture.

Goodbye, Brazil

1

The Boys (and Girls) from Brazil

Brazil is a country of out-turned eyes, our gaze is always aimed abroad. We lack
any sense of self-recognition of our legitimate values and that's why we don't
have our own identity or maturity. We're like an adolescent who doesn't yet
know who he is and is always looking for role models outside his home while all
he had to do was look to his own parents' generation.

    Silviano Santiago (1994, 90)

It is Sunday, September 6, 2009, and the twenty-fifth annual Brazil Day
Street Fair commemorating Brazilian Independence Day on September
7 is in full swing on Little Brazil Street and on adjacent thoroughfares in
the heart of Midtown Manhattan. Brazilian flags are strung across West
Forty-Sixth Street, and large "Visit Brazil" signs loom overhead; Brazilian
music booms from various locations, and a large-screen TV on Sixth Avenue
shows the featured entertainer to the lively dancing throngs. Meanwhile,
hundreds of vendors hawk their wares from street-side booths. The pot-
pourri of items ranges from *pão de quejo* (cheese bread), *pasteis* (savory
stuffed pastries), *guaraná* (a soft drink), *feijão tropeiro* (black beans mixed
with manioc flour), and other Brazilian specialties to such mundane
street-fair items as costume jewelry, socks, and onion-sausage hoagies.
Interspersed are vendors featuring green and yellow soccer T-shirts (Brazil's
national colors), hats, purses, jewelry, and key chains adorned with Brazilian
flags and minuscule bikinis—consummate Brazilian beachwear.

Meanwhile, thousands upon thousands of exuberant green-and-
yellow-clad Brazilians mingle among local American aficionados of Brazil
and dazed tourists—both foreign and domestic—wondering just what they
have wandered into. The festival is an eye-catching glimpse of one of the
recent and mostly hidden waves of immigrants to the United States. Tens
of thousands of Brazilians from all over the northeastern United States

flock to the annual event—the largest celebration of Brazilian ethnicity outside Brazil. By 2009, an estimated one million people participated in Brazil Day, and Rede Globo, Brazil's largest television network, beamed the extravaganza back to Brazil (Sá 2009). This is not the only such gathering. There are carnival parades in San Francisco, New Orleans, and London; Brazilian Independence Day celebrations in Boston, Toronto, London and Tokyo; and wild spontaneous revelry in several cities in the United States, Europe, and Japan when Brazil wins a World Cup soccer match. All are indicative of the same phenomenon—Brazilians leaving Brazil to seek their fortunes abroad.

Historically, Brazil has been a country of immigration, *not* emigration— far more people arrived in Brazil than left to move elsewhere. In the late nineteenth and early twentieth centuries, only the United States and Argentina received greater numbers of migrants from Europe. To be sure, after the military coup in Brazil in 1964 and the stranglehold that the military placed on free speech and free expression, hundreds of academics, musicians, artists, and politicians fled the country for the United States, Europe, and several countries in Latin America (Green 2010). However, until 1980, Brazilian demographers believed there was neither immigration nor emigration from their country; but since the late 1980s—for more than three decades now—Brazilians have been leaving Brazil as the nation has weathered a series of intense economic crises. Only in recent years have economic stability and growth returned. So the questions are: Have the economic conditions that led so many Brazilians to leave their homeland in the first place been reversed? And, if so, are they now returning home? What about the tens of thousands of Brazilian revelers so evident at the Brazil Day street fair in New York and similar events elsewhere? Are they just here today, and will they be gone tomorrow? These are some of the questions that I plan to answer in this book.

Numbers

First, some figures that can provide insight into the size of the Brazilian diaspora worldwide: in 2011, Brazil's Ministry of Foreign Affairs estimated that major concentrations of Brazilians were living in the countries outlined in table 1.

In an effort to gauge the magnitude of the exodus, Brazilian embassies and consulates around the world collected these figures. In marked contrast

Table 1 Brazilians living abroad: Major populations, 2011

Region	Number
North America	
United States	1,380,000
Canada	30,000
South America	
Paraguay	200,000
Argentina	37,000
Venezuela	26,000
Uruguay	30,000
Bolivia	50,000
Suriname	20,000
French Guiana	8,000
Europe, England, and the Republic of Ireland	
England	180,000
Portugal	136,000
Italy	85,000
Spain	159,000
Switzerland	57,000
Germany	91,000
France	80,000
Republic of Ireland	18,000
Pacific	
Japan	230,000
Australia	45,000
Total	**3,100,000**

Source: Ministério das Relações Exteriores 2011.

to them, the 2010 Brazilian Census attempted to determine the size of the Brazilian population living abroad by including in its household survey a question asking whether anyone who had resided in the household was now living in another country. The result of this inquiry, which has been widely criticized, found an absurdly low total of 491,645 Brazilians living abroad, a number that is said to include Brazilians living in *all* countries outside Brazil (IBGE 2011)!

Accurate figures are clearly difficult to come by, particularly in countries like the United States, where many Brazilians—an estimated 63 percent in 2007—are undocumented. In fact, by 2009, Brazil was among the top ten countries sending unauthorized migrants to the United States. At the same time, an estimated 44 percent of Brazilians living in Canada, most of whom were undocumented, were missed by the census, and about half of the Brazilians in Spain lacked the legal papers to work there. Even more difficult to measure is the number of Brazilians living in countries bordering Brazil, such as Brazilian gold and diamond prospectors in Bolivia and Venezuela (*O Globo* 2007; Marcelli et al. 2009; Goza 1994; Noguera and Coelho 2005; De Almeida 1995).

People who are living in a country illegally are loath to stand up and be counted in national censuses and surveys, which is one reason why these numbers are problematic. As such, with the exception of Japan, the figures presented here represent the midpoints of estimates of the size of the Brazilian population in any given country. In Japan, in contrast, since the early 1990s, the vast majority of Brazilians—most of whom are of Japanese ancestry—have been legally authorized to live and work there, so the numbers are likely to be more accurate (Margolis 1995a).

Are there other figures besides official ones that might shed light on the magnitude of Brazilian emigration? Some comparisons can be useful. While in 2011 the American Community Survey counted a mere 280,000 Brazilians in the entire United States, TV Globo, Brazil's largest and most influential television network, which has been available in the United States since 1999, estimates that it has some 420,000 individual subscribers in this country. And if, at a minimum, two or three Brazilians live in the household of each subscriber? That translates into anywhere from 850,000 to 1.2 million Brazilians. Or take a similar statistic, albeit one on a local level. A representative for TV Globo claims to have installed more than 20,000 Globo satellite dishes in the Atlanta area alone since 2000. If, again, one assumes that there are two or three Brazilian viewers for every TV Globo subscription, that could come to more than 60,000 Brazilians in the area, compared to the mere 7,677 in the entire state of Georgia counted in the 2011 American Community Survey (Kottak 2009; Marcus 2009b).

While the numbers on Brazilian immigrants are uncertain, it is clear that the migration stream of Brazilians to various countries differs in its particulars. So, while most Brazilian migration to Japan is legally based and is sanctioned by the Japanese government and Japanese industry, a significant number of the Brazilians in Portugal are not authorized to work there. Still, since they speak Portuguese, they are much more likely to work in jobs for which they were trained than are Brazilian immigrants in other countries like Japan. Although a relatively modest immigrant community in terms of size, the Brazilian presence in Portugal looms large because of the country's small population and because of the high profile Brazilian immigrants maintain there. Many immigrants work in advertising, marketing, computing, and television production. And there is also the highly publicized wave of Brazilian dentists practicing in Portugal, a wave that has been dubbed "the dental invasion" (Soares 1997). As in Portugal, many Brazilian immigrants in Australia are middle class and have professional jobs, working as doctors, dentists, lawyers, and teachers (Rocha 2006).

These examples suggest that Brazilian immigrants in Portugal and Australia—in contrast to those in other countries—can often work in the fields in which they were trained. In Japan, in contrast, despite the high educational level of many Japanese Brazilians, they are employed in what is known as the "three K" sector of the Japanese economy—they hold jobs that are *kitui* (arduous), *kitanai* (dirty), and *kiken* (dangerous), jobs that are shunned by the Japanese themselves. The admission of Brazilians of Japanese ancestry was viewed as a way to help solve the labor shortage in jobs considered undesirable by the Japanese, while at the same time not diluting the native population's strong sense of its distinct "race."

Again, contrast this with the situation of Brazilian immigrants in Paraguay. The flight of Brazilians to Paraguay and other nations sharing a common border with Brazil took off in the mid-1980s, the same era that the exodus to the United States and other industrial countries increased. The emigration of Brazilians to neighboring South American countries, however, had different roots—primarily landlessness and the lack of agrarian reform—than those that led Brazilians to more distant lands. From the early 1970s, the mechanization of agriculture and the consolidation of land in Paraná state in southern Brazil led to the expulsion of agricultural workers and their move to an adjacent region in Paraguay (Margolis 1973). Many small farmers in Paraná state sold their holdings and bought larger tracts in Paraguay, where the cost per unit of land was about one-tenth the cost in Paraná. Other Brazilian immigrants in Paraguay found jobs as day laborers and tenant farmers. Similarly, Brazilian rubber tappers, miners, and cultivators—sharecroppers, renters, and small holders—also crossed international frontiers in the northern and western Amazon and the Southern Cone. In sum, the motivations behind these flights to countries bordering the homeland were very different from those of Brazilians migrating great distances to developed nations abroad.

Why They Go

What, then, are the primary reasons why Brazilians left and are still leaving Brazil and heading to industrialized countries in North America, Europe, and Asia? To understand international migration flows, we must look at the cause of the original flow, as well as the factors that maintain it. What are the conditions in the country of origin, in this case Brazil, that led to emigration in the first place?

As mentioned at the start of this chapter, Brazil has weathered a series of economic crises over the past three decades. Since the mid-1980s, Brazilians have been buffeted by high rates of unemployment and underemployment, low wages, a high cost of living, and, until 1994, out-of-control inflation. The Brazilian middle class was particularly hard hit by these conditions, making it much harder to maintain its standard of living and thus undermining its class expectations.

Hyperinflation is a good example of an issue that confronted middle-class Brazilians during the first decade of significant emigration from Brazil—roughly 1985 to 1994. While Brazil had long had a history of high inflation, prices soared during the late 1980s and early 1990s; by 1994, inflation had reached more than 2,500 percent annually. Then, in 1994, the Brazilian government put in place an economic plan that brought down the rate of inflation, but, within several months, prices for goods and services soared and it was widely noted that middle-class Brazilians were again suffering. These conditions were made worse by the fact that Brazilian salaries had long been in decline. In the decade after the inception of the new economic plan in the mid-1990s, discounting the effects of inflation, workers' incomes lost one-third of their real purchasing power (Cohen 1988; Brooke 1990, 1991a, 1991b, 1994a, 1994b).

Unemployment, particularly among the young, was another goad to emigration. In 1991, 15 percent of those eighteen to twenty-four years old were without jobs in Greater São Paulo, the wealthiest region of Brazil. A decade later, that figure had jumped to 25 percent in São Paulo and 30 percent in some other metropolitan areas of the country (Brooke 1991c).

Besides high prices, low wages, and unemployment, the inability of many educated Brazilians to find jobs in the fields in which they were trained was another powerful incentive to leave home. In New York City, Boston, Lisbon, Nagoya (Japan) and other immigrant destinations, a significant number of Brazilians who are university graduates—some trained as professionals—were unable to find employment with decent salaries in their own fields in Brazil. While far more Brazilians than ever before are attending universities and receiving degrees, the number of jobs that call for higher education has not kept up with the growing number of young people seeking them. The nation's economic troubles beginning in the mid-1980s have meant that fewer jobs requiring university training have been created. Many Brazilians with college degrees could therefore find only positions with lower status and lower pay than their educational qualifications had led them to expect (De Moura Castro 1989).

All these conditions—inadequate pay, the high cost of living, few good job opportunities, and ongoing economic uncertainty—shadowed the lives of many Brazilians. When they looked to the future and saw little hope of improving their economic circumstances in Brazil, emigration became a "What have I got to lose?" opportunity. Said one researcher about this situation: "Innumerable Brazilians are no longer finding perspectives of a dignified and secure existence in their own country" (De Carvalho 1996, 13). All of these "push" factors are analyzed in more detail in the next chapter.

Who are these émigrés from the land of soccer and samba? During the early years of emigration, the first wave of Brazilian immigrants were primarily male; men accounted for 70 percent of Brazilians "missing" from the 1990 census, and the assumption was that they had left Brazil. During the 1990s, more and more Brazilian women began seeking opportunities abroad, and by the turn of the new millennium the sex ratio had balanced out—about as many women as men had left home.[1] These early emigrants were also young. Again, by far the largest cohort absent from the 1990 census was composed of those between the ages of twenty and forty-four. And many were educated. Of the 1.3 million Brazilians who disappeared from the country between 1991 and 2000, most had at least a high school education, and many were college graduates.

Where do these immigrants come from in Brazil? During the first years of emigration, if a Brazilian had been asked this question, the automatic response would have been: "They're *mineiros*, of course" (natives of the Brazilian state of Minas Gerais). And this statement would have been correct. Most pioneer immigrants hailed from this state in south-central Brazil. But beginning in the 1990s more and more Brazilians from other parts of the country began leaving home to seek their fortunes abroad, and since 2000 emigration has become a truly national phenomenon. Writes one researcher, "It would not be an exaggeration to suppose that, except in the poorest regions of Brazil, there is no one who has [not] heard the topic discussed, or who does not have . . . an acquaintance, friend, or relative who in the last fifteen years has gone to 'live in another country'" (Martes 2010, 4).

Minas Gerais, the state that most pioneer immigrants call home, is also the site of the famed immigrant-sending community Governador Valadares, sometimes called "Governador Valadólares" for the large sums of money sent there by the town's natives who are living and working in the United States. Over the past two decades, perhaps a quarter of this city's population of 230,000—as well as many thousands of Brazilians from the surrounding region—have immigrated to the United States or to Europe. And in Brazilian discourse the quintessential Brazilian emigrant is a *valadarense*—a native of Governador Valadares. So, while on a national scale the remittance money sent back to Brazil has been no more than a drop in the bucket because of the size of the Brazilian economy and its huge population—by 2012 it was the sixth-largest economy in the world and had fewer than 2 percent of its nearly two hundred million citizens living abroad—in places like Governador Valadares, with large numbers of emigrants, entire industries have grown up and become dependent on the money sent home.[2] Housing and apartment construction and renovation are two obvious examples, but there is also an entire sector of the local economy that has developed to meet the needs of would-be and actual emigrants—money exchanges, remittance and travel agencies, and "*cônsuls*," members of the local elite who have relationships with Mexican *coyotes* and who arrange for travel between Brazil and Mexico or Guatemala and on to the United States and Canada.[3] Governador Valadares is not alone in its reputation for exporting residents. Towns like Criciúma in the southern Brazilian state of Santa Catarina and Piracanjuba in the central Brazilian state of Goiás also have seen masses of their citizens travel abroad, and they too have "cultures of migration" whereby young people grow up expecting to migrate abroad someday (Assis 2003; Inman 2011; Prada 2010; Marcus 2008b).

Identity and Community

While the specific conditions and catalysts for the exodus from Brazil to other countries, as well as its timing, vary, certain issues seem to have posed similar problems to Brazilians no matter where they live. One such issue is ethnic identity within the context of international migration. In the United

States, for example, Brazilian immigrants have vociferously complained about the fact that Americans routinely confuse them with Hispanics, insisting that they are *not* Hispanic—because they speak Portuguese, not Spanish. Researchers have noted the frequent attempts by Brazilian immigrants to differentiate themselves from the Spanish-speaking population in this country. In a similar vein, many Brazilians of Japanese ancestry in Japan become irate when the Japanese confuse them with immigrants from Peru who also have Japanese antecedents.

These attempts by Brazilian immigrants to distinguish themselves in terms of language and culture from other Latin Americans are based not only in their experience in the United States or Japan but also in attitudes brought from Brazil, where feelings of cultural pride, of the distinctiveness of the Brazilian "race" (*raça*), as they call it, are marked. As the Brazilian anthropologist Darcy Ribeiro ([1995] 2000, 126) observed years ago, "The Brazilian people see themselves as unique, as singular." This observation helps explain why it is so difficult for Brazilians to accept their inclusion in other groups.

Anyone concerned with the massive undercount of the Brazilian population in the United States cannot fail to make reference to the question of Brazilian identity. Brazilian identity is an indistinct and ambiguous category within the context of immigration, which helps explain the general invisibility of Brazilian communities in the United States and elsewhere. Confusion over identity also has practical consequences. Although Brazilians widely reject the Hispanic label and affirm their distinct national identity, what are the consequences of this rejection for their political life? As the Hispanic population in the United States grows and its political activities and organizations multiply, will Brazilians continue to separate themselves from these efforts?

Another issue widely noted by researchers is the fractured nature of so many Brazilian immigrant communities. Several fissures that inhibit community solidarity are present among Brazilian populations in the United States and elsewhere. Evidence suggests, for example, that Brazilians who arrived earlier in the migration stream—say, two decades ago—tend to disparage more recent arrivals for being less educated and for coming from more modest backgrounds than their pioneer countrymen and women. Brazilians in places where immigration began earlier sometimes have a negative image of their newly arrived compatriots, whom they see as opportunists who lack a sense of community. A similar divide exists between the relatively few Brazilians who have become American citizens and those who have not. These "Brazilian Americans" sometimes attribute the same negative characteristics to the Brazilian immigrant population as a whole that Brazilians attribute to Hispanics. That is, those "other Brazilians" are "not to be trusted" and are "out only for themselves."

Again, such fissures are not unique to Brazilian communities in the United States. They have also been reported among Brazilians in England, where distinctions are based on social and legal status, origin, and employment. In London, the fault line is between the "political and economic elite"—employees of the Brazilian Embassy and Consulate and large Brazilian companies—and ordinary immigrants, most of whom are in the country illegally (Torresan 1994).

In the United States, the problematic issue of community among Brazilian immigrants and community-based institutions—or rather the lack thereof—has been dubbed "Brasphobia." This involves what I call the "discourse of Brazilians bad mouthing each other" (Margolis 2003). Part of the discourse is the refusal of some Brazilians living in the United States to identify themselves as Brazilian. I found this in the Brazilian community in New York City, and it also has been reported by researchers in Boston and Florida (Margolis 1994a; Martes 2000; Resende 2002, 2005).

Brazilian immigrants themselves complain of the lack of a community ethos and compare themselves unfavorably to other immigrant groups in this regard. However, partly contradicting the litany of complaints is actual behavior, that is, the reality that Brazilians could hardly survive the immigrant experience without the aid and comfort of other Brazilians. One of the most salient features of Brazilian immigrant populations is the apparent contradiction between ideology and behavior. While examples of non-communitarian actions certainly exist, it is also true that Brazilian immigrants overwhelmingly rely on one another to navigate the multiple hurdles of immigrant life.

Another topic that has received a good deal of attention is religious participation among Brazilians abroad. Most of those who have done research on Brazilian communities in the United States are struck by the burgeoning number of churches in them, particularly evangelical churches. Just one example: a team of researchers from the University of Florida located thirty-nine churches with Brazilian congregations in a single county in south Florida, only one of which was Catholic; the rest were Protestant, the majority evangelical (Alves and Ribeiro 2002).

Likewise, there are at least three evangelical churches serving the

Brazilian community in London. In little Gort, a town of some three thousand, in the west of the Republic of Ireland, where Brazilians once made up an estimated 25 to 30 percent of local residents, Mass is celebrated in Portuguese at the local Catholic church, and an Assembly of God church was established to serve Brazilians there (Healy 2008). And, in several cities in Japan with Brazilian populations, Portuguese-language services are held in Baptist, Assembly of God, and Catholic churches.

How can we explain the plethora of religious institutions? Part of the appeal of these ethnically based churches is that they are not limited to an exclusively religious dimension—they play important social and support roles as well. The ethnic churches augment social life through different kinds of recreational activities—parties, community meetings, national celebrations, sports events, and the like. These activities help construct ethnic identity in public spaces so that, in essence, they re-create "Brazilian-ness" in a foreign setting.

The churches, moreover, are often sources of critical information about jobs, housing, and other aid intended to help Brazilian immigrants. The social role churches play as sources of information and solidarity may explain why in the United States—in contrast to Brazil—roughly as many men as women attend church services. And the support can be very specific. Immigrants from the same church or the same town in Brazil may receive material assistance from church members from the same region (Alves and Ribeiro 2002).

In Boston, the Brazilian churches are not only the center of social life; they also provide a good deal of practical aid to immigrants. The success of the evangelical churches, in particular, may result from the fact that, un-like the Catholic churches, the evangelical churches are entirely dependent on their own members for financial support, which makes them less hier-archical and less centralized than their Catholic counterparts. Since evan-gelicals fund church facilities themselves, a strong feeling exists that this is "our space," one built especially for Brazilian believers. Moreover, the religion emanating from these churches is "nonterritorial" and, therefore, well suited to transnational migrants because it is not linked to a specific locale and does not rely on a highly trained professional clergy or national church structures like dioceses. Finally, the actual discourse of the evangeli-cal churches is comforting to immigrants; by encouraging hard work and lauding prosperity and social mobility, such religious discourse is decidedly attuned to their own aspirations (Freston 2008; Martes 2010).

Here Today and Gone Tomorrow?

Given the numbers involved, to leave Brazil—to try to better one's life in another country—is no longer an isolated decision of a few individuals or a small group of people. Rather, it is a social trend. While emigration may amount to only 1 or 2 percent of Brazil's population of close to two hundred million, that still involves the movement of a great number of people. In fact, as early as the mid-1990s, studies of Brazilians living abroad and the remittances they sent home dashed "the hope that the phenomenon [i.e., emigration] was transitory." The portrait that emerged from these studies suggested that emigrant Brazilian communities "already have taken root" abroad (Klintowitz 1996, 26).

So the question then becomes: Are Brazilians "here today"—that is, in New York, Boston, Miami, Los Angeles, Toronto, Lisbon, London, Tokyo, and elsewhere—and "gone tomorrow"? Or will they become permanent fixtures of a widespread diaspora? It is difficult to say, because, in the years ahead, much depends on economic conditions in Brazil, as well as in the countries to which Brazilians have immigrated. Will the Brazilian economy sustain the growth it achieved in the late 2000s? And, more important, will that growth lead to an increase in well-paying jobs? What does the future hold for the economies of Spain and Japan, for example, major destinations of Brazilian immigrants? Will ongoing unemployment in them spur Brazilians to return home?

Aside from economic factors, family matters are often central in the decision to stay or to go. What is the role of second-generation Brazilians in such decisions? That is, will children of Brazilian parents who were born in a host country or brought to the United States, Portugal, Italy, or Japan as infants or toddlers be willing to return to Brazil, a country they barely know and whose language they may not speak well? And, in turn, will their unwillingness to "go home" anchor their parents and perhaps other relatives more firmly in their immigrant destinations? Again, it is too soon to tell. The relative recency of Brazilian emigration means that 1.5- and second-generation Brazilians are just now coming of the age to make such weighty decisions.[4]

The final issue concerning the durability of the Brazilian diaspora is a political one. What does the future portend for those lacking the documents that would allow them to live and work legally in the nations of the industrial world? Will the post-9/11 crackdown on undocumented immigrants in the United States continue, or will Congress eventually pass immigration legislation that allows them to emerge from the shadows? Will an unending threat from Al Qaeda and political measures to contain it dampen the movement of people seeking to better their lives through emigration? And will the borders of nation-states become ever more fortified and difficult to cross?

None of these questions has a definitive answer. But in the pages that follow we will learn a great deal more about who these emigrants are, why they left home, the means by which they traveled abroad, where they immigrated, and what they encountered at their final destinations. We will look at the nature of far-flung Brazilian communities and community institutions and focus on one of the famed "sending communities" in Brazil. We will also analyze the Brazilian government's response to this phenomenon. Finally, we return to the question posed earlier: Will Brazilians sojourners be here today and gone tomorrow, or are they true immigrants who see their lives and futures in their adopted lands?

2

Why They Go

In Brazil if you want a $50 dress, you can only buy it by paying on credit over twelve months. But by the time it's paid for, the dress is worn out. But in the United States, if you want a $50 dress, you just go out and buy it for cash.

Brazilian immigrant in New York City (quoted in Margolis 1994a, 79)

Brazilians rarely talk about "emigrating" or say that a friend or relative "is working in another country." Rather, they say that "he [or she] is living in another country" or that a friend or relative is "doing America" (*fazendo América*). For some Brazilian families, having a relative in the United States is considered "chic," a sign of status. This highlights the fact that most Brazilians living abroad do not see themselves as immigrants. Initially, at least, most see their stays outside Brazil as temporary (Martes 2010; Margolis 1998).

The denial of immigrant status may be linked to the general malaise that many Brazilians felt during the 1980s, the first decade of emigration, an era that has been labeled the "lost decade." The middle class had grown in size in the 1970s during the heady years of double-digit annual economic growth. But, by the 1980s, the consumption level of the middle and lower-middle classes was declining as prices far outpaced income. It was a time not only of economic stagnation and hyperinflation but also of heightened political expectations that went unrealized, a period of re-democratization and mass mobilizations that demanded direct elections after the long nightmare of military dictatorship (1964–85). But the decade was marred by the scandal surrounding Brazilian president Fernando Collor de Mello and the utter failure of his plan to tame hyperinflation. It was a time of both profound hope and bitter political and economic disappointment.

It was within this setting in the late 1980s and early 1990s that—for the first time in the nation's history—Brazilians began leaving Brazil in significant numbers. These immigrant pioneers, many from the middle strata of Brazilian society, began traveling to the United States, Japan, Portugal, and a handful of other European countries. For some, emigration served as an escape valve from unemployment and underemployment, while for others it was the irresistible lure of higher wages paid in even menial jobs in the United States, Japan, and other industrialized nations that convinced them to leave home (Klagsbrunn 1996). For still others, emigration was a result of frustration with dead-end jobs that offered little hope of social mobility. Aside from relative economic deprivation, during those years many middle-class Brazilians had feelings of alienation and stagnation, of disillusionment with the economic and political situation in Brazil. They decried the lack of opportunities or, in the words of one researcher, had "a sense that their citizenship was being undermined" by "a level of incongruence between [their] aspirations and the reality in which they lived" (Torresan 2012, 111–12).

For still others, emigration was an alternative to higher education. Many young Japanese Brazilians who had had access to a guest worker program in Japan since 1990 chose to work there for a few years after finishing high school. This was seen as an alternative to trying to pass the difficult college entrance exam (*vestibular*) and then attempting to get a "top job" in Brazil. Most such immigrants were low-wage white-collar workers or students who viewed temporary migration to Japan as a chance to improve their economic situation.

Still, there was more to the motives of many immigrants than mere economic gain. There was also the adventure of living in a foreign country and perhaps learning a new language. Nowhere was the "pull" of adventure stronger than in the United States. Beginning in the 1940s, the United States captured the "geographical imagination" of Brazilians who admired American movies, music, and technology, while viewing American lifestyles through rose-tinted glasses. By saturating the Brazilian public with representations of the good life, American style, the Brazilian media played an inadvertent role in the emigration flow. It is not surprising that the opportunity to visit the source of these fanciful images was a potent lure to aspiring immigrants. This was, in the words of one scholar, a "game of seduction" consummated by immigration to this country. Moreover, in Brazil there is a widespread ideology that all that is "modern" is located abroad—in the United States and in western Europe. From this perspective, Brazil still has not metaphorically shifted into what is thought of as "modernity." Brazilians can achieve such a transition only by moving to an industrialized country, that is, relocating away from all that is Brazilian (Tota 2009; Marcus 2009c, 2011b; Martes 2010).[1]

As we have seen, several so-called push factors—that is, conditions that led them to leave Brazil—have been implicated in Brazilians' decisions to emigrate. The overarching one has been the long-term Brazilian economic crisis and its impact on the nation's middle and lower-middle classes. Job opportunities (particularly for the educated middle class), wage levels, purchasing power, and prospects for advancement were all affected by the economic maelstrom of hyperinflation, high levels of unemployment and underemployment, and the general lack of well-paying jobs.

Perhaps the biggest initial "push" was the hyperinflation that squeezed the middle class and made its standard of living very difficult to maintain. Over an eighteen-month period beginning in 1987, the real income of the Brazilian middle class declined by 30 percent as rents rose, the price of newspapers doubled overnight, and canned goods in supermarkets were thick with price stickers—stuck one on top of the other—as store managers struggled to change prices to keep up with inflation. Always high, inflation soared during the late 1980s and early 1990s, reaching almost 1,400 percent annually between 1990 and 1994. Since salaries in Brazil typically are paid once a month, it is very difficult to plan expenditures in such a highly inflationary situation (Brooke 1993; Roett 2010).

That hyperinflation and the conditions of economic uncertainty that accompanied it were a major reason for this growing exodus is supported by the fact that the emigration floodgates opened in 1986 at about the time that the *Cruzado* Plan, the Brazilian government's initial effort to deal with runaway inflation, failed. According to government figures, in that year nearly 40 percent of Brazilians who left the country never returned (*Folha de São Paulo* 1990). Or, as one Brazilian émigré put it, that economic reform plan "was our last hope for a better life."

Then, in 1994, the *Real* Plan (Plano Real) was launched by Minister of Finance Fernando Henrique Cardoso, soon to be elected president of Brazil. The plan introduced a new currency—the *real*—but, more important, it finally tamed inflation after years of wild price increases. Still, it was not a panacea. Although the annual rate of inflation between July 1994—when the *Real* Plan was introduced—and July 1995 was 35 percent, the price of several services used by the middle class increased far more; domestic service was up 150 percent, club membership fees 84 percent, restaurant meals 66 percent, medical services 60 percent, and school fees 56 percent. Even tickets for soccer games—Brazil's national sport—were up by over 100 percent (Araújo 1995; *Veja* 1995)![2]

Moreover, the plan certainly did not appear to change the rate at which Brazilians were leaving home; they continued to arrive in the United States, Japan, and elsewhere much as before the *Real* Plan was established. One researcher suggests that the economic conditions in Brazil that motivate emigration are broadly structural and that hyperinflation was only one "push" factor. Since many would-be emigrants had made plans to leave Brazil well before steps were taken to stem inflation, the imposition of the *Real* Plan was not enough to change their intentions to emigrate. At the same time, with the stabilization of the Brazilian currency, it became easier to afford airplane tickets to travel abroad (Martes 2010).

The lack of jobs paying reasonable salaries and offering chances for advancement was another powerful influence on some Brazilians' decision to leave Brazil. By the 1990s, many professionals—dentists, journalists, filmmakers, librarians, and others, especially those in the arts and communication—were abandoning Brazil for other countries because they could not find remunerative work in their fields. One example: Brazil produces about twelve thousand students a year with computer science specialties, but there are only about five thousand new jobs available annually in those areas. Then, too, while starting salaries in this field were about $1,000 a month in Brazil, they were $5,000 a month in the United States. In my own research in New York City in the early 1990s, I met Brazilian psychologists, agronomists, lawyers, economists, and teachers who simply could not find jobs in Brazil in the areas in which they were trained. Said one immigrant, "It is not difficult to enter college there [in Brazil], but the problem is that there are limited jobs available once you have [completed] the university" (Forjaz 1993; Margolis 1994a).

When I visited Governador Valadares in 1990, I met one woman—a middle-class English-language teacher—whose daughter had been working as a nurse at two local hospitals for ten years and was then earning only $200 a month. Another daughter, a kindergarten teacher, had quit her job because of the ridiculously low pay. Similarly, her son, with a degree in agronomy, simply could not find work in his profession after finishing university and traveled to New York, where he took a job as a chauffeur and cook for a wealthy elderly woman on Manhattan's East Side. He hoped to save money to buy a farm and cattle, but his parents told me he will probably remain in the United States.

Consider immigrants who had held more modest jobs in Brazil. Data on Brazilian women in Boston, for example, suggest that many were schoolteachers, bank employees, secretaries, housewives, and students in Brazil. Those who had been employed in Brazil had earned between $100 and $400 a month, while in the United States they were earning four to ten times as much. Or consider the bricklayer who earned about $184 a month in Governador Valadares but earned $10 to $20 an hour in Boston. And, as one resident of that town pointed out, with Brazilian wages it takes a year to save enough money to buy a bicycle, but with U.S. wages one can save enough money in that time to buy a car (Martes 1996c; Paiva 2001).

Thus, migration was also spurred by the decline in opportunities for social mobility and the difficulty of even preserving the social and economic patterns of earlier years. So migration could be a way of *maintaining* middle-class status; through emigration, Brazilians could once again afford middle-class levels of consumption. In fact, what has been called the "citizenship of consumption" is one of the main reasons immigrants say that in the United States they are better rewarded for their work than they are in Brazil, even though they have jobs that they would never have back home. Just one example: A Brazilian trained as an engineer and lawyer had earned $3,000 a month before he lost his job with a multinational food company in Brazil. During his nearly five-year sojourn in the United States, he was able to save the amount of money it would have taken him ten to fifteen years to earn in Brazil. Emigration, he said, "was the only way to maintain a middle-class lifestyle" once he was laid off (Maisonnave 2005e; Assis 2011; Mineo 2006b).

A glance at actual salaries in Brazil in the mid-1990s illustrates how paltry they were even for prestigious, white-collar positions requiring years of schooling. While the average salary in Brazil's six largest cities was about US$420 a month during that period, the average for an experienced computer programmer was $1,300, for a senior accountant a little over $1,800, for a veteran attorney just under $2,000, and for a senior systems analyst about $2,200. Of course, lower-level jobs paid considerably less. For example, the average receptionist earned $350 a month, while an administrative assistant took home about $850. One Brazilian immigrant I met in New York, after returning to her home town, Rio de Janeiro, in 1997, became head of housekeeping for a luxury apartment hotel and earned around $400 a month for a six-day, forty-eight-hour work week, while another former immigrant, a medical secretary with twelve years' experience, earned $470 a month. Working for an American company in Brazil did not mean higher wages. Yet another returned immigrant worked as head of training in customer service for United Airlines in Rio de Janeiro. His salary was $900 a month (*O Globo* 2001).

Even a decade later, the situation had not improved much for educated professionals in Brazil. For example, economists there averaged about $26,000 annually in 2010, agronomists $22,000, lawyers about $20,000, dentists and accountants about $16,000, and clinical psychologists $11,000 annually (Salariômetro 2010).[3]

To make matters even more challenging, prices for many consumer goods used by middle-class Brazilians were far more expensive in Brazil than in the United States. Some examples: a Sony TV cost twice as much as the same model in the United States; a pair of Levi 501 jeans was three times more expensive in Brazil; and Reebok sneakers cost nearly four times as much. Even Big Macs and Cokes cost one and a half times as much in Brazil as in the United States! These price differentials were aggravated, of course, by the fact that Brazilian salaries, on average, were considerably lower than those in the United States. Because of their relatively meager incomes, many in the middle class began paying for basic expenses with credit cards. But, with high interest rates, bounced checks and unpaid credit card bills soared, and bankruptcies became common (Cristina 1995; *O Globo* 1995).

Growing unemployment and slowed productivity also put a damper on the mood in Brazil. In São Paulo, for example, Brazil's industrial heartland, unemployment grew to nearly 17 percent by the mid-1990s and to just under 20 percent by 2003. Then, too, despite forecasts of economic growth of 4 to 5 percent, the actual figure was barely 1 percent. All of this translated into a loss of faith in the *Real* Plan on the part of many Brazilians. By mid-1997, only about one-third of those polled thought the plan was a success (Schemo 1998; Mugnatto 1997).

These gloomy economic conditions were part of the emigration equation, that is, the analysis of the costs and benefits of leaving Brazil. Monetary costs were relatively low for the middle class because the capital needed to migrate was accessible to many Brazilians, particularly in places like Governador Valadares, where an "immigration industry" not only sold plane tickets and provided information needed for emigration but also made loans to help emigrants meet travel expenses. Even for those who lived in large cities without a history of emigration, the costs of leaving, at least through the 1990s, were not unreasonable—perhaps $1,000 to $1,500 for airfare and $1,500 or $2,000 for initial expenses getting settled in the host country. Then, too, the costs of emigration were lowered for those who were linked to the migration networks of friends and relatives who were already living abroad. As the sociologist Douglas Massey wrote some years ago, "Every new migrant reduces the cost of subsequent migration for a set of friends and relatives, and with the lowered costs some of these people are induced to migrate" (1988, 397).

The psychological "cost" of leaving Brazil and living far from loved ones who remained behind was softened by a discourse that legitimized emigration for immigrants and for their families and friends. This discourse painted emigration as a type of personal investment, a way to improve one's lot in life by going abroad for a few years, experiencing a foreign culture, and, most notably, saving money to devote to some future project in Brazil. Like any investment, emigration involved gathering information and resources and exposing oneself to risk. And yet, as we have seen, Brazilians rarely use the mundane term "emigration." Rather, as this discourse suggests, their travel abroad is viewed in an idealized light, as a way of bettering themselves, a means of improving their future lives back home in Brazil despite the ongoing barriers to economic ascent there (Martes 2000).

What They Do: The United States

However the move abroad was couched, what conditions greeted Brazilians in the countries to which they immigrated? Because this book covers more than two decades of Brazilian emigration and includes various destinations—North America, several countries in South America that border Brazil, and a number of nations in Europe and Asia—the answer must be that it depends on time and place.[4] As a general rule, Brazilians who left home earlier in this migration stream found more welcoming conditions in terms of job opportunities and overall reception than those who left Brazil in more recent years, particularly after the attacks in the United States on September 11, 2001.

Since the vast majority of Brazilians leaving Brazil have sought employment upon reaching their destinations, it seems reasonable to begin by describing the job markets they encountered, including some of the specific sectors in which they have been employed. Brazilians in North America and Europe usually work in the low-wage service sector of those nations' economies, while those in Japan are commonly employed in manufacturing jobs. In chapter 8 I will discuss the very different job situation in the countries that border Brazil.

Perhaps no segment of the labor market has hired more Brazilians than domestic service, a decidedly female job niche. In my own research in New York City, 80 percent of the Brazilian women I interviewed had been employed at one time or another as housekeepers, nannies, and/or babysitters. This employment sector is critical for Brazilian women not only in the United States but also in Canada and in several European countries; and one segment of this niche, housekeeping, is of particular interest for two reasons. First, housekeeping is the most highly remunerated position to which most Brazilian women have access. Second, for some Brazilian women, being a *faixineira* (housecleaner) is not just a job but a business and a path to financial success. Most women working as housecleaners have a high school education, although some have gone to university. In either case, their earnings as housecleaners in the United States and in Europe are far greater than what they could earn in white-collar jobs in large cities in Brazil. Indeed, housekeeping can be such a lucrative line of work that Brazilian immigrants rarely leave it except to return home (Margolis 1994a; Martes 1996c, 2010).

How does this employment sector work? I will use the Boston metropolitan area as an example because domestic service has been meticulously researched there. Immigrants who have lived in the area for a while and have some command of the English language build cleaning routes. That is, over time they come to "own" ten to twenty houses that they clean on a regular basis. Housecleaners with too much work to do themselves either hire assistants or charge aspiring owners—other Brazilian immigrants eager to start their own cleaning businesses—hundreds of dollars to turn over their extra jobs to them (Martes 2000; Fleischer 2002).

A housecleaner can earn $2,000 or more a month. This is net income, since taxes and Social Security are very rarely deducted from wages. One housecleaner in Boston describes the financial returns of the job this way:

> A teacher here [in the United States] doesn't earn a third of what we earn. Secretaries . . . are poorly paid and have money withheld. I charge $15 to $25 an hour. For an apartment with two bedrooms I charge between $45 and $55 . . . on average there are three bathrooms and three bedrooms. This will give me $60, $65. I stay two hours when I go with an assistant. . . . I

pay her $15 for the house. I have two steady assistants and two
who come when the regulars can't make it. (quoted in Martes
1996c, 22)

More recent immigrants with fewer social contacts find work as cleaning
assistants through word of mouth. Such jobs are appealing because they
are flexible and require little English and no work papers; in addition, undocumented immigrants employed in private homes can avoid detection
more easily than those in public workplaces. A cleaning assistant earns
minimum wage or somewhat more working alongside or in place of the
owner of the cleaning route. Indeed, there is usually a large gap between
what owners and assistants earn. So it comes as no surprise that many
assistants would like their own cleaning routes but lack the money to "buy"
the jobs owned by more established immigrants.

Using the terms "buying" and "selling" in reference to cleaning jobs
requires an explanation. In the Boston metropolitan area, where the practice
appears to be most highly developed, selling housecleaning routes dates at
least to the early 1990s, but the practice is also found in other Brazilian
communities such as those in San Francisco and Atlanta. How does the
system work? Let us say that on average a housecleaner has ten houses she
cleans on a weekly basis. When a house is "sold," its average price is the
amount earned from cleaning it over a three-month period. For example, a
housecleaner cleans a house once a week and receives $100 for each cleaning
job, or $400 a month. This comes to $1,200 over a three-month period—so
that $1,200 is the price for buying the house. The price for multiple houses
or an entire cleaning route can reach thousands of dollars. As such, buying
and selling cleaning jobs involves a great deal of money (Millman 2006;
Ribeiro 1996; Marcus 2008b).

When a "buyer" appears, the job "owner" tells her boss, usually the
"lady" of the house, that a friend or relative—in either case, a person of
trust—is interested in the job. For about a month, the job owner and would-
be buyer go to the job together, during which time the owner explains the
cleaning routine to the buyer, who also meets the homeowner, who evalu-
ates her work. If the buyer is acceptable to the homeowner, then cash
changes hands, and the job is sold. The employer has no knowledge of this
transaction, that is, that the job to clean her house is being sold.

Typically, such sales occur when an immigrant is getting ready to
return to Brazil. A housecleaner planning to return home spreads word
among her friends and acquaintances that she is selling the houses where

she works. At times, the buying and selling of houses even occurs among family members. In any case, the housecleaner leaves for Brazil with a tidy sum of money. Writes one researcher, "The work of house cleaning . . . is transformed into merchandise that is bought and sold among the immigrants themselves" (Martes 2010, 132).

Brazilians with well-established housecleaning businesses usually do not clean themselves but enlist as many as a dozen workers and fill out their client lists as word of their reliability spreads. When they have too much business to handle efficiently, they can carve out "starter" routes to pass on to family members newly arrived from Brazil. Or, as we have seen, they can sell the routes via a well-developed informal market. The most industrious assistants may eventually save enough to purchase their own ready-made routes. Aside from buying houses to clean with money saved from first jobs, immigrant housecleaners also need a car—in metropolitan Boston, the majority work in the suburbs, which lack reliable public transportation—and at least some English to be able to communicate with their employers.

Aside from buying expensive cleaning routes, some Brazilian immigrants seek out new clients on their own. One means of acquiring additional business is by cruising well-to-do suburbs during the day and noting which houses appear to have no one at home. These are presumed to be the homes of two-job families that might need a housecleaner. Flyers advertising the immigrant's services are then stuffed in their mailboxes or under the front door (Millman 1997).

Clearly, the more houses one cleans, the greater the income. And these cleaning businesses can be lucrative indeed. One Brazilian who has lived in the Boston area for two decades earns more than $100,000 annually servicing the homes of some seventy clients. A few she cleans herself, but mostly she pays other Brazilian immigrants—many of them, like her, well-educated English speakers—to do the work. Or take the example of a married couple, who working together can clean an average house in two to three hours. A house is cleaned once a week, and a full complement would be about fifteen houses per week. This works out to some $1,500, figuring an average of $100 a house. Even after expenses for gas and a cleaning assistant, a couple can easily net more than $1,000 a week. And such earnings are not limited to Brazilians in Boston. In the Atlanta metropolitan area, for example, one Brazilian woman was earning $8,000 a month from her housecleaning business (Maisonnave 2005f; Millman 1997; Marcus, personal communication).

Thus, housecleaning and job selling are a business for many Brazilian immigrants. In Florida, estimates suggest that cleaning businesses account for nearly 30 percent of Brazilian-owned businesses in the state, while in California the figure is about 15 percent. And despite the low status that such work has in Brazil, for Brazilians living abroad it can be a ladder to both financial and professional success. Besides being lucrative, housecleaning also has an appealing autonomy. Housecleaners do not have bosses; they have clients. Then, too, the housecleaner who hires assistants becomes an employer herself; she is essentially running a business (Siqueira 2007; Martes 1996c).

Brazilians who do this work emphasize the differences between being a housecleaner in Brazil and a housecleaner in the United States. Since immigrants generally view housecleaning in the United States as a business, relations between employer and employee are far more egalitarian than they are in Brazil. Many Brazilians say they value their relationships with their employers, pointing out that they are trusted with house keys and other valuables in their employers' homes. Even Brazilians who assert that their employers treat them in a cold, formal manner value this as a sign of their professionalism.

Brazilian housekeepers also consider housecleaning in the United States as less physically demanding and time consuming than it is in Brazil. They can clean a house or apartment in two or three hours, while in Brazil cleaning is an all-day affair. In the United States, a housecleaner has established tasks she is expected to do: vacuum or sweep the floors, clean the bathrooms and kitchen, and dust. This contrasts with Brazil, where a maid is expected to do whatever tasks her employer asks of her, which can include washing and ironing clothes, cooking meals, and caring for children (Martes 1996c; De Jesus 2003).

One researcher suggests yet another reason why Brazilians view housecleaning in the United States in a favorable light: they do not have a clear understanding of American class structure. While they clean the homes of middle- and upper-middle-class Americans, they view their employers as "*gente rica*" (rich people) and take photos of their homes to send to Brazil to demonstrate to friends and relatives the wealth of the families that employ them. This is reminiscent of a practice documented by the Brazilian filmmaker Tania Cypriano in her incomparable film *Grandma Has a Video Camera* (2007), on the transnational lives of Brazilians living in San Francisco. There, during real estate open houses, Brazilian immigrants videotape the interiors of luxurious residences for sale in the Bay area and send the videos back to Brazil to highlight the wealth of the "average" American home (De Jesus 2003).

While, in a number of countries, housecleaning among Brazilian immigrants is a largely female affair, with the occasional male joining his spouse or partner in such endeavors, what major job sectors employ most immigrant men? Again, it depends on their destination. In cities in the United States and Europe, probably the most common male occupation is restaurant work, while, in American suburbs, many Brazilian men are employed in civil construction—primarily renovation, carpentry, roofing, and painting—as well as landscaping. In Japan, on the other hand, most men have manufacturing jobs. They typically work in small and midsize subcontracting businesses that supply parts to automobile and home electronics companies (Koyama 1998).

The kind of work that Brazilian men do is varied indeed. They are dishwashers, home care attendants, office cleaners, and house painters in Boston; landscapers in Danbury, Connecticut; street vendors, restaurant workers, and call car drivers in New York City; and car washers and valet parkers in south Florida (Martes 1996b; Sales 1998b; Menezes 2003; Margolis 1994a; Oliveira 2003). Then, too, some specific locales have their own male specialties—pizzeria owners and pizza deliverers in San Francisco; shoe shiners in New York City; carpenters in Riverside, New Jersey; pool builders in Pompano Beach, Florida; and "hurricane chasers" in New Orleans—part of a "rapid response labor force" that arrived in the city to work in reconstruction after Hurricane Katrina (Meihy 2004; Costa 2004a; Ribeiro 1998; Pedroso 2008; Fussell n.d).

The variety of male occupations in one major region of Brazilian settlement, south Florida, is illustrative of more general patterns. When Brazilians first arrive in the area, they usually do entry-level work for a few months in car washes, landscaping, and unskilled construction jobs that require little English and little or no prior experience. In landscaping, for example, those willing to put in very long hours can earn $80 to $100 a day. Washing cars is another entry-level job in which earnings vary from about $5 to $7 an hour plus tips. The vast majority of Brazilians holding such jobs in south Florida are undocumented. Some work fifteen-hour days but are not paid overtime; work hours are determined by the employer, and labor laws are often flouted (Pedroso 2008).

As time passes, immigrant men find work in other areas. Jobs building pools, waterproofing, and tiling require some experience and are usually better paid than landscaping or car washing. In these jobs, earnings range from $80 to $140 a day. Brazilians are often not directly employed by Americans. Instead, relative newcomers and those not fluent in English are typically hired by Brazilian middlemen who arrived in the United States earlier, have green cards, speak English well, and have the necessary capital to buy the equipment and vehicles to transport material to job sites. This is true, for example, in pool construction. Since these middlemen are then subcontracted by American-owned companies, the companies do not have to worry about the fact that employees hired by middlemen are undocumented and may lack Social Security cards (Pedroso 2008).

As we have seen in the case of some housecleaners, Brazilian immigrants are employers as well as employees. In one survey of Brazilians in the Boston area, for example, nearly 23 percent owned their own businesses, which included construction, painting, remodeling, landscaping, cleaning, and insurance companies, as well as restaurants, bakeries, and "ethnic retail," that is, retail stores that carry Brazilian products and appeal to the ethnic community. Brazilians are especially involved in residential painting in Boston, and many small nonunionized painting companies are Brazilian owned (Siqueira and Jansen 2008; Kirshner 2004).

Perhaps nowhere is the impact of Brazilian businesses greater than in Framingham, Massachusetts, a city of sixty-five thousand people, including some ten to fifteen thousand Brazilians. According to the city's secretary of human relations, Framingham would be a "ghost town" if it weren't for the Brazilians. During my own visit to Framingham in 2005, the Brazilian presence was everywhere—every third or fourth store or business on Main Street, perhaps fifty in all, was Brazilian owned or catered to the local Brazilian community. There were Brazilian bakeries, groceries, restaurants, jewelry stores, beauty and nail salons, auto repair shops; a children's clothing store, an electronics store, a language school, real estate offices, dentists, accountants; and small stores featuring Brazilian CDs, soft drinks, clothes, and cosmetics, all businesses displaying Brazilian flags and signs noting "*falamos portugues*" (we speak Portuguese). A large, modern supermarket displayed an array of Brazilian products, including a butcher featuring Brazilian cuts of meat and a snack bar selling *salgadinhos* (savory snacks) and *cafezinhos* (Brazilian-style espresso). The market even sold laundry detergent and other cleaning products imported from Brazil! Framingham is not unique in the northeast. In Danbury, Connecticut, another major Brazilian destination, immigrants have been responsible for transforming the once-moribund Main Street with businesses that largely cater to their immigrant compatriots (De Oliveira 1996a; Swift 2002).

South Florida, with a substantial Brazilian population, also has a wide range of Brazilian-owned businesses, including gas stations, restaurants, snack bars, travel and remittance agencies, moving companies, cell phone and furniture stores, and, of course, the ubiquitous shops selling Brazilian products including *tangas*, the minuscule Brazilian bikinis sometimes referred to as "dental floss" (*fio dental*). South Florida is also home to many Brazilian professionals—doctors, dentists, lawyers, and accountants—who serve a largely Brazilian clientele.

The west coast is another major site of Brazilian settlement and, therefore, Brazilian business. The Brazilian Mall in metropolitan Los Angeles is a large shopping center complete with waterfall and tropical Brazilian décor. Anchored by the Supermercado Brazil, the mall has fifteen shops, along with a cultural space that features Brazilian films, music, cultural exhibitions, and cooking demonstrations. Los Angeles and San Diego are awash in dozens of Brazilian-owned businesses, including upscale restaurants and nightclubs, snack bars, food markets, motels, travel and remittance agencies, and newspapers and magazines aimed at both the local Brazilian community and aficionados of Brazil.

And southern California is not the lone nexus of Brazilian business and culture in the state. The San Francisco Bay area, aside from its much touted Brazilian-owned pizzerias, is also home to some dozen samba schools, the most in the nation.[5] The samba schools perform during the Carnaval celebration, held annually on Memorial Day weekend in the city, and, while many of the area's ethnic groups are represented, the Brazilian and Caribbean contingents are the most dazzling in an event that features five thousand dancers and musicians and attracts close to a half-million spectators (Ribeiro 1997).

As a sideline, some Brazilian members of San Francisco's samba schools give *batucada* and samba lessons, mostly to American devotees of things Brazilian.[6] As such, they are engaged in what has been called "informal self-employment," informal in that they lack separate places of business and may or may not pay taxes on their earnings (Raijman 2001). Other examples of informal self-employment among Brazilians include housekeeping and babysitting jobs, catering, street vending, and craft sales. In New York City, for example, there are several women who make Brazilian culinary specialties—*pão de queijo* (cheese bread), *pasteis* (savory meat- or shrimp-filled pastries), and a variety of desserts—that they sell to fellow immigrants. These are less visible than ethnic retail sales because they are not associated with a physical space like a storefront. Narrow definitions of self-employment often ignore such informal economic activities, many of which are carried out by immigrant women. And, as we have seen, these activities can lead to successful business formation, as in the case of housecleaning.

There are also examples of Brazilian immigrants who have "made it big" in the United States in businesses unrelated to their ethnicity. In New York City, these include the owner of an upscale Manhattan furniture store and the proprietor of a chic beauty salon, the clothes designer with her own shop in SoHo and the manufacturer of pricey handbags sold in New York department stores. Then there are the hugely successful seven sisters who began offering "Brazilian bikini waxes" to women at their exclusive Manhattan salon, the popular personal trainer working at a fashionable East Side gym, the society florist, the interior designer, and the art gallery owner—Brazilian immigrants all turned entrepreneurs. Examples in Atlanta include Brazilians who own upscale restaurants as well as large pool construction and pool service companies, while in Los Angeles some Brazilians who have "made it" are employed in the recording, movie, and music industries (Marcus 2008b; Beserra 2003).

Emigration can also mean decisive moves up the social ladder. There is, for example, the Brazilian from a modest background who worked as a waiter and then as a maître d' in a restaurant in New York's Little Brazil and who now owns his own restaurant in Midtown Manhattan. Then there is the immigrant who began transporting goods with a small, rented van. In time, his business grew, and today he has more than ten trucks making deliveries around the New York metropolitan area. There is also the Brazilian couple with two American-born children who worked their way up from sous-chef and housecleaner to owners of a highly rated Brazilian restaurant in Queens. Finally, there's the divorced woman who was a licensed cosmetologist but never practiced her trade in Brazil. After arriving in New York, in 1999, she worked as a housekeeper and babysitter and cleaned a beauty salon. Today, now documented and married to an American, she owns her own hair salon on Manhattan's East Side. These examples of "moving on up," especially for immigrants of modest roots, are instances of social mobility that Brazilians often complain are impossible in Brazil. Without the cleaning business in the United States, said one immigrant, her family never would have succeeded. "Here, it's hard," she said. "There, it's impossible" (Menai 2007, 77).

What They Do: Japan and Europe

We now turn to Brazilian employment in destinations outside the United States—in Japan, for example, where Brazilians of Japanese ancestry (*nikkejin*) are heavily involved in the manufacturing sector of the economy. There, as we have seen, they work in the difficult blue-collar jobs that are shunned by the Japanese themselves. About half of Japanese Brazilian immigrants in Japan—both men and women—are employed on assembly lines in factories that manufacture car parts, electronics, and foodstuffs. Others work in cleaning firms or hotels, as security guards and home care attendants, or in construction jobs; some *nikkejin* women are employed as caddies on golf courses. However, unlike the job market for Brazilian women in the United States, where, at least initially, a majority are employed as domestic servants, the typical Japanese family does not employ domestic help, so these kinds of jobs are not available to immigrant women there (Roth 2002; Tsuda 2003; Rossini 1995; Koyama 1998).

Wages earned by Brazilians in Japan compare favorably to those earned in the United States. Trading their "third-class Brazilian currency" for the "first-class yen," Brazilian immigrants eagerly took jobs that, they believed, would allow them to save in one year what it took ten years to earn in Brazil (Ishi 2003). In the early 1990s, when *nikkejin* first immigrated to the land of their ancestors, the average immigrant male factory worker earned $3,000 a month. Wages fell with the recession during the decade that followed, and, by 2001, income had declined on average by about one-third, with reduced opportunities for overtime pay. Nevertheless, *nikkejin* still earned five to ten times what they were earning in Brazil. The typical middle-class monthly income in Brazil is equal to the pay for about five days' work in Japanese factories. Today the wages of Brazilians in Japan range from $1,500 to $2,500 a month; the latter figure is higher than the average income of doctors, lawyers, and university professors in Brazil (Yamanaka 1996a, 1996b; Salgado 2001; Tsuda 2002).

Nikkejin women are regularly paid 20 to 30 percent less than men for the same jobs. For example, during the period of top pay in the 1990s, women in manufacturing averaged $2,000 a month, whereas men earned an average of $3,000. These pay differentials appear even in want ads published in Portuguese-language newspapers in Japan. Still, despite such gender discrimination, the income of *nikkejin* women was far more than what they had earned in Brazil as white-collar and professional workers (Yamanaka 1997).

Some older women who emigrated from Brazil to Japan were actually born in Japan, having arrived in Brazil as children after World War II. Because they speak Japanese, they returned to Japan to work as home care attendants. These jobs paid an average of $140 a day in the 1990s, again far more than these women or their families had ever earned in Brazil. In effect, because of their knowledge of Japanese, older *nikkejin* women created an economic niche for themselves as health care aides in hospitals and private homes. These large wage differentials were and still are the primary catalyst for the exodus from Brazil to Japan (Yamanaka 1997).

Despite the decline in wages and the return of unknown numbers of *nikkejin* to Brazil—a return discussed in chapter 12—some researchers have suggested that these immigrants have become structurally embedded in the Japanese labor market and that the introduction of relatively cheap foreign labor has created a reliance on such labor in Japan, generating a self-perpetuating demand for immigration (Kashiwazaki 2002).

In contrast to the situation in Japan, where few *nikkejin* immigrants speak Japanese well, in Portugal, where Brazilians constitute about 20 percent of foreigners in the country, they obviously are fluent in the local language, and in many instances this fluency affects the sort of jobs they hold there. Portugal is one of the only nations where highly trained Brazilians are able to secure jobs in their own fields of expertise, a situation that is rare or impossible in most immigrant destinations. Take the famed "dental invasion" (*invasão odontologica*), for example, in which significant numbers of dentists trained in Brazil immigrated to Portugal, where they came into direct competition with their local Portuguese counterparts, much to the latter's chagrin (Moura 2010; Soares 1997).

Dentists are not the only Brazilian professionals attracted to Portugal. Estimates suggest that close to 20 percent of Brazilian immigrants there are in the liberal professions, with large numbers in computing, communications, marketing, advertising, and television production, all fields in which skilled workers were in short supply locally. In other words, Brazilian immigrants in Portugal are much more likely to work in the fields in which they were trained than those in the United States, Japan, or other destinations in Europe (Bógus 1995a, 1995b).

This is not to suggest that all Brazilians in Portugal are employed as white-collar professionals. Recent immigrants there have diverse roots and varied employment situations. They range from working-class Brazilians from small towns in Minas Gerais who live and work on construction sites in Lisbon; to Brazilian women employed as housecleaners, home care attendants, and hotel and restaurant workers; to highly trained professionals from São Paulo who work for large computer companies. As a general rule in Portugal, as in the United States and Japan, the employment of Brazilians in relatively menial jobs has meant downward mobility in terms of social status and prestige while providing a higher income than was possible in Brazil (Padilla 2007; França 2010).

Money Sent Home

Given the decline in status that most Brazilians suffer when they emigrate—compensated for to some extent by their higher earnings—it's useful to examine their goals for this money. What is it used for? How much of what they earn is sent back to Brazil in the form of remittances? These are really two separate but interrelated questions. The first focuses on individual goals and personal behavior; the second analyzes the impact of these individual decisions on the macroeconomic level for the nation as a whole.

In my own research, I found that about half of the immigrants I studied sent money home irregularly or occasionally. But most of those who sent frequent remittances were not, in fact, sending money to support their families in Brazil. Rather, they were sending it to build a nest egg for their own use when they return home—to buy a house or an apartment or start a business—or to pay off a personal debt incurred for their trip to United States. In other words, I found very few Brazilian immigrants in New York who provided routine financial support for their families in Brazil (Margolis 2009).

This is similar to the findings of Ana Cristina Braga Martes (1996b, 2008), who has done research for more than a decade on Brazilian immigrants in Boston. While most of those she interviewed belonged to the lower-middle class in Brazil—a segment of the population that lost buying power during the last decades of the twentieth century—and 80 percent of them sent remittances with some regularity, their main motivation for sending money home was, in her words, "not for relieving poverty, but for avoiding it" (2008, 130). While the infusion of money certainly helped family budgets, most of the cash was used to buy land or to start businesses in Brazil.

Many Brazilians who used remittance money to start new businesses lost everything—mostly because of their inexperience—so the more rational alternative was to invest money in real estate. Buying a house or apartment could relieve the family in Brazil of having to pay rent and also could supplement the family income by renting out the property. Then, too, purchasing real estate, including land, was seen as a long-term investment by emigrants who eventually planned to return to Brazil (Siqueira 2008).

Brazilians in other immigrant destinations also send money home. Estimates suggest that about 65 percent of the Brazilians working in Japan send remittances to Brazil. Another proposes that each Japanese Brazilian worker sends home an average monthly remittance of $2,000. And, over time, they often send a considerable amount of money—on average $30,000 to $50,000—with a few salting away as much as $100,000 during the course of their sojourn in Japan. While most save to buy a house, a car, or real estate, or to start a business in Brazil, some professionals—doctors, dentists, lawyers, accountants, engineers—use their savings to open their own clinics and offices there. In the early 1990s, a time of peak salaries, Japanese Brazilians were estimated to send home up to $4 billion to Brazil annually, but, by 2009, that figure had fallen to about $1.7 billion, still a significant sum (Amaral 2005; Patarra and Baeninger 1995; Yamanaka 1996b; Koyama 1998; Martes 2008; Sasaki 2009).

Brazilian government officials are clearly interested in facilitating the transfer of these funds back home. In 2009, for the first time, Brazilians in the United States had access to the Bank of Brazil's new remittance service, BB Money Transfer. With this new service, one does not need a bank account to receive remittance money in Brazil. One can simply go to a teller to make the withdrawal at any of the thousands of branches of the Bank of Brazil around the country; all that is needed is an identity card and proof of address. Money becomes available immediately at no charge because of the technology used by the service. A remittance that is sent on weekends, for example, can be withdrawn at the same time by a beneficiary who has an account at the Bank of Brazil or at any bank branch or ATM. Similarly, Bradesco, Brazil's largest private-sector bank, began offering financial services in Portuguese to Brazilian immigrants in Japan, with plans to install ATMs there in areas with large Brazilian populations (*Comunidade News* 2009b).

Then, too, in 2008, the Bank of Brazil began offering Brazilians living abroad lines of credit to allow them to buy homes in Brazil. Immigrants could receive financing over fifteen years for up to 60 percent of the cost of the property they wished to purchase. According to the bank, this new line of credit was meant to meet the demand of Brazilians who had migrated abroad and who wanted to save money to acquire their own homes in Brazil (Fernandes 2008).

The government's concern is, of course, related to the effect these monetary transfers have in Brazil. What do these individual remittances mean for the nation as a whole? As we have seen, the impact of remittance money is evident in small cities like Governador Valadares and Criciúma, large numbers of whose residents live abroad. Take Governador Valadares, for example. It is estimated that two-thirds of its citizens living outside Brazil remit money to the town, and nearly 40 percent of those invest in real estate locally, most in houses and apartments. This adds up to a lot of real estate transactions indeed. From the mid-1980s to the mid-1990s, nearly half of all real estate sales there involved emigrants (Soares 1995a, 1995b).

In more recent years, while it is estimated that around $72 million annually was being sent back to the city—a sum that represents nearly 60 percent of the $127 million municipal budget—when the exchange rate of the Brazilian *real* to the U.S. dollar reached a low in 2007, Governador Valadares and two dozen towns in the surrounding area felt the economic impact and experienced significant declines in real estate and other local investments. The sector most affected by the drop in remittances was construction. The ripple effects of changes in the exchange rate were felt throughout these immigrant-sending communities, which stagnated economically (Mineo 2006a; Peixoto 2007; Moreira 2007).

These are the impacts of remittances in relatively small communities, but, since most of the money sent home is widely dispersed to many parts of Brazil, remittances have not had a noticeable effect on larger population centers. For example, many thousands of Brazilians from Belo Horizonte, the capital of the state of Minas Gerais, have emigrated abroad and sent money home. But, given the size of the city, Brazil's third largest, with some 5.5 million inhabitants in the greater metropolitan area, their monetary contributions are virtually invisible locally.

Nevertheless, while perhaps not evident outside smaller immigrant-sending communities, the sums sent back to Brazil are impressive indeed, with 1.3 million Brazilians receiving remittances from relatives or friends living abroad. To cite just one statistic: the Brazilian Congress estimated that in 2004 the $5.6 billion sent to Brazil by emigrants abroad—just under 1 percent of the nation's gross domestic product—was roughly the same amount that the country earned from soybeans, its leading export.

This was the largest transfer of money sent to any country in Latin America or the Caribbean except for Mexico. However, because most of these remittances were sent informally, Brazil's Central Bank officially registered only $2.4 billion dollars remitted that same year (Rohter 2005; Martes and Soares 2006; Luna 2005; Langevin 2010).[7]

These figures make clear that there are wide discrepancies between informal remittance figures and official ones. However, what is known with certainty is that, because of the worldwide economic crisis in the late 2000s, the valorization of the Brazilian *real* vis-à-vis the dollar, and the improved economy in Brazil, a significant but unknown number of Brazilian emigrants have been returning home in more recent years. This is reflected in a nearly 24 percent drop in remittances sent to Brazil between 2008 and 2009, the largest decline in more than a decade (Bernstein and Dwoskin 2007; Peixoto 2010).

Whatever the amount of remittances sent home, has the much-heralded economic boom in Brazil that began in the first decade of the new millennium created new jobs, and has this, in turn, impacted emigration? This question is explored more fully in chapter 12, but it is worth noting here that, by 2007, after years of economic crises, the Brazilian economy was growing, as was optimism about it. According to government data, Brazil's gross domestic product grew by 5.4 percent that year and has grown at a similar rate through the first decade of the new millennium (*Economist* 2009).

Yet this rosy scenario does not seem to have convinced a flood of Brazilians abroad to return home. "If Brazil were so good, people would not be working until the wee hours to save money," one Brazilian in London told BBC Brasil in 2008. "I only see Brazilians arriving. Those who returned to Brazil want to return here. . . . I think the situation is only improving there for the rich" (quoted in Pereira 2008b). It is apparent that, at least for the time being, Brazil's economic growth is still not capable of anchoring educated immigrants to their homeland. Many college graduates in Brazil are still struggling to get jobs that offer compensation equal to what a restaurant worker earns in immigrant destinations in the industrialized world (Pereira and Salek 2008).

Wilson Fusco, a Brazilian demographer, notes that Brazil's economic boom has not brought an immediate reaction on the part of immigrants. "Their relatives and friends in Brazil need to feel these economic changes in order to incentivize the return of these Brazilians," he says. "Newspaper accounts [of the improved economy] don't have the same impact as [the opinions of] those who stayed in Brazil" (quoted in Pereira 2008a). Nevertheless, he believes that ongoing good news about Brazil will eventually impact emigrants' decisions to return. It will be one more factor to be considered, along with growing unemployment in the industrialized countries, greater fear and difficulties caused by crackdowns against undocumented immigrants, and the strength of the *real* against the dollar, the euro, and the yen (Pereira 2008b).

Brazil's Government Takes Notice

Since emigration from Brazil began in earnest in the late 1980s and Brazilian émigrés began sending billions of dollars home annually, the Brazilian government, most particularly Itamaraty, Brazil's Ministry of Foreign Affairs, has taken notice. Itamaraty established a series of programs in an effort to meet the needs of Brazilians abroad. But these initiatives were not directed at all citizens living outside Brazil; rather, they were largely intended for Brazilians in the United States, Europe, and Japan, not those in the countries that border Brazil. The citizens councils, itinerant consulates, and other schemes launched by Itamaraty have had less impact on Brazilian immigrants in Paraguay, the second-largest Brazilian immigrant community outside the United States, or on any of the other countries that border Brazil (Sprandel 2006).

One of the earliest indications of the Foreign Ministry's interest in Brazilians abroad took place in Lisbon in 1997 at a conference on Brazilian emigration. There the diplomat charged with Itamaraty's outreach to Brazilians living outside Brazil told the assembled academics and community leaders that Brazilian consulates around the world were no longer interested only in issuing visas for foreigners traveling to Brazil but also wanted to serve the nation's citizens abroad. Or, as reported in *Veja*, Brazil's equivalent of *Time* magazine, it took more than a decade for the foreign office to recognize that its job was not just to "sit next to the superpowers in the UN." The diplomat then pointed to several policies aimed at this constituency: the Brazilian constitution was altered to recognize dual citizenship; itinerant consulates were established to travel to smaller cities and towns that have immigrant populations, and to factories in Japan that employ large numbers of Brazilians; educational books and TV programs in Portuguese were distributed to immigrant communities, along with information on education and health; and finally, in answer to the complaints of some Brazilians about their poor reception at Brazil's consulates, he concluded by saying that citizens have the "absolute right to good treatment" by Brazilian consular personnel (Klintowitz 1996, 29; Amorim 1997).

In the mid-2000s, Itamaraty established a division, the Sub-Secretariat for Brazilians Living Aboard, and sponsored a conference on emigration two years later. In 2009, the Foreign Ministry held a second conference at which a website, Brazilians in the World: Portal of Brazilian Immigrant Communities Abroad (Brasileiros no Mundo: Portal das Comunidades Brasileiras no Exterior), was launched. This three-day meeting, held in Rio de Janeiro, was attended by more than 400 delegates, including more than fifty consuls general representing Brazilian communities around the world. There were formal sessions, including talks titled "Health, Social Welfare and Work," "Consular Services," "Education and Culture," and "Political Representation." The conference's most important measure was the approval of the election, in 2010, of sixteen official representatives of Brazilian communities abroad who would then form the Council of Community Representatives. Although the government agreed to cover travel and other expenses to meetings of the council, which would take place at least twice a year, the positions would be unpaid and open to Brazilians who had lived for at least three years in the foreign community that they were representing. The platforms of candidates would be posted online, and voting would also be electronic. Each region—North America (including the United States and Canada), Europe, Asia-Oceania (including Japan and Australia), and Africa–Middle East—would have four representatives. Brazilians living in Paraguay and other nations that border Brazil were neither invited to participate in the conference nor awarded representatives on the council (Langevin 2010; Nublat 2010).

Itamaraty was not the only government organ interested in Brazilians living outside Brazil. In 2008, a member of Brazil's House of Deputies, citing the estimated 2.5 million Brazilians living abroad, proposed that Brazilian emigrants have the right to elect their own representatives to Brazil's National Congress. They would constitute the "State of Emigrants" (Estado dos Emigrantes). The deputy argued that Brazilians abroad constitute the "twenty-eighth state in the Brazilian federation" and said that emigrants "have earned recognition for their notable contribution to our economy"—citing estimates that they send home $10 billion a year— "and spread of our culture" (Câmara dos Deputados 2008).

This was followed by yet another Itamaraty-sponsored gathering, the Conference of Brazilians in the World (Conferência Brasileiros no

Mundo), this time held in Brasília, to discuss the creation of a twenty-eighth state. This was, in part, a response to the more than twenty thousand individuals who had signed a petition requesting that Brazilians living abroad have the right to directly elect their representatives, and a proposal to amend the Brazilian constitution to this effect was made before Congress. Here Brazil was following the example of other countries, including France, Portugal, and Italy, all of which had created councils of emigrants with elected representatives (*Comunidade News* 2009a).

These plans provoked considerable discontent among some Brazilians living abroad. Said one: "Brazilian emigrants have already formed a virtual State of the Emigrant [the website] and now we want a Secretary of State of Emigrants and emigrant representatives in Brasília." Moreover, these emigrant representatives should be entirely independent of Itamaraty. "An emigrant is an emigrant, a diplomat is a diplomat. The politics of emigration should not be run by diplomats but by emigrants themselves" (quoted in Weiden 2011).

Then there was the protest concerning who could vote. Some activists noted that this was not to be a universal vote but one open only to those who had computers and knew how to use them, an emigrant elite they referred to as "class A." "What sort of representation is this if, out of 2.5 million, only the 18,000 with computers vote?" demanded one emigrant. And the complaints continued. "Recall the Citizens Councils created by the government of FHC [President Fernando Henrique Cardoso] that only gathered elites together probably to drink whiskey with the Directors of Varig Airlines, the Banco of Brasil, and big shot lawyers. These were the people who represented us immigrants!" Other objections arose concerning the North American representatives, all of whom were from the east coast of the United States, with none from Canada. And emigrants from Africa? Said one activist: "I haven't seen a photo of all those elected but it seems to me . . . that there was not a black or mulato among them, even though the majority of Brazilian emigrants 'have a foot in Africa'" (quoted in Martins 2010).

Indeed, the citizens councils mentioned previously were an early effort to organize emigrants and were made mandatory at all consulates representing a minimum of five thousand Brazilians. By the late 1990s, there were thirty-eight citizens councils worldwide. In Boston, for example, the council included religious leaders, businessmen, community organizers, and professionals and met twice a year to discuss community issues. The council distributed bilingual books to local schools and lobbied the Bank of Brazil and Varig Airlines to begin serving the Boston area. Such "innovations [were] directed at migrants as settlers not sojourners," note two academics. Still, there was also grumbling because the consuls general appointed all twelve council members, so that questions of representativeness quickly arose (Levitt and de la Dehesa 1998, 18).

In contrast, Itamaraty's program of itinerant consulates, started in the mid-1990s, has not been the subject of dissent and appears to be functioning as intended. According to a consul general in New York, the goal of the itinerant consulates is to bring "the presence of the government to the isolated Brazilian abroad." Itinerant consulates make one or two trips a month to smaller communities of Brazilians within each consular district. The first itinerant consulate was in Paraguay in the mid-1990s, one of the few examples of Itamaraty outreach to Brazilians in that country. There are now itinerant consulates in many parts of the world, including several dozen operating in the United States alone (Sekles 1997; Assumpção 1997b).

In 2007, I accompanied New York's consul general and his wife on an itinerant consulate to Danbury, Connecticut. The Danbury event was held in the Brazilian American Catholic Center, and, when we arrived, more than 200 people, including infants and young children, were waiting to be assisted by five consular employees who had also traveled to Danbury from New York City. As their numbers were called, they went into another room to have their documents processed—passport renewals and replacements, registration of births and marriages, and other paperwork needed for various transactions in Brazil. The forms were made available by local Brazilian volunteers prior to the arrival of the consular personnel so that those waiting could be served quickly and efficiently. At the time, the itinerant consulate traveled to Danbury from New York twice a month, but, with the 2010 inauguration of the Brazilian Consulate in Hartford, Brazilians in Connecticut no longer needed the services of New York–based consular personnel.

Several initiatives to assist Brazilian immigrants have been undertaken by individual consulates. The Brazilian Consulate in New York City started a project called "Você é Legal, para Nós Você É Muito Legal" (You are legal, for us you are very cool). This is a play on the word "*legal*" in Portuguese, which means both "legal" and, colloquially, "cool." It was intended to make undocumented Brazilians less fearful about their legal status in the United States. Likewise, consulates began issuing *carteiras de matrícula consular* (consular registration cards) so that Brazilians would have at least one official form of identification with a picture ID.[8] Although

U.S. authorities have not formally recognized the *carteira* as a legal document, for those without green cards who were unable to acquire or renew driver's licenses because of their undocumented status, the *carteira* meant that they could open a bank account, rent an apartment, enter a federal building, board an airplane, and so on. The *carteira* is highly prized because, as an official form of identification, it can forestall the impression that its holder is "out of status." Said one Brazilian of her *carteira*: "I give thanks for the miracle of this little card. I felt like a prisoner inside this country and I was afraid to travel because I didn't have papers and they were asking for two photo IDs. But once I showed the little card, airline personnel didn't ask for anything else and I happily embarked for Florida" (quoted in Costa 2004a, 9).

Another initiative undertaken by several Brazilian consulates in the United States arranged for health insurance at a group rate for immigrants holding a Brazilian passport, regardless of their legal status. Most immigrants lack insurance, and the group plan was much cheaper than what could have been purchased individually. Finally, in 2004, a well-attended ceremony was held at the City University Graduate Center in New York City, where the Brazilian president, Luis Inácio Lula da Silva, inaugurated the Service for the Remittance of Resources for Brazilians Living Abroad (Serviço Caixa de Remessas de Recursos de Brasileiros Residentes no Exterior). Through this program, Brazilian immigrants could facilitate the transfer of remittances to Brazil via the Internet in a secure manner that was less costly than other alternatives. As a result of these programs, one consul general believes that the perception among Brazilians living abroad of their government representatives is shifting. Before "we were viewed as arrogant and elitist, but this has changed a lot" (quoted in Sekles 1997).

According to the New York Consulate's former liaison to the immigrant community, some Brazilians who become unemployed or have no place to live or have financial problems demand that the consulate help them because they are "Brazilian citizens." They view themselves as economic refugees who left Brazil because of their government's failure to provide them with economic opportunities. This attitude is summarized by one Brazilian who told the consulate's liaison that "the Consulate is Brazilian territory so that you are obliged to help me because I moved to America because the Brazilian government did not provide me with the conditions to live in Brazil" (Costa 2004a, 25).

Despite Itamaraty's role in immigrant affairs, Brazil's state-led policies have not encouraged immigrants to participate in politics back home.

Then, too, relatively few Brazilian immigrants appear to be interested in Brazilian politics. In the presidential elections in Brazil in 1998, only fifty thousand Brazilians living abroad registered to vote, and, of these, only half actually cast ballots. Still, in more recent years, with a potential electorate of up to 3 million, some political candidates have appealed for their votes. In 2010, both presidential candidates reached out via Twitter and blogs to encourage Brazilians abroad to vote for them, while the electoral commission advised Brazilian immigrants on how to register to vote at their respective consulates (Levitt and de la Dehesa 1998; *O Globo* 2010).

3

Who They Are

Brazilians [in the U.S.] are angry all the time. They come here to make a life but it is hard for them to accept that everyone is the same here, even if you are a "doctor" in Brazil. Here, you lose your title, everyone is the same, and it makes them angry.

Brazilian immigrant in New York City (quoted in Strategier 2006, 26)

In the previous chapter I mentioned that improvements in the Brazilian economy have not yet been sufficient to create enough jobs with good wages to secure well-educated Brazilians to their homeland. But are all Brazilian immigrants well educated? Just who are these immigrants, and what is their background in terms of social class, education, and origins in Brazil? These are the questions to which we now turn. Once again, I will describe only Brazilians who are immigrating to North America, Europe, England, and Japan here because they are very dissimilar in social and economic terms from those who go to countries that border Brazil. Those are covered in chapter 8.

In many ways, the initial exodus from Brazil was composed of that nation's "best and brightest" in the sense that a lot of Brazilians in the first decade or so of emigration were among the nation's most educated. When I did my research in the early 1990s, for example, I was quite stunned to find the high education level of most Brazilian émigrés in New York City. More than three-quarters of those in my sample had at least a high school education, while just under one-third were university graduates. And this at a time when only 28 percent of Brazilians had completed high school, and a mere 12 percent went on to university (Margolis 1994a).[1]

Nor were the Brazilians living in the Big Apple unique. Brazilians in Florida and California had educational attainments similar to those of

Brazilians in New York, with just under 40 percent of Brazilians in south Florida and just over half of those in Los Angeles having at least some university training. But such high levels of education were not uniform across the country. One study of Brazilian immigrants in Boston found that more than one-third had not completed high school, while 15 percent were university graduates. Nevertheless, the picture that emerged of Brazilians nationally in the 2000 U.S. Census showed them to be a decidedly educated group, especially when compared to other recent immigrants. Only 9 percent of Brazilians living in the United States in 2000 had failed to complete high school, according to census figures, while a majority of Mexicans and Central Americans in the country lacked high-school diplomas. Almost one-third of Brazilians were university graduates, and 12 percent had graduate or advanced degrees.[2] The latter two figures were notably higher than those for native-born Americans, of whom 25 percent have college or postgraduate degrees (Oliveira 2003; Beserra 2003; Martes 1997; Lima and Siqueira 2007).

Tables 2 and 3 present an overview of the educational attainment of Brazilians in the United States and in other countries. What little research has been done on Brazilians in Canada also found them to be mostly middle class and well educated. One study of the Brazilian community in British Columbia established that just under 60 percent had worked as "highly qualified professionals" in Brazil, while 9 percent had been entrepreneurs and only 2 percent had worked in blue-collar jobs before immigrating to Canada. This class standing was reflected in their educational attainment; close to 70 percent had had at least some higher education, while just 2 percent had completed only primary school. Still, the Brazilian population in other parts of Canada, especially Toronto, appears to be more mixed in

Table 2 Educational profile of persons born in Brazil living in the United States

Educational level	Percent
Less than high school	15
High school graduate	31
Some college	21
College graduate	21
Graduate or professional degree	11

Source: American Community Survey 2007–9.

terms of social class and education, with less-educated immigrants from Minas Gerais included in the mix (Botelho 1998; Shirley 1999).

And elsewhere? We already know that the educational level of Brazilian immigrants in Portugal also was generally high, at least during the first decade or so after their arrival in the mother country, and that many Brazilians were able to find jobs there that used the professional qualifications they had attained in Brazil. Of course, one important condition for their high-level employment in Portugal was fluency in the language. But this was the exception. For the most part, the relatively superior educational levels of Brazilian immigrants elsewhere in Europe, in England, and in Japan did not translate into white-collar and professional jobs.

To cite a few figures: During the early years of emigration nearly three-quarters of Brazilians living in Madrid had completed their secondary schooling, and about 13 percent were college graduates. The numbers are similarly high for Brazilians in Italy during the same period, where more than 80 percent had high school diplomas and 12 percent had college degrees. A 2010 survey of Brazilians in England found that nearly three-quarters had attended a university and that, of those, slightly more than half had obtained undergraduate degrees. Finally, about 70 percent of the *nikkejin* who emigrated from Brazil to Japan in the 1990s and shortly thereafter had completed secondary school, and of these 30 percent had gone on

Table 3 Educational levels of Brazilian immigrants in other countries

Country	Educational level
Canada (British Columbia)	70%, at least high school 2%, only primary school
Spain (Madrid)	75%, at least high school 13%, university graduates
Italy	80%, at least high school 2%, university graduates
England	75%, some university 8%, university graduates
Japan	70%, at least high school 30%, at least some university

Sources: Diverse.

to university. Interestingly, more female than male *nikkejin* were university graduates. Typically, they were unmarried eldest daughters who had gone to work in Japan to help their families in Brazil buy real estate or to fund higher education for a younger sibling (Fernandes and Rigotti 2008; Rossini 1995; Evans et al. 2011; Yamanaka 1996b; Nishida 2009).

As we will see in the discussion of social class that follows, the average level of education of Brazilians in some areas of the United States, in Portugal, and perhaps elsewhere appears to have declined after 2000. But first I want to establish that Brazilian immigration to the United States, Japan, and several European countries was a distinctly middle-class phenomenon, at least for the first decade or so of the flight from Brazil. This is hardly surprising, given that educational level and social class are closely related.

My research in New York City two decades ago suggested that the vast majority of Brazilians who arrived there belonged to their nation's middle sector. As such, they represented only a portion of Brazil's total social hierarchy, with the poorest and wealthiest segments absent from the mix. In Brazil, about 40 percent of the population then belonged to some sector of the middle class—upper, middle, and lower—while about 90 percent of Brazilian immigrants in New York City fell into that category. We see nearly the reverse of these proportions when we look at the bottom rungs of Brazil's social ladder. While the poorest classes accounted for 60 percent of the Brazilian population in the 1990s, only 10 percent of the immigrant population in New York did so at that time. In sum, Brazilian immigrants in the city were decidedly more middle class than their compatriots back home (Margolis 2009).

This is also true elsewhere in the United States. Brazilian immigrants in Danbury, Connecticut, are reported to be largely middle class and more affluent than other immigrant groups in that city, such as Ecuadorians. Prior to migrating to the United States, Brazilians in Framingham, Massachusetts, held archetypal middle-class positions—teacher, sales clerk, accountant, student, business owner, bank teller, journalist. Similarly, the majority of Brazilians in Pompano Beach and Deerfield Beach, Florida—significant sites of Brazilian settlement—were members of the lower middle class back home, while those farther south in Miami-Dade County were generally upper middle class. Then, too, research on Brazilians in the Los Angeles area found that most were middle class and, as we have seen, quite well educated (Swift 2002; Marcus 2011a; Alves and Ribeiro 2002; Oliveira 2003; Beserra 2003).

Still, there is no question that the issue of social class among Brazilian immigrants in the United States is a complicated one. As one researcher queries, "How does one categorize those Brazilian immigrants who were considered 'lower-middle class' or 'lower class' in Brazil, and after migrating to the United States generate over $8,000 in monthly revenues as house-cleaning business owners? Or those Brazilian immigrants who were once lawyers, engineers, or physicians in Brazil, and who, after migrating . . . to the United States, now work as housecleaners, construction workers, or pizza-delivery drivers?" (Marcus 2011a, 62).

Examining social class from the sending side of the transnational map, one researcher grouped the population of Governador Valadares into five social classes, using kilowatt consumption as a proxy for socioeconomic data. He found no current or former immigrants from families in the highest and lowest reaches of the local social pyramid; all came from the three middle sectors of the community (Goza 1994).

Similarly, in Japan, most *nikkejin* belong to the urban lower-middle and middle class and held white-collar and professional jobs before leaving Brazil; they were engineers, lawyers, dentists, secretaries, sales clerks, teachers, and students. Like most other Brazilian emigrants, they saw the move abroad as a personal investment opportunity, rather than as a neces-sity, because their relatives back home did not depend on a regular influx of cash to meet their basic needs. To be sure, given their middle-class roots and the university training of many, they experienced a "professional identity crisis" in Japan, where most work in blue-collar jobs at the bottom rung of Japanese society (Yamanaka 1996a; Sasaki 1996; Ishi 2003).

Generation and language also come into play in the experience of Brazilian women in Japan. As we have seen, one job niche filled by older *nikkejin* women with few skills other than fluency in Japanese is work in convalescent homes or as private attendants for the elderly. Younger *nikkejin* women who are educated but do not speak fluent Japanese usually work in small factories. Their reasons for coming to Japan also differ. Many senior women travel to Japan to experience Japanese culture first-hand, while younger women generally come for economic reasons—to save money for their education or to start a business. Some Brazilian women not of Japanese ancestry accompany their *nikkejin* husbands to Japan (Yamanaka 1996b, 1997).

Turning to Brazilians in Europe and England, they too were almost uniformly middle class for at least the first decade of emigration, although this has changed somewhat over time. In Portugal, for example, two stages of migration have been identified. The first wave of Brazilians, those who arrived in the 1980s through the mid-1990s, were upper middle class, with high levels of education. As we have seen, they went to Portugal because there were opportunities for skilled jobs in the booming Portuguese economy of the day. By the late 1990s, however, with the closing of Portugal's job market to foreign professionals from outside the European Union and the sharpening of immigration controls, the profile of incoming Brazilians began changing from a majority of professional middle-class workers to less-educated, lower-middle-class job seekers, most of whom worked in the informal economy as domestic servants, in commerce, and in restaurants. Moreover, by 2009, women made up 65 percent of the Brazilian immigrant population in Portugal, likely because women have an easier time than men getting jobs there (Fernandes and Rigotti 2008; Padilla 2007; dos Santos, Mendes, Rego, and Magalhães 2010).

Similarly, during the 1990s and until about 2000, Brazilians in London were young, largely middle class, and from Brazil's south and southeast, especially São Paulo. But, in more recent years, immigrants to the city have come from more humble backgrounds, with many from Minas Gerais, Goiás, and Paraná. The new arrivals, who have been dubbed "migrant workers," know little English and hope to earn money to help their families back home or to save to invest in some future project there. This later wave of immigrants has initially followed much the same path as the better-educated middle-class Brazilians who preceded them. Both arrived on tourist or student visas that they overstayed and hold similar kinds of jobs—in restaurants and bars, as housecleaners and nannies and delivery "boys." Those who stay on sometimes find jobs in construction, as electricians, or eventually open small businesses patronized by fellow immigrants (Evans et al. 2011; Brightwell 2010; Frangella 2010).

Perhaps nowhere in recent years has this downward shift in social class among Brazilian immigrants been more apparent than in the United States. Evidence for this comes from a variety of sources. According to the former liaison to the Brazilian immigrant community in the four-state region served by the Brazilian Consulate in New York City—New York, New Jersey, Pennsylvania, and Delaware—there has been a change in the socioeconomic backgrounds of Brazilians assisted by the consulate.[3] From the late 1980s through the 1990s, most belonged to the urban middle class, but, from 2000 on, more had working-class origins and at most a high school education. They were also more likely to come from small towns and rural areas in Brazil than their pioneering counterparts (Costa 2004a).

Once in the New York metropolitan area, many of these recent arrivals took jobs that were not very different from jobs they had in Brazil. An analysis of post-2000 consular data found that about a quarter of the Brazilian women employed as maids in the United States had been domestic servants in Brazil, while some 10 percent of the men working as waiters had held similar positions back home (Costa 2004b). Of course, the attraction of American jobs, however undesirable from the vantage point of working conditions, is that they pay wages that are many times what similar jobs pay in Brazil.

Others have also pointed out that recent immigrants come from more modest roots than their predecessors. A Brazilian in Massachusetts remarked that when he first came to the United States in the late 1980s, other Brazilian immigrants with whom he worked were lawyers, geologists, and engineers by training. But, when he returned to Massachusetts in the late 1990s, in his words, "the social class worsened." Most of his fellow countrymen were now from rural areas and were unfamiliar with Brazil's large cities (quoted in Marcus 2008a, 298). Similarly, the founder of the local Brazilian Women's Group noted that poorer, less-educated Brazilians from interior towns began arriving in Boston around 2000. Nevertheless, one researcher found that, although Brazilians in Boston said that many of their fellow immigrants were "uneducated farmhands," immigrants from small farms made up only between 1 and 2 percent of the population she sampled from the mid-1990s to 2005. In other words, Brazilians tended to exaggerate this portion of the immigrant community (Souza 2002; Martes 2010).

Then there are the new Brazilian émigrés living in Newark, New Jersey, and in Mount Vernon, a town in Westchester County just north of New York City. They too are from small towns, have working-class roots, and are almost all undocumented. Their intention is to be in the United States as short a time as possible to earn money to build a better life back home in Brazil. They live crowded together in order to increase their savings and are loath to spend money on shows, museums, or other entertainment in New York City; indeed, some have never even been to Manhattan (Strategier 2006).

Finally, the most recent immigrants from the far reaches of Brazil's western Amazon—the states of Rondonia and Acre—appear to be from more humble backgrounds and are much less educated than their pioneering compatriots from other parts of the country. The majority of *amazonenses*, as they are collectively called, have completed grade school but not high school. Most held unskilled jobs back home, working as truck drivers, supermarket checkouts, and gas station attendants, while many had small land holdings on which they raised cattle (Pedroso 2008; Gibson 2010).

Social Class and Emigration

How might we explain this downward drift in social class? Social scientists observed some years ago that, over time, the costs of migrating fall because each additional migrant who becomes part of a migration stream makes it more likely that others will follow. In other words, as the social networks of migration mature and expand, they reduce the financial and personal costs of migration, thus allowing for a more diverse migrant population. Decreased migrant selectivity over time is well documented. By lowering the costs and increasing the returns of migration, social networks help create a migrant demographic profile that increasingly reflects the population at the point of origin. Simply put, poorer immigrants who have not had access to the information and resources needed to emigrate abroad earlier now have both, thanks to the monetary assistance and advice provided by friends and relatives who were already established abroad. With more family members earning money overseas, a greater pool of financial assistance and information is available on which potential migrants can draw (Massey et al. 1998; Massey 1990; Massey et al. 1987).

Emigration for the middle class often means a fall from grace because of the low-status jobs many hold in host countries. Or, as one researcher put it, "Migrants with the greatest human capital fall farthest in status in the United States" (Mahler 1995, 126). But, as the migrant pool widens and becomes more diverse in terms of social class and education, emigration for others can mean a move up the social ladder; it can be a path to success in terms of both earnings and empowerment. Consider the Brazilian who returned home with the $50,000 he had saved working as a carpenter in Florida. He built a modest house, started making payments on a car and a few head of cattle, and opened a small food market with the money he had made in the United States. Before emigrating, he had earned $200 a month making deliveries for a pharmacy in his hometown. Another case in point from the other side of the emigration equation is the woman who stayed behind in Brazil and lived in a down-and-out neighborhood in Governador Valadares. She was eventually able to buy a modern three-bedroom house with the money two of her children earned in Massachusetts (Margolis 1990; Padilla 2007; Pedroso 2008; Mineo 2006b).

So now that the Brazilian immigrant population has become more diverse in terms of social class and education, have there been repercussions for relations within Brazilian communities abroad? After all, as the Brazilian anthropologist Roberto Da Matta noted some time ago, Brazil is a "society with an enormous preoccupation with social position and a tremendous awareness of all the rules and resources having to do with its maintenance, loss or threats to it" (1991, 143). These preoccupations are, indeed, carried abroad and are evident among Brazilians in New York, south Florida, and the greater Atlanta area—at least they have been well documented in those locales. Just one example: the arrival of less "elite" Brazilians in the city has disturbed the owner of a chic Brazilian restaurant on Manhattan's East Side. He said to me of the restaurants in Little Brazil, the street long associated with Brazilian immigrants, "It's fine if people want to go there, but we attract a better class of people."

Social class is also a divisive issue among some Brazilians in south Florida. Brazilians in Miami, many of whom claim they come from a "higher level" of Brazilian society than their poorer, less-educated compatriots in Pompano Beach and Deerfield Beach, often denigrate the latter by referring to them as the "*mineirada*," the "gang from Minas Gerais." This is meant as a slight to the many working-class and lower-middle-class Brazilians there who hail from that state, unlike their countrymen and women in Miami, who are more often from cosmopolitan Rio de Janeiro or São Paulo. According to one researcher, such distinctions by social class, place of residence in Florida, and place of origin in Brazil "permeate" the local Brazilian population (Resende 2009; Oliveira 2003).

This sort of elitism is also subtly reflected in the discourse of an organizer of the Brazilian International Press Awards, which have been given out in Miami for more than a decade. He presents a nearly idyllic portrait of Brazilians living in this country, while ignoring the "complex economic, political and social motivations that precipitated mass migration to the United States" (Butterman 2008, 3–4). Choosing to overlook the stark differences in economic condition and lifestyle among Brazilians in the United States, he castigates those who do not participate in events celebrating "Brazilianness" and maligns those who dare to suggest that U.S.-based Brazilians lack a sense of community. It is worth noting, however, that members of the "Brazilian community" at large are not welcomed to the awards ceremony, which is by invitation only (Butterman 2008).

If we turn to the Brazilian population in the Atlanta metropolitan area, we find that those from southeast Brazil—primarily Rio de Janeiro and

São Paulo—view Brazilians from the central western state of Goiás as "international laborers," while they see themselves as "globalized entrepreneurs who have become integrated into U.S. society" (Marcus 2008a, 159). Like the *mineirada* in south Florida, Brazilians from Goiás are referred to by their more sophisticated compatriots as "*o povão*"—the masses.

This sort of boundary-making has been interpreted as an attempt by Brazilian immigrants to reposition themselves within the local social hierarchy. Again, it is well to remember the singular importance of social class in Brazil. In the United States all are immigrants, many are undocumented and have limited English-language abilities, and a majority have low-level, unskilled jobs, but these boundary-setting efforts obscure these commonalties and seek to re-create the sharp social distinctions that permeate Brazilian society. Through the creation of boundary markers, the immigrant son of an elite family from Minas Gerais who is working as a dishwasher in Boston, or the immigrant daughter of a middle-class family from Rio de Janeiro who cleans apartments in New York, or the university graduate from São Paulo who is a short-order cook in Miami can distinguish himself or herself from a vague but assuredly less desirable Brazilian "other" (Martes 1998, 2000).

Race, another social construct, sometimes comes into play in the immigrant scheme of things. I believe that my own data on the racial composition of Brazilians in New York City can be generalized to other Brazilian communities in the United States. Recall the largely middle-class make-up of New York's Brazilian immigrant community, since it also holds the key to its racial make-up. Here, too, New York's Brazilians are not representative of their nation's population because most cluster at the lighter end of the color spectrum. In my study, 83 percent of the Brazilians interviewed were white, 8 percent were light mulatto or mulatto, and 8 percent were black. Thus, blacks and other "people of color," to use the Brazilian phrase, accounted for only about 16 percent of the city's Brazilian immigrant community, a fraction of the nearly 52 percent reported in the 2009 National Household Sample for Brazil as a whole (Pesquisa Nacional por Amostragem de Domicilio 2009).

This reflects the relationship between race and class in Brazil. Brazilian racial types are not randomly distributed across the nation's social classes, and people of color are overrepresented at the lower ranks of Brazilian society, underrepresented in the middle sectors, and nearly absent among the nation's tiny elite. Thus, if Brazilian immigration is mostly a middle- and lower-middle-class phenomenon—as it appears to have been in New

York City and elsewhere at least for the first decade or so of immigration—it is not surprising that the immigrant population is lighter than the nation as a whole. It is also true, however, that, as the Brazilian immigrant population in the United States becomes more diverse in terms of social class, it is likely that this will be reflected in more racially diverse Brazilian communities.[4]

Gender and Emigration

This brings us to another variable in the immigration equation: gender. Here there are three basic issues: the actual gender makeup of Brazilian communities abroad, family structure in the context of international migration, and the relationship between the sexes under the exigencies of living in a new land.

During the very early years of emigration, in the mid to late 1980s, evidence suggests that men accounted for perhaps 70 percent of the Brazilian immigrant population in the United States. Similarly, in Japan, in the late 1980s and early 1990s, the typical *nikkejin* was a lone male sojourner. We find similar ratios when we look at sending communities in Brazil, for example Governador Valadares and Criciúma in Santa Catarina, where almost two-thirds of the residents of both towns going abroad were male. Thus, Brazilians followed a common pattern in new migration streams; men tended to emigrate first.

By the 1990s, however, sex ratios among Brazilian immigrants began to balance out. By then, New York City's Brazilian community had only slightly more men than women, and this also seems to have been true elsewhere in the United States. Likewise, in Japan, by the mid-1990s, the sex ratio of *nikkejin* had changed from a pattern in which working-age males predominated to one more balanced in age and sex. And sex ratios have continued to evolve. By 2000, according to data collected by the Brazilian Consulate in New York City, women began outnumbering men in the consular district by roughly 54 percent to 46 percent. But, even early in the exodus from Brazil, women made up 60 percent of the Brazilian immigrant population in Spain and 70 percent in Italy, special cases that we consider in chapter 6 (Yamanaka 1997; Costa 2004a; Fernandes and Rigotti 2008).

Before we turn to family structure and relations between the sexes in the context of international migration, we must know with whom men and women travel abroad, that is, alone or with friends or in family groups. As we've seen during the very early years of emigration from Brazil, the great majority of immigrants were male; they traveled alone or with close male relatives and friends. By the time female immigrants began arriving in the United States in large numbers, many were accompanied by husbands, partners, or parents. A study of Brazilians in south Florida found that, in many cases, entire nuclear families had emigrated together, about half accompanied by their children. Today more women come alone—women who are unmarried, divorced, or widowed (Martes 1996c; Oliveira 2003; Goza 1994).

The marital status and hence the family structure of Brazilian immigrants has also varied over time. In the early 1990s, 60 percent of the immigrants in my research sample were single when they came to New York, about one-quarter were married, and the rest were separated, divorced, or widowed. Many immigrants married only *after* coming to the United States. Although the evidence is somewhat contradictory, these rates may not have changed very much as this immigrant stream has aged. For example, a random sample of four hundred Brazilians in Framingham, Massachusetts, in the early 2000s found that only about 20 percent of the women were married, as were some 30 percent of the men. Still, other research suggests that Brazilians in the United States today are more likely to be married than those who came in earlier years (Marcus 2004; Goza 1994; Badgley 1994).

In the early 1990s, children made up a small part of New York's Brazilian immigrant population, but, as time has passed, their numbers have been on the rise. This is true in other Brazilian communities in the United States, as well. While there are still very few Brazilians under the age of fifteen registered in the four-state region covered by Brazil's New York consular district, this may be an artifact of children being American-born or too young to vote, with no pressing need, in either case, for their parents to register them.

Another reason for the dearth of children registered at the New York Consulate is that some remained behind in Brazil. An unknown number of married men have come to the United States alone with the sole purpose of saving money to take back to their families in Brazil. Relatively few women have followed this path, and those that have are usually divorced or separated or have a very specific objective, such as earning money to pay for a son or daughter's university tuition. These patterns, in turn, are likely related to the socioeconomic class and financial resources of emigrants and their families prior to leaving Brazil. That is, if financially able, married couples generally travel to the United States together, but families with fewer resources who have difficulty paying for the trip tend to stay behind in Brazil (Costa 2004a).

We see similar familial changes among Brazilian immigrants in Japan. By the mid-1990s, the modal family had become a married couple with children under the age of fifteen. In fact, by the early 2000s, a majority of *nikkejin* were married with children, and many had brought over close female relatives—primarily grandmothers or aunts—to help with child care and other domestic chores while both parents work. This is comparable to the emerging pattern I noted a decade earlier in New York City—what I termed the Brazilian "grandmother-child minder phenomenon" (Koyama 1998; Salgado 2001; Margolis 1994a).

Less data exists on family structures in other countries where Brazilians have immigrated, although evidence suggests that in Portugal in recent years there has been a growing tendency for Brazilian women to migrate alone or to migrate as part of a "family strategy." One researcher suggests that even for single, divorced, or separated women who migrate alone, migration is a "family project" because they maintain ties with relatives in Brazil helping them financially or having them care for the children they left behind (Padilla 2007).

We now turn to the more contentious topic of shifts in gender roles under the exigencies of international migration. A good deal has been written about this as it relates both to Brazilians and to other international migrants. Let me begin by giving one telling quotation from a study of Brazilians in the greater Atlanta area, a major site of Brazilian settlement: "Brazilian immigrant women are generally happier in the United States than their male counterparts since levels of female social capital and economic empowerment increase after migration" (Marcus 2008a, 314–15).

According to Alan Marcus, the researcher just quoted, some Brazilian men feel "emasculated" as a result of their spouses' newfound financial independence and the social freedom it affords. He suggests that immigrant women are "almost defiantly asserting their perceived and newly found . . . independence," which he sees reflected in the remark of one housecleaner he interviewed: "Now the check comes in *my* name!" she told him proudly (Marcus, personal communication).

As a consequence, Brazilian men generally have a more difficult time adjusting to the exigencies of the immigrant experience than Brazilian women. Men who work in construction jobs in enclosed environments with other immigrants, for example, have less exposure to American society and less opportunity to speak English than do women who work as house-keepers and who necessarily interact on a daily basis with their employers (Marcus 2008a).

These findings are borne out to some degree in other Brazilian immigrant communities, and they often create friction between the sexes. As the quotation suggests, the main catalyst for changes in gender roles is the fact that nearly all Brazilian immigrant women hold jobs. While it is not unusual for married women in Brazil to be employed, their earnings are seen as "supplemental" to those of their husband, and their primary responsibility still centers around home and children. Even in middle-class families that have domestic servants, it is understood that the household is the woman's domain, and the man as the "family provider" takes little or no responsibility in it (Margolis 1992; DeBiaggi 2002).

Thus, under the aegis of immigration, Brazilian women gain greater financial autonomy, setting the stage for a reformulation of traditional gender roles. In Boston, for example, nearly all immigrant women work outside the home, sometimes earning more than their husbands or partners. It is within this context that the traditional household division of labor in Brazil, including child care, can become a source of conflict. Because female immigrants are in a different place financially than they were in Brazil, and because they are now living in a new, more liberal setting in terms of what are deemed appropriate gender roles, they begin to question the old pattern of relations with their husbands or partners, including, perhaps most important, the prior domestic division of labor. Then, too, because domestic servants are no longer in the picture in the United States, middle-class Brazilian couples come to rely on each other to a greater extent than they did in Brazil to accomplish the myriad quotidian tasks that surround their working lives (DeBiaggi 1996; H. Galvão 2005).

The reaction to these novel circumstances varies. In some cases, the fact that women not only have jobs but may earn more than their spouses is cited as a primary source of contention that leads couples to separate and divorce. Women, say such men, become "greedy" and "only think about money" (Assunção 2011, 164). Other couples not only maintain but actually increase the rigidity of their traditional gender roles in order to avoid conflict. More frequently, women simply no longer accept inequality in the division of household tasks; the traditional structure itself is questioned. When women gain financial clout by working outside the home all day and men still refuse to take on "female" tasks, discord often ensues. Too often, men perceive these shifts as transitory and, when they return to Brazil, expect everything to go back to the way it was before emigration. For some, this leads to discord in the relationship and eventual separation and divorce. Reconciliation—if it occurs—usually results from the adoption of what Brazilians themselves call an "American-style relationship," that is, a more egalitarian partnership when it comes to domestic issues. Said one immigrant husband: "The fact is that in Brazil women never demand these things [i.e., men sharing household tasks]. The women change here. . . . I think that in Brazil owing to their financial situation, there they are women" (Siqueira 2011; quoted in DeBiaggi 1996, 25).

Where They Come From: Hometowns and Cities

This is only a partial portrait of Brazilian immigrants. What is missing is place of origin in Brazil because, like social class, geographical residence prior to emigration and the regional stereotypes that that often entails are key status markers for Brazilians living abroad. Mirroring the importance of this social signifier, towns, cities, and states of origin in Brazil are frequently reflected in the names of stores, restaurants, and food markets in Brazilian immigrant commercial districts in the United States.

One researcher has characterized relations among compatriots in Brazilian communities in the United States as "fragmented interactions," a reference to the fact that regional and rural-urban distinctions seem to be magnified in the context of emigration (Marcus 2008b, 306). Regional stereotypes that lead to such fragmented interactions are myriad. In the Atlanta metropolitan area, for example, immigrants from the state of Goiás, in Brazil's central west, are considered unsophisticated, indeed coarse, by *cariocas* and *paulistas* (natives of Rio de Janeiro and São Paulo). *Goianos*, in turn, see their big-city compatriots as elitists. Goiás is deemed a peripheral, rural agricultural state with a provincial, uneducated population by urban immigrants from Rio de Janeiro, São Paulo, and Belo Horizonte who consider their region the "core" of the nation (Marcus 2008b).[5]

The same is true in New York City, although there immigrants from Minas Gerais, *mineiros*, replace *goianos* as objects of derision. While *mineiros* are sometimes lauded as pioneers, they are more often vilified for a variety of real or imagined transgressions by their countrymen and women from other parts of Brazil. *Mineiros* are the butt of endless jokes, and natives of the state are the victims of unflattering stereotypes. They too are said to be provincial and are described as unrefined rubes, especially in comparison to their cosmopolitan compatriots from Rio de Janeiro and São Paulo. And so it goes. As we've seen, in south Florida, the dividing line is between Brazilians in Miami, most of whom are from Rio de Janeiro and São Paulo, and their fellow countrymen in Pompano Beach, who are dismissed as provincial, unlettered *mineiros* who are best avoided (Margolis 2009; Oliveira 2003).

Such negative stereotypes are rooted in geographical and rural-urban distinctions brought from home. What we see here is a revamping and updating of the traditional discourse of urban Brazilians, especially those from major metropolitan areas like Rio de Janeiro and São Paulo, who have a long tradition of maligning people from the interior of their country, calling them *caboclos*, *caipiras*, or *sertanejos* (hillbillies, hicks, or backwoodsmen).

Regional stereotypes aside, what are the specific origins of Brazilian immigrants in their vast nation of sprawling cities, lush tropical forests, dazzling beaches, immense savannahs, semi-arid scrub forests, and luxuriant farmland, a nation, in fact, as vast and varied as the United States? The question of their geographical roots was a fairly simple one in the early 1990s. Then, more than 40 percent were *mineiros*, natives of Minas Gerais, as we have seen, a state that is often associated with international migration. Yes, *paulistas* and *cariocas* were also important, together accounting for another 45 percent of the Brazilians I interviewed; the rest were from a few other states in Brazil, primarily Espírito Santo and Paraná. Similarly, a majority of Brazilians in south Florida came from Minas Gerais, Rio de Janeiro, and São Paulo, as did those in Los Angeles, with representatives of Rio Grande do Sul, Brazil's southernmost state, present there, as well. Likewise, nearly all *nikkejin* going to Japan are from São Paulo and Paraná, the home states of most Japanese Brazilians. But *mineiros* still dominate in some areas. A random sample of four hundred Brazilians in Framingham, Massachusetts, in 2004 found that half were from Minas Gerais. In sum, the vast majority of immigrants through the 1990s came from the south-central and southern parts of the nation (Margolis 1994a; Oliveira 2003; Beserra 2003; Higuchi 2001; Marcus 2004).

The more recent exodus from Brazil is more diverse in terms of geographical reach, and in most areas *mineiros* no longer constitute the majority of immigrants as they did during the first decade or so of out-migration. We can see this growing diversity in New York, where, by 2005, immigrants from Minas Gerais accounted for no more than a quarter of Brazilians in the city, and new sending states had been added to the mix—Goiás in the central west, Bahia in the northeast, and Roraima and Rondonia, in the far northern and western reaches of the Amazon Valley. Today there are also more immigrants arriving from rural areas in Brazil than in earlier years, when a majority came from urban centers (Amaral 2005; Costa 2004a; Gibson 2010).

Brazilian immigrants from the same small towns and cities have tended to cluster in the same regions abroad. Take metropolitan Atlanta, for example, where many immigrants are from Piracanjuba, a town of about 25,000 in the state of Goiás. Immigrants from that state also account for a significant percentage of Brazilians in the San Francisco Bay area. In fact, it is said that, after Minas Gerais, Goiás is now the second-largest exporter of immigrants to the United States (Marcus 2009a; Huamany 2004; Ribeiro 1997).[6]

In focusing on origins from the vantage point of sending communities in Brazil, we should mention Criciúma, a town of about 170,000 in the state of Santa Catarina that, since 1990, has been an important source of immigrants to the United States. The initial impetus for emigration was the decline in carbon mining in the area, which threw thousands out of work. Then, in 1999, the textile industry that had replaced mining was adversely affected by the devaluation of the Brazilian currency, prompting a second wave of émigrés. In fact, nearly half of all immigrants from the town made their first trip to the United States between 1998 and 2000. Some twenty thousand former residents of Criciúma and the nearby region now live in the greater Boston area, while some locals of Italian ancestry have immigrated to Italy (Assis 2003; dos Santos 2001; Siqueira, Assis de Oliveira, and de Campos 2010).[7]

Two new sources of immigrants, Acre and Rondonia, states in the far western reaches of the Brazilian polity, began sending significant numbers abroad only after 2000. In Rondonia's case, these were often secondary migrants, that is, natives of Minas Gerais—specifically from the area around Governador Valadares—who first went to Rondonia seeking a better life, only to migrate again later on, this time to the United States. In Jaru, for example, a town of about sixty thousand in Rondonia, some residents who first migrated there from Minas Gerais in the 1980s later headed to south Florida, Boston, Newark, or Riverside, New Jersey. Today it is rare to meet someone in town or the surrounding countryside who does not have a relative or friend in the United States. Then, too, residents of Rondonia often have relatives in Minas Gerais who are thought to have predisposed them to move abroad (Moroz 2005b; Pedroso 2008).

Others from this region without roots in Minas Gerais also have been migrating to the United States. For example, in 2002, Acrelandia, a community of about fifteen thousand that has been dubbed the "Valadares of Acre," began exporting its citizens to the United States. The exodus from the town, which picked up in 2005, has been so great that Acrelandia has sent more immigrants to the United States than has any other locale in Acre, including Rio Branco, the state capital (Pedroso 2008).

One notable difference between immigrants from the two Amazonian states and those from elsewhere in Brazil is that this latest migration stream is largely male. As we will see in the chapter to follow, after the attacks on New York and Washington, DC, in 2001, it became ever more difficult to secure tourist visas to travel to the United States. Since the vast majority of immigrants from the Amazon region left home after 2000, they were far more likely to arrive in the United States by crossing over the border from Mexico than to fly in with tourist visas in hand. Since the Mexican route is far more dangerous and costly, this may explain the relative dearth of women among these recent arrivals from the Amazon region relative to arrivals from elsewhere in Brazil (Pedroso 2008).

So what can we conclude from the foregoing review of the social composition and origin of Brazilian emigrants? What started as a middle- and lower-middle-class phenomenon centering around the state of Minas Gerais and some specific locales in it became a more generalized, albeit still largely middle-class exodus from the urban areas of southeast Brazil, especially Rio de Janeiro and São Paulo. But, in time, with the inclusion of emigrants with more modest roots in small towns and rural areas in far-flung outposts of the country—in the central-west, northeast, and Amazon regions—the source of émigrés expanded to the extent that emigration became a truly national phenomenon.

4

How They Arrive

I tell them God made the earth, and Man made the borders. To go anywhere in
the world to better yourself is God's way. To not go because of borders and law is
Man's way. We follow God's way.

  Brazilian priest, Framingham, Massachusetts

In recent years, many Brazilian immigrants coming to the United States
entered the country by crossing over the border from Mexico, a
decidedly dangerous and costly route. For some immigrants, securing a
tourist visa to the United States has always been difficult, but, after
September 11, 2001, the barriers to traveling to this country as a tourist
mounted. Since the beginning of the new millennium, going to several
western European countries and England to find work also has become
more problematic for Brazilians and other would-be immigrants. The lone
exception for Brazilians—at least those of Japanese ancestry—is Japan,
where the vast majority of those who have traveled there to work have
done so with the official blessing of the Japanese government and Japanese
industry. The means of entry is important, since the conditions under
which international migration takes place can have long-term and far-
reaching consequences for immigrants' legal status.

As we will see in this chapter, how Brazilian immigrants enter the
United States, Portugal, Italy, other nations in western Europe, and
England—places favored by Brazilians—is linked to their social class and
financial resources, their level of education, and their place of residence in
Brazil. In a few cases, it also depends on their ancestry. As a general rule,
Brazilians of more modest means and those with less education have more
trouble acquiring tourist and student visas. Then, too, applications for
tourist visas from certain towns and states in Brazil raise red flags. Applicants from places well known as major immigrant-sending locales, such as

Governador Valadares and the surrounding towns in Minas Gerais and Criciúma, in southern Santa Catarina, are calls to arms for American consular personnel in Brazil. For example, in a group of fifty aspiring "tourists" from Governador Valadares who sought visas at the American Consulate in Rio de Janeiro, only five were successful. The town has such a suspect reputation among consular personnel that even people with considerable resources may be denied visas. One local man representing the Industrial Federation of Minas Gerais who owns, among other property, a pasta factory that employs two hundred people, was turned down for a visa. Similarly, in recent years it has become extremely difficult for residents of Criciúma to get tourist visas at the American Consulate in São Paulo, the one closest to their town. Some have opted to travel greater distances to establish "residence" in Rio de Janeiro by briefly renting an apartment there and then going to the local American Consulate in hopes of obscuring their actual hometown and being approved for a visa (Dos Santos 2006).

When I visited Governador Valadares in the early 1990s, the difficulty of getting tourist visas from the American Consulate was a constant topic of conversation. People liked to trade horror stories about who was the latest local resident to be denied a visa. Most of the stories centered around wealthy doctors and landowners—people with no intention of staying and working in the United States—who were denied tourist visas, which they sought as legitimate tourists. One man, a wealthy *fazendeiro* (rancher) who is also a lawyer, and his daughter were denied tourist visas to visit Disney World. Another man, an engineer who had previously studied in the United States, wanted to return to take a three-month short course but was also turned down. Then there was the tale of one young woman I met who was invited to a conference of Presbyterian youth to be held in Panama City, Florida. She was denied a tourist visa after she took time off from work to travel to Rio and was interviewed at the American Consulate. Despite her vehement protestations that she was going to the United States only to attend the conference and did not intend to stay on and get a job, the visa was still denied. In contrast, young people from São Paulo had no problem getting visas to attend the same conference, and this young woman is convinced, with good reason, that she was denied solely because of where she was from.

A 2003 National Public Radio report noted that more than one-third of Brazilians applying for tourist visas to come to the United States were being turned down. In fact, the number of visas issued to Brazilians plummeted from about 500,000 annually in the late 1990s to 100,000 by

2002. One foreign service officer at the American Consulate in São Paulo claimed that he ran into trouble when he refused to comply with his superior's demand that he increase the rate of visa refusals from 15 to 30 percent of applicants. In a 2005 internal dispatch unearthed by WikiLeaks, the then consul general at the same American Consulate suggested a system for dividing Brazilian applicants for tourist visas into three categories: "the good, the bad, and the ugly." The "good" were described as well-educated, middle-class kids who wanted to go to the United States to work in hotels, ski resorts, and casinos with the goal of earning money, improving their English, and returning to Brazil. The "bad" were friends and relatives of undocumented Brazilian immigrants in the United States looking for low-level jobs there. They were a risk because once they had a tourist visa, they would not return to Brazil. Finally, the "ugly" were the unkempt, uneducated, and desperate poor who, instead of paying $10,000 for travel to the United States via Mexico, had forked over $3,000 for fraudulent work papers to present to U.S. consular officers (Shenon 1997; Donahue 2005; Galvão 2011).

As securing a tourist visa has become more problematic, some Brazilians have been entering the United States as tourists on European passports. Brazilians of Portuguese and Italian descent, for example, have the right to passports from their ancestral homelands. In essence, Europe has become a jumping-off point for entry into the United States because Italy and Portugal are countries in the "U.S. Visa Waiver Program," whose citizens do not need tourist visas to travel here. Such nations have what are considered "low-risk populations," that is, those unlikely to overstay their visas and seek employment. Brazilians who have passports from these countries can travel freely to the United States by entering the country as "European" tourists. Indeed, some Brazilians of Italian descent from Criciúma have gotten Italian passports and then entered the United States via this route (Rygiel 2010; Assis 2003).

Just what does it take to be approved for a tourist visa to come to the United States? It takes time, for one thing. By 2011, the average wait for an interview for a tourist visa at the American Consulates in Rio de Janeiro and São Paulo was nearly two months. Once an applicant does get an interview, U.S. consular personnel will not grant visas to would-be tourists who fit an "immigrant profile"—that is, those who are young, single, and without a steady job. To receive a tourist visa, an applicant must have a round-trip plane ticket, proof of income and residence, and an income tax declaration. Then there is what Brazilians jocularly term "the law of three suits" (*a lei dos três ternos*), which goes like this: if a would-be tourist has the same suit on in his passport and two visa pictures rather than three different suits, this means he is poor and really intends to go to the United States to seek work rather than just visit as a tourist (Stellin 2011).

This tale, albeit apocryphal, highlights the fact that financial resources do indeed play a major role in determining whether an applicant will be granted a U.S. tourist visa, and numerous accounts in the Brazilian media point this out. In the *Jornal do Brasil*, a major newspaper in Rio de Janeiro, an article titled "Consulate Bars Mulatto Athlete" reported that the American Consulate in Rio denied a tourist visa to a teenage jujitsu champion who wanted to compete in the Pan American Games in Hawaii. A boy from a poor family, he found a sponsor to pay his way to the United States, and his family claimed the denial was racially based since he was the only non-white athlete and the only one turned down for a visa. The American Consulate refused comment. Sometimes a visa is denied arbitrarily. This is what happened to the subprefect of Arpoador, a small, expensive beach community adjacent to Ipanema in Rio. This man—who is also a dentist— was denied a tourist visa to travel to the United States to attend a dental congress in Philadelphia although he had previously visited this country many times. When a reporter called the visa section to inquire about this, he was told curtly that there would be no explanation for the denial. In fact, a Brazilian who works at the American Consulate in São Paulo told me that one of her American coworkers in the visa section prides herself on the number of visas she turns down for no apparent reason (*Jornal do Brasil* 1997a, 1997b).

The "selection" process for U.S. tourist visas received widespread head-lines in Brazil and the United States in the late 1990s when a former foreign service officer at the American Consulate in São Paulo sued the U.S. State Department for $750,000 after being dismissed for denouncing a policy that he said used codes to mask racial and ethnic discrimination in the awarding of tourist visas to Brazilians for travel to the United States. He claimed the codes recommended that nonwhites, descendants of Koreans, Palestinians, and people between eighteen and thirty-five who did not appear to be from wealthy families be denied visas or at least be subjected to rigorous interviews. The U.S. State Department, he said, had an internal coding system that classified Brazilians into five groups: "LP" meant "looks poor"; "LR" meant "looks rough," used for those who appeared to be un-educated; "TP" meant "talks poor" and was applied if the person expressed himself or herself poorly; "TC" meant "take care," used if the person was considered suspect; and "RK" meant "rich kid." The State Department conceded that the codes were in effect but asserted that they were "sensible tools" to weed out visa applicants who were likely to stay on in the United States illegally (Epstein 1997; Shenon 1997, Assumpção 1997a).[1]

What about other countries where Brazilians have immigrated over the past two decades? Have they pulled in the welcome mat in similar fashion? Yes, in most cases, they have. In 2007, for example, the European Union began conducting an operation specifically aimed at undocumented immigrants from South America. A year earlier, Spain blocked the entry of nearly eight thousand Brazilians—40 percent of all foreigners denied entry at Madrid's airport. After the laws were toughened, even more Brazilians were barred from the country—nearly ten thousand in 2007. Then there was the notorious case of a group of Brazilian graduate students who were traveling to Lisbon to attend an academic conference. The trip required a change of planes in Madrid, where several were detained and deported to Brazil on suspicion that they had actually traveled to Spain to look for work (Guedes 2007; Nidecker 2008; Infante 2008).

England has also received some notoriety in the Brazilian media on this score. Brazil led all other nationalities in the number of its citizens denied entry to England—about five thousand annually in 2004—a number that has risen every year since 2001. As it became more difficult to enter the United States as a tourist, England became the alternative for some Brazilians seeking job opportunities abroad, with many traveling there on tourist or student visas, which could be obtained upon entry into the country. Others arrived in England with European passports in hand, most from Italy (Cariello 2008; Evans 2010; Evans et al. 2011).

As we have seen, pressure from other members of the European Union led Portugal to close its job market to foreign professionals from outside the EU and to deter immigrants from the developing world in general. Portugal has reacted by sending increasing numbers of Brazilians back home before they leave the airport in Lisbon. And Brazil, in turn, has countered by sharply restricting the work of Portuguese immigrants in Brazil and subjecting them to fines and deportation if they take jobs without an approved work permit (Fernandes and Rigotti 2008; Luis 1993).

Italy is a special case because it permits Brazilians of Italian ancestry to apply to become citizens. *Jus sanguineus* (citizenship through blood) can be transmitted via the paternal line to grandchildren, great-grandchildren, and even more distant generations.[2] However, on the maternal side, only those born after 1948—the year men and women gained equal rights in

Italy—can be considered for citizenship. By 2008, a half-million Brazilians were waiting for their citizenship to be approved by the Italian Embassy in Brasília, and almost twice that number had already been granted Italian citizenship over the previous decade. Because the Italian Embassy in Brazil is understaffed, the wait for approval can take years, so some Brazilians travel to Italy and send their citizenship applications directly to a local city hall; they simply have to prove their residence in that locale. It is estimated that three to four hundred Brazilians a month journey to Italy on Italian passports, but only about 10 percent remain there; 40 percent go to England, and another 40 percent go to other EU countries, primarily Spain and Portugal. Some 10 percent return home to Brazil (Rey 2008a).

As a consequence of these restrictions, many Brazilians in Europe have undocumented status. In Spain, for example, estimates suggest that, of the forty-five to fifty thousand Brazilians in that country, about half were living there illegally until 2005, when some ten thousand of them were legalized in an amnesty program for undocumented immigrants. Or take the case of Portugal, where, of the fifty-two thousand Brazilians living there in 2001, only about 30 percent were there legally, having received amnesty in the mid-1990s (Noguera and Coelho 2005; Salgado 2001).

The situation of Brazilians in Japan stands in marked contrast to the entry and legal scenarios just described. The reason is that, in 1990, the Japanese government passed immigration reform that allowed Brazilians of Japanese ancestry to work legally in Japan for a specified period of time. The new law reflected the *jus sanguineous* principle of Japan's Nationality Law, which granted descendants of Japanese emigrants (*nikkejin*) up to the third generation, along with their spouses and children, the right to reside in Japan. All had the status of "guest residents," not "guest workers," even though the vast majority came to Japan to take jobs. The reform was intended to solve the dilemma of attracting cheap, compliant labor to fill the essential but undesirable jobs that the Japanese themselves were unwilling to do—the aforementioned *kitui, kitanai*, and *kiken* (arduous, dangerous, and dirty) jobs. The law was also an attempt to avoid importing an unwanted "alien" (i.e., non-Japanese) element into the nation. In essence, the legislation was meant to maintain Japan's supposed ethnic homogeneity in the face of its need for labor (Fox 1997; Yamanaka 1996a, 1996b).

In sum, with the notable exception of Japan, since the start of the new millennium it has become ever more difficult for aspiring Brazilian immigrants to gain access to jobs in the industrialized nations of North America and Europe. But these difficulties pale next to the trials and tribulations encountered when attempting to enter the United States via the border with Mexico, a topic to which we now turn.

The Mexican Route

In the early 1990s, it was the rare Brazilian who entered the United States via the border with Mexico. In those days, the vast majority of Brazilians arrived in this country by flying to New York, Miami, or Los Angeles on valid tourist visas. But, soon after the turn of the new millennium, reports began surfacing about the growing number of Brazilians resorting to the far more expensive and dangerous route of flying from Brazil to Mexico City, making their way overland to the U.S.-Mexican border, and then crossing illegally into the United States. Official U.S. immigration figures reflect this surge; the number of Brazilians detained by U.S. immigration agents at the border jumped from just over 400 in 1997 to about 3,500 in 2001 (Souza 2002; Kammer 2002).

For the first time, Brazilians began appearing in official statistics in significant numbers. Of the more than one million people apprehended trying to cross the border each year, about 93 percent are Mexican nationals. But, among the groups referred to as "other than Mexican" (OTM), the number of Brazilians rose far faster than the number for any other nationality—from some three thousand in 2002 to nearly thirty-one thousand by the end of fiscal year 2005. Untold thousands of others likely eluded capture.[3] According to the U.S. Border Patrol, the increase in illegal entrants from Brazil may be related to the fact that locally based smugglers targeted that nation; it is not unusual for smugglers to seek would-be immigrants from distant lands because there is more money to be made on longer journeys (Rohter 2005; U.S. Department of Homeland Security 2005; Machelor 2002).

What, then, is the fate of those detained at the border? According to international law, when "other than Mexicans" are stopped at the border, they cannot be sent back to Mexico; they must be returned to their own countries. Since the United States has long had a severe shortage of detention space, very few of those apprehended were imprisoned before being sent home. Instead, they received a summons and were ordered to appear in court on a specific date.

Brazilians referred to these summons as "diplomas." After receiving one, they would call a friend or relative already in the United States and request money; then they would travel to their final destination. Even before leaving home, Brazilians knew that if they were stopped at the U.S.-Mexican border, they would not be jailed but would be released on their own recognizance. Of the 2,500 Brazilians detained in Texas in April 2005, 2,400 were released with a promise to appear at a later judicial hearing; nearly 90 percent failed to do so and remained in the United States illegally. There is also the—perhaps apocryphal—story that the number of illegal border crossers became so explosive that when a call was placed to the Brazilian Consulate in Houston, the one closest to the border, the first selection on the recording informed the caller (in Portuguese): "If you have been arrested on the border and need assistance, press 1" (Almeida 2010; Kammer 2005; Meirelles 2005).

The number of Brazilians detained within Mexico before reaching the U.S. border also skyrocketed. Between 2000 and 2005, the Mexican government counted more than twenty-four thousand Brazilians it deemed "irregular migrants." Under strong pressure from the American government, Mexican authorities began trying to stop undocumented immigrants headed for the United States by detaining them at the airport in Mexico City. One such attempt led to the apprehension of more than a dozen Brazilians who were trying to enter Mexico as tourists but who had no luggage, hotel reservations, or credit cards (Maisonnave 2005b; Thompson 2004).

Just how did these would-be immigrants make it all the way from their homes in Brazil to the U.S.-Mexico border and then on to their final destinations in the United States? To answer this question, the Brazilian Congress appointed a Parliamentary Inquiry Commission on Illegal Emigration. Its report cited nearly forty smuggling rings that brought potential immigrants from Brazil to the United States via Mexico. According to the inquiry, this "smuggling mafia" was well organized and highly profitable and operated in several Brazilians cities, primarily those with a long tradition of sending residents abroad (Mineo 2005b).

Immigrants paid for the journey in one of two ways—either before they left home or after they arrived at their final destination. Smuggling rings offered loans to Brazilians who wanted to travel to the United States but could not afford their $10,000-and-up fees. Members of the ring were called *"cônsuls"* in Portuguese, an ironic reference to the fact that they served a function similar to that of an American consul in facilitating entry to the United States—albeit illegally. *Cônsuls* loaned money to would-be immigrants willing to put up their houses, cars, or other property as collateral. They were expected to repay the loan—along with up to 10 percent interest a month—from their wages in a year or two after arriving in the United States. Most *cônsuls* worked with *agenciadores*, fixers who enlisted Brazilians who wanted to work in the United States. In sending communities like Governador Valadares, smugglers sometimes also worked closely with travel agencies that allowed immigrants to pay for plane tickets on time (Costa 2004a; Mineo 2005b, 2006e).

In 2005, the cost of being trafficked to the United States was about $10,000, divided as follows: $5,000 to the local *cônsul* who arranged the trip but had no expenses other than a few phone calls; around $700 for airfare to Mexico City; $400 for hotel and food in Mexico; $500 for travel to the U.S.-Mexican border; and $2,000 for the *coyote*, the guide who led the crossing into the United States. The remaining $1,400 was divided between the local fixers who convinced the would-be immigrant to make the trip to the United States and the *receptadores* (receivers), those who met the immigrant in Mexico (Rodrigues and Filgueiras 2005).[4]

Gang members in several Brazilian states made the arrangements that allowed undocumented immigrants to travel abroad. In Minas Gerais, false passports were provided; in Rio de Janeiro and Paraná, gang members purchased airline tickets; in São Paulo, a group was in charge of housing would-be immigrants and escorting them to the airport. Co-conspirators at the airport made sure that Brazilians with bogus passports or fraudulent tourist visas could board planes, while others made certain that clients encountered no problems with Mexican immigration officials upon arrival in Mexico City. Immigrants were met at the airport by gang members and taken to a hotel. After an overland trip to the border, entry into the United States was carried out by swimming across the Rio Grande, crossing the desert on foot, or, for an additional charge, being transported across by car or truck (Hisayasu 2005; Costa 2004a).

The actual "smuggling package" from Governador Valadares—which offered "door-to-door service"—included a lengthy bus trip from the town to Rio de Janeiro or São Paulo, a flight to Mexico City, *coyote* escorts to cross the Mexican border into the United States, and rides in vans that eventually carried immigrants to the address of relatives in Massachusetts or other destinations in the United States. The trip from Governador Valadares to the American city or town of choice lasted, on average, a little over seven days. "They deliver you to Framingham [Massachusetts] or anywhere else in the United States almost like the United Parcel Service or Federal Express," said one appreciative resident of Governador Valadares (quoted in Mineo 2006e; see also Mineo 2006g).

Of course, entering the United States via Mexico is not only more costly and time consuming than flying into the country on a tourist visa; it is also far more dangerous. Although firm numbers do not exist, at least six Brazilians lost their lives attempting to enter the United States in 2003 and 2004, with an additional five deaths in 2005 and still others in more recent years. In El Centro, California, near the border with Mexico, there is a cemetery for approximately five hundred unidentified immigrants who died while trying to cross into the United States; of these, up to one hundred are believed to be Brazilian. Conjectures about countries of origin are based on the brands of clothes the immigrants are wearing and their physical appearance. Bodies are rarely discovered with any clear identification on them. There are also reports of Brazilian women being raped as they make their way across difficult terrain in Mexico and of *coyotes* kidnapping Brazilians and holding them for ransom. And it is well to remember that at least two Brazilians were among the seventy-two immigrants massacred in northern Mexico in August 2010 (*Folha de São Paulo* 2005a; *Comunidade News* 2008; Rodrigues and Filgueiras 2005; Motta 2010).

Horrific tales of passage through Mexico provided in firsthand accounts by Brazilians tell of constant demands for bribes by Mexican officials, days without food or water, temperature extremes in desert crossings, and abandonment by *coyotes*. Some Brazilians report that Mexican police and border agents have excellent systems of communication that identify would-be border crossers by their appearance even before they arrive at the U.S.-Mexican border. They particularly seek out Brazilians, who they know will be carrying considerable sums of cash. Brazilians are advised by *cônsuls* to carry as much as $3,000 in cash to bribe Mexican police (Almeida 2010).

Even as the border has become more difficult to traverse, estimates suggest that about one-third of all prospective border crossers make it into the United States on their first try, 60 percent make it in on their second through fifth tries, and only 8 percent eventually give up and return home. Still, because of stepped-up border patrols, immigrants are now more reluctant than ever to go home, fearing that they will not have another chance to enter the United States. In the case of Brazilians, the loans of some smugglers were supposed to be voided if, after three attempts, entry was unsuccessful. Still, success was not guaranteed. If the immigrant was arrested at the border and never reached his or her final destination, smugglers sometimes tried to dun the immigrant's family back in Brazil for whatever money was still owed for the journey (Porter and Malkin 2005; Bautzer and Moreira 2003).

As these smuggling rings received increased media attention and the number of Brazilians caught on the U.S.-Mexico border climbed to more than thirty thousand by the end of fiscal year 2005—nearly triple the number stopped the previous year—a series of raids, one dubbed "Operation Bye Bye Brazil," were organized by the federal police in São Paulo in cooperation with the U.S. Department of Homeland Security. The raids also targeted "Operation Stork," a gang that over time purportedly earned $1.3 million bringing Brazilian children across the Mexican border to the United States to be reunited with their immigrant parents. The gang produced fraudulent documents that were meant to show a relationship between the children and the individuals responsible for escorting them abroad (Clendenning 2005; Costa and Dutra 2006).

Again with the urging of the American government, in October 2005, Mexico reinstated a visa requirement—which had lapsed in the 1980s—for Brazilians entering Mexico. Community leaders and academics disagree about the result. Estimates of an 80 to 90 percent decline in the number of Brazilians entering the United States via Mexico since the visa requirement went into effect come from community leaders in Massachusetts, one of whom insisted that, in the four months following the imposition of this new obstacle in late 2005, he had not encountered a single Brazilian who had entered the United States via Mexico. Other data also indicate that the new constraint on travel was having the desired effect. In 2006, just under three thousand Brazilians were deported from the United States; the number was much higher the year before. Nevertheless, one study of Brazilian immigrants in Massachusetts found that, to the contrary, the new hurdle "appears to have had little effect on the number of Brazilians crossing the Mexico-U.S. border" and settling in the Boston metropolitan area (Marcus 2008b; Sotero 2006; Nidecker 2008; Marcelli et al. 2009).

At about the time that the visa requirement for Brazilians traveling to Mexico was instituted, the U.S. government adopted a new tactic, called "rapid removal," in which deportation of undocumented immigrants was accelerated and new facilities were built to detain those picked up on the border. "Rapid removal" partially replaced the "catch and release" method in which all "other than Mexicans" stopped at the border were released with the promise to appear for a future court date. As a consequence of these new obstacles, many Brazilians who had planned to travel to the United States via Mexico now feared imprisonment and deportation and decided not to risk it and to stay home (Dantas 2005; Fornetti 2011).

None other than then President George W. Bush defended the hardening of U.S. immigration policy by citing statistics on the decline in the number of undocumented Brazilians picked up on the U.S.-Mexico border:

> We're . . . pursuing . . . common-sense steps to accelerate the deportation process. . . . We recently tested the effectiveness of these steps with Brazilian illegal immigrants caught along the Rio Grande Valley of the Texas border. The effort was called Operation Texas Hold 'Em. It delivered impressive results. Thanks to our actions, Brazilian illegal immigration dropped by 90 percent in the Rio Grande Valley, and by 50 to 60 percent across the border as a whole. (Bush 2005)

One result of the crackdown along the U.S.-Mexico border and the new visa requirement was that some Brazilians eager to immigrate to the United States sought alternate, more costly, more complex, and more dangerous routes. Today one can encounter Brazilians who have crossed as many as eight countries in Latin America before arriving at the U.S.-Mexico border. One route used by a number of Brazilians is to fly from Rio de Janeiro to Havana and then on to Mexico City. In 2010, six Brazilians were among the nineteen would-be immigrants from Haiti, Jamaica, and Sri Lanka picked up off the Florida coast by the U.S. Coast Guard. Brazilians are also using routes through Panama, the Bahamas, and, most commonly, Guatemala.[5] Guatemala has no visa requirement for Brazilians, and at least sixty Brazilians were picked up near the Guatemala–Mexico frontier just days before they were required to have visas to enter Mexico. They hailed from seven far-flung states in Brazil, suggesting that a widespread smuggling scheme using this new route was already in place. In this case, Brazilians were flying a circuitous route though Peru and El Salvador and sometimes Honduras and Costa Rica before arriving in Guatemala. They then slipped over the border into Chiapas, Mexico, before making their way to the U.S. border, a distance of more than 1,200 miles. This route has been used for years by other immigrants, especially those from Central America. The new path to the United States costs Brazilians at least $11,000, up to $1,500 more than the more direct route via Mexico (Maisonnave and Guimarães 2005; Gibson 2010; Mineo 2006e, 2006f).

Who Comes through Mexico?

Just who are these Brazilians so determined to enter the United States by almost any means necessary that they risk life and limb, not to mention a stunning amount of money? A majority of those coming over the border are lower-middle- and working-class Brazilians from immigrant-sending communities like Governador Valadares and Criciúma, individuals who were denied tourist visas because of an inability to demonstrate financial resources and because of their suspect towns of origin.[6] In fact, of the Brazilians imprisoned in Mexico, 70 percent came from Minas Gerais, followed by Goiás and Paraná with 10 percent each. And, as we have seen, it is in these same locales that the complex networks allowing frontier entry to the United States are most highly developed (Maisonnave 2005b, 2005c, 2005d; Goza 2005).

Mexican authorities found that many of these Brazilian nationals had similar profiles. They tended to be twenty- to thirty-year-old lower-middle-class males with new passports. They carried a suitcase with a change of clothes and had reservations in the same hotels. This common experience "creates an identity apart," according to one Brazilian who has long worked with his fellow immigrant nationals. "The immigrant who comes via Mexico sees the crossing as a symbol of courage which distinguishes him from other [Brazilians]. . . . People introduce themselves with the phrase 'I came through Mexico'" (Campell 2010; Mineo 2005a; quoted in Maisonnave 2005a).

As a consequence of these diverse paths to this country, a large but unknown number of Brazilians in the United States are undocumented, that is, living in this country illegally. As we have seen, since the late 1980s, thousands of Brazilians have either traveled to the United States on tourist visas that they then overstayed or entered over the border from Mexico; in either case, they are "out of status," in immigration parlance. And the number has almost certainly grown over the past decade. According to the U.S. Department of Homeland Security, between 2000 and 2008, the number of unauthorized Brazilians in the United States increased 72 percent, the second-largest percentage increase for any undocumented population. Although almost certainly an undercount, the official number of undocumented Brazilians in the United States rose from 100,000 in 2000 to 180,000 by 2008. Yet, despite such a significant increase, Brazilians still account for only about 2 percent of undocumented immigrants in the United States (Hoefner, Rytina, and Baker 2009; Pereira and Salek 2008).

Figures on undocumented Brazilians in specific locales provide a fuller picture. In the Boston metropolitan area, for example, more than 70 percent of Brazilian residents were undocumented in 2009, or more than two of every three Brazilian adults and more than 15 percent of their children. Similarly, in the New York metropolitan region, a majority of Brazilian immigrants were undocumented at the start of the new millennium, although there had been a slight increase in the number who arrived on work visas.[7] Undocumented Brazilians refer to themselves and to others in similar circumstances as "those without papers"—*os sem papel* (Sacchetti 2009; Marcelli et al. 2009; Menai 1999; Costa 2004a).

Occasionally, Brazilians "without papers" receive unwelcome media attention. This happened in 2010 when it was discovered that more than thirty undocumented Brazilians living in the Boston area were taking flying lessons from a local flight school. Since the attacks on September 11, federal law has prohibited undocumented immigrants from receiving training as pilots. The Brazilian owner of the flight school also turned out to be undocumented (Goodnough 2010).

Figures in specific job niches are also instructive. Estimates suggest, for example, that about 20 percent of the nearly 2.6 million chefs and cooks working in U.S. restaurants are undocumented immigrants, while well over 25 percent of the nation's 360,000 dishwashers lack work papers. These numbers sounded low to a Manhattan chef and restaurateur. "We always, always hire the undocumented workers," he said. "It's not just me, it's everybody in the industry. First, they are willing to do the work. Second, they are willing to learn. Third, they are not paid as well. It's an economic decision. It's less expensive to hire an undocumented person" (quoted in Kershaw 2010, D3).

What does it mean to have undocumented status in the United States in recent years, a time when the issue of illegal immigration has reached a fever pitch? For families made up of legal and undocumented immigrants—an increasingly common scenario among Brazilians with American-born children—life can be a dizzying series of obstacles. Those with green cards or work visas can lawfully hold jobs, get driver's licenses, and leave the country on short notice to visit an ailing parent, attend a wedding, or see friends and relatives in Brazil—none of which is possible for those without papers. If they travel home, undocumented Brazilians run a very high risk of being denied re-entry to the United States even if they have valid visas and passports. The reason: having overstayed the time limit of their visas in the past, they were living in the United States illegally and are therefore prohibited from returning (Margolis 2008b, 2009).

Then, too, since the events of September 2001, there has been growing fear among undocumented immigrants due to increasing enforcement of immigration laws. Beginning in 2006, U.S. Immigration and Customs Enforcement (ICE), an arm of the Department of Homeland Security, has been targeting many undocumented immigrants who do not have criminal records, despite the fact that the stated purpose of increased funding for enforcement was to ferret out foreign-born criminals and terrorists. Moreover, some local officials have taken it upon themselves to challenge the residence in their communities of Brazilians and other immigrants who lack driver's licenses or documents that prove that they are living in the United States legally. For example, although immigration control is a federal responsibility, in Danbury, Connecticut, which, as we have seen, has a sizeable Brazilian population, the Republican mayor sought to deputize the state police to enforce immigration laws. Similarly, the police chief in a small town in New Hampshire has invented his own border control policy; he has given orders to arrest undocumented immigrants, charging that they are "trespassing" in his community (Marcelli et al. 2009; O'Leary 2005; Powell 2005).

While the Brazilian presence is very evident in the downtown business district of Framingham, Massachusetts—many stores have Brazilian flags, signs in Portuguese, and yellow and green decor—this is not true in the city's residential areas. According to one Brazilian resident, this is because the many undocumented Brazilians fear attracting attention to themselves. In the past, immigrants sometimes placed Brazilian flags in their apartment windows and cars, but, since 9/11, with increased activity by ICE and growing anti-immigrant sentiment, Brazilians have avoided such displays. Business owners are more likely to be legal than other Brazilian residents of Framingham, so they have less fear of exhibiting their ethnicity (Skorczeski 2009).

Despite these fears and barriers, some Brazilians maintain that the problems they face living "out of status" are worth the sacrifice as long as they have jobs that pay what they consider to be good wages. And then there is the always distant hope of a green card. With or without green cards, Brazilians are now turning up in a variety of far-flung places in the United States. In "doing America," as they call it, Brazilians live in cities large and small, and it is to these specific locales that we now turn.

5

"Doing America"
Big Cities and Small

It has nothing to do with green. It's rose color, like a new born child. . . . It's like a very rosy child when it's born. The green card gives you a sense of free passage. . . . A lot of people [in the United States legally] don't know this, that it means a free road just like when a traffic light turns green it's okay for you to go ahead.

Brazilian immigrant in Boston (quoted in Sales 1998a, 15)

This chapter looks at the specific locations of *brazucas* in North America. "*Brazuca*" is a slang term for "Brazilian," but it has come to have the more specific meaning of Brazilians living abroad, especially those who have immigrated to the United States. At any given moment, approximately three million Brazilians are abroad; half are living overseas, and the other half are traveling for business or pleasure. "Few for the world, but a lot for Brazil," opined the Brazilian demographer José Magno de Carvalho (quoted in Beting 1997, 54). This is a large number indeed, but it represents only some 1.5 percent of Brazil's 2012 population of nearly 200 million. The United States, Japan, and Paraguay account for about 70 percent of Brazilians living outside Brazil, with most of the remainder in Canada, Portugal, Italy, Spain, France, Switzerland, and England. There are also small Brazilian communities in other South American and European countries, as well as in Australia and New Zealand (Gomide 2009; Assumpção 1997b).

Hard data on the number of Brazilians in any given country except Japan are difficult to come by. As we know, counting people living in a country illegally is difficult at best, so official statistics on the number of Brazilians in any particular locale are necessarily suspect. Perhaps the most

Table 4 Comparative censuses: The United States and Brazil

State/ Consular District	2011 American Community Survey (state) Number	2011 Itamaraty (consular district) Number
New York	63,489	300,000
Massachusetts	65,719	355,000
Florida	66,213	300,000
California	30,433	123,000
Georgia	7,677	80,000
Texas	11,865	50,000
Washington, DC	20,298	26,000
Illinois	3,795	40,000
Connecticut	13,771	60,000
Total	280,080	1,334,000

Sources: American Community Survey 2011; Ministério das Relações Exteriores 2011.

Notes: The figure for New York includes those for New Jersey and Pennsylvania, both of which are also in Itamaraty's New York consular district. The figure for Washington, DC, includes Virginia and Maryland; both are in the Washington, DC, consular district.

striking contrasts in this regard are between official U.S. government data and the population estimates of Brazilian consulates in the United States provided by Itamaraty, Brazil's Ministry of Foreign Affairs. It is worth comparing counts of Brazilians in the 2011 American Community Survey (ACS) to Itamaraty's 2011 estimates of Brazilians living in various consular districts in the United States (table 4).

Comparative Censuses: The United States and Brazil

Clearly the units measured by Itamaraty and the ACS are not coterminous, because consular districts often encompass more than one city. Brazil's New York consular district, for example, spans the greater metropolitan area and includes Newark, New Jersey, a site of significant Brazilian settlement. Nevertheless, the differences in these statistics are striking. One way of putting these figures in perspective is as follows: according to data from the U.S. government, more than thirty million immigrants were living in this country in the decade following 2000. During that time, Brazilians ranked twenty-fourth in the number of foreign-born residents in the United States. However, *if* the United States used Itamaraty's far larger estimate of 1.33 million Brazilians, that group would represent the eighth- or ninth-largest foreign-born population in the country rather than the twenty-fourth—outpaced only by Mexico, China, the Philippines, India, Vietnam, El Salvador, and Korea. In short, while from a Brazilian perspective the United States is certainly a major focus of migration, from an American viewpoint Brazilian immigration is quite insignificant. Nevertheless, while their numbers are uncertain, Brazilians spend an estimated $4 billion annually on consumer goods and services, contributing significantly to the American economy (Buarque 2009; Grieco and Trevelyan 2010; Marcus 2011a).

Destinations: New York, New Jersey, and New England

Brazilians speak of "doing America" (*fazendo América*) when they come to the United States as immigrants. But where exactly do they live in this country? We already know that they are heavily concentrated in a handful of states—New York, New Jersey, Massachusetts, Connecticut, Florida, and California—that account for perhaps 70 percent of Brazilians in the United States but, as we will see, they are considerably more dispersed than that figure suggests.

First we will look at areas with large concentrations of Brazilians, none bigger than New York City—the "Big Apple," as it is often called. This was the site of my own research on Brazilian immigrants in the early 1990s, the first in-depth study of this new immigrant stream. New York is home to one of the largest Brazilian communities in this country, and yet, once again, in the 2000 U.S. Census, Brazil was not in the top thirty source countries of foreign-born in the city, meaning that, according to the census, fewer than twenty thousand Brazilians were counted there. Even in Queens, the area of the greatest concentration of Brazilians in New York City, they were not listed among the top twenty source countries of the foreign-born, which translates into fewer than sixteen thousand Brazilians in the entire borough. And in Astoria, the Queens neighborhood with the largest Brazilian community by far, they were said to account for less than

4 percent of the foreign-born. Yet, in a single supermarket in Astoria that sells food products from fifty nations, sales of Brazilian goods average $40,000 a month, making them the third most popular line of ethnic products sold there (Margolis 1994a; Lobo and Salvo 2004; C. Santos 2006).

It is true that it is not that easy to spot Brazilians in Astoria, a very heterogeneous, multiethnic, largely working-class neighborhood with Greek, Italian, south Asian, and Hispanic enclaves whose attractions are relatively low rents and proximity to Manhattan. Yet today Astoria has a multitude of Brazilian-owned businesses with largely Brazilian clienteles. As I predicted in my research two decades ago and as immigration trends have continued, a distinctly Brazilian commercial presence has indeed become a more visible part of Astoria's ethnic mix. By 2010, there were at least sixteen restaurants—both take-out and full service—offering Brazilian cuisine, a Brazilian bakery, six stores selling Brazilian food products, four travel agencies specializing in travel to Brazil, and three Brazilian beauty salons, as well as Brazilian-owned remittance agencies, call car companies, auto repair shops, and boutiques and shops featuring Brazilian fashions and gift items. And on a Sunday in early September, when thousands of Brazilians flood into Astoria's streets to celebrate Brazil's Independence Day, their presence is noisily apparent. While the festival is far smaller than the better-known and older Independence Day Street Fair on West Forty-Sixth Street (Little Brazil Street) in Manhattan, the joyous exuberance of Astoria's Brazilian community is difficult to miss.

From 2001 on, Brazilians became more dispersed in the greater New York metropolitan area, and today they live in a number of cities and towns that constitute the metropolitan region. Several factors account for these internal moves. Foremost is the greater difficulty finding work in New York City as low-wage service jobs declined after 9/11 and those that remained became saturated with immigrants from other countries. Then, too, the cost of living in New York—especially the cost of rent—is a good deal higher than in other areas outside the city (Costa 2004a).

One key to where Brazilians live in the greater New York metropolitan area is the presence of what the Brazilian Ministry of Foreign Affairs calls its "itinerant consulates," consular personnel who regularly travel to smaller cities and towns to serve the needs of their Brazilian citizens. Today the Brazilian Consulate in New York City oversees itinerant consulates in Mineola on Long Island; Mount Vernon and Port Chester in Westchester County, just north of the city; Schenectady in upstate New York; in

Newark and Long Branch, New Jersey; and Philadelphia and Pittsburgh, Pennsylvania.

Mount Vernon, New Rochelle, and Port Chester, all towns in Westchester County, have significant Brazilian communities. Brazilians ranked second in the number of foreign-born in Mount Vernon, making up about 10 percent of the town's population of seventy-two thousand. About two-thirds of them hail from Poços de Caldas, a resort city in the state of Minas Gerais; today Poços de Caldas and Mount Vernon are official "sister" cities. With the growth of the Brazilian community, especially after 2000, the town made plans to hire a Portuguese-speaking police officer to communicate with Brazilian victims of crime who were reluctant to come forward because of their undocumented status. Today the Brazilian presence is evident along Mount Vernon's commercial strip, with restaurants, a nightclub, a butcher shop, a bakery, a beauty salon, and remittance and travel agencies catering to the local Brazilian community. In fact, Brazilians have become such a significant element in town that they are lobbying to change the city's Office of Hispanic Affairs to the Office of Latino Affairs—Brazilians, after all, are *not* Hispanics, but they *are* Latinos (Lobo and Salvo 2004; Grand and Castillo 2004; F. Santos 2006).

Moving farther north in New York State, the Catskill Mountains have long been home to a small Brazilian community of about two thousand; most work as busboys, waiters, or housekeepers in Catskill-area resorts. Largely natives of Governador Valadares and the surrounding towns, they constitute an old migration stream that began in the mid-1960s. According to one account, an American woman who worked at an employment agency in New York City encountered Brazilians looking for work when she frequented a Brazilian restaurant on Little Brazil Street. She sent one Brazilian and then others to work at the Catskill resorts, and a chain migration was soon under way. Brazilians were welcomed by resort owners as hard workers who were willing to work year round (*New York Times* 1995).

The first media mention of the Brazilian presence in New Jersey was in a 1995 *New York Times* article about how successfully undocumented Brazilians blended into the larger Portuguese population in the Ironbound section of Newark, a historically Portuguese enclave. The article noted that the undocumented immigrants of the past were nearly all Portuguese but that things have changed: "You see a lot of Brazilians now," said one Portuguese resident of the area. "They are going through the same phase as the Portuguese 30 years ago." In fact, today Brazil ranks third as the source country of foreign-born in that city, and Brazilians outnumber Portuguese living there (quoted in Dunn 1995, 1; Lobo and Salvo 2004).

While Brazilians live in a number of locales in New Jersey—Elizabeth, Kearney, Cliffside Park, Long Branch—perhaps nowhere has their presence received more extensive media coverage than in Riverside, a town of some eight thousand residents in northwestern New Jersey, not far from Philadelphia.[1] Brazilians began arriving in Riverside in 1999, attracted by local Portuguese-owned businesses and the construction jobs available in the then-booming housing market. Portuguese subcontractors hired Brazilians, some of whom started their own businesses. "Growing demand for cheap construction labor . . . kept friends and relatives coming" (Moroz 2005a, 2005c).

At first, the newcomers constituted a youthful and largely male migration—virtually all of whom came to the United States via Mexico—of whom the great majority worked as carpenters. Then women began arriving; many found work as housecleaners, and, by 2005, some twenty-five Brazilian children were attending Riverside's local elementary school. Brazilians revived Riverside's main street with more than a dozen Brazilian-owned stores and restaurants; as one resident put it, "Brazilians are taking over this whole town" (quoted in Moroz 2005a).

Many of the newly arrived immigrants in Riverside were from the Brazilian states of Mato Grosso, Rondonia, and Roraima—none of which were sources of immigrants to the United States in earlier years. As previously noted, a Minas Gerais-Rondonia connection seems to have existed in this migration flow. That is, many immigrants to the United States from Rondonia have relatives back in Minas Gerais, where their parents or grandparents once lived. Two or three decades ago, they left Minas Gerais and sought land in Rondonia, a frontier region in the western Amazon. But when success eluded them there and few opportunities existed for the next generation, some of these young *rondonenses* followed the path of their *mineiro* relatives to the United States (Moroz 2005a).

So why the media's wide-ranging attention to Brazilians in this small New Jersey town? The publicity about Brazilians in Riverside stemmed from the often ugly discourse and actions of some of the town's residents. A rowdy meeting of the town council in July 2006 approved the so-called Illegal Immigration Relief Act, an ordinance banning employers and landlords from hiring or renting to undocumented immigrants, with fines starting at $1,000 and the threatened loss of business licenses for up to five years. The law's authors cited overcrowded apartments, packed parking lots, and strained social services, all purportedly a result of the presence of undocumented immigrants in town (Capuzzo 2006).

Soon after its passage, nearly four hundred opponents of the new law protested outside the town hall and were heckled by some five hundred counterdemonstrators with chants of "Go Home." As immigration supporters accused the town council of racism, opponents chanted "USA, USA" and waved placards reading "Scram" and "Stop Illegal Immigration." A passing pickup truck flying a Confederate flag with the motto "The South Will Rise Again" drew loud cheers from ordinance supporters. As violence appeared imminent, police were called in to separate those who opposed the law from those who supported it. Then several Brazilian residents claimed their cars were firebombed, an action confirmed by local police. Finally, an anti-immigrant faction organized by the Minutemen and armed with baseball bats and guns appeared in Riverside and declared that undocumented immigrants had seventy-two hours to get out of town (Capuzzo 2006; Hurdle 2006).

The situation had turned so ugly that, in 2007, Riverside's town council rescinded its never-enforced ordinance. One reason was rising legal fees—which had already reached $100,000—for defending the law. Additionally, a story on the front page of the *New York Times* reported on the other high costs of the town's draconian efforts to curb undocumented immigration. According to the mayor and the parish priest who celebrated Mass in Portuguese at Riverside's Catholic Church, after the threats began, nearly all Brazilians left town; the few remaining were those who owned small businesses there. The local economy suffered as restaurants, hair salons, and other businesses catering to immigrants saw their sales plummet and some closed their doors. One estimate suggested that local business was down by $50,000 a week (Capuzzo 2007; V. Galvão 2005; Belson and Capuzzo 2007).

Many Brazilians from Riverside fled to an immigrant neighborhood in northeast Philadelphia; others went to Maryland, Delaware, or Massachusetts. Philadelphia was chosen as a haven because many Brazilians already had Pennsylvania driver's licenses, since they were easier to obtain than New Jersey licenses (Moroz 2005a, 2005d).

None of this stopped some local residents, including a former mayor of Riverside, from expressing anti-immigrant venom. "The business district is fairly vacant now," said the former mayor, "but it's not the legitimate businesses that are gone. It's all the ones that were supporting the illegal immigrants or, as I like to call them, the criminal aliens" (quoted in Belson and Capuzzo 2007, 23).

Connecticut is another major destination for Brazilians in the northeast United States. By 2010, the state had a large enough Brazilian population to warrant its own Brazilian Consulate. This was intended to lessen the workload of the Brazilian Consulate in New York City, which had previously served the Brazilians who are concentrated in a handful of Connecticut locales, most notably Danbury. Waterbury and Bridgeport also have significant numbers of Brazilian residents, and all three Connecticut cities were attractive places for Brazilians because of their long-established Portuguese communities.

Brazilians are the largest segment of the foreign-born in Danbury, a city of some seventy-five thousand. But their official number—around five thousand—underestimates what locals believe are actually some ten to fifteen thousand Brazilians, or up to 20 percent of Danbury's population. As in Riverside, Brazilians, who began arriving in Danbury around 1990, helped transform what had become a moribund downtown into a thriving business district with at least twenty Brazilian-owned shops and restaurants. Several Brazilian women started home-based day care centers. Originally intended for their own children and those of their friends and relatives in the Brazilian community, the centers began enrolling American children and other immigrant children and have turned into lucrative enterprises for several Brazilians (Lobo and Salvo 2004; Swift 2002; Musante 1996; Menezes 2000).

However, all has not been peace and light among Danbury's Brazilians, and here, unlike in Riverside, the animus has been mostly internal, that is, within the Brazilian community itself. In 2005, the city's newly re-elected Republican mayor—citing simmering anti-immigrant tensions—requested permission from Connecticut's governor to deputize local police, an action that would allow them to arrest undocumented immigrants. Although his request was denied, the editor of *Tribuna*, a local Brazilian newspaper, supported the mayor's position, a stance that did not sit well with most of Danbury's Brazilian residents.

Sometime after the mayor's request, a local TV news report—on the basis of an undercover investigation—suggested that the owner of a popular Brazilian travel agency was selling counterfeit documents to his undocumented compatriots, a report that further inflamed the immigrant community. Again, the editor of *Tribuna* came out on the side of "law and order" and wrote an opinion piece deploring the fact that "people are able to get social security or green cards on the street. It's a shame that a majority of people providing these services are Brazilians" (quoted in Dávila 2005).

Danbury's two other Brazilian newspapers responded with headlines blazing "Traitor!!" and "Community Revolt!" The editor of one paper demanded to know whether the editor of *Tribuna* had not herself been undocumented until receiving a green card three years earlier. And, within days, the *Tribuna* began receiving threatening phone calls and e-mails; a group called "I Hate the *Tribuna* Newspaper" was created on Orkut, a social networking site popular with Brazilians. Then came talk about a conversation overheard in a local Brazilian restaurant in which a group of diners—speaking Portuguese—agreed that someone "should kill this woman," that is, the editor of the newspaper. While a police inquiry was begun, the incident was left unresolved. Nevertheless, many Danbury Brazilians claimed that the only reason an investigation was even started was that "this woman is aligned with a Republican politician who persecutes immigrants" (Dávila 2005).

"Bring Brazil to Your House"
Ad for TV Globo and Dish Network on a city bus in Boston

Perhaps nowhere have Brazilians received more attention from both the media and academic researchers than in Massachusetts, which, according to the 2011 American Community Survey, had the second-largest Brazilian population in the United States. Here, too—as in Newark and Riverside, New Jersey, and in Danbury and Bridgeport, Connecticut—Brazilians have settled in areas of prior Portuguese immigration. The presence of Portuguese speakers has been an especially strong draw for Brazilians in this case because 800,000 Massachusetts residents speak the language, the most of any state in the country.[2] Massachusetts is home not only to Portuguese and Brazilians but also to sizeable communities of Azoreans and Cape Verdeans who also speak Portuguese (Millman 1997).

Brazilians are indeed attracted to the state. The *Boston Globe* published a report indicating that, during the early 2000s, one of every five immigrants arriving in Massachusetts was Brazilian. But here, as elsewhere in the United States, precise numbers are elusive. After careful calculations, a group of researchers estimated that some 73,000 Brazilians were living in the greater Boston metropolitan area in 2007. This is not too far from the nearly

66,000 counted in the 2011 American Community Survey but not the Brazilian Ministry of Foreign Affair's 2011 figure of a whopping 355,000 for the same region. What is not in doubt is the notable shift that has taken place in Boston's Brazilian community from one that was predominantly male during the early years of emigration in the 1980s to one that was more balanced in terms of gender by the 1990s. Then, too, while about nine out of ten Brazilians in Massachusetts were natives of Governador Valadares and surrounding towns in the first years, by the end of the millennium fewer than half hailed from that region, and immigrants to Boston were now more likely to come from Rio de Janeiro, São Paulo, or Paraná than were those who arrived earlier in the migration flow (Abraham 2005; Marcelli et al. 2009; Souza 2002).

In Boston, new immigrants from Brazil often settled in East Boston, considered a marginal area by some. Then they moved on to other parts of the city—to places like East Cambridge, a traditional Portuguese neighborhood and the site of some of the first Brazilian-owned businesses. Allston and Somerville—which has been described as "a family place"—are also neighborhoods with significant Brazilian communities (Souza 1992, 3).

While Brazilians live throughout the greater Boston area, nowhere have they had a larger impact than in Framingham, a city of some sixty-seven thousand about twenty miles west of Boston. Framingham may have the largest number of Brazilian immigrants of any American city of its size. Somewhere between ten and fifteen thousand of its residents, or up to 20 percent of the population, are Brazilian. Then, too, they are densely concentrated in the area. In the 2000 U.S. Census, the Brazilian-born population made up more than 57 percent of one south Framingham census tract, a likely undercount given the large number of undocumented Brazilians in the region. According to a city official, Framingham would be "a ghost town if it weren't for the Brazilians" (Skorczeski 2009; quoted in de Oliveira 1996a).

Brazilians in Brazil who typecast Governador Valadares as *the* archetypal immigrant-sending community need look no further than Framingham to confirm this stereotype. Today about 40 percent of Brazilians in Framingham are from Governador Valadares. The *Diário do Rio*, a newspaper published in Governador Valadares and largely devoted to local news, began biweekly distribution in the United States from an office in Framingham. And in the 1990s—because of the close ties between the two towns—Framingham and Governador Valadares became official "sister cities" (Mineo 2006j).[3]

Framingham also provides evidence that Brazilians from a variety of backgrounds in Governador Valadares are emigrating abroad. One report about Framingham cites the following residents, all from Governador Valadares or the surrounding small towns: a young woman with a university degree in accounting, a man who was a farm laborer back home, and a sixty-five-year-old retired civil servant who could not live on the "miserable pension" he received after working for thirty-three years for the Cia. Vale do Rio Doce, the largest employer in the area (De Oliveira 1996b).

Since Framingham is home to many long-time Brazilian residents who have developed access to networks outside the immigrant community, some immigrants have been able to abandon the jobs typically associated with newer arrivals—housekeeping and construction, in particular—and have been able to return to conventional middle-class occupations as teachers, bank tellers, secretaries, and business owners. Teaching, in particular, has become an important source of employment because of the local need for bilingual Portuguese-English teachers. Since Framingham is one of the oldest sites of Brazilian settlement in the United States, with a large 1.5- and second-generation Brazilian demographic, the demand for such teachers is evident. And the fact that so many were also teachers in Brazil and then immigrated to the United States suggests the deep dissatisfaction with the teaching profession back home because of its very low salaries (Marcus 2011a).

While I will analyze the return of Brazilians to Brazil from the United States and elsewhere in more detail in the last chapter of this book, it is worth noting here that, since 2007, the number of Brazilians living in Framingham has dropped off. Local estimates vary widely, with some suggesting that up to 40 percent have left. The owners of businesses in town that cater to Brazilians are worried that, with many Brazilians leaving, their businesses will suffer. In contrast, the four Brazilian-owned moving companies have never been busier, and travel agencies report increased sales in one-way tickets to Brazil. The reasons for the departure are many: the loss of jobs, especially in construction, because of the crisis in the U.S. housing market; the decline in the value of the dollar vis-à-vis the *real*, which negatively impacts remittances; the failure of the U.S. Congress to pass meaningful immigration legislation that would have provided a path to legalization for the many undocumented Brazilians in Framingham; and burgeoning anti-immigrant sentiment in the town (Barnes 2009; Mineo 2007; *Comunidade News* 2007).

It is, indeed, the case that Framingham has become the site of some virulent anti-immigrant rhetoric, although there—unlike Danbury—the tensions created by the malicious discourse have roots outside the Brazilian community itself. In 2004, Joe and Jim Rizoli, identical twin brothers and natives of Framingham, gained notoriety for their public-access cable TV show *Illegal Immigration Chat*. Their targets were undocumented immigrants, with particular emphasis on Brazilians. On the show, the Rizolis accused Brazilians of overburdening local schools and other public institutions at taxpayers' expense and of bringing crime and disease to town. To wit: "Reading the daily police blotter these days one cannot help but notice which 'culture' is getting the most police attention," Jim Rizoli told his TV audience. "Another major concern," he went on, "is the introduction or in some cases the re-introduction of long-eradicated diseases coming to the area. A special delegation of doctors from Brazil recently came to the area offering their services because TB is making a comeback." This sort of talk is reminiscent of some heard during past congressional hearings on immigration reform in which undocumented immigrants were maligned as catalysts for crime and agents of disease (quoted in Woodridge 2006; Chock 1995).

Public declarations like "Framingham has been raped by Brazilians," "We're not targeting Brazilians; Brazilians are targeting Framingham," and "Illegals have made Framingham an outlaw town" and claims that the city "has been turned into a Brazilian slave camp" understandably outraged both Brazilians and their local supporters. The brothers even attacked Governador Valadares, calling it "the most corrupt city in Brazil—its biggest export is illegal aliens and document fraud." But the Rizolis' venom was not limited to words. The brothers were also instrumental in founding the group Concerned Friends of Illegal Immigration Law Enforcement, whose members began targeting Brazilian gatherings. In June 2006, for example, the Rizolis and other members of the group videotaped and harassed hundreds of Brazilians celebrating in downtown Framingham after Brazil's national soccer team won a World Cup game. And, in 2010, much to the chagrin of many locals, Jim Rizoli decided to run for a seat in the Massachusetts legislature. It is no surprise that some Brazilians could no longer tolerate this toxic atmosphere and decided to leave town and move elsewhere in the state (Kocian 2005; Sanchez 2008; McDonald 2010).

Framingham is not the only city in Massachusetts in which Brazilians have been subject to anti-immigrant rhetoric and actions. In 2011, a

Brazilian, an undocumented immigrant and construction worker living in Boston, was stopped by a traffic officer because his brake light was burned out. When he was unable to produce a valid driver's license, he was arrested and subsequently led away in ankle and foot chains by immigration agents. This action was taken under the federal Secure Communities Program, a program which is supposed to arrest and deport only "criminal aliens." The Brazilian agreed to be deported to Brazil along with his Brazilian wife and five-year-old American-born son. "I am not a criminal and my wife and little son are not criminals. They did not have to humiliate us like this," he said (Preston 2011b).

At least since the mid-1990s, Brazilians have not been limited to the greater Boston area that includes Framingham; they have been moving throughout Massachusetts and now live in 250 of the state's 350 towns and cities. It appears that Brazilians first settle in larger hubs but that, as they become more familiar with life in the United States and less dependent on ethnic networks, many move to smaller towns and suburbs. Then, too, some Brazilians are leaving the Boston area because of the high cost of housing there (Siqueira and Jansen 2008; Souza 2002).

One region in Massachusetts that has become a major Brazilian destination is Cape Cod and neighboring Martha's Vineyard. Estimates suggest that between eight and twelve thousand Brazilians live on Cape Cod, more than half in the Hyannis area. The economic impact of Brazilians on the Cape is mostly anecdotal, but it is difficult to miss in Hyannis, where there are about two dozen Brazilian stores and restaurants, as well as home-based businesses such as cleaning services. The local branch of one savings bank hired Portuguese speakers; before the housing crisis, the bank was marketing mortgages to Brazilians in the area. The community college in Hyannis began offering classes in conversational Portuguese that attracted staff from the local hospital and other large employers, as well as owners of smaller businesses that have Brazilian employees (Catholic Social Services 2001; Moeller 2003).

The Brazilian community also mushroomed on Martha's Vineyard.[4] Brazilians began arriving in droves shortly after President Bill Clinton adopted the island as his summer vacation retreat in the 1990s, and the roughly 3,500 Brazilians living there in 2010 accounted for about one-fifth of the island's winter population of some 16,000. Brazilians also provide much of the labor to support the Vineyard's summer population of more than 100,000. The impact of Brazilians there is highlighted by the fact that, in 2007, almost one-third of babies born on the island were born to Brazilian mothers (Seccombe 2011).

Brazilians work long hours painting, renovating, and landscaping. "The contractors love them because they're cheap, they're off the books, they're disposable, and there is like an unlimited labor supply," said one contractor (quoted in Gerson 2004). They work in the island's myriad hotels and restaurants and also provide the bulk of domestic service as housekeepers, babysitters, and nannies, especially during the summer months. When the Clintons vacationed on the island, attracting scores of visitors and celebrities, countless Brazilians began cleaning the homes of the rich and famous. Although work is scarcer in the winter, many Brazilians remain on the island getting by on reduced hours or travel to places like Miami to find temporary jobs, as did one Brazilian I met on the island who was working as a waiter in a pricey restaurant that catered to summer residents and tourists.

"Until recently their efforts were welcome and their legal status"—up to 70 percent are undocumented—"largely ignored," writes the journalist Daniela Gerson (2009) of the Brazilian community on Martha's Vineyard. But a house fire in 2002, where up to fourteen Brazilians were staying, focused attention on the severely overcrowded conditions in which many of the immigrants live; they often pay $400 a month just for a bed in a jam-packed room. Then, in the fall of 2003, immigration officers came to the island and arrested eleven Brazilians who had ignored deportation orders, sending them back to the mainland on a Coast Guard cutter. The deportations unnerved many in the Brazilian community, but it did not halt the flow. Although some Brazilians left for Brazil, other Brazilians— including some who had lived in Florida—continued to arrive. Thus, there was not a significant decline in the Brazilian population on the island, although now very few Brazilians arrive directly from Brazil (Gerson 2009).

One prominent feature of the Brazilian population in Massachusetts, in general, is that perhaps in no other state where Brazilians live are there more small businesses owned by Brazilians offering goods and services to their fellow co-ethnics. During the early years of immigration, small stores that sold Brazilian food products, along with beauty salons and ethnic restaurants, opened in several Boston neighborhoods. These were followed by more varied businesses, and, by the mid-1990s, there were Brazilian-owned medical and dental offices; travel, remittance, and insurance agencies; and English-language schools, most still catering to Brazilians, in an ever-expanding geographical radius. But, from about 2000 on, Brazilian-owned businesses in Massachusetts not only opened in the downtowns of cities large and small, from Cape Cod in the south to Lowell in the north, but also many began attracting a non-Brazilian clientele. Some of these businesses, such as cleaning services and painting and renovation companies, no longer catered to the ethnic community. By 2010, in fact, there were an estimated 400 Brazilian-owned businesses in the state. As the sociologist Ana Cristina Braga Martes (2010) notes in her study of this facet of the Brazilian community, most of these businesses were started with money saved from housecleaning, restaurant work, construction, delivery, and other jobs open to new immigrants.

Some towns in northern Massachusetts have become bedroom communities for Brazilians who work in New Hampshire. There is, in fact, a notable Brazilian presence, especially in the Nashua area, in that small New England state. While no data exist on the number of Brazilians working or living in New Hampshire, in July 2007, while visiting a well-known resort outside Portsmouth, I met four Brazilians working as chambermaids, who told me that several more of their compatriots were also employed at the resort. They said that all of the Brazilians who work there are bused in from Peabody, Massachusetts, about an hour away. When I inquired (in Portuguese) where they came from in Brazil, one replied "Resplendor," a tiny town not far from Governador Valadares. When I prompted her, asking, "In Minas Gerais?" she said, "Yes." What was remarkable about this response was that she identified her hometown in Brazil, a literal speck on the map that only Brazilians from the immediate area would ever have heard of—rather than the state of Minas Gerais—suggesting to me a person with humble roots. One woman was from São Paulo, and another was from Blumenau, in the southern state of Santa Catarina, while the fourth woman was from Ipatinga, a town in the region of Governador Valadares. I was surprised by this variety of origins because Brazilians from the same locale usually work together. The dispersal of hometowns suggested that this was a recent place of employment and that Brazilians from the same towns had not yet had a chance to recruit their own friends and relatives for jobs there.

This, then, is the picture of Brazilians in the northeast United States and New England, the region that has the largest concentration of this relatively recent immigrant stream. We now turn our attention to the South, a region of the country with a growing Brazilian presence—but not always in the places that one might expect.

Destination: The South

In the past two decades or so, metropolitan Atlanta, an area not traditionally associated with immigration, has been attracting new immigrants to the United States, Brazilians among them. While fewer than eight thousand Brazilians were counted there in the 2011 American Community Survey, estimates of their actual presence range up to ten times that number. The growing population of Brazilians is made plain by the 2008 decision of Brazil's Ministry of Foreign Affairs to re-open its Atlanta consulate; it had been closed a few years earlier due to budgetary constraints. Then, too, there are now so many Portuguese-speaking children enrolled in the public schools in Cobb County—which encompasses part of greater Atlanta—that, in the summer of 2007, the school system sent several language teachers to take an intensive Portuguese course at Middlebury College in Vermont (White 2008; Brent Berlin, personal communication).

Atlanta is the second home in the United States to a number of Brazilians who first lived in Framingham, Massachusetts. Most say they came south for the weather, rather than to escape the sort of anti-immigrant unpleasantness in Framingham described earlier. I have often heard that Brazilians commonly perceive New England and the northeast, in general, as less friendly and inviting than the southern United States, which is more to their liking in terms of both climate and sociability (Olmsted 2010; Marcus 2009b).

Most Brazilians live in Marietta, Roswell, Alpharetta, and other bedroom communities north of Atlanta. However, a clear residential pattern has emerged in the region. Less-educated Brazilians from more modest backgrounds—most of whom are undocumented—tend to live well north of downtown Atlanta. They are fairly recent arrivals in the United States and usually come from small towns in Goiás and Minas Gerais. Being undocumented, they cannot visit Brazil because, if they did, they would run the serious risk of not being able to return to the United States. Given the restrictions on traveling to their homeland, they place less emphasis on their children's retention of Portuguese. Better-educated, middle-class Brazilians, on the other hand, often live within the city of Atlanta and usually have lived in the United States for a longer period of time. They are more often from urban areas in Brazil, including Rio de Janeiro and São Paulo, and they are likely to be legal residents of the United States. As such, they can travel freely to Brazil, so their children's continued ability to speak Portuguese is important to them. Because of residential separation and differences in social and educational history, these two communities of Brazilians rarely interact (Pickel 2000; Olmsted 2010; Vasquez, Ribeiro, and Alves 2008).

As in other parts of the United States, the immigration crackdown has taken a toll on the Brazilian community in Atlanta, and, by 2008, more Brazilians were said to be leaving Atlanta than were arriving. Estimates suggest that as many as five thousand Brazilians may have either returned to Brazil or headed for North or South Carolina, where immigration enforcement has been less draconian than in Georgia. In Cobb County, where most Brazilians live, when a car is stopped by police and the driver cannot produce a driver's license—which is increasingly difficult to obtain if one lacks legal residency—he or she may be reported to Immigration and Customs Enforcement (ICE) and may eventually face deportation.[5] This is a very serious problem, since no public transportation exists in the county. The downturn in the housing market also may have been a catalyst for the exodus, since many Brazilian men with construction jobs either worked fewer hours or lost their jobs entirely in the slower economy. It is difficult to assess whether it was problems with immigration or difficulty finding work that caused many to leave the area (Vasquez, Ribeiro, and Alves 2008).

My most striking encounter with Brazilians took place in a part of the South where I least expected it. In 2004, while visiting friends near Charleston, South Carolina, I encountered several Brazilians who were living in Goose Creek, a working-class suburb of about thirteen thousand people north of the city. There are also small Brazilian communities in Mount Pleasant, another Charleston suburb, and in Myrtle Beach, South Carolina. An estimated five thousand Brazilians live in Goose Creek, which grew during the early years of the new millennium. Men were the first to arrive; they generally found work in construction-related jobs as carpenters, painters, and installers of aluminum siding. Women followed and were hired as housecleaners in some of the well-to-do suburbs and beach communities outside Charleston. At one time, this small population supported three stores that sold Brazilian products and two bakeries that featured Brazilian specialties. There is also what Brazilians call a "kilo restaurant," one in which customers select from a variety of dishes served buffet-style and then are charged for their food by weight (Goyette 2008).

According to a Brazilian woman I met from Goose Creek who has a housecleaning business that employs her recently arrived compatriots and whose husband owns a siding company, most of the newcomers to the community—all of whom are undocumented—came through Mexico and paid around $10,000 for the trip. But, as in Atlanta, some began leaving Goose Creek in 2007 as jobs in construction became scarcer, the dollar lost its value against the Brazilian currency, and there was a crackdown on undocumented immigration in the state (Goyette 2008).

"Come to Florida! The Brazil That Worked Out!"
Ad in Atlanta yellow pages for a real estate company (quoted in Marcus 2008b, 106)

Brazilians in Brazil usually are more aware of the Brazilian immigrant communities in Florida than of those elsewhere in the United States. Not only do Florida's Brazilians receive more media attention in Brazil than those in other U.S. locales, but also Florida, especially Disney World, in Orlando, is a very popular destination for Brazilian tourists; as one tour operator put it, taking one's children to Disney World is "the dream of every person in Brazil." During the first nine months of 2011, an estimated 1.1 million Brazilians spent $1.6 billion in the state, an increase of nearly 60 percent from the previous year. Among foreign nations, only Canada sends more visitors to Florida. About one-third of Brazilian visitors made their way to Orlando, a city with a sizeable population of their compatriots who, among the other jobs they hold, are hired to cater to Brazilian visitors and other tourists alike. But, in terms of numbers, Orlando, in central Florida, pales in comparison to south Florida, where the great majority of Brazilians in the state live. There are also small Brazilian communities in Tampa and St. Petersburg (Clark 2010; Alvarez 2011; Fries 2005).

Since Florida has long attracted Brazilians of varying social stripes, Brazilian communities in south Florida might best be described as a "tale of two cities," in this case the adjacent towns of Pompano Beach and Deerfield Beach on one hand and Miami on the other. The reason for the "tale of two cities" is that Florida has a more diverse Brazilian population in terms of social class than any other region of the country. Officially, Florida also has the largest population of Brazilians of any state in the United States—66,000—according to the 2011 American Community Survey. But, here again, this is almost certainly an undercount, and it is a far cry even from the conservative figure of 150,000 Brazilians in the Sunshine State that is the estimate of the Brazilian American Chamber of Commerce in Miami and the much larger number of 250,000 to 300,000 suggested by the Brazilian Consulate in Miami (Brinkley-Rogers 1998; Whitefield 2011).

The varied social roots of Brazilians in Florida have been noted by several researchers. There is "the economic elite" or simply "the rich," for one. Propelled by a lack of lucrative job prospects back home, high interest rates, and a genuine fear for their personal security, tens of thousands of well-to-do Brazilians began arriving in south Florida, particularly Miami, in the late 1980s and early 1990s. One real estate broker estimated that 10 percent of the apartments sold in south Florida in the late 1990s were bought by Brazilians, and by 2010 Brazilians were the most important foreign buyers in that real estate market.[6] "The Brazilians walk in, they don't even negotiate," said one Miami real estate agent. "It's a no-brainer for them." Some very wealthy Brazilians were buying multiple units in high-rise condominiums in upscale places like Williams Island, Key Biscayne, and Boca Raton. Then there were the Brazilian builders, developers, and assorted entrepreneurs who descended on Miami to take advantage of the Brazilian capital flowing into the area. They began building luxury condos for the Brazilian elite, who are said to be particularly active in the market for homes costing $1 million and up. In all, Brazilians own an estimated fifteen thousand pieces of real estate, including houses and apartments in the greater Miami area as well as two hundred business establishments in central Miami alone (Magalhães 2004; Resende 2009; Brinkley-Rogers 1998; Longa 1994; Streitfeld 2011; Whitefield 2011).

Some of these privileged families live divided lives. In one family, for example, the mother and son—a university student—reside in Miami, but the father, a financial consultant in São Paulo, commutes between Brazil and the United States. This pattern is not uncommon for this elite segment of the Brazilian population in south Florida. Families worried about their security and their bank accounts buy property in south Florida and send their children to school there but commute to Brazil to run their businesses or maintain close contact with them via e-mail, phone, and fax. They are reminiscent of the so-called Chinese astronauts, the wealthy Chinese whose families live in the United States or Canada and who frequently travel back to their homes in Hong Kong or Taiwan. Just like their Brazilian counterparts, they are well-educated professionals, business executives, and entrepreneurs (Brinkley-Rogers 1998; Almeida 1994; Wong 1997).

Another slice of the south Florida Brazilian community consists of white-collar workers and their families. Mostly residents of Miami, they are employed by multinational companies, hold executive positions in banks and corporations, or own sizeable businesses; in all cases, they are financially secure. Well educated and coming from middle- or upper-middle-class families in Brazil, others work as doctors, lawyers, accountants, journalists, translators, and college teachers (Magalhães 2004).

Then there are the owners of the myriad small businesses that dot the south Florida landscape. Perhaps as many as three thousand Brazilians in Miami-Dade and Broward Counties (Pompano Beach and Deerfield Beach) own modest travel, remittance, real estate, and insurance agencies, gas stations, restaurants, food markets, and stores that sell Brazilian products. Generally of somewhat more modest backgrounds than the Florida Brazilians just mentioned, most are legal residents of the United States, having lived here for quite some time. In fact, almost none of those in the upper rungs of the Brazilian population in south Florida have problems with documentation. Nearly all live in the United States legally and are able to travel freely between their country of origin and their adopted land (Magalhães 2004).

Finally, there is the tale of the "other" city, the Broward County beach communities that are home to Brazilian blue-collar workers. One appeal of the area is that, since Broward has a smaller Hispanic population than Miami, there is less competition for jobs there. Still, most of the jobs are low level and require little more than an (often bogus) Social Security card. While some Broward residents who have lived in the United States for a decade or more have green cards, most do not. They hail from Brazil's middle and lower-middle classes and have varying levels of education. The newest arrivals among them are all undocumented—having almost invariably arrived in the United States through Mexico—and have even more modest backgrounds and less schooling than their Broward compatriots who came earlier (Magalhães 2004).

It is important to point out, however, that the jobs Brazilians have in Florida are often not commensurate with their class roots and level of education. While a majority of Broward County Brazilians labor in unskilled construction jobs or make food deliveries or clean houses, most are high school graduates. And there are examples of even more glaring mismatches between employment and education. There is the university graduate in public relations, for example, who distributes flyers on the street, the lawyer who took a job as a private chauffeur, the psychologist who became a receptionist in Miami, and the one-time business manager who works as a waiter in Fort Lauderdale. These are the same sort of disparities between jobs and schooling that I discovered earlier in my own research in New York City (Neto and Bernardes 1996; Margolis 1994a).

Finally, as in Atlanta and as elsewhere in Florida, many Brazilians in Broward County are secondary migrants, having lived in the northeast, including New England, before moving to the Sunshine State. Brazilians are especially partial to south Florida because its balmy climate and beaches remind them of home. Then, too, the similarity between the Spanish and the Portuguese languages and between Brazilian and Latin cuisine make for an easy familiarity in an otherwise alien setting (Suarez 2003; Bustos 1995).

Moving farther west, Brazilians in New Orleans have been dubbed "hurricane chasers." They were part of a "rapid-response labor force" put together after Hurricane Katrina, in 2005, that was composed largely of fairly recent Latino immigrants who spoke little English but had relatively high levels of education. These geographically mobile groups—Brazilians among them in this case—are quick to respond to sudden labor demands, such as those that occur after natural disasters. Then, too, because of the enormous need for workers in New Orleans following Katrina, legality was not an issue, and the majority of Brazilians who flocked to the city were undocumented and worked off the books. Because of the crisis, immigration enforcement was also much more lax than in other parts of the country, and immigrants were generally not targeted or harassed (Fussell n.d.; Nolan 2008).

Most Brazilians who went to New Orleans were recent arrivals in the United States, having lived in this country on average three years or less and having entered through Mexico. Many of their hometowns in Brazil were in the interiors of Minas Gerais, Goiás, Rondonia, and Pará, the states sending the largest number of immigrants to that city. As secondary migrants nearly half traveled south from Massachusetts, while most of the rest were former residents of Florida and Georgia; fewer than 10 percent came directly to New Orleans from Brazil (Fussell 2007; Gibson 2010).

This was largely a male migration—men looking for better-paying jobs in post-Katrina reconstruction. While Hispanics worked mostly in demolition, Brazilians often took skilled jobs. Brazilian workers with construction-related skills, like flooring, tiling, and roofing—what Brazilians called "*roofeiros*" in Portuguese—were attracted by salaries of up to $30 an hour, although most earned about $150 a day, and, because of unscrupulous contractors, a few were not paid at all. Brazilians helped rebuild the Superdome, Tulane and Loyola Universities, Riverwalk, and many restaurants and bars in the French Quarter, along with innumerable private homes. As the Brazilian population in New Orleans expanded, some Brazilian men began working in jobs to service the needs of their compatriots. They became car salesmen, mechanics in body shops, and computer repairmen exclusively for other Brazilians. Fewer than 20 percent of the Brazilians coming to post-Katrina New Orleans were women; many of them took jobs as domestic workers, although some were employed in construction. At the height of reconstruction, from 2005 to 2007, women began selling Brazilian food at job sites, particularly during these early years when there were no Brazilian restaurants in the city. Later on, as New Orleans slowly emerged from the shadow of Katrina, Brazilian women began working as chambermaids in hotels and started housekeeping businesses in private homes. In short, this was a decidedly young, single population, with few children or older people in the mix (Fussell 2007; Kaste 2006; Nolan 2008; Gibson 2010).

New Orleans is home to several groups of so-called fraternity among friends (*cónsorcio entre amigos*) in which, each month, group members put a certain amount of money—usually between $50 and $100—into a joint pot. The pot goes to a different member each month, allowing the winner access to a large sum of money to pay off debts or to make purchases like a car to drive to work or to make a down payment on real estate or a business in Brazil (Gibson 2010).

One of the most striking facets of this migration stream is the way Brazilians seem "pre-adapted" to New Orleans. Brazilians say they feel more at home there than in other American cities. In addition to their appreciation of the mild climate, they appear to adjust more readily to the Big Easy because of the similarity between some aspects of New Orleans popular culture—zydeco, carnival, street parades—and that of Brazil. Some Brazilians depict New Orleans as a sort of cultural middle ground between the United States and Brazil. Many say they prefer New Orleans because of its laid-back ambience in terms of social liberty: police look the other way at public drinking, loud parties, and "disorderly" conduct in general. The city is also a place where bars and restaurants stay open until the wee hours of the morning (Gibson 2008, 2012).

Brazilians take part in the city's famous social life, including its Mardi Gras parades, for which they organized a *bloco*, a group of costumed singers, dancers, and musicians, in the style of Brazilian *carnaval*. Brazilians are said to have "a cultural kinship" with New Orleans because it is the "most sensual, most European" American city. Said one Brazilian living there: "There's a natural fusion of New Orleans culture and Brazilian culture. It's a good blend" (Gibson 2010; quoted in Nolan 2008).

Before the hurricane devastated the city, there were no more than a few hundred Brazilians residing in New Orleans. At its peak, in 2007, the Brazilian population reached an estimated ten thousand Brazilians, but by 2010 the number living and working in the city had fallen to between three and five thousand. Because of the recession, many lost jobs, and, once work was hard to find, they left the city for other locales in the United States or returned home to Brazil. Still, the community is far from disappearing, although its future in New Orleans is uncertain. What becomes of it will depend on the ongoing demand for construction labor and the continued tolerance of undocumented workers (Gibson 2010; Corrêa 2010).

Destination: The West

The presence of Brazilians in California appears to go back a long way. During World War II, an American army base was built in Natal, a coastal city in northeastern Brazil. After the war, a number of Brazilians accompanied their American friends and/or employers back home to California. Thus, it is said that some Brazilian old-timers in the state can trace their residence in California to this decades-past connection to Natal (Osmar Freitas, personal communication).

The three poles of Brazilian settlement in California are San Francisco, Los Angeles, and San Diego. About forty thousand Brazilians are served by the Brazilian Consulate in San Francisco, but, since that number includes all of northern California, Washington, and Oregon, it is difficult to determine how many Brazilians live in the San Francisco Bay area. Once again, official U.S. statistics are of no help, since the 2011 American Community Survey counted only thirty thousand Brazilians in the entire state. The most common estimate is that there are about fifteen thousand Brazilians scattered around the San Francisco Bay area, with their most prominent presence in the Mission district, which is known for its ethnic diversity (Ribeiro 1996).

San Francisco has a distinctly Brazilian ethnic niche: pizzerias. Brazilians are pizzeria owners, pizza makers, pizza servers, and pizza deliverers. In fact, when one does a Google search for pizzerias in San Francisco, two types are listed: Italian and Brazilian. To be sure, this ethnic niche provides work for relatively few Brazilians. This is similar to other quintessential ethnic fortes—shoe shining and go-go dancing in New York City—in which only a few hundred Brazilians are actually employed. Most of San Francisco's Brazilians have jobs similar to those their compatriots hold in other American cities; they are cab drivers, restaurant workers, house-cleaners, nannies, and takeout food and newspaper deliverers (Ribeiro 1996; Margolis 1994a; Maia 2012).

Some Brazilians make their living through what has been called "the commoditization of their culture," and those who perform "their culture" at clubs and private and corporate parties have been hailed as "cultural workers." They cook Brazilian food, teach samba, and offer instruction in *batucada*, Afro-Brazilian drumming, and in *capoeira*, the Brazilian martial art, to American fans of all things Brazilian. A majority of those who participate in Brazilian cultural activities are, in fact, American. Although many of San Francisco's Brazilians are from the state of Goiás, in the United States they turn into *cariocas*, archetypal natives of Rio de Janeiro in the sense that they adopt American stereotypes of Brazilian culture—samba, *carnaval*, and soccer (Ribeiro 1996, 5; 1998).

As we have seen, the San Francisco Bay area is home to some dozen samba schools. Samba classes are targeted at Americans, since Brazilians are presumed to be "naturals" at dancing samba. Along with their newly trained American *sambistas*, Brazilian men usually hold lead positions as drummers in samba parades, while Brazilian women are featured "almost completely naked" on the floats. Writes the Brazilian anthropologist Gustavo Lins Ribeiro of San Francisco's Carnaval: "Brazilian visibility is highly based on the exposure of women's bodies. . . . There is no doubt that this is a powerful factor in attracting both the media and the public and that it clearly distinguishes . . . Brazilian participation in the parade" (1997, 14).

Between sixty and seventy thousand Brazilians are served by the Brazilian Consulate in Los Angeles, which covers southern California, including San Diego, Arizona, New Mexico, and Utah. An estimated thirty-three thousand Brazilians live in the greater Los Angeles metropolitan area. While the Brazilian community in Los Angeles is still relatively small when compared to communities of other Latino immigrant groups that live there, in the past two decades, thousands of Brazilian immigrants have made Los Angeles their home. Many live in West Los Angeles, the locale of a Brazilian cultural center, as well as in Santa Monica, Venice, and Chico. Other small enclaves of Brazilians are also found in the region. For example, attracted by the bilingual education available to their children there, Brazilians have settled in Artesia, a town in Orange County near Disneyland that is the site of a decades-old Portuguese community (Beserra 2003).

Because of Brazilians' long involvement in the recording and film industries in Los Angeles, dating from the heyday of Carmen Miranda, it is said that L.A.'s Brazilian community has had a singular influence in diffusing Brazilian culture abroad. Perhaps the popularity of samba schools in Los Angeles—as in San Francisco—is an outgrowth of California's association with the entertainment industry. And, as in San Francisco, samba schools in Los Angeles thrive, attracting primarily American fans of Brazilian culture; only 20 percent of the students in one samba school are Brazilian, and the rest are American (Beserra 2003; Munoz 1995).

An estimated ten thousand Brazilians live in San Diego, many having moved there from other regions of the United States. "A lot of people from the East Coast are coming down to start businesses," said one Brazilian resident of San Diego. But, as elsewhere in the Sun Belt, "the main thing is the weather. Brazilian people are fond of good sunshine and good beaches," he opined (quoted in Kammer 2002).

Most of what we know about Brazilians in other states in the United States—other than those described in this chapter—comes from indirect evidence, because little or no research exists on Brazilian populations elsewhere in the country. An example: the Brazilian Consulate in Los Angeles periodically sends itinerant consulates out to Las Vegas, Salt Lake City, and Phoenix, indicating that there are sizeable Brazilian communities in those cities. The Brazilian consul general in Los Angeles estimates that some eight thousand Brazilians live in Utah, many of them Brazilian women married to American Mormon men whom they met when the latter were missionaries in Brazil. Another example: the editor of a major Brazilian immigrant newspaper in Atlanta claims to have a circulation of fifty thousand; he says that twenty thousand copies are distributed to Brazilians in Tennessee, North Carolina, South Carolina, and Texas (Marcus 2008b).

Washington, DC, and adjacent suburbs of Maryland and Virginia also have sizeable Brazilian communities. In November 2010 I was an invited participant in an all-day gathering of Brazilian families from the area that was organized by Bryan McCann, a professor of history at Georgetown University; several hundred Brazilians attended the event. If one includes Maryland and Virginia where most Brazilians live, more than twenty thousand Brazilians were counted in the District of Columbia in the 2011 U.S. Census. Similarly, Houston and Chicago are said to have large Brazilian populations on the basis of data from both the U.S. Census and the Brazilian consulates in those cities.

Before leaving North America, we should mention another site of Brazilian settlement: Canada.

Destination: Canada

The Brazilian Ministry of Foreign Affairs estimates that about thirty thousand Brazilians were living in Canada in 2011, well over half of them in Toronto, with a few thousand more largely divided between Montreal and Vancouver. Still, this figure should be viewed with caution, because, as one researcher suggests, perhaps half of the Brazilians living in Toronto were not counted in the Canadian census (Ministério das Relações Exteriores 2011; Shirley 1999; Goza 1994).

Until 1987, Brazilian tourists did not need visas to visit Canada, but visa requirements were subsequently put in place in a bid to crack down on unofficial immigration by Brazilians who claimed to be political refugees or who came as tourists but stayed on and sought work in Canada. Nevertheless, would-be immigrants from Brazil continued to arrive, and, for the first time, Brazilians were entering Canada without support from employers or relatives already in the country. Most of these newcomers found work in the informal sector, often in Portuguese-owned businesses. They were employed in construction, in the cleaning industry, as restaurant workers, or in other low-paying service positions (Paoletti 1987; Shirley 1999).

The Brazilian population in Toronto, the largest in the country, has several distinct social levels. A small Brazilian elite that has lived in Canada for decades is tied to the nation's well-to-do English-speaking establishment through business and marriage. An educated middle sector includes professionals, business owners, and others with comfortable employment positions. The last and most recent group to arrive in Canada are the Brazilians mentioned earlier. Coming from more modest backgrounds, many of them lack work papers. Some members of this group have become closely allied with the Portuguese, who were already well established in Canada. Portuguese social workers and religious personnel helped the new immigrants find places to live and assist them in their dealings with Canadian authorities (Goza 1999; Shirley 1999).

Each of these social levels has its own economic foundation, its own links to Canadian society, and its own places of business and leisure. It is apparent here, as it is in some Brazilian communities in the United States, that many Brazilian immigrants in Canada use class and regional affiliations to distinguish themselves from their fellow countrymen and women. There is little awareness of or communication among the various segments of Brazilian society in Toronto, which appears to be the only Canadian city with Brazilians from such diverse backgrounds (Shirley 1999; Brasch 2007).

Indeed, contrast this situation with that of the small Brazilian community in Vancouver. One researcher estimates that approximately 1,500 Brazilian-born residents, nearly all of whom are legal, live in Vancouver. Arriving in the late 1980s and early 1990s, about 70 percent came as landed immigrants, and another 20 percent acquired that status after arrival. To be approved as a landed immigrant or permanent resident—the term that is now more commonly used—one is expected to have the skills, education, work experience, language ability, and other qualities needed to get a good job in Canada (Botelho 1998).

Given their social and educational background and their legal status as permanent residents, it is no surprise that the income level of Vancouver Brazilians is well above that of other immigrant groups in the city. And, while many initially experienced a drop in occupational status after arrival in Canada, over time about 80 percent began to hold professional jobs that met their pre-migration training and aspirations. The vast majority work in areas that demand high skill levels, including various medical fields, computer and other technical areas, and administrative and business positions (Botelho 1998).

Most Vancouver Brazilians already are or plan to become Canadian citizens, and more than three-quarters intend to make Canada their permanent home. But this does not mean that they have forsaken Brazil. The great majority visit Brazil at least occasionally, and they keep close contact with relatives and friends there by phone, e-mail, and other means. In this sense, they are akin to Brazilians in the United States and elsewhere; they are transnationals tying home and host country into a single social field. While they have left Brazil, they are still most emphatically Brazilian (Botelho 1998).

We now turn to Brazilians in Europe. Although they are fewer in number and less studied than those in North America, their presence is increasingly felt, and one can assume that many Brazilians in Europe, like their counterparts in the United States and Canada, are there to stay.

6

Other Destinations

Europe, England, and the Republic of Ireland

The modernity Brazilians were bringing to Portugal was not viewed as equivalent to cultivated European taste. It was a hybrid, third world kind of modernity. . . . It was also volatile and unpredictable, for Brazil was seen as a young country lacking strong cultural and moral traditions to counteract the cultural excesses of modernization.

Angela Torresan (2007, 114)

Just how many Brazilians are there in various European nations, in England, and in the Republic of Ireland? As in the United States numbers are illusive because many Brazilians are in their host countries illegally. Still, estimates exist, such as the one published by Itamaraty, Brazil's Ministry of Foreign Affairs, in 2011 (table 5).

Table 5 Brazilians in Europe, England, and the Republic of Ireland

Country	Number
Portugal	136,000
England	180,000
Spain	159,000
Germany	91,000
Italy	85,000
France	80,000
Switzerland	57,000
Republic of Ireland	18,000

Source: Ministério das Relações Exteriores 2011.

Brazilians in Europe

Although the number of Brazilians in Europe is relatively modest when measured against the number in the United States, evidence suggests that several catalysts re-oriented many Brazilian immigrants and their facilitators—primarily travel and remittance agencies—away from the United States and toward Europe and England. Foremost among them was the greater difficulty securing tourist visas for travel to the United States following the September 2001 attacks in New York and Washington, DC, along with the increased controls at U.S. borders. The high cost, uncertainty, and outright danger of illegal entry via Mexico certainly put a damper on the allure of the United States. The strength of the euro vis-à-vis the U.S. dollar also played a role in that the value of remittances sent back to Brazil was enhanced when sent in the European Union's currency.[1] And, as noted in chapter 4, the possibility that Brazilians could acquire Portuguese, Spanish, or Italian passports because of their ancestral roots in those countries and their resulting ability to immigrate legally made these destinations attractive to many would-be immigrants (Salek 2002).

Destination: Portugal

Perhaps nowhere did this re-direction away from the United States and toward Europe have a greater impact than in Portugal. It is not surprising that Portugal, Brazil's "mother country," is home to what is likely the largest number of Brazilians on the European continent. After all, Brazilians speak the language, albeit with a distinct accent and somewhat different vocabulary from those of the Portuguese themselves. Since 2007, Brazilians have been the largest immigrant group in Portugal, accounting for 25 percent of all immigrants in that country (Dos Santos et al. 2010; Moura 2010).

A good number of Brazilians headed for Portugal after being prevented from traveling to the United States. Recall that residents of Minas Gerais are routinely denied U.S. tourist visas, which explains why an estimated 30 percent of Brazilians in Portugal are from that state. Portugal became an inviting destination for Brazilians for three reasons: the relative ease of entry into the country; the strength of the euro in relation to the U.S. dollar; and, of course, the language. Portugal did indeed beckon many Brazilians who had not previously considered immigrating to the United States because they did not speak English; at least in Portugal they would be able to communicate (Padilla 2007; Pinho 2010).

When Brazilians first arrived in Portugal in the late 1980s and early 1990s, the nation needed their skills in highly visible fields associated with modernization, such as marketing, advertising, and television production. And so, as was noted earlier, they were not restricted to typical immigrant job niches as were Brazilians elsewhere. To be more precise, in Portugal, a demand existed for middle-class Brazilians in mainstream jobs, so they were not forced to sacrifice the status associated with their prior employment and education back home in Brazil. To these Brazilians, the very thought of being a housecleaner or dishwasher in Portugal—so common elsewhere—was anathema. Then, too, unlike the United States, Great Britain, and other western European countries, Portugal was seen by Brazilians as "not quite" a first-world nation, so there was not much in the way of financial rewards for taking unskilled jobs there (Torresan 2007).[2]

The early years of Brazilian immigration to Portugal were also a time when the Portuguese were becoming more familiar with things Brazilian. First to arrive were the wildly popular soap operas (*telenovelas*) produced by Brazil's giant television network TV Globo. Beginning in 1977 with the showing of *Gabriela, Clove and Cinnamon* (*Gabriela, Cravo e Canela*), which crowds gathered to watch at Lisbon cafes, many popular *telenovelas* provided the Portuguese with extravagant rose-tinted views of contemporary Brazilian society. There was also the establishment of Brazilian-owned enterprises like the Rio-based supermarket chain Pão de Açúcar, which carried a variety of Brazilian products, and the ever-growing popularity of Brazilian music and Brazilian entertainers, who played to packed houses in Lisbon and other Portuguese venues (Silver 2005; Torresan 2007).

For some middle-class Brazilians who arrived during the first wave of migration to Portugal, this destination was not seen solely in economic terms but also was a way of increasing one's social and cultural capital. After all, one was living in a European country, albeit a country without the cachet of a France or an Italy. Europe was viewed by many Brazilians as more egalitarian, better educated, more urbane, safer, and less corrupt than their homeland. Then, too, because of their relatively privileged position in Portuguese society, middle-class Brazilians were the most visible and articulate immigrant population in Lisbon, and they used this visibility—in marked contrast to the invisibility of Brazilians in New York and London—to campaign for their right to remain in the country and to highlight their own contributions to the national economy. Brazilians also occupied a symbolically privileged position in the nation vis-à-vis African immigrants from Portugal's former colonies. The organization of immigrant populations in Portugal essentially followed the hierarchical pattern established by the old colonial order, with the addition of immigrants from eastern Europe, who, as Caucasians and because of ongoing racial preferences, were classified somewhere between African and Brazilian immigrants in local ethnic rankings (E. Rodrigues 2010; França 2010; Machado 2003, 2006).

Yet, despite their position at the apex of the immigrant social order and much to their surprise and chagrin, most educated Brazilians did not become an integral part of the Portuguese middle class. Still viewed as foreigners, they found that it was no simple matter to attain the social acceptance warranted by their economic success. Some Brazilians saw having Portuguese friends as a way to achieve their desired status within Portuguese society. In essence, having Portuguese friends symbolized migratory success; it signaled that Brazilians were not isolated from the larger society and were not limited to socializing with and living among other immigrants (Torresan 2006).

Thus, Brazil and Portugal's shared language and culture, both tied to their past colonial connection, did not always provide middle-class Brazilian immigrants with the necessary "cultural competence" to be welcomed with open arms into the local urban middle class. Many Portuguese viewed Brazilians as being insufficiently "Europeanized" in manner and values and also complained about their insensitivity to Portuguese traditions and national identity (Torresan 2007).

Brazilians in Portugal are viewed by many Portuguese as exotics associated with samba, soccer, sexuality, and miscegenation. Such stereotypes usually have more negative connotations for Brazilian women than for Brazilian men. In the minds of some Portuguese, Brazilian women dress too provocatively because of their purported sensuality, making them "easy" and linking them to prostitution. One Portuguese magazine mirrored this view, asking why Portuguese men "love" Brazilian women and Portuguese women "hate" them. But Brazilian women are also positively cast as warmer and more communicative than the Portuguese themselves or members of other immigrant groups meaning that they are particularly "well suited" to jobs as housekeepers, nannies, and caretakers of the elderly (Machado 2003; Beleli 2010; Padilla 2007; Moura 2010; França 2010).

In fact, Brazilians have had to contend with a rash of widely held stereotypes about what "being Brazilian" means in Portugal, a small country where their presence looms large. Consequently, the experience of Brazilians there differs from that of their compatriots in other countries. Brazilians are not "invisible" in Portugal as they are in the United States; nor are they confused with other immigrant or minority groups. Their distinctiveness is evident as soon as they open their mouths because their accents and vocabulary mark them as Brazilians and not part of an undifferentiated mass of "Latinos" or South Americans, as is the case in the United States and elsewhere (Padilla, Selister, and Fernandes 2010).

This is not meant to imply that most Brazilians want to integrate into Portuguese society to such an extent that they would lose their own distinct national identity. They are said to resist behaviors and attitudes that would put their sense of being Brazilian at risk. For example, Brazilian teenagers living in Portugal try to maintain their Brazilian accents and speech patterns and their "Brazilian verve" (*ginga brasileira*), a sign of their desire to remain distinct from their Portuguese contemporaries. Linked to the quest to preserve Brazilian identity is their disapproval of what many Brazilians regard as the cheerless reserve of the Portuguese, a diffidence stemming from the conservative formality of Portuguese society—so different from their own vibrant cultural traditions (Bela Feldman Bianco, personal communication; Torresan 2006).

Destination: England

An illuminating segue between the experience of Brazilian immigrants in Portugal and their lives in England is the contrast between the experience of middle-class Brazilians in Lisbon and that of those in London. In Portugal, Brazilians' middle-class status is recognized both back home in Brazil and in Portugal, their host country. But, in London, the simple fact of living in England—a first-world nation—connotes middle-class status independent of the type of jobs Brazilians hold there. Then, too, Brazilians in London—middle class and otherwise—are seen as part of an undifferentiated mass of immigrants from Latin America, just as they are in the United States. In contrast to their situation in Portugal, they are invisible to most people in England, and their privileged middle-class status is recognized only by fellow Brazilians by virtue of the fact that they live in London, a cosmopolitan first-world city (Torresan 2007).

Brazilians do indeed hold jobs in England that would be unthinkable in Brazil. Despite the high education level of many immigrants, they take whatever unskilled, low-paid employment is available to them. Brazilians work as chambermaids in hotels, as dishwashers and waiters in restaurants, as office cleaners, housecleaners, au pairs, and babysitters in private homes, as drivers and pizza deliverers, and in construction. The meaning of being a housecleaner or waiter in London is entirely different from its meaning in Brazil. Taking such jobs in Brazil would imply a grim plunge in status that would be intolerable to educated, middle-class individuals. Yet, in London, for Brazilians with similar social roots and education, such jobs are the norm. One survey found that about one-third of Brazilians in London have jobs cleaning offices and private homes, one-quarter work in restaurants and hotels, about 10 percent are drivers and couriers, and roughly the same number work in construction (Evans et al. 2007, 2011; Torresan 1994).

While hardly welcomed into the country with open arms, Brazilians do mesh with the needs of a segment of the labor market in England. They are seen as temporary workers who plan to stay in the country for only a few years to work and study and then return home. Such a labor force fits nicely with the sort of immigrant worker acceptable to the British government: young, temporary, and middle class, a docile labor force that can be easily controlled and that is unlikely to demand rights or cause problems (Torresan 1994).

Because of the utility of such workers, it has been suggested that British authorities look the other way when young Brazilians arrive in the country as students or tourists and then seek work.[3] About 10 percent of these arrivals hold European passports and come to live and work in England legally. Other Brazilians who have lived in England for many years or who marry British citizens or citizens of other members of the European Union also have the right to paid employment. Nevertheless, more than half of the Brazilian population in England—53 percent—was undocumented in the mid-2000s (Torresan 1994; Evans et al. 2007).

As in Portugal and other European countries, Brazilian immigration to England increased in late 2001 after additional restrictions on travel to the United States were put in place. While numbers are uncertain, evidence for this increase comes from various sources. A 2006 survey of Brazilians in London found that just under 70 percent had arrived within the preceding five years. Said one very long-term Brazilian resident there: "Before it was so unusual to encounter a Brazilian that it was cause for a party. Now there's no more novelty and one meets Brazilians all the time" (quoted in Torresan 1994, 114). Brazilians who had lived in London for a decade or more also remarked on the increase in the number of their compatriots during the first decade of the new millennium (Evans 2010; Frangella 2010).

This population increase is also reflected in the growth, mostly dating from the early 2000s, in the number of businesses catering to Brazilians in the London metropolitan area, where the vast majority of Brazilians in England live. While during the early years of immigration many Brazilians made Bayswater—dubbed "Brazilwater"—their home, today Brazilians reside in several locations in the city, including neighborhoods like Brent, especially Kensal Rise in London's northeast and Stockwell in the south. There, stores offering Brazilian products may be owned by people of other nationalities who use symbols like Brazilian flags to indicate that they carry ethnic specialties. The rising Brazilian population created new spaces for a variety of businesses for London's Brazilians—bars and restaurants, travel and remittance agencies, clubs, beauty salons, and law and immigration services, as well as stores featuring Brazilian apparel and other imported merchandise. Some of the appeal of these Brazilian-tinged goods and services stems from what has been referred to as "the economy of longing" (*a economia de saudade*) (Frangella 2010; Evans et al. 2007; Evans et al. 2011; Brightwell 2010, 27).

The Brazilian cultural scene in London also has grown dramatically since 2000. That year, to celebrate the five-hundredth anniversary of Brazil's discovery by Pedro Álvares Cabral, the Brazilian Embassy promoted extensive programs at the Barbican and in the Royal Albert Hall and arranged to have Brazilian films shown commercially. In 2004, Selfridges, the well-known London department store, dedicated a month to Brazilian fashions and products. Windows were dressed with lush tropical Brazilian scenes, and a local samba group performed next to the store's escalators. The following year, the Paraiso Samba School, one of three samba schools in London, won recognition in the famed Carnival Parade in Notting Hill, an event traditionally dominated by immigrants from the Caribbean. Then there are the "Brazil nights" at more than a dozen London nightclubs and the three *capoeira* associations with aficionados of varying ethnicities. In short, Brazil has become quite fashionable in the British capital (Frangella 2010).

Destination: The Republic of Ireland

It all began in 1999 when a meatpacking plant near the city of Anápolis, in Goiás, in west-central Brazil, closed down, leaving its workforce unemployed. At about the same time, an Irishman who had moved to Brazil to work in meatpacking learned of a labor shortage in the Irish meatpacking industry. Soon thereafter, he and his Brazilian wife became labor contractors, locating workers willing to travel on work permits for jobs in meat processing in the Irish Republic, specifically jobs in the town of Gort, in County Galway, in the west of the country. The couple used their Irish and Brazilian meatpacking contacts to initiate a flow of skilled blue-collar Brazilian workers from the Anápolis area to Ireland. Then the owners of another Irish meat-processing plant applied for work permits for still more Brazilians from that region. Later, meatpacking companies in other parts of Ireland recruited Brazilian workers from the state of São Paulo (Healy 2008; Cade 2010).

While the meat-processing plants were the original catalysts that brought Brazilians to Gort, other Brazilians came to work in different jobs in town; men filled labor demands in construction, farming, fisheries, and manufacturing, while women found jobs in retail sales, catering, restaurants, hotels, and nursing homes or worked as housecleaners and child minders. For several years, as many as one hundred Brazilians a day would appear in the town square, and farmers and construction foremen would hire them. "There was always work," said one resident. And, although the first Brazilian arrivals were from Goiás, the Brazilian community in Gort later included immigrants from elsewhere in Brazil (Healy 2008; Cade 2010; Sheringham 2009).

Gort, a town of some three thousand, grew into a key center for Brazilians in Ireland, where they accounted for an estimated 25 to 30 percent of local residents. The town had also become a "first stop" for many Brazilian immigrants new to Ireland who traveled to Gort to find information about employment and accommodations before moving on to other parts of the country. The town had turned into such a lively hive of Brazilian activity that the Brazilian community is mentioned in a Lonely Planet travel guide to Ireland, and a 2008 *New York Times* article on travel to the country cited Gort as a place where "you might wade into a celebration of Brazilian culture. The impact has been extraordinary: Brazilian music nights in one of the pubs, Brazilian necessities—from *maracujá* (passion fruit) to *mandioca* (manioc)—in the shops and a Sunday Mass said in Portuguese"

(Barry 2008, 8). In essence, a Little Brazil bloomed in Gort, where Brazilian-owned businesses included two clothing stores, three laundromats, several food shops, and a beauty salon, along with Internet cafes and remittance agencies. In addition to the Portuguese Mass at the local Catholic church, several evangelical churches in town served the needs of Brazilian devotees. Brazilians also played on the local soccer team, and a Brazilian-style carnival was celebrated every summer (Healy 2008; Cade 2010; Sheringham 2010a).

Despite their numbers, Brazilians do not appear to have socialized very much with Gort's Irish residents. In one study, most Brazilians interviewed said that, while they had Irish acquaintances made through contacts at work, they did not have any close Irish friends. Brazilians rarely frequent Gort's many pubs—the centers of social life for most of the town's Irish residents—either because they are evangelicals who do not drink or because they spend such long hours at work that they have little time for leisure. But respondents also said they could not understand *why* the Irish drink in pubs, which they describe as dark, dreary, enclosed spaces. Brazilians much preferred to socialize at home by having barbeques—weather permitting—or parties with spirited Brazilian music and dancing (Sheringham 2009).

While some Brazilians came to Gort without their families, spouses and children soon followed, and, in time, 40 percent of the children in Gort's main primary school were Brazilian, as were 10 percent of those in the town's high school. Both schools took steps to accommodate the growing number of Brazilian students, employing Portuguese-speaking teachers and establishing an English-immersion year for new arrivals. Education was clearly a key factor in the decision of many Brazilians to remain in Ireland longer than originally planned (Healy 2008; Sheringham 2009).

Most Brazilians arrived in Gort with the intention of staying for a few years and then returning to Goiás with their savings—to build a house, start a business, or pay for their children's education. But some signs of greater permanency began to surface as Brazilians helped to bring relatives to Ireland and found them jobs there. Still, this shift in plans could be problematic. Many Brazilians had temporary one-year work permits, and their continued right to live and work in Ireland was uncertain. Although it is better for an immigrant to have such a limited permit than to have no permit at all, the permits, which are essentially Ireland's contracts for lower-level jobs, tie the employee to a single employer. Nevertheless, after having lived in the country continuously for five years while doing arduous jobs like those in meat processing, an immigrant who holds a work permit has the right to submit an application for Irish citizenship—an opportunity some Brazilians have taken advantage of—which, if granted, also entitles them to automatic citizenship in the European Union (Healy 2008; Helen Marrow, personal communication).

One study reported a distinctly positive quality-of-life issue for Brazilians and other Latin American immigrants in Ireland. It found that many of these immigrants felt "advantaged" because of the range of neutral to positive stereotypes the Irish hold of Latin Americans in general. This, they said, gave them an edge not only over other immigrant, refugee, and racial groups who were deemed "less desirable" by the Irish but also over Latin American immigrants in the United States, in Spain, and, for Brazilians, in Portugal. These respondents believed that, in those countries, Brazilians were situated on a lower rung of the local social hierarchy than they were in Ireland. This may be why Brazilians in Ireland did not appear to exhibit the strong distancing behavior from other Latin American immigrants that is so well documented in the United States and elsewhere. Brazilians further contrasted the use of relatively nonracialized national origin and pan-ethnic terms employed in Ireland with the more constricting and racialized terminology found in the United States and Spain (Marrow 2012).

So, while Brazilians in Ireland usually do not have to contend with the sort of negative stereotypes they encounter elsewhere, does social class partly account for this differential treatment? The Brazilian population in Ireland appears to be heterogeneous in terms of background. There are middle-class students who have traveled there to study English, a few professionals seeking jobs in Dublin, and the far larger community contracted to work in meatpacking plants around the country. As a general rule, then, the Brazilians in Ireland are from more humble backgrounds and are less well educated than a majority of those in the United States. And this, in turn, is related to how they came to Ireland, that is, because of the links between the Brazilian and Irish meatpacking industries (Cade 2010; Helen Marrow, personal communication).

It is ironic, indeed, that although most Brazilians have lower levels of skills and education than their countrymen and women in the United States, Ireland *does* provide a path to legality for Brazilians as long as they can tolerate the difficult and demanding work available to them for five years before they can apply for Irish citizenship. Nevertheless, more restrictive immigration measures have been put in place in recent years: the number of deportations has increased, there is a growing scarcity of permits for non-European Union workers, and "birth-right citizenship" is being denied to the immigrants' children born in Ireland (Sheringham 2009).

Destination: Spain

Brazilians began arriving in Spain in large numbers during the 1990s, particularly after 1997, and the Brazilian population continued to grow through the 2000s. By then Brazilians, some of whom had re-migrated from Portugal and Italy, were the third fastest-growing foreign community in Spain, with women accounting for nearly 60 percent of Spain's Brazilian residents. Nevertheless, although there were as many as 125,000 Brazilians in Spain by 2009, they were essentially unseen. When the Spanish media and researchers focused on immigrants, Brazilians were not among those mentioned. Then, too, the Spanish public does not recognize Brazilians as immigrants; Brazilians are soccer players, entertainers, or students. Immigrants, from the Spanish point of view, are Ecuadorians, Moroccans, Senegalese, and so on. Brazilians also appear to be more tolerated than other, more numerous immigrant populations—Moroccans and Ecuadorians, for example—who are far more visible than Brazilians. Still, in Spain, Brazilians with darker skin tones are often confused with Africans and Arabs and are more stigmatized than those of European appearance (Teixeira 2007; Organização Internacional para as Migrações 2010; Badet 2010; Pires 2010; Cavalcanti 2005, 2007, 2008).

Most Brazilians in Spain live in Barcelona and Madrid. They go largely unnoticed in Barcelona because of their relatively small number and because they are not concentrated in any one neighborhood in the city. Some Brazilians who live there have dual nationality because of their Spanish roots, while others arrived on tourist visas and are not authorized to work. But they are a heterogeneous lot, indeed, in terms of age, origin in Brazil, professional training, level of education, and social class. They range from construction workers who share beds—one person working by day and the other working at night—to those with bank accounts who can count on receiving money from home should they need it (Cavalcanti 2005, 2008).

What is striking about Brazilian immigrants in Barcelona and, perhaps, elsewhere in Spain is that when a group of Brazilians gets together socially, one can note the marked disparities among them in terms of schooling, professional training, economic background, regional origin, and phenotype.

In Brazil, these differences probably would have been the motive for maintaining a separation, for avoiding social interaction with the "unlike." In contrast, in Spain, such distinctions tend to be minimized. In their shared condition as immigrants, individuals of widely varying backgrounds get together to eat a *feijoada* or go to a musical event or watch a soccer match (Cavalcanti 2008).

Brazilians in Spain hold more white-collar and professional jobs than any other immigrant group except immigrants from other European Union member countries, suggesting a relatively privileged position in the national labor market. Perhaps this is why growing numbers of Brazilian workers signed up for Spain's social security program, particularly during the country's economic crisis in 2008 and 2009, in contrast to the decrease in number of immigrants in general who did so. Still, as elsewhere, Brazilian women are concentrated in domestic service and other jobs in the service sector, while Brazilian men have more diverse employment; the majority work in services, with a smaller percentage in construction. Again in contrast to most immigrant groups in the country, some of Spain's Brazilians are "business immigrants," those who own enterprises with up to thirty employees. Many sell products and services that cater to the Brazilian community itself, while others market to the Spanish public at large (Masanet and Baeninger 2010; Fernandes and Rigotti 2008; Cavalcanti 2007).

One matter related to the employment of Brazilians in Spain was highlighted in a 2008 study of the Spanish media, which found that Brazil was the country most often cited in reference to the problem of prostitution in Spain. Similarly, a 2005 report in *Veja*, the Brazilian equivalent of *Time* magazine, focused on Uruaçu, a city of thirty-three thousand in Goiás, some two hundred kilometers from Brasília, where prostitution was said to be responsible for the town's economic prosperity. The town's economy once centered around the manufacture of wooden rosary beads, but in recent years this new, much more lucrative activity has meant that a large portion of Uruaçu's wealth has come from remittances sent by residents living abroad, in this case, local women working as prostitutes in Spain (Badet 2010; Nascimento 2005).

The *Veja* report suggested that the traditional prejudice surrounding prostitution was overcome by the wealth that this activity afforded the town. As a result, what was once a hidden profession became an accepted occupation like any other. Many of the women's relatives were aware of what they were doing in Spain; the women were dubbed the "*espanholas*" by townspeople. One local man, although a fervent Catholic, was not bothered by the chosen profession of his two daughters. Seven years earlier, they had left for Mallorca, and they had sent back enough money to build four houses in Uruaçu, one with a swimming pool. "I never liked the idea but they had no work here," he said. "But it's better that they go there than run around with married men here" (quoted in Nascimento 2005, 52).

Upon their return home, the *espanholas* are the main patrons of the local beauty salons; they own one-third of all rental property in town; and they build homes in the town's most upscale neighborhood. Moreover, the tales of women who earned good money in Spain have had a multiplier effect. The New York School, one of the foreign-language schools in town, began offering a course in Spanish, and among its thirty-four students were nearly a dozen who planned to join their mothers in Spain. The earnings of the *espanholas* must be seen in the following context: a producer of rosary beads in Uruaçu earns 11 centavos per piece. Working all day long, she can earn 150 *reais* a month, less than half of what an *espanhola* can make during a twenty- or thirty-minute assignation (Nascimento 2005).

The economic success of the *espanholas*, however, is only the rosy part of the picture. The women typically were underwritten by local travel agencies, so they arrived in Spain in debt to the agencies for their travel expenses and room and board. Cases of debt servitude and mistreatment were not uncommon, and some women turned to local Spanish authorities for help. "Some return in despair and disgraced by the aberrant forms of sex they have to practice to earn money," said the local priest, well known in town for being both a psychologist and a father confessor to the *espanholas*. "We need to find a way of showing the bad things that can happen [in Spain] — becoming involved in criminal networks, drugs and other crimes" (Nascimento 2005, 53).

Unlike the *espanholas*, some Brazilian women in Spain were sex workers *before* migrating to Europe. Several were involved in sex tourism and were helped financially by foreign clients they met in Brazil. The cost of the trip for others was financed by nightclub owners abroad, while a third group paid its own expenses. Prior to emigrating, most of these women belonged to the lower middle class, and they claim that, rather than being forced by dire poverty, they entered the sex industry because they wished to. "I came [to Spain] because I wanted to," said one woman. "I turn tricks because I want to" (quoted in Piscitelli 2008, 126).

The lack of opportunities in Brazil was cited by many *espanholas* as the reason for their migration to Spain, and they made the decision to go into the sex industry there because it meant they could earn a great deal more money than was possible in Brazil. The women contrasted their lives at home and in Europe, highlighting their changed circumstances after migration. They gained not only economic power in Brazil from the money earned in Spain but also prestige because they had experience living in a "first-world" country. For these women, migration was part of a well-planned strategy for social ascension and for achieving an improved lifestyle for themselves and their families back home (Piscitelli 2008).

Destination: Italy

In Italy, as in Spain, Brazilian women outnumber Brazilian men by more than two to one, and, as in Spain, some work as prostitutes. Some women, like the *espanholas*, travel abroad with the intention of becoming sex workers, while others find themselves attracted to the profession after becoming discouraged by their paltry earnings in more traditional jobs. Housecleaning, for example, in both Spain and Italy pays as little as one-fifth of what women can earn as sex workers. This was made clear in a report on BBC Brasil that recounted the experience of one Brazilian woman in Rome:

> The 24-year-old from São Paulo says that while she is not proud of being a prostitute she considers the work like any other, the only difference being that it is far more lucrative than most jobs open to Brazilian women in Italy. Three years ago she decided that she had had enough of smelling of disinfectant and having broken fingernails with little money—$12 an hour—to show for her exhausting work cleaning houses. Without leisure time to go to the gym or money to buy new clothes, she decided to follow the advice of some of her friends; she left house cleaning and entered the sex industry in Rome.
> She dyed her dark hair blonde, bought more revealing clothes, had her picture taken in a bikini and put it up on the Internet. At first she lived and worked in a house with four other Brazilian sex workers and later rented her own apartment in the historic city center. Her clients include businessmen, actors, soccer players and politicians and she arranges dates with them via cell phone. She meets clients between noon and 8 p.m.—outside of these hours she charges more—with her pay ranging from $140 to $425 per encounter. It is not difficult, she says, to earn $2,000 a day and one month she earned over

$42,000. Some clients ask her to play Brazilian music, dance the samba and say dirty words [*palavrões*] in Portuguese. She has clients who visit her every week and the only thing she will not do is work for no pay. (Rey 2008c)

Not all Brazilian prostitutes in Italy work independently or earn as much money as this *paulista*. Many arrive in Rome or Milan typically owing more than 3,000 euros (about $4,200) to friends or agencies that have funded the cost of obtaining a passport, paying the airfare, and providing money to tide the immigrants over while they settle in the country. Many are exploited by pimps who keep a large percentage of their earnings while they work in clubs or out of apartments and make less than half of those who work independently. In one instance, the police in Rome cracked down on a gang that specifically exploited Brazilian sex workers (Rey 2008c).

According to the anthropologist Adriana Piscitelli (2008, 2009), who has studied Brazilian sex workers in Spain and Italy, these women's motives for going abroad are invariably economic. Most of the women she interviewed in Italy were from Fortaleza, a city in Brazil's northeast, where they had held low-paying service-sector jobs. The women told her that they had left Brazil for Italy after being invited to do so by foreign sex tourists they met in Fortaleza. Their Italian "boyfriends" provided plane tickets, money for a passport, and a place to stay upon arrival. Such invitations to travel abroad were welcomed because they gave the women an opportunity to start a new life in Italy and were seen as relatively safe and debt-free. Some eventually bought houses or apartments in Brazil, which they rented out or used when they went home on vacation (Piscitelli 2008).

Other women Piscitelli interviewed engage in circular migration; they travel to Italy for a few months at a time as tourists and, once there, seek out clients they had met in Brazil. They go home with money and gifts and return to Italy on a regular basis. Others follow a more ad hoc routine. They visit their lovers/clients in Italy and, once there, try to persuade them to help them remain in the country. If they do not succeed, they still return home with elegant clothes, watches, perfume, and so on and then go in search of new foreign lovers who might help them leave Brazil. Most of those interviewed, however, managed to stay in Italy and married their sex tourist clients. After marriage, they left sex work behind and became legal residents of the country (Piscitelli 2008).

Sex work performed by Brazilians, despite its relatively high visibility in Spain and Italy, accounts for a small fraction of the jobs Brazilian women hold in those countries. In Italy, far more women take jobs as manicurists, hair dressers, child minders, housecleaners, or caretakers of the elderly or work at jobs in hotels and restaurants (Rey 2008b). In September 2011, while in Rome, my husband and I had dinner at a small restaurant near the Pantheon that had been recommended by a friend. The waitress who took our order appeared to speak Italian with a Portuguese accent. When I inquired about this, she said she was indeed Brazilian and then introduced me to her friend, another Brazilian who also worked there.

Estimates suggest that nearly 80 percent of Brazilian women in Italy work at one time or another as housecleaners and nannies for families or in institutions that care for children and the aged. Civil construction, agriculture, and restaurant work are the primary types of employment undertaken by Brazilian men. Agricultural jobs, in particular, are seen as entry-level work for those who have just arrived from Brazil and have not yet found better prospects. Whatever the work, in all cases, the pay is significantly higher than these immigrants were earning in Brazil (Tedesco 2008).

While the jobs Brazilians hold in Italy are known, the number of Brazilians there is not; estimates range from 45,000 to 130,000. More confounding is the fact that, according to the Brazilian Ministry of Foreign Affairs (Itamaraty), there were 130,000 Brazilians in Italy in 2007 but only 70,000 two years later, a decline that is not explained. Also in 2009, the official statistics of the Italian government recorded the presence of just over 44,000 Brazilians in the country. However, the government's data include only officially registered foreigners and do not take account of undocumented immigrants or those with dual citizenship, which many Brazilians living in Italy have (Bogus and Bassenesi 2000; Tedesco 2008; Zanin 2010).

One reason for the uncertain numbers, then, is the internal differentiation of Brazilian immigrants in Italy. There are those of Italian ancestry (*oriundi* in Italian) who have returned to the land of their grandparents or great-grandparents and who have dual citizenship. Other Brazilians are in the process of legalization, while another 15 to 20 percent remain undocumented. Ancestry helps explain why a number of Brazilians live in northern and northeastern Italy, in Vêneto, Trento, Friuli, and Lombardy. They are said to be sought after as hard workers but are also welcomed because of their status as *oriundi* whose ancestors left those areas one or two generations earlier (Bogus and Bassenesi 2000; Tedesco 2008).

Europe: Other Destinations

As in Italy, immigration researchers in other European countries—France, Switzerland, and Germany—often note the number of Brazilian women in those countries who are married to men who had once been sex tourists in Brazil. Then, too, as elsewhere in Europe, Brazilian women outnumber Brazilian men. In Germany, for example, according to German government data, the ratio is nearly four to one, the likely result of love matches between German men and Brazilian women. Some women met their future husbands in Brazil, while others met them touring Germany. For women without work permits, the simplest path to legality is finding a German husband (Zanin 2010; Netto 1997; Gerson 2005).

Many Brazilians in Germany are indeed there to work. They quickly find jobs cleaning, babysitting, and working in restaurants in Germany's flourishing shadow economy. Kitchen jobs, construction work, or tending to Germany's growing senior citizen population are often the only jobs available. Still, unlike in other European countries, there are relatively few undocumented Brazilians in Germany. Perhaps this is because some 70 percent of Brazilians in Germany are from southern Brazil, a region of German settlement, and are themselves of German ancestry. In other words, like the *oriundi* in Italy, they can legalize their status because of their German antecedents (Gerson 2005; Klintowitz 1996).

Germany's Brazilian community, which began to emerge after 1990, is one of the fastest-growing immigrant communities in the country. Signs of its presence are marked. Several stores now carry Brazilian products like *farinha de mandioca* (manioc flour) and *guaraná* (a soft drink), samba and *capoeira* are immensely popular, and there are church services conducted in Portuguese in most major German cities. While largely middle class in origin, Germany's Brazilians are socially and financially diverse; they range from academics to restaurant workers and from au pairs to engineers (Gerson 2005).

One European country, France, has what might be dubbed a "Brazilian specialty." France was once the preferred destination of Brazilian transvestites (*travestis*), who were well known around Paris. Called "hermaphrodites in high heels," a purported ten thousand Brazilian transvestites lived there at one time, many of whom had left Brazil during the military regime and remained after the return to democracy. In 2000, after loud complaints from residents near the Bois de Boulogne about the traffic and the noise created by flamboyant Brazilian transvestites peddling their wares to passing motorists, some left the city and headed to Milan, site of another thriving Brazilian transvestite community (Henley 2000; Fernandes 2003; Abud 2010).

This, then, is a snapshot of Brazilian communities in England, the Irish Republic, and other parts of western Europe. We now turn farther afield to a third global destination of Brazilian immigrants: nations bordering the Pacific.

7

Other Destinations
Pacific Bound

Upon arrival, most appeared to be suitably Japanese, but on closer acquaintance
they proved to be distressingly alien: Latin American in language, culture,
personality and behavior.
  Keiko Yamanaka (1996a, 68)

The largest Brazilian population in the Pacific region by far is in Japan.
In contrast to what happened in Europe, there is no evidence that
the number of Brazilians going to Japan increased after September 11, 2001,
in response to the strictures placed on immigration to the United States.
Also, in contrast to other countries where Brazilians have settled, the official count of the Brazilian presence in Japan is quite accurate. The reason is
that a large majority of Brazilian immigrants to Japan traveled to the country with the official sanction of the Japanese government and Japanese industry. Because of this, the official tally of 230,000 Brazilian residents in
Japan, which is the 2011 estimate of Brazil's Ministry of Foreign Affairs, is
likely close to the mark. In contrast, the Ministry's count of Brazilians in
Australia and New Zealand that same year is probably too low (table 6).

Table 6 Brazilians in the Pacific Rim

Country	Number
Japan	230,000
Australia	45,000
New Zealand	8,000

Source: Ministério das Relações Exteriores 2011.

Destination: Japan

Every day Tam Flight #8084 departs from São Paulo for Tokyo's Narita airport. Since the early 1990s, each twenty-eight-hour flight has brought a new contingent of *dekasseguis* to Japan to seek economic opportunities in the land of their ancestors. The term *"dekassegui,"* once used as a pejorative, refers to Brazilian immigrants of Japanese descent who are living in Japan. It is a combination of the Japanese verbs "to leave" and "to earn." In Japan, the term *"dekasseguis"* (*dekasegi* in Japanese) once referred to the rural workers who went to Tokyo in winter to look for odd jobs to make ends meet. It now refers more generally to people who leave their hometown to seek work elsewhere in order to earn money.

To explain the flow of Brazilians to Japan, I must backtrack and clarify the legal framework that allows them to do so. In 1990, the Japanese passed a law that was an attempt to ameliorate the labor shortage in those industrial jobs that the Japanese themselves shunned. These were the disagreeable "three K jobs," the *kitui* (arduous), *kitanai* (dirty), and *kiken* (dangerous) jobs mentioned in chapter 1. This reform permitted Brazilians (and others) of Japanese descent, that is, *nikkeijin*—Japanese people who had emigrated from Japan and their descendants—to work legally in Japan. Parenthetically, by 2008, Brazil had the largest Japanese population outside Japan, with an estimated 1.5 million Japanese and their descendants living there. The law created the category "long-term resident" for *nikkeijin*. It allowed both *nisei* (children of people born in Japan) and *sansei* (grandchildren of people born in Japan) to live and work in Japan for up to three years. After the reform was passed, a majority of the Brazilians who went to Japan were young *nisei* and *sansei* in their twenties and thirties. The reform also strengthened the prohibition on hiring illegal workers; it now imposed a two-year prison sentence or a fine of up to two million yen—about $20,000 at the time (Sasaki 2010; Yamanaka 1993, 1996b).

The value of the *nikkeijin* was twofold: as a large pool of relatively cheap labor, they would help solve Japan's labor shortage, while, at the same time, they would not disturb what was perceived as the nation's racial and social homogeneity. Because most Japanese pride themselves on belonging to a single, cohesive ethnic group, *nikkeijin* were preferred over other foreign workers because it was thought that their "race," regardless of nationality, would allow them to assimilate to Japanese culture with ease. As a result of this legal reform, company owners were not just worried about fines incurred for hiring illegal workers; many also felt that hiring foreign laborers—who looked foreign—might hurt their company's image (Yamanaka 1993; Fox 1997).

In 1989, approximately 29,000 Brazilians, many of whom were older and also held Japanese citizenship, were admitted to Japan. The following year, after passage of the new law, more than 67,000 were admitted, and, in 1991, the high point of Brazilian immigration to Japan, some 96,000 *nikkeijin* entered Japan. With growing unemployment in Japan in the mid-1990s, there was a cooling of this immigrant flow, and the number of Japanese Brazilians in Japan appears to have stabilized between 1993 and 1994. Nevertheless, by that date, the size of the *nikkeijin* population was considerable, with some 160,000 living in Japan, representing about 10 percent of Brazil's residents of Japanese ancestry. And, for a time, the number continued to grow. According to Japanese government figures, there were more than 176,000 *nikkeijin* living in Japan by the late 1990s. In other words, in less than a decade, this immigration stream nearly equaled the 189,000 Japanese who had immigrated to Brazil in the forty-two-year period that ended right before World War II. Even more remarkable is that, by the mid-2000s, close to 20 percent of the entire population of Japanese Brazilians was living in Japan (Klagsbrunn 1996; Yamanaka 1996a; Koyama 1998; Corrêa 1994; Tsuda 2004).[1]

How did Japanese Brazilians come to travel to Japan? Some were recruited by Brazilian travel agencies, but most were contracted by labor brokers (*empreiteiros*) who found not only jobs but also housing for the *nikkeijin* they contracted; some loaned them money to cover passports, airfare, and other travel expenses, as well. Previously, many of these Brazilian labor brokers had themselves been immigrants in Japan. They signed up would-be immigrants wherever they found them in southern Brazil—home to most Brazilians of Japanese descent—and sent them to wherever there was a demand for workers in Japan. For this reason, unlike in the United States, where friends and relatives help immigrants who come from the same town or city in Brazil and then settle in one locale in the United States, in Japan it was labor recruiters who determined where to seek immigrants in Brazil and where to send them in Japan. Recruiters, who received fees from Japanese companies for each immigrant contracted, welcomed all comers regardless of where they lived in Brazil. Even immigrants contracted by the same recruiter might be dispersed in Japan, since they were sent where their labor was needed. As a result, Japanese Brazilians from the same town in Brazil did not necessarily settle in the same city in Japan. This pattern suggests that *nikkeijin* in Japan were necessarily less dependent on family and friends than were Brazilian immigrants in the United States and elsewhere (Higuchi 2001; Sasaki 2006; Roth 2002).

Since *nikkeijin* were legally foreigners, most were hired through labor brokers, which meant that their terms of employment were less advantageous than those of Japanese workers. Although they often received negligible benefits and lower salaries than Japanese who held the same positions, because of their legal status, *nikkeijin* were usually paid more than undocumented Asian workers. Working under labor contracts meant that they had no paid vacations or holidays and lacked access to the Japanese social security system. It also meant that Brazilian women were paid less than Brazilian men doing the same job. Probably the greatest disadvantage of being contracted by an employment broker was the lack of health insurance and the denial of compensation for injuries suffered on the job. Although Brazilians were originally employed because of the labor scarcity that developed during the economic boom of the early 1990s, even after the boom ended, Brazilians could still find jobs because, as foreigners, they were hired as a highly flexible labor force that could be easily laid off (Fox 1997; Sasaki 2010; Higuchi 2001).

One interesting—although perhaps not unexpected—outcome of Japan's new labor law is what I call "Green Card marriage, Japanese style." As we have seen, to work legally in Japan, one must be of Japanese ancestry. After the law passed, there was a surge in the number of marriages between *nikkeijin* and non-*nikkeijin* Brazilians, since, with marriage, the non-*nikkeijin* gained the same right to work in Japan as his or her Japanese-descended spouse. After arriving in Japan, these couples often separated.[2] Another ploy involved counterfeit identification papers purporting to show Japanese ancestry. In at least one case, the same document "proving" Japanese descent—a grandparent born in Japan—was reproduced and presented to the Japanese Consulate in São Paulo by dozens of would-be immigrants seeking work in Japan (Rossini 1995).[3]

Just who are these *nikkeijin* who travel to an unknown land, albeit the home of their forebearers? We have already noted that, at the start of the emigration surge in 1990, most emigrants were young second- and third-generation descendants of Japanese immigrants. We also have observed that they had fairly high levels of education by Brazilian standards, with more than half having at least completed high school. Most were middle and lower-middle class and had been white-collar workers or students in Brazil. Whereas earlier Japanese immigrants from Brazil were mainly *issei*, first-generation *nikkeijin* who retained their native language and culture, the newer arrivals were born and raised as Brazilians and spoke little or no Japanese. Interestingly, the *issei* who did speak Japanese used an outmoded form of the language dating from the Meiji period, before numerous English words were introduced. Many Japanese were amused by the use of this antiquated style, although some *issei* were insulted by the laughter their speech evoked (Sasaki 1995; Koyama 1998; Lilli Kawamura, personal communication).

About equal numbers of men and women have traveled to Japan. Like their male counterparts, most *nikkeijin* women are young, from the middle strata of Brazilian society, and quite well educated. A small percentage of them are non-*nikkeijin* who came to Japan as the spouses of Japanese Brazilian men. The experience of Brazilian women in Japan differs primarily according to generation and language ability. Older *nikkeijin* women with few skills other than fluency in Japanese usually work in Japan as home health aides and attendants to the elderly. While wishing to earn money, these women went to Japan primarily to live in and experience Japanese culture. Younger *nikkeijin* women, both *nisei* and *sansei*, are well educated but do not speak fluent Japanese, and most often hold factory jobs. These women traveled to Japan largely for economic reasons—to save money to establish a business back home or to pay for their education or that of a family member (Yamanaka 1996b, 1997).

The initiation of the labor program in 1990 provided an opportunity for whole families to pick up and leave the economic chaos then raging in Brazil. As long as parents could prove they were *nisei*, they could bring their *sansei* children with them to Japan. In time, more and more *nikkeijin* children traveled to Japan with their parents, and, by 2008, an estimated thirty-three thousand such children of school age were living there, while 17 percent of the Brazilian population in Japan was composed of children age fourteen and under. Brazilian children are not subject to compulsory education laws in Japan, although about one-third of them do attend Japanese schools. The rest go to one of the numerous Portuguese-language schools in Japan or do not attend school at all. For many families, the tuition at Portuguese-language schools, which are private, is simply too expensive to enroll their children. And, according to one Brazilian official, "The Brazilian schools prepare people for their past in Brazil, not their future in Japan" (Sasaki 2010; quoted in Brooke 2001).

A diplomat in Brazil's Ministry of Foreign Affairs told me that both her own government and the Japanese government were very concerned about the children and adolescents of Japanese Brazilians in Japan. Those who have lived in Japan for several years are "neither Brazilian nor Japanese," she said. "The major problem is schooling. Children need to know 8,000 Japanese characters to be minimally literate in Japan, to be able to read a newspaper and eventually get a job." Many Brazilian youth do not have this ability, and some are literate in neither Portuguese nor Japanese. Those who do not attend Japanese-language schools may feel alienated from Japanese society because of their inability to communicate with facility in Japanese. Culture shock for Brazilian immigrants in Japan is greater than elsewhere, said the diplomat, because of the stark contrast between Brazilian and Japanese culture and the isolation of Brazilian immigrants in Japan. Many adolescents suffer an identity crisis in Japan that can lead to emotional problems. As a result, some get involved with drugs and gangs, she noted ruefully (Vera Machado, personal communication).

Whether seeking individuals or families, labor recruiters set their sights on southern Brazil, which, as we have seen, is home to most Japanese descendants in the country. Some 65 percent of the Brazilians in Japan are from São Paulo, and just under 20 percent are from the neighboring state of Paraná. One city in particular, Maringá, in the northern part of that state, has an especially large number of its residents living in Japan. In fact, it has been said that Maringá is to Japan what Governador Valadares is to the United States, a quintessential sending community with a growing culture of out-migration. Labor recruiters representing large Japanese companies came to Maringá to recruit would-be *dekasseguis*. One company, a Japanese food manufacturer, hired some two hundred townspeople (Amaral 2005; Sasaki 2009). One such émigré explains Japan's attraction by recounting his own story:

> I went [to Japan] when I was 50. I was a peddler and was at the age when things were not going to change. I took my wife. We both went to work in a plant that manufactured Ford parts. One year and eight months later I bought two farms in Maringá. But it wasn't enough. We went back again for another year and a half. Then I bought an apartment in a good condominium . . . and 47 alquieres of land [about 280 acres]. My father, who came from Japan at age 13, is now 82 and working all these years in farming was never able to amass so much land. (quoted in Corrêa 1994, 74)

We know where Japanese Brazilians come from in Brazil, but where do they settle in Japan? About half of the *nikkeijin* population lives in five prefectures in central Japan that have high concentrations of labor-intensive industries such as manufacturers of automobile parts and electrical appliances. These include cities like Toyota, Nagoya, and Hamamatsu. Take the latter, for example. About twenty thousand Brazilians live in Hamamatsu, and most of them work for subcontractors that supply parts to larger manufacturers. In some smaller cities like Ota and Oizumi, *nikkeijin* make up almost 10 percent of the local population (Yamanaka 1996b; Sasaki 2006; Roth 2002).

Prior to 1990, when Brazilians began arriving, these cities had very few foreign residents, and the arrival of *nikkeijin* set the stage for many well-documented examples of cultural misunderstanding and conflict. While the *nisei* and *sansei* look Japanese, most do not speak the language well, if at all. Estimates suggest that some 20 to 30 percent of *nikkeijin* can communicate in Japanese, but only about 5 percent actually study the language. But it is not just a lack of language skills that leads to friction between *nikkeijin* and their Japanese hosts. Cultural clashes with Japanese — the fact that Brazilians often play loud music, do not keep appointments on time or recycle properly — have abated in some areas as Japanese disturbed by such behavior have moved away from large housing complexes like those in Toyota City, where Japanese Brazilians make up half of the residents (Tsuda 2001; Onishi 2008).

Yet these conflicts are ongoing, and miscommunication and misunderstanding are rife. Another public housing complex in Toyota City, home to thousands of workers at Toyota and its subsidiaries and suppliers, with eleven thousand residents, including three thousand *nikkeijin*, has signs posted in Japanese and Portuguese that read: "Don't turn up your television or radio early in the morning or late at night." And: "Don't barbecue on the balcony." There are reportedly daily disputes over noise, garbage, and parking. A report in a 1999 online issue of *Time* magazine summarized the sources of many of these contretemps:

> To Japanese in one densely populated public housing complex, it feels as if the foreigners are closing in on them, the smoke from the barbecues suffocating them, the Latin music drowning out an imagined tranquility. Ten years ago there were 200 Brazilians in the complex. Today there are 3,500. "There's no room for us anymore," said one Japanese woman. . . .
>
> After a dispute with a . . . street vendor got out of hand, about 100 supporters of a right-wing nationalist group paraded around the housing complex where [many] Brazilians live. They shouted through a loudspeaker, "Foreigners go home,"

[and] taunted the Brazilians to come out and fight. . . . "I was really scared to leave my flat to even go to the store to buy food," recalls one Brazilian. "I was afraid that I would be beaten up."

"A lot of the Brazilians work very hard," says . . . Toyota City's deputy police chief, adding that this is because "they are of Japanese descent." But as the Brazilian population grew . . . the cherished peace was disrupted. "They thought they would be getting people like them who would fit in," says one Brazilian who has lived in Japan for nine years. "They found out we are more Brazilian than Japanese." . . .

The Toyota City government has formed a committee to work on improving relations between the two nationalities. The committee does not include any Brazilians. (Larimer and Tashiro 1999)

A primary source of discord is the *nikkeijin* habit of hanging out on the street, outside grocery stores, train stations, and other public spaces. Japanese cities do not have the familiar meeting places where casual contact is made—the *praça* (public square) and the *botequim* (neighborhood bar)— that are so ubiquitous in Brazilian towns and cities. There is none of the easy neighborhood sociability that is so much a part of daily life in Brazil, no similar public space where people run into each other and schmooze. As a result, it is a mystery to many Japanese why these immigrants spend so much time hanging out on the street. On the other hand, from the Brazilians' perspective, while they very much appreciate the safety of Japanese cities—so different from those in Brazil—they do not like their formality, their lack of novelty and spontaneity (Linger 2001b).

Another common Brazilian behavior, public displays of affection between couples, such as holding hands and kissing on the street (*namorando na rua*), is something rarely or never seen in Japan. What *nikkeijin* see as coldness on the part of Japanese, a lack of human warmth, the Japanese view as politeness. In short, the Japanese take on all of this can be summed up as follows: "They look like us, but *they certainly don't act like us!*"

Some of these misunderstandings and conflicts are also linked to the *nikkeijin*'s general segregation from Japanese workers in the companies where they are employed, reinforcing their position as outsiders. The system of labor brokers, with the tacit agreement of manufacturers and the Japanese government, serves to segment and differentiate between *nikkeijin* and Japanese. And this too leads to discord. Brazilians are often criticized by the Japanese for not being "hard workers" and for "goofing off." They are accused of being disloyal to the companies that employ them when they switch jobs for higher pay, a marked contrast to the traditional lifetime employment of Japanese in a single company (Roth 2002).

The isolation of Brazilians in Japan is not just based on their segregated employment. Brazilians are also isolated because they are culturally and linguistically excluded from the mass media, from all forms of Japanese entertainment, and from Japanese life in general. In fact, 60 percent of *nikkeijin* report little or no contact with Japanese. Their marginalization is both ethnic—as culturally defective Japanese—and economic, since they are largely confined to the despised "3 K job" sector of the labor market. One could say, then, that Brazilians in Japan live *among* the Japanese but not *with* the Japanese and that there is very little interaction between the two populations either at work or at play (Linger 2001b; Ikegami 2001; Tsuda 2002).

Part of this isolation may be tied to the relative invisibility of the *nikkeijin*. Even in communities with large concentrations of Japanese Brazilians—Hamamatsu, Nagoya, and Toyota City—their presence is not obvious. There are no "Brazil Towns" with distinct ethnic community centers, schools, or churches. Other than Brazilian flags in some windows, there are no indications of their presence, especially on weekdays, when everyone is at work. It is only on weekends, when they gather at places like train stations and shopping malls, that they are conspicuous—groups of Japanese-looking individuals animatedly conversing in Portuguese (Koyama 1998).

Some *nikkeijin* try to surmount this invisibility by asserting their ethnic roots through dress and behavior. They wear distinctive clothes in Brazil's national colors—green and yellow—along with T-shirts displaying the Brazilian flag and Brazilian icons like Corcovado, the outstretched arms of its Christ statue looming over Rio de Janeiro. Collective rituals like samba parades are unmistakable signs of Brazilian ethnicity. Some say the *nikkeijin* present culturally deficient performances because they rarely or never participate in samba schools or carnival parades in Brazil. But, while both their dancing and their makeshift costumes would be considered wanting by Brazilian standards, they have turned out to be popular spectacles in Japan because the Japanese know even less about samba parades and the like than do the *nikkeijin* (Tsuda 2002).

The Japanese media pay a disproportionate amount of attention to Japanese Brazilians, whom they exoticize, treating them as "amusing anomalies." Generally portrayed in a favorable light, the immigrants are expected to absorb Japanese culture because of their physical appearance. But, when they fail to do so, they are derided as "inadequate Japanese." The Japanese media can be regarded as a conservative force that supports rather than challenges cultural assumptions by stressing the potential for cultural disorder caused by foreigners—even those who look like "real" Japanese (Tsuda 2001).

In the Japanese scheme of things, North Americans and Europeans tend to be treated with more respect as *gaijin* (foreigners) than are Japanese Brazilians. The former are complimented even when they speak broken Japanese because Europeans and Americans are expected to be culturally incompetent but nevertheless are admired because they come from "modern" first-world nations. But when expectations of Japanese Brazilians' "Japaneseness" are contradicted by their behavior, they are sometimes verbally abused and called "stupid, uncivilized people from a backward country." They are particularly ridiculed when they use Japanese incorrectly. Says one researcher about the Japanese view of the *nikkeijin*, "Their Brazilianess [*sic*] is at best a mystery, at worst a sad third-world affliction" (Yamanaka 1997; Linger 2001b, 6).

While these negative stereotypes are rife and perhaps stronger in Japan than in other destinations where Brazilians settle outside Brazil, Japanese Brazilians do enjoy one distinct advantage over their compatriots in other countries. Until the last few years, they could easily travel between Brazil and Japan and back again because such travel was legal. And there is a lot of evidence that they did just that. At one point in the mid-1990s, for every ten Japanese Brazilians applying for a Japanese work visa, nine were applying for re-entry. Other *nikkeijin* returned to Japan two or three times after they could not find decent job opportunities in Brazil. Their salaries in Japan in unskilled jobs—even during the recession—were many times those offered in Brazil even for more highly skilled positions. This stark contrast in earning potential undoubtedly contributes to the sense of rootlessness, the back-and-forth travel between Japan and Brazil, the disquieting feeling of not being quite satisfied in either place. For this reason, and because of the absence of strictures like those in the United States that prevent the free flow of Brazilians between the two countries, Japanese Brazilians can leave Japan temporarily for Brazil to vacation, for family reasons, or for any other reason with the assurance that they can return to their jobs in Japan (Klintowitz 1996; Koyama 1998; Sasaki 2006, 2009).[4]

Evidence suggests that many *nikkeijin* engage in what I have previously termed "yo-yo migration" in reference to the behavior of Brazilian immigrants in the United States. Yo-yo migration is the re-migration of immigrants who, in their own words, had returned home "for good." Economic insecurity led a number of *nikkeijin* who said they were going home permanently to re-migrate to Japan after their new businesses in Brazil failed, businesses established with savings from their prior work in Japan. Others returned to Brazil with the intention of staying, lived on the money they saved in Japan until it was exhausted, and found poor prospects for new employment in Brazil. As one Japanese Brazilian told the anthropologist Daniel Linger, "Many people here say they're going [back to Brazil] once and for all, never to return. And in three, four months . . . they're back again" (Margolis 1994a, 263; Yamanaka 1997; quoted in Linger 2001b).

The effortlessness of circular migration between the home and the host country enhanced transnationalism among *nikkeijin*. Some *nikkeijin* travel back and forth between Japan and Brazil and are unsure where to settle. They literally find themselves suspended between two nations, feeling they do not quite belong in either one. Others have returned to Brazil permanently; still others have begun to settle in Japan while maintaining their identification with all things Brazilian. By the mid-1990s, the figures on those leaving Brazil for Japan and those in Japan returning home suggested that the wave of sojourning (staying abroad for a defined period of time) had begun to wane and that circular migration and its concomitant transnationalism—in which immigrants move from home country to host country and back again—was on the rise (Basch, Glick Schiller, and Szanton Blanc 1994; Margolis 2001b; Linger 2001a; Roth 2002; Yamanaka 1996a).

Transnationalism rests, in part, on modern transportation and communication technologies that allow immigrants not only to travel great distances across international borders but also to follow what is happening at home via the Internet, e-mail, Skype, homeland TV channels beamed into their host countries, phone, and fax. Since 1996, satellite TV from Brazil has been available in Japan, and videos of Brazilian *telenovelas* are widely available for rent. At least four Portuguese-language newspapers with news of home are published weekly in Japan, and the *nikkeijin* are said to be international telephone companies' "best customers" (Margolis 1995b; Brooke 2001; Koyama 1998).

Like Brazilians in the United States and elsewhere, most *nikkeijin* traveled to Japan envisioning immigration as a temporary journey to take advantage of a specific opportunity that would improve their lives in Brazil. For most, at least initially, there was simply no doubt that Brazil was their homeland where their real lives would be lived. Japan was no more than a way station, a temporary workplace where they could acquire the means to better their lives upon their return home. As such, most *nikkeijin* went to Japan planning to stay from one to three years and then to return to Brazil to build a house, start a business, pay for their education, buy a car, or have a comfortable retirement. While many did return to Brazil within the time frame planned, others extended their stay. The cost of living in Japan was higher than expected, and, in the mid-1990s, the recession reduced wages and overtime pay, so many had to stay longer to meet their savings goals or to pay off the debt incurred for travel to Japan. While most still expressed the desire to return to Brazil eventually, others began to consider staying in Japan longer than originally anticipated (Yamanaka 1996b, 1997).

Brazilians who did put off the return home were less willing to work overtime and traded night shifts for more regular working hours. Some began traveling as tourists in Japan and elsewhere in Asia and spending more money on leisure in bars and restaurants. The growing rootedness of some *nikkeijin* in Japan is highlighted by how they spend their money. Where they once bought bicycles to get around, several began buying costly Japanese cars. Other signs of permanence include investing resources locally and the purchase of major consumer items in Japan that are not easily transported back to Brazil. In short, they were no longer saving every yen for the return home (Roth 2002; Sasaki 2009).

Over time, enhanced job opportunities also tied some *nikkeijin* more closely to Japan. In the past few years, a number of Japanese Brazilians found themselves no longer limited to unskilled jobs in factories. They moved into a variety of professions catering to the ethnic market, a result of the local growth of the Brazilian community. Such new opportunities also changed the outlook of some. Rather than saving money for the return home, many began investing in Japan. Nevertheless, there was and still is a definite limit to their social mobility as immigrants, to wit: "Becoming upwardly mobile in Japanese society seems almost impossible," notes Angelo Ishi, a *nikkeijin* journalist who has lived in Japan for several years. "They lack the language fluency and Japanese companies seem reluctant to accept foreigners into skilled jobs: lawyers, doctors, or engineers in Brazil have little chance of working in their own profession in Japan," he concludes. This is one of the reasons they are anxious to earn as much money as possible for the return to Brazil. "Our life in Japan, is *not* our *real* life" (Ishi 2004, 2003, 81).

During the first several years of the current millennium, an additional 10,000 Brazilians annually established permanent residence in Japan, apparently altering their initial migratory project and becoming more at home in the land of their ancestors. But are *nikkeijin* limited to only two choices in terms of their futures—to stay in Japan for the long term, try to assimilate to Japanese culture and make the best of being confined to low prestige jobs, as most still are, or, alternatively, to leave for home and resume their lives as Brazilians? It is perhaps too soon to tell which path most Japanese Brazilians will take, but one researcher, Joshua Hotaka Roth (2002), suggests a third alternative: that *nikkeijin* may remain in Japan for the long term but retain a strong sense of themselves as Brazilians. Recent statistics suggest the greater permanence of Brazilians in Japan, especially among the young. Still, it is impossible to say what this means for maintaining their national identity over time (Sasaki 2009).

Destination: Australia

Not all *nikkeijin* who leave Japan are headed home to Brazil. Many travel to Australia, instead. In this instance, Japanese Brazilians are said to be using Japan as a "trampoline" to expand their travels. Because of its strong currency and Japanese Brazilians' ability to work there legally, Japan, in effect, becomes a place to put away enough money to travel the world and perhaps settle somewhere else. In this sense, Australia is a third node in the circulation of Japanese Brazilians between Japan and Brazil. Australia's attractions are many. There is the cultural cachet associated with a modern English-speaking country and the multicultural policies of the Australian government—so unlike Japan's discourse of racial and ethnic homogeneity and exclusion. Then, too, whereas upward mobility is very limited in Japan, this is not the case in Australia. For those who held professional positions in Brazil as engineers, dentists, economists, architects, and the like, factory work in Japan can be an interlude after which, in Australia, many can reclaim their former professions and attendant class identity. As a consequence, it is said that, for some young Japanese Brazilians, "Japan is the place of work while they decide what they will do next." However, not all Japanese Brazilians think of Japan as an intermediate stop. For many in the 1.5 generation who grew up and were educated in Japan and have permanent residence there, after a sojourn in Australia, they return to Japan, which continues to be home (Perroud 2007, 59; Rocha 2009).

Japanese Brazilians are by no means the only Brazilians traveling to Australia. Other Brazilians go for the mild climate, the nation's "beach culture," and the laid-back lifestyle that is reminiscent of Brazil's. They also view Australia as a modern, youthful, friendly nation that lacks the crime and economic instability that blight their homeland. According to an official Australian census count, there were twelve thousand Brazilians living in Australia in 2006, and Australia's Brazilian consulates estimate that there were forty-five thousand Brazilians in Australia in 2011. Well over 40 percent were living in New South Wales, primarily in the Sydney metropolitan area (Rocha 2009, 2010; Duarte 2005).

The first Brazilians to arrive in Australia were a small number of working-class Brazilians who immigrated in the late 1970s. Many knew little English and interacted mostly with members of Australia's Portuguese immigrant community. Today, however, the Brazilian community in Australia is composed largely of educated middle- and upper-middle-class professionals and students who are fluent in English and have gained resident status. Many of these students took advantage of the 2001 Australian law that allows for permanent residence after two years of study in the country. This group began arriving in the late 1990s, several traveling to Australia for other than economic motives—to learn English, for a taste of adventure, because of disillusionment with Brazil, or simply to have a better quality of life (Rocha 2006, 2009; Duarte 2005).

The split between the earlier and the later arrivals suggests that, as was true in New York, Boston, Atlanta, and south Florida, social class supersedes ethnicity in importance within the context of Brazilian emigration. The differences in social class and education have meant that the two waves of Brazilian immigrants seldom interact. Rather, the latter group socializes with middle-class Australians, often working alongside them. In essence, the two sets of immigrants have partially re-created the social hierarchy that is so much a part of Brazilian society (Rocha 2010; Margolis 2009; Martes 2010; Vasquez, Ribeiro, and Alves 2008; Resende 2009).

Despite its relatively small size, the Brazilian community has made its mark in Australia. Brazilian music, Brazilian restaurants, and certain Brazilian products—*havaianas* (flip-flops), *açai* (a tropical fruit), *guaraná* (a soft drink), and *caipirinhas* (a potent mix of Brazilian alcohol muddled with fresh limes and sugar)—along with *capoeira*, have become popular among Australians, who tend to view Brazil as a cosmopolitan and exotic nation. Then, too, a number of Australians have traveled to Brazil for what has been called "spiritual tourism," primarily an interest in Brazilian Spiritism.[5] They then connect with the Brazilian community upon their return to Australia, especially its spiritual centers and their Brazilian adherents (Rocha 2009, 2010).

Destination: New Zealand

In Aimorés, a small city near Governador Valadares, one Brazilian journalist noted that "it is difficult to find anyone among its 22,000 inhabitants who does not have a friend or relative . . . in the USA or New Zealand, the new destination for those in search of opportunity" (Menconi 2004, 92).

Indeed, since about 2000, the number of Brazilians in New Zealand has been growing, and Brazil's Ministry of Foreign Affairs estimates that eight thousand were living there in 2011. Still, there is no published research on New Zealand's Brazilian community, so only anecdotal evidence suggests why Brazilians go to this distant land not known for attracting immigrants and what they do once they get there. Despite its relatively small size, this population deserves to be mentioned as another node in the Brazilian diaspora because of some notable differences between New Zealand and the other destinations of Brazilian émigrés. The following information relies on the personal accounts of two Brazilians—one a journalist and the other an anthropologist—who have spent time in New Zealand.

Sandra Lobo, a journalist, notes that, when she lived in Auckland in 2006, a substantial number of Brazilians could be heard speaking Portuguese on the street, especially on Queen Street, the city's main thoroughfare. She also points out that, in the Mexican restaurant where she worked, close to 90 percent of the employees were Brazilians and that, after the restaurant was cited for employing undocumented immigrants, the owners helped legalize the Brazilian employees who wanted to continue working there.

Why do Brazilians travel to New Zealand? One reason is that the doors of other desired destinations are closing. Moreover, New Zealand does not require a visa, making it easier for would-be immigrants to enter as tourists or students. Then, too, for some Brazilians—specifically those living in the southernmost Brazilian states of Santa Catarina and Rio Grande do Sul—it is simpler and somewhat less costly to get there than to reach other destinations. Since they do not need visas, they save the time and expense of traveling to New Zealand's consulate in either Rio de Janeiro or São Paulo to apply for one; they also need not go to those cities to catch international flights to New Zealand. Rather, a Brazilian who lives in Florianopolis (in Santa Catarina) or Porto Alegre (in Rio Grande do Sul) can fly directly from those cities to Buenos Aires and from there connect to a flight to Auckland, New Zealand.

New Zealand also has a number of inexpensive language schools—some of dubious quality—which provide a convenient way for Brazilians to enter the country as students. Then too, in one New Zealand city, Queenstown, a tourist center that features skiing, bungee jumping, and power boating, employers are allowed to hire foreigners to fill peak-season labor shortages. Because of the city's liberal work-permit program, foreign guest workers can be earning money within days of arriving there. And, over time, roughly two thousand young Brazilians have taken advantage of this; of the three thousand permits issued in 2006, for example, more than eight hundred went to Brazilians. Some Brazilians work in resorts year-round in violation of the country's immigration statutes, and the powers that be have ordered a review of the program, claiming that Brazilians may be taking jobs from "Kiwis," as native New Zealanders are called (3News 2007).

The anthropologist Cristina Rocha, who lives in Australia and has done research on Brazilians there, found that some New Zealand Brazilians differ from those in Australia who, as we have seen, are largely middle class. Since New Zealand has no visa requirement, many Brazilians immigrating there are from modest backgrounds, since they do not have to demonstrate their financial well-being to obtain a visa as they do for the United States. Most borrow money to travel to New Zealand and register for an English course—often of questionable quality—with the ultimate goal of staying on and finding work. The authorities are now aware of this ploy, so there are cases in which would-be immigrants arrive at Auckland's international airport only to be turned back. Referring to Brazilians with such humble roots, Lobo concludes that, for them, "New Zealand has become a new migratory route for [those] who are fleeing from the lack of opportunities in our country" (Sandra Lobo, personal communication).

The goals of another group of Brazilians in New Zealand are quite different. They are students from middle-class families who enroll in established English-language schools and, like most of those in Australia, journey to the country for both study and adventure. Many return home after their language course is over or take temporary jobs in places like Queenstown that hire young foreigners in the hospitality industry. Rocha encountered large numbers of young Brazilians on that city's streets and in parks, bars, and restaurants and met some who were employed in local hotels and shops.

And so Brazilians travel to New Zealand for both adventure and jobs, which is not the case for those who journey to countries bordering Brazil. We now turn to a very different kind of immigrant, one who leaves home not just to earn money for some specific project—to start a business, purchase a house, or finance an education—but, rather, an immigrant who is desperate to find work, even for subsistence wages, in agriculture or mining or who longs to own a small plot of land on which to eke out a meager living.

8

Other Destinations
And for the Poor

The first impression one has who visits these "Brazilian communities" in eastern Paraguay is that the international border has been dislocated since the 1970s. The strong presence of Brazilians in this frontier region makes it seem like a piece of Brazil inside Paraguay or a state inside another state.

  Brazilian visitor in Paraguay (quoted in Albuquerque 2009, 162)

A wave of emigration distinct from that previously described has been taking place over the past four decades as immigrants from Brazil have been moving to adjacent nations in South America. These figures in table 7 provide some sense of the size and scope of this exodus.

Some 400,000 Brazilians live in the ten countries bordering Brazil, according to estimates. Although the first exodus from Brazil to Paraguay occurred in the late 1960s and the 1970s, the emigration of Brazilians to

Table 7 Brazilians in South America

Country	Number
Paraguay	200,000
Argentina	37,000
Venezuela	26,000
Uruguay	30,000
Bolivia	50,000
Suriname	20,000
French Guiana	18,000
Guyana	7,500

Source: Ministério das Relações Exteriores 2011.

neighboring countries took off in the mid-1980s, about the same time that the departure for the United States and other nations abroad intensified. What some have called an "internal exodus" to South American nations that border Brazil had very different roots—landlessness, land consolidation, the mechanization of agriculture, and the absence of agrarian reform—from those that led Brazilians to more distant parts of the world. It was in those years that rubber tappers, miners, and small cultivators—sharecroppers, tenant farmers, and landless day laborers—crossed international frontiers in the northern and western Amazon and the Southern Cone. Some suggest that this interchange involved an "exportation of social tensions" and served as an escape valve that moved Brazilians to neighboring countries to reduce tensions generated by Brazil's internal problems of agrarian structure (Klintowitz 1995; De Almeida 1995, 28).

The principle of nationality comes into play in these population movements in that the laws that divide and distinguish national entities in such cross-border travels are ignored. Many of them have involved conflicts—along the borders of Venezuela, Colombia, Bolivia, Guyana, and French Guiana—between natives of those countries and Brazilian miners, rubber tappers, landowners, and indigenous populations. The Brazilian press has taken to calling these same areas "our agricultural frontiers abroad" (*nossas fronteiras agrícolas no exterior*), and the Brazilian immigrants who journey there are said to be "the last *bandeirantes*," a reference to the adventurers and trailblazers who crisscrossed Brazil in the sixteenth through the eighteenth centuries (quoted in De Almeida 1995, 35).

Destination: Paraguay

Today the approximately 200,000 Brazilians in Paraguay make up fewer than 5 percent of that country's population but may occupy as much as 10 percent of the nation's territory. In some eastern areas that border Brazil, such as Alto Paraná, where Brazilians have long settled, there are an estimated four Brazilians for every Paraguayan. It is thought that 60 percent of the population living in that general region is either Brazilian or of Brazilian parentage. The initial move of Brazilians to Paraguay was not spontaneous; rather, it was instigated by the authorities in both countries. The government of the long-lived Paraguayan dictator Alfredo Stroessner sought to open up the sparsely populated eastern region of Paraguay that borders Brazil and encouraged the settlement of Brazilians there. In 1975, he and Brazil's president, Ernesto Geisel, a general appointed by the armed forces to preside over the country, signed a treaty agreeing to the occupation of an area of nearly 122,000 square kilometers in Paraguay adjacent to the nearly completed Itaipu Dam on the border between the two countries, an area that represented one-third of Paraguay's total land area. In the military thinking of the day, a large local population would ensure the security of the Itaipu project. The end result is that the eastern border region has been caught in a kind of "pincer movement" between the Paraguayan government's ambitious plans for development there and the inexorable expansion of the Brazilian frontier (Wilson, Hay, and Margolis 1989; Alves 1990; Cortêz 1994).[1]

The classic push-pull motivation for emigration is clearly discernible in the cross-border settlement of Brazilians in Paraguay. Among the "push" factors was the expansion and mechanization of soybean and wheat cultivation as well as the spread of cattle ranching in the 1970s in adjacent northern Paraná. This was at the expense of coffee cultivation, which is more labor intensive, and, as a consequence, many sharecroppers, tenant farmers, and day laborers were thrown out of work. Then, too, during the same decade, the construction of the huge Itaipu hydroelectric dam in southwestern Paraná displaced about 20,000 small farmers and agricultural workers. In sum, an estimated 350,000 Brazilians left Brazil in the 1970s, expelled by the introduction of mechanized agricultural production, the expansion of cattle ranching, and the construction of the Itaipu Dam (Margolis 1973; Wilson, Hay, and Margolis 1989; Sprandel 2006).

The lure of Paraguay for Brazilians was clear. It meant having access to new areas of fertile land close to frontier towns in the Brazilian states of Paraná and Mato Grosso, so close that one that could easily pick up radio and television broadcasts from Brazil. Then, too, if one sold three hectares of land in Brazil, one could easily purchase thirty hectares in Paraguay. This was an attractive proposition for many small farmers in Brazil—the majority of immigrants in Paraguay—who could not afford to buy additional land to divide among their many heirs (Sprandel 2006; Wagner 1990; Wilson, Hay, and Margolis 1989).

Two groups of Brazilians moved to Paraguay. The first were natives of Minas Gerais and several states in northeastern Brazil who had earlier traveled south to São Paulo and Paraná and found work there as day laborers, tenant farmers, and sharecroppers. Some were employed clearing the land of its dense forests, while others were engaged in cultivating coffee and mint. For this group of Brazilians, Paraguay was merely a detour along the route of the great internal migrations of agriculturalists to new frontiers in Brazil. Many subsequently left Paraguay seeking fresh land and opportunities in recently opened frontier regions of the northern and western Amazon (Margolis 1973; Sales 1995; Wagner 1990).

The second group of emigrants hailed from the southernmost Brazilian states—Paraná, Santa Catarina, and Rio Grande do Sul—where they owned small and medium-size properties. It is estimated that about 85 percent of the Brazilians in Paraguay are from these three states. After selling their land, they were able to buy lots in eastern Paraguay, where the cost per hectare was about one-tenth the cost of land in their native states in Brazil. The vast majority of emigrants in this latter group were the descendants of Italians and Germans who had immigrated to Brazil in the late nineteenth and early twentieth centuries (Albuquerque 2009; Silva 2003).

By the late 1970s and early 1980s land concentration and agricultural mechanization began to increase in the areas of Brazilian settlement in Paraguay. A combination of subsistence farming—corn, manioc, beans, and so on—along with cash crops like mint, gave way to soybean monoculture, and both Brazilians and Paraguayans were dislodged in the process. Some moved further into Paraguay's interior while others went to live on the outskirts of cities. By the mid-1980s an estimated 60,000 of the 350,000 Brazilians then living in Paraguay were landless. This number likely doubled over the following decade, a result of dividing up too little land among too many heirs (Albuquerque 2009; Wagner 1990).

One Brazilian described what happened next: "Opportunities only existed for those who could buy land, register it in Asuncion, and continue investing in Paraguay. The poorer people were transformed into sharecroppers and many families began to think about returning to Brazil." In essence, once large agro-industries introduced the same methods of agricultural modernization into Paraguay that had led many Brazilians to leave Brazil in the first place, these practices became the main catalyst that led Brazilians to consider returning home. Around the same time, the Brazilian government came out with an agrarian reform plan that erroneously had many Brazilians believing that land would be readily available once they went back to Brazil (quoted in Cortêz 1994).

In late 1985, problems with legalization, mechanization, and land consolidation came to a head and led to a social crisis for many Brazilians in Paraguay. As a result, more than one thousand Brazilian families returned en masse to Brazil. Encouraged by the Landless Workers Movement (Movimento Sem Terra or MST) and the Pastoral Land Commission

(Comissão Pastoral da Terra), they set up encampments in the Brazilian state of Mato Grosso do Sul, near the border with Paraguay. They were harassed by police and hired gunmen and eventually expelled. Over the next several years, other groups of Brazilians in Paraguay planned well-organized returns to Brazil. Meetings were held, leadership emerged, and strategy was planned. All were aware that both Paraguayan and Brazilian authorities would make the return difficult. Somewhat later, another group of nearly one thousand families from several different locales in Paraguay crossed the border into Brazil, joined the MST movement, and demanded land. They too set up camp in Mato Grosso do Sul and remained there for several months (Cortêz 1994; Wagner 1990).

The border crossing was eventually closed to prevent the arrival of still more Brazilian families, and the attitude of the state government of Mato Grosso do Sul hardened toward the repatriated Brazilians. In the following years, they continued to return quietly, but now in small groups, and joined the settled families in the occupations and encampments near the border in Brazil. Their numbers continued to grow as more and more sharecroppers were thrown out of work in Paraguay. Many of these landless laborers had no legal documents to prove their citizenship in either Brazil or Paraguay.[2] They had crossed over the border into Paraguay some years earlier without ever having official documents of any kind in Brazil. They were essentially stateless (Cortêz 1994; Wagner 1990).

With the fall of the Stroessner dictatorship in Paraguay in 1989, the struggle for land grew, and many large ranches were occupied by landless workers including Brazilians. And, with the economic crisis in Argentina that followed, thousands of Paraguayans who had been working there were let go and returned home. There they began to compete with immigrants, especially Brazilians, for jobs. Most Brazilian farmers, in turn, were never able to amass enough capital to buy more land in Paraguay, and, as had happened in Brazil, their properties were divided into smaller and smaller holdings among their offspring. Then, too, many never had clear title to their land, which caused all kinds of difficulties, including precluding them from being approved for agricultural loans (Wagner 1990; De Oliveira 1995).

The economic crisis in Paraguay deepened in 1990, and thousands of small farmers went bankrupt as mechanized agriculture also forced share-croppers off the land. Over the following two years, nearly 1,500 Brazilian sharecroppers were forced to leave farms where they had worked. As a result, thousands of Brazilians returned to Brazil in the 1990s, while others, primarily young people in Paraná, migrated to eastern Paraguay in hopes of finding work in the commercial or service sectors of the Paraguayan towns colonized by Brazilians (Cortêz 1994; Albuquerque 2009).

By the mid-1990s, as unemployment grew, undocumented Brazilians began to be threatened with expulsion by Paraguayan authorities. Yet regularizing their status would be a costly bureaucratic nightmare, since they had to have birth certificates and identity cards sent from Brazil, both of which had to be registered in Asuncion. They were also required to show proof of current residence and employment in Paraguay. Brazil's Ministry of Foreign Affairs tried to convince Paraguayan authorities to simplify the process because a poor Brazilian who had lived in Paraguay for fifteen or twenty years would have trouble proving prior residence in Brazil. Moreover, it cost about $90 for the paperwork to legalize one's status at a time when most landless Brazilian day laborers were only earning $5 or $6 a day (Cortêz 1994; De Oliveira 1995).

To be sure, not all Brazilians in Paraguay are poor and lack legal papers. Some business owners, most of whom are *gauchos*, natives of Rio Grande do Sul, are at least moderately prosperous thanks to their enterprises, which mainly serve the Brazilian community. Other Brazilians own large farms and ranches that produce 90 percent of Paraguay's soybeans, 80 percent of its corn, 60 percent of its beef, and 50 percent of its cotton. In recent years, enormous Brazilian-owned cattle ranches have been partly responsible for forest destruction in the Chaco, in western Paraguay. However, the great majority of Brazilians have relatively modest holdings, averaging between 30 and 50 hectares (about 75 to 125 acres) of land. Both production and consumption are closely tied to Brazil. While some goods of Paraguayan manufacture are sold locally, most are of Brazilian origin, and it is Brazilian middlemen who buy soybeans and other crops that are then exported to Brazil (Klintowitz 1995; Wilson, Hay, and Margolis 1989; Romero 2012a; Wagner 1990).

Those Brazilians who have ascended socially over the past decades have come to control important sectors of the local economy in the Paraguayan towns where Brazilians have settled. Some entered politics, and by 2005 there were four Brazilian-born mayors in the region. Yet it is not only local economies and politics that have been impacted by the Brazilian presence. Indeed, in those counties in eastern Paraguay where Brazilians and their descendants are the majority, they dominate society, and it is Paraguayans who are obliged to adapt to Brazil's language and culture. In the schools in these locales, 95 percent of the students are Paraguayan by birth, but they are the children or grandchildren of Brazilians and speak more Portuguese than Spanish, although they study both Spanish and Guarani in school, as well as Paraguayan history and geography.[3] The presence of Brazilian television in the region over the past two decades also has reinforced the use of Portuguese. In addition to language, Brazilian tastes in food, music, and dance are also firmly entrenched. The music played in bars is Brazilian, as are the bands that perform at local dances. Catholic Mass is conducted in Portuguese, and Brazilian Independence Day is celebrated with the singing of Brazil's national anthem. Even the clocks in these communities are set on Brazilian time, which is an hour ahead of Paraguay (Alves 1990; Wagner 1990).

Brazilians in Paraguay are often referred to as "*brasiguaios*," a term that was coined in 1985, when the first group of Brazilians returned to Brazil from Paraguay. The term came to be associated with Brazilians as foreigners and small cultivators who were excluded from social and political rights on both sides of the international border. As such, they were stigmatized by some in the elite sectors of Brazilian society who feared the return of large numbers of *brasiguaios* from Paraguay as threats to the social order in the Brazilian towns and cities where they settled (Albuquerque 2009).

Brasiguaio, in fact, encompasses diverse groups of Brazilians, including small landowners, tenant farmers, sharecroppers, and rural laborers. The poorest Brazilians in Paraguay accept the term as an important marker that may allow them to receive social benefits in both countries. But a sense of stigma also adheres to the term, and most Brazilians or those of Brazilian ancestry prefer to be called "Brazilian" or "Paraguayan." Then, too, the rubric is generally rejected by wealthier Brazilians and those with political power because it is associated with the undocumented, the poor, and the marginalized (Sprandel 2006; Albuquerque 2009).

By the end of the Stroessner regime, in the late 1980s, *brasiguaio* also took on a decidedly negative political connotation as it came to signify "invader" and "land usurper," with Brazilians also being dubbed "imperialistic intruders." Paraguayan authorities were urged by some politicians, university students, and Paraguayan farmers to declare the area of Brazilian occupation along the international frontier with Brazil a "national security zone," which would have meant ousting foreigners. There was pushback, however, from powerful segments of Paraguayan society that feared the loss of cheap labor if Brazilians were expelled from the country (Albuquerque 2009; Alves 1990, 9).

It is clear from this discussion that relations between Brazilians and Paraguayans are not all sweetness and light. Most Paraguayan peasants speak Guarani, not Spanish, further isolating them from Brazilians, who view local Paraguayans as "the other." Seeing themselves as hardworking pioneers from a more developed country, some Brazilians assert that they are in Paraguay as "missionaries of civilization," there to modernize the nation, which will happen only when immigrants hold local and national political positions. "If it wasn't for us Brazilians, they would still be growing manioc around here," claimed a Brazilian soy exporter as he pointed to the twenty-five-thousand-ton soy silo that he had built in a town in eastern Paraguay. Some Brazilians contrast their work ethic with that of Paraguayans, whom they claim are "lazy" and "corrupt." I find the parallels striking here between these stereotypes of Paraguayans and those held by some Brazilians in the United States with regard to Hispanics. This is discussed in chapter 11 (Barrionuevo 2008; quoted in Brooke 1991d; Albuquerque 2009, 9).

The conflicts between Brazilians and Paraguayans are very real. Over the past two decades, disputes over land between Paraguayan peasants and Brazilian landowners have erupted in eastern Paraguay. Many land titles are dubious, and a plot of land may be claimed by several "owners." Moreover, it is widely believed that some large Brazilian landowners illegally acquired additional land from Paraguayan peasants. Another source of conflict is the accusation that Brazilians are poisoning the environment with toxic chemicals used in mechanized soybean production. Then, too, some Paraguayans resent lighter-skinned Brazilians, many of whom are descended from German and Italian immigrants. Says one observer of such conflicts: "These tensions related to land, the environment, and local political power on the 'brasiguaian frontier' can be seen as class conflict, ethnic disputes, nationalist tensions and the clash between western capitalist civilization and peasant and indigenous cultures" (quoted in Albuquerque 2009, 147).

With the election of Fernando Lugo, a former priest and a leftist, as president of Paraguay in 2008, many landless peasants had hopes of reclaiming land from Brazilian soybean farmers. Amid a good deal of anti-Brazilian sentiment and some armed conflicts, Brazilian farmers, many of whom practice large-scale mechanized agriculture that provides few jobs, have been accused of contaminating local water supplies. But attitudes toward Brazilians are complicated. On the one hand, they have been praised for helping Paraguay's economy boom; on the other, they have been demonized as "foreigners" who control large tracts of land. At times, disgust with the status quo has led activists to burn Brazilian flags. And resentment against Brazilians continues to grow. "Paraguayan identity in the border provinces is being diluted because of the predominance of foreigners who speak their own language, use their own currency, hoist their own flag and are masters of the best lands," wrote a columnist in Paraguay's *Ultima Hora* newspaper in 2001 (Barrionuevo 2008; Romero 2011; quoted in Rohter 2001).

Today, no one knows how many of Paraguay's 6.5 million people are Brazilian because, as we have seen, an estimated 20 percent lack either Brazilian or Paraguayan documents. However, Brazilians in Paraguay without papers are likely to benefit from the new Mercosul agreement legalizing citizens of all member states who live in one of the other Mercosul countries. The six member nations of Mercosul—Brazil, Chile, Argentina, Paraguay, Uruguay, and Bolivia—have approved a plan to allow their 250 million citizens to live and work in all other Mercosul countries and be given the same rights and protections as citizens of those countries (Kantowitz 1995; Rohter 2002).

Destinations: Other South American Nations

What of the other nations that border Brazil, including those that belong to the Mercosul pact? None have a Brazilian presence of the size and influence of Paraguay's Brazilian population. Nevertheless, since Brazil has common borders with nine other nations in South America, it is not surprising that there are Brazilian communities, albeit some comparatively small ones, in all of them.

Brazilians who immigrate to other Mercosul countries are of two general types. There are rural property owners, some with very large holdings, and there are rural workers, including those made landless by the mechanization of agriculture in Brazil. A majority of Brazilians who go to Argentina and Uruguay are of the first type. In Uruguay 50 percent of rice production is in the hands of Brazilian producers, and in Argentina about 25 percent of that crop is also grown by Brazilians. The attraction of both countries is that land in them is considerably cheaper than it is in Brazil, particularly in the state of São Paulo (Sales 1996).

In Uruguay, which has a population of only 3.3 million, Brazilians attracted by the fertile soil and relatively cheap prices in the northern and northeastern regions of the country have been renting and buying land there. Today Brazilians own about one million hectares or more than 6 percent of Uruguay's arable land, and some thirty thousand resident Brazilians raise a half-million head of cattle, along with a number of cash crops. To be sure, these Brazilians, some of whom have vast land holdings, bear little resemblance to their impoverished compatriots in Paraguay, although several Brazilian landowners do employ landless Brazilian laborers on their properties (Klintowitz 1995).

Brazilians have followed two independent migratory paths in Argentina, one to the greater Buenos Aires metropolitan area and the other to Misiones in Argentina's northeast. In terms of social class and education, Brazilians in Buenos Aires are more akin to those who have immigrated to the United States, Europe, and Japan, while those in Misiones have more in common with the poor agricultural workers in the nations along Brazil's periphery. Many Brazilians in Buenos Aires—like those in Portugal and Australia—are able to find white-collar jobs in line with their educational credentials. As such, unlike the majority of middle-class Brazilian immigrants who have settled elsewhere, they do not suffer a decline in occupational and concomitant social status after emigration (Hasenbalg and Frigerio 1999).

In recent years, because of the difficulty of getting a tourist visa to go to the United States, some Brazilians who had planned to travel there have been heading to Argentina instead, especially to Buenos Aires, to find work. In general, Brazilians in that city receive better salaries than they do in Rio de Janeiro or São Paulo for similar jobs. Then, too, craftsmen hired by construction firms in Buenos Aires can earn about 40 percent more than they were earning in Brazil for the same work. Still, they are paid less than the average salary for Argentine workers. Another drawback of taking such jobs is that prices are higher for food and other essentials in Argentina than they are in Brazil (Espinoza 1994).

Buenos Aires is also home to a considerable number of mostly middle-class Brazilian women who have married Argentine men they met while they vacationed in Brazil. As a result, almost two-thirds of Brazilians in greater Buenos Aires are women. Another group of Brazilians earn a living through what has been called *trabalhos de brasileira*, that is, "Brazilian work." They are singers, dancers, and musicians who specialize in Brazilian entertainment, as well as performers and instructors of *capoeira* (Braga 2003).

The emigration of Brazilians to Misiones is linked to the agrarian structure in parts of southern Brazil, especially the concentration of land in large holdings and the increasing cost of arable land there. Most Brazilians going to Misiones usually plan to stay a short time, save money, and return to Brazil. An estimated twenty thousand Brazilian agricultural workers travel there for the harvest and then return home. Here and elsewhere in Argentina, Brazilians generally encounter few problems finding jobs, and borders can be crossed quite easily. Brazilians routinely receive permits to stay in the country for three months, but if they stay longer they rarely have problems with the authorities (Hasenbalg and Frigerio 1999; Espinoza 1994).

Borders also do not present much of a problem elsewhere in South America in nations that adjoin Brazil. In the densely forested Amazon, thousands of Brazilian workers lose any sense of national frontiers. Take the *brasivianos*, for example, as Brazilians are called in Bolivia. There is a long history of border crossings in both directions between Acre, in Brazil's far northwest, an area that once belonged to Bolivia, and that country's current frontier with Brazil. In the 1970s, twelve thousand families were expelled from Acre into Bolivia when the forests of rubber trees where they worked as *seringueiros* (rubber tappers) were cut down and transformed into cattle ranches. Today, an estimated fifteen thousand Brazilians tap rubber in Bolivia, and, as in most other Mercosul countries, there are also prosperous Brazilians with large tracts of land in the area near the Bolivian city of Santa Cruz (De Almeida 1995).

Similarly, several thousand Brazilians toil as *seringueiros* in French Guiana, and several thousand more work in that nation's capital, Cayenne. Nearly all of them are in the country illegally. Mostly poor, single men with low levels of education, they are from Brazil's Amazon region, and, besides rubber tapping, they are also employed in unskilled jobs, primarily in construction. They travel to French Guiana for better wages that can reach as high as $1,000 a month. Other Brazilians have been successful opening small businesses there. It appears that, when there is a labor shortage, the authorities look the other way when it comes to the illegal entry of Brazilians (and others), but, when there is no need for additional labor, the welcome mat is withdrawn. Like their compatriots in Paraguay, Brazilians in French Guiana and other countries bordering Brazil maintain contact with their homeland via satellite dishes, which enable them to regularly tune into TV Globo, Brazil's large television network, and to keep up on the latest news, sports scores, and *telenovelas* from back home (Organização Internacional para as Migrações 2010; Ferraz 1996).

Not rubber but gold is what draws Brazilians to Suriname, although the actual number of Brazilian immigrants, which has been rising in recent years, is open to dispute. While the Brazilian Embassy in Paramaribo puts it at fifteen thousand, other estimates range as high as fifty thousand. What is not in dispute is what brought them to Suriname: gold. Most Brazilian gold miners are from northern Brazil, people of little schooling who crossed the border in search of better economic opportunities than they had at home. While the migration is largely male—men going to the mines in search of gold—some Brazilian women travel to Suriname and work as prostitutes in the mining region or in Paramaribo. Most miners come with the object of saving money and returning to Brazil, although few seem to return home permanently. With the influx of Brazilians, there are now areas in Suriname where Portuguese is widely spoken, and there are hotels, restaurants, and other businesses that cater to the immigrants. To meet the needs of these miners, Brazilian soft drinks, DVDs, clothes, and even performers are imported from Brazil (Romero 2000, 2008; Soliani 2004).

In the mid-1990s, the state of Roraima in far northern Brazil attracted immigrants, mostly from Brazil's impoverished northeast. Roraima was dubbed the "new Eldorado" because of the boom in gold mining there, and, when the boom ended a few years later, some miners traveled across the border to Guyana to try their luck at mining. Today, some ten thousand Brazilians work in the mines in Guyana. Some chose to stay even after their jobs in the mines ended and are now involved in that nation's gold and diamond trade (Pereira 2006; Romero 2000).

Finally, there is Venezuela, which until the early 1990s was not a primary destination for Brazilian immigrants, most preferring other countries that border Brazil. Those who immigrated there are dubbed *brazuelanos*, Brazilians living in frontier regions of Venezuela. Here, too, the source of most immigrants is the adjacent Brazilian state of Roraima. The first few Brazilians arrived in the 1970s with the decline of diamond mining in Roraima. Many of them eventually established businesses that bought and sold gold and diamonds in the southern Venezuelan cities of Ciudad Bolivar and Santa Elena do Uairen, and current estimates suggest that 35 percent of Santa Elena's population is Brazilian (Rodrigues 2006).

The second wave of Brazilians arrived in the 1980s and was also linked to the decline of the mining boom in Brazil. Venezuela is one of the world's major gold producers, and there are estimates that some fifteen thousand Brazilian prospectors and miners there produce as much as 80 percent of the country's gold and 90 percent of its diamonds. They also dominate the gold and diamond trade in the country (Brooke 1992; Klintowitz 1995).

A third wave of Brazilian miners in Venezuela received wide media coverage in the 1990s. Many of these Brazilians had left Roraima as surveyors began demarcating a thirty-six-thousand-square-mile reserve to protect the Yanomami Indians who lived there. Rich in gold, diamonds, and bauxite, the area had attracted thousands of miners, but, with demarcation, the Brazilian government started a campaign to evict miners from the Yanomami reserve. As a result, thousands of impoverished Brazilian gold miners crossed over the border into Venezuela and set up mining camps, some in that country's own newly created Yanomami reserve (Brooke 1992).[4]

"The *garimpeiro* [miner] problem is resented by all of Venezuela's population," said a retired army general. "They are taking our mineral sources and deforesting our most important watershed." Amid an outcry about a "Brazilian invasion," it was widely reported in the news media that border guards in Venezuela had attacked and burned more than one hundred mining camps, detained hundreds of Brazilian miners, and sent others fleeing through the dense forest and over the border back to Brazil. Other reports strongly suggested that a plane carrying Brazilian miners was shot down by the Venezuelan authorities. The ensuing contretemps between the Brazilian and Venezuelan governments nearly led to a break in diplomatic relations (quoted in Brooke 1992).[5]

These, then, are the destinations of Brazilian immigrants in countries that have common borders with Brazil. We now turn to one major source of Brazilian immigrants, the pioneering immigrant-sending community of Governador Valadares, in the state of Minas Gerais in south central Brazil, which as early as the 1960s began sending immigrants to the United States and, later, to several European countries as well.

9

Quintessential Emigrants
Valadarenses

It's a rare household in the county that doesn't have someone who went to the
United States, who lives there, or at least, who is thinking of going.
   Rector, University of the Vale do Rio Doce, Governador Valadares
        (quoted in Corrêa 1994, 70)

Governador Valadares is a quintessential emigrant-sending community. This town of some 260,000 persons, located three hundred
kilometers northeast of Belo Horizonte, is also the regional economic
center of eastern and northeastern Minas Gerais and the neighboring
state of Espírito Santo. Governador Valadares and the surrounding towns
in the Vale do Rio Doce constitute what has been called a "sending hub"
because by 2007 just over half of local households had at least one member
living abroad. In fact, the number of passports held by the citizens of
Governador Valadares would be average for a city of one million, not a city
one-quarter that size. Thoughts about emigrating are always on the minds
of townspeople—not necessarily doing it but at least considering emigration
as a possibility (Siqueira and Jansen 2008; Beraba 2007).

If the area surrounding Governador Valadares is included, some forty
thousand people in the region are living outside Brazil. With almost no
industry, the municipality basically lives on services and commerce, both
of which are sustained by money earned in the United States and elsewhere.
By the mid-2000s, some $5 million a month or $60 million annually was
being sent to the city in the form of remittances. This is why it has been
dubbed "Governador Valadólares": about 60 percent of the money flowing
through it is directly or indirectly sent from abroad. Viewed from a national
perspective, natives of the Vale do Rio Doce region sent back about 14

percent of the $6.4 billion remitted to Brazil in the mid-2000s. In contrast, the São Paulo metropolitan area, with an estimated twenty million residents, was the recipient of just 4 percent of these funds (Reel 2006; Peixoto 2007; Scheller 2008c).

While Governador Valadares is the focal point of emigration activity, numerous small towns and villages in the Vale do Rio Doce also have been bitten by the migration bug. Take Capitão Andrade, for example, some twenty-two miles from Governador Valadares. An estimated 1,000 of its 3,200 residents are living abroad and are sending back $500,000 a month— $100,000 or more than the entire municipal budget. Then there is Tarumirim, a town of 12,000 people that is less than an hour from Governador Valadares; nearly one-third of its residents are living in the United States. The relative prosperity they see in Governador Valadares is the catalyst for the exodus from these small towns, an exodus that consists largely of young men. So many have left that it has become difficult to find workers to hire to do farm labor, and women are said to have a hard time locating potential spouses (Mineo 2006a, 2006c).

Emigration and related topics—such as the exchange rate for dollars— are so pervasive in Governador Valadares and the surrounding towns that some locals got together and wrote and produced a play about the phenomenon. The play, which ran for nine consecutive days, was a huge hit. Titled "The Last One to Leave Turns Out the Light" (*O Ultimo a Sair Apaga a Luz*), the play included songs with lyrics that recounted the trials and tribulations of emigration, set to tunes like "New York, New York," "California Dreaming," and "Monday, Monday," which was retitled "Money, Money." Although the play is a musical comedy, one of the play's authors told me that it was meant to be a tragicomedy and was intended to show some of the real difficulties immigrants from Governador Valadares face when confronted with life in the United States.

Setting the Stage

Just how did Governador Valadares develop into what is undoubtedly the most famous immigrant-sending community in Brazil? We need to look back several decades for a full understanding of the town's evolution as a font of immigrants. After a transitory period in the 1920s when it was based on coffee cultivation, an era that ended after a crisis in that industry, the regional economy became focused on mineral extraction, especially the mining of mica, and the commercialization of wood. During the 1930s, the region was firmly linked to the outside world by railroad for the first time, and, with the arrival in the early 1940s of the Companhia Vale do Rio Doce, a huge mining company and still a major employer in the region, its economy took off (Soares 1995b).[1]

The 1940s and 1950s were largely prosperous decades, particularly the World War II years, when there was a huge demand for mica, which was used as insulation for radio tubes, detonators, and other war products. During the war, American engineers and technicians from the Boston area arrived in Governador Valadares to work in mineral extraction, particularly the mining of mica. The town was also the center of mica processing, and the processed mica was exported directly from there to the United States. The importance of mica as a war material also led the U.S. government to send American advisers to take part in a program to combat malaria in the region and to aid in the construction of modern water and sewage systems. At about the same time, a group of American businessmen established contacts with the Vale do Rio Doce because of their interest in the trade of semiprecious stones mined there. All these events brought *valadarenses* into contact with Americans and their culture, and "the USA went from being a 'foreign world' to a concrete reference point" (Millman 1997; Soares 1995b, 43).

During the 1950s, a North American company was contracted by the Companhia Vale do Rio Doce to build a railroad connecting Minas Gerais to neighboring Espírito Santo. The company also built a housing compound for its American workers in Governador Valadares, and locals were impressed by the houses, which contained such then-unfamiliar appliances as electric mixers. During this period, according to the researcher Glaucia de Oliveira Assis, "the North Americans brought with them everything that is modern—electric lights, a railroad and consumption habits. They brought with them contact with the world" (Scheller 2008; quoted in *Folha de São Paulo* 1997a).

The extractive economy experienced a crisis in the 1960s as sawmills closed and the demand for mica dwindled. During the decade, more than 80 percent of the county's land was gradually turned into pasture, and the cattle industry became its most important enterprise. Cattle ranching, however, was incapable of absorbing the growing number of unemployed in the area because, as the Brazilian saying goes, "where cattle enter, men exit" (*onde o boi entra, o homem sai*). Then, too, the region was not suitable for agriculture because of its relatively sparse rainfall and a topography unsuited to mechanization. As a result, only about 7 percent of county lands were under cultivation. After the decline of mica, mining continued on a much reduced scale and centered around the extraction of cassiterite and semiprecious stones. By the 1960s and 1970s, Governador Valadares and the other small towns in the Vale do Rio Doce had become problem areas and had gained a reputation as "pockets of poverty and social tension" (Soares 1995a, 23).

The contact between the citizens of Governador Valadares and Americans during World War II and the years following the war appears to have intensified during the 1960s. Several creation stories dating from that period claim to be about the "first" *valadarenses* to travel to the United States. Some examples: At some point early in the decade, a group of about ten young people from the town decided to "have an adventure" and "spend some time" in the United States, long considered the "land of dreams." They left for New York and moved up the East Coast as far as Boston, taking jobs in hotels along New England's tourist route. A few returned to Brazil, but others remained in Boston, encouraging family members to join them there. Then there is the tale of the "first four immigrants from Governador Valadares" who left for the United States in 1964. They sent home letters and photos describing the opportunities and wonders of the new land. And they, in turn, provided the support for others who wanted to follow. Then, too, an anecdote is often recounted about a group of students from Governador Valadares who left town to take advantage of scholarships to study in the United States and then returned home with stories of all the money to be made there (Martes 2004, 40; Siqueira, Assis, and de Campos 2010; Beraba 2007).

Another, more elaborate creation story goes like this: In 1967, the daughter of one of Governador Valadares's pioneer settlers—a man with vast land holdings and the founder of its faculty of law—was hired as the local representative of Varig, Brazil's national airline. The Varig office was maintained in such a small city as a "tribute to national integration." To drum up business, she came up with the idea of selling one-way tickets to the United States to the town's citizens, allowing them to pay for their plane tickets in installments. As a result of this scheme, some three hundred international passengers became customers of her small agency in the Brazilian interior. She essentially financed their plane tickets; when the travelers arrived in the United States and got jobs, they would pay her back. She claimed never to have had a bad debt. But when this scheme caught the attention of officials of the American Consulate in Rio de Janeiro, they summoned her there. If consular officers expected an apology for her "fly now—pay later" program, they were badly mistaken: "You [Americans] arrived there first. What you have taken in mica, timber, iron ore and precious stones is enough to pay for the stays of all the *valadarenses* in your country for the rest of the century!" (quoted in Corrêa 1994, 77).

What these stories have in common is that the earliest immigrants, by reporting their experiences to those back home and showing evidence of their "migratory success," helped construct an image of the United States as a land of milk and honey while also creating the first social networks that linked Governador Valadares, the Boston area, and other immigrant destinations in the United States. And, more important, they provided information, contacts, and financial support for the immigrants who followed. This was the start of a long series of migration narratives disseminated throughout the community, accounts that seduced others into "trying their luck" at the migrant experience. These tales infused the geographical imagination of local residents and served as powerful enticements to those who had never before thought of leaving Brazil (Siqueira, Assis, and de Campos 2010; Marcus 2009a).

Stories of more recent migratory success also are rife in the community. For instance, there was one elderly couple in town who had trouble remembering the names of all thirty-two of their family members living in the United States. These included their six children, eight grandchildren, three great-grandchildren, sons-in law, daughters-in-law, and several nephews. The couple administered the nearly thirty properties in Governador Valadares bought by relatives with dollars earned in the United States. Their daughter, who had lived in the United States for eight years, was one of the most successful family members. She owned a house in Governador Valadares, a two-hundred-hectare *fazenda* (ranch) ten minutes from the city, and more than two hundred head of cattle. Working as a housecleaner in the United States, she planned to stay there for two more years, which would be enough time, she calculated, to earn the money to build a house with a pool on the *fazenda* where she intended to retire (*Folha de São Paulo* 1989).

The Culture of Migration and the Migration Industry

In no other place in Brazil does the United States have a greater sway on the imagination than in Governador Valadares. "Boston and New

York are closer to *valadarenses* than other Brazilian cities like São Paulo," notes Weber Soares (1995a), a demographer who has done research on immigration's economic impact on the community. The evidence for this close connection is plentiful. The local post office receives around four hundred pieces of mail a month from the United States, while other towns of similar size elsewhere in Brazil might receive thirty such pieces of mail a month. Major purchases can be paid for in dollars. In the *Diario do Rio Doce*, the local newspaper, perhaps half of the prices of houses and apartments are quoted in dollars. Several local bars accept dollars, as do some pharmacies and a number of cab drivers, and the town is said to be the only one in Brazil where beggars ask for alms in dollars. Many businesses are named after towns and cities in the United States where immigrants once lived, and some parents are giving their newborns "American" names like Michelle, Jennifer, and Michael. Even a seven-year-old in town was heard saying that he was "going to America" to join his four cousins who live there. And, as the local joke goes, "when Christopher Columbus arrived in America there were already *valadarenses* there" (Caitano 2010b; Mineo 2006a; Sperandio 2012; quoted in *Folha de São Paulo* 1997a).

During the so-called lost economic decade of the 1980s, while many poor Brazilians left their rural homes to search for jobs in Brazil's large coastal cities, the citizens of Governador Valadares were much more likely to seek their fortunes abroad. This is why the town has been called the "cradle of *brazucas*" (*o berço do brazucas*); "*brazuca*" is a term for Brazilians living in the United States. The focus on the United States is not surprising, given that 82 percent of townspeople going abroad immigrate to what they call "the land of *Tio* Sam" (Uncle Sam), and locals joke about the number of townspeople who go there.[2] It is said that Governador Valadares is a "phantom city" (*cidade fantasma*) that does not really exist because nearly everyone has left for the United States and that "mass is said in English" for the few people who remain (Soares 1995b).

According to the sociologist Sueli Siqueira, who has done long-term research in Governador Valadares, so dense are the social networks built up between the town and various locales in the United States that it is possible for a person who knows no English, has never traveled more than a few hundred kilometers from the Vale do Rio Doce, and is unfamiliar with the great cities of Brazil like São Paulo and Rio de Janeiro to get off a plane in New York, travel to a town, such as Framingham, Massachusetts, and be working at a job there a day or two later.

Fully half of the *valadarenses* who immigrated to the United States left home between 1985 and 1993. "Valadares lived through cycles of mica and coffee exports in earlier decades. In the 1980s, the city exported people," said one researcher (quoted in *Folha de São Paulo* 1997b). By the early 2000s, one of every nine residents in town had migrated to the United States at one time or another, and one in four residents knew at least one person who had lived there. What does this look like in terms of total numbers? In 2005, the mayor of Governador Valadares, Jose Bonifácio Mourão, estimated that some forty thousand townspeople were living in the United States—or about 15 percent of the population. "Almost every family, including mine, has relatives in the United States," he said (Soares 2002; quoted in Rohter 2005, 3).

Some of the very first people to leave were members of the local elite, upper-middle-class individuals who had the information and resources to make the trip abroad. Most of the *valadarenses* in a 1989 random sample of immigrants came from the middle and upper-middle classes and had, at a minimum, a high school education. Some locals joke about young women from middle- and upper-middle-class families going to the United States to work as housecleaners. When they arrive, it is said, they do not even know how to make a bed since at home they have always had domestic servants to do such chores. There is a great deal of evidence, then, that it was people from the middle sectors of *valadarense* society that went first, but, with the maturing of a "culture of migration," especially from 2000 on, the class affiliation of immigrants became more diverse. Then, too, the huge influx of dollars sent home by immigrants undermined the traditional economic ascendancy of the upper-middle-class families, whose wealth was based on their herds of cattle and extensive land holdings. Waiters, cooks, and attendants at one of the local hospitals were now going to the United States, as did a physician, an orthopedist, who immigrated there with his family. While away, he maintained his clinic in town and hoped to save enough money while working in the United States to buy a large ranch in the Vale do Rio Doce. Indeed, even children of *fazendeiros* (large landowners) were trying their luck in the United States (Siqueira 2007; Goza 2003; Beraba 2007).

Given the numbers involved, it is no surprise that an entire industry has grown up to help would-be immigrants attain their goals.[3] By 2003, for example, there were seventy registered travel agencies in town. Prior to the mid-1990s, these agencies sold only airline tickets, but then some began to help finance immigrants' trips to the United States and to aid those seeking forged documents. These travel agencies, in turn, work hand in hand with the local "passport and visa industry." The passport "chop shops" substitute photos, doctor places of origin, and insert pages with U.S. tourist visas awarded to someone other than the passport holder. As a consequence, the town has earned the reputation as *the* "center of false passports" in Brazil. The visa industry, in turn, produces bogus financial documents meant for the eyes of American consular personnel; these documents indicate that the visa applicant is a person of considerable means who, of course, has *no* interest in taking a job in the United States. Most of those involved in these enterprises are themselves former migrants (Martes 2010; Paiva 1997).

The manufacture of bogus documents in the city has led to several investigations by Brazil's federal police, resulting in the confiscation of three hundred counterfeit passports along with the questioning of six hundred individuals allegedly involved in their production and distribution. A bogus passport with a U.S. visa stamped in it can cost as much as $7,000 for a professionally produced, high-quality document. Said a spokesman for the American Embassy in Brasília: "Brazil has the best falsifiers of visas on the planet." Some passports are stolen, preferably ones with valid visas already attached, and then the name and photo are altered. The industry is so well organized that, in the mid-1990s, four armed men stole three hundred passports with U.S. tourist visas stamped in them from employees of the Association of Travel Agents in Rio de Janeiro (quoted in Paiva 1997).

Beyond passports and visas, there are also specialized intermediate agents called "counsels" (*cônsuls*), without whom undocumented immigration from Governador Valadares to the United States via Mexico would be much more difficult, if not impossible. The *cônsul* "is the key Brazilian broker who has transnational connections with Mexican coyotes," according to researcher Alan Marcus. As we have seen in an earlier chapter, *cônsuls* will arrange the entire trip to the United States for fees of $10,000 and up. They are among the wealthiest individuals in Governador Valadares, some with newly built houses costing $1 million or more (Marcus 2009b).

Just who are these travelers from Governador Valadares? We already know that the city's pioneer émigrés largely came from the middle sectors of local society but that since 2000 they have had more diverse social and economic roots. Most were between twenty and forty years old, and a majority had completed high school. As such, they were better educated than the average city resident, about half of whom have only a primary school education. Seventy percent were employed before emigrating, and most earned from three to five minimum salaries a month (wages in Brazil are expressed in multiples of the official minimum salary per month). In the United States, they earn an average of four times as much as they did in Brazil. Nearly 40 percent used their own resources to pay for the trip, demonstrating that they were hardly impoverished before leaving home and emigrated either to maintain their standard of living or to improve it. Those who borrow money for the trip arrive in the United States owing between $8,000 and $12,000, and they typically pay off the debt in about eighteen months with money earned in their new country (Siqueira 2009b; Soares 1995a).

Remittances and the Remittance Economy

Just what becomes of the dollars *valadarenses* earn in the United States after any debts owed for the trip are paid off? Immigrants are more likely to invest their savings in real estate than in businesses. More than two-thirds of immigrants put their money in real estate—apartments, houses, and land. By 2006, these real estate transactions accounted for nearly half of all such transactions in town. According to research by Weber Soares, between 1984 and 1993 émigrés bought just under eleven thousand plots of land, nearly six thousand houses, and more than two thousand apartments in Governador Valadares. This added up to quite a sum of money indeed: nearly $150 million in land and housing (Mineo 2006a; Soares 1995b).

Of those persons who invest, 60 percent buy residences. This is evident from the enormous boom in apartment and house construction in the city. Entire sections of town are referred to as "*bairros americanos*" (American neighborhoods) because they were built with money sent from the United States. A common pattern is for an émigré to purchase two apartments, one for personal use and the other to rent out to produce income. In fact, locals say that initially, at least, the single most important reason for going to the United States is to save money to buy a place to live. Although salaries in Brazil are low, "rent is what weighs you down," says one resident; a large portion of one's income pays for rent. But if you are a homeowner, you do not have the expense of rent, and you are better off even with the same salary. One result of these purchases is that the price of land in the Vale do Rio Doce increased 300 percent between the late 1980s and the end of the first decade of the new millennium (Soares 1999; Siqueira 2009b).

The impact of the influx of dollars on the local economy is immense. A number of townspeople told me that the building boom created vast numbers of jobs in the construction industry and that it also has had a huge impact on the local sale of building materials from wood and bricks to asphalt, tiles, and kitchen appliances. At least through the mid-1990s there was said to be very little unemployment in the city because of the surge in building, and wages were higher there than in comparable cities because of the demand for labor in construction.

During my visit to Governador Valadares, I was told that families often work together to construct new condo buildings in which they will own apartments. First, several sets of parents of children who are immigrants to the United States get together to draw up plans for a small apartment building. How many sets of parents depends on how many apartments are to be built. The parents jointly hire an engineer and decide on the type and size of the apartments, the building's exterior material, and so on. The interiors of each apartment can vary. Blueprints are then sent to their children in the United States, who approve the plan or make changes to it. In order to begin construction, the families make a down payment of around $3,000 for each apartment. After that, the children send their parents a pre-agreed sum each month. As the money arrives, another stage of construction proceeds. For example, one month's collective remittances might be used to buy and install windows and window frames, another might pay for the purchase and installation of bathroom tiles, and so on. The whole process usually takes about eighteen months from start to finish, but it can take less time if everyone agrees to make a larger initial down payment. Typically, the parents living in town keep an eye on the construction and report back to their children through letters and phone calls (in the 1990s) and via e-mail and Skype today.

While far fewer people invest in businesses than in real estate, some returned migrants do start enterprises with the goal of becoming economically independent. While they worked as waiters or in construction in the United States, they have no intention of holding such jobs upon the return home. And so, for example, the first laundromat in town was built and equipped with money the owner earned in the United States. Similarly, there are a number of stores built with dollars: supermarkets, fast-food outlets, restaurants, several pharmacies, a stationery store, a video rental store, and a gasoline station at a busy intersection that serves buses and trucks traveling along the Salvador–Rio de Janeiro Highway (Duffy 2008).

For some successful entrepreneurs, investments made with immigrant dollars lead to a significant increase in monthly income. Before going to the United States, just under 70 percent earned, on average, three minimum salaries; after they returned home and started businesses, nearly 40 percent began earning the equivalent of around six minimum salaries, while another 21 percent made more than ten minimum salaries. Not surprisingly, those successful upon their return feel their stay in the United States was very worthwhile (Siqueira, Assis, and de Campos 2010; Siqueira 2009b).

A number of immigrants return with money but are uncertain how to invest it because they are unfamiliar with the local market. They often want to own a business in an area that might have appeal in the United States but that does not necessarily mesh with local needs. A good example is the aforementioned laundromat, with its modern washers and dryers. Dryers are unnecessary in Governador Valadares; because of its warm climate and low humidity, clothes dry very fast on the line, and the owner ultimately went bankrupt. Others bought land but were unsure what to do with it; land often turned into a "symbolic investment" that produced little or no return.[4] A survey of immigrants who started local businesses between 2007 and 2009 found that nearly 40 percent of them encountered problems. Almost three-quarters had done no research to define what area would be best to invest in locally, and most lacked managerial skills. Another study found that more than 70 percent of such businesses failed within two years, leaving returnees without any savings. The plan of the majority of these unsuccessful business owners was to try again, that is, to return to the United States, save money, and start a new business in Governador Valadares at some future date (Siqueira 2009b; Peixoto 2007).

One variable that distinguishes immigrants who succeed in their investments when they return home from those who do not is gender. More than 87 percent of those who are successful are men. The sociologist Sueli Siqueira (2009b), who did an in-depth study of the investments of returnees, believes the reason that more women fail at business than men is that, upon their return to Brazil, women once again become the exclusive caretakers of hearth and home and have little time to devote to other activities, including any businesses they may have started with their savings from the United States.

Another significant difference between those who succeed in their investments and those who do not is knowledge of the market in which they are investing. Due to the high rate of returnee failure because of a lack of experience and planning and in order to better ensure that the money earned in the United States is invested wisely, the municipal government of Governador Valadares, along with the Western Union Company and the Bank of Brazil, created the Center of Information and Support for Families and Workers Abroad, or Ciaat (Centro de Informação, Apoio e Amparo à Família e ao Trabalhador no Exterior), a program intended, in part, to help would-be investors. And, in recent years, at least two other organizations have addressed the challenges faced by immigrants when they return to their communities in Brazil. One, the Federation of Industries of the State of Minas Gerais (Federação das Industrias do Estado do Minas Gerais), has set up a technical assistance program to help migrants who want to start businesses in their hometowns. These programs were all attempts to halt the wave of business failures in these locales and to help deal with growing unemployment in them as the construction boom ebbed (Scheller 2008a; Marcus 2009a; Levitt 2001).

Despite the difficulties many immigrants encounter in business and otherwise when they return home, these troubles tend to be downplayed because of a propensity in Governador Valadares and other sending communities to view Brazilian immigrants as hometown "heroes." The local image of the "hero immigrant" especially adheres to those audacious citizens who faced the perils of entering the United States clandestinely via Mexico. Indeed, the mayor's office in Governador Valadares has put up a plaque in the town square lauding emigrants as local "heroes." Not coincidentally, in Governador Valadares, the "Day of the Immigrant" (Dia do Emigrante) is celebrated on July 4 (Siqueira 2007; Marcus 2009b).

Such attitudes echo the findings of research conducted in several evangelical churches in Governador Valadares. While church doctrine explicitly condemns the emigration of Brazilians from the city to the United States because it is known to be "illegal" in most cases, the churches continue to provide strong support both to these immigrants and to their families who stayed behind (Duarte, Amorim, Dias, and Siqueira 2008).

Some of the stickiest problems surrounding immigration involve families and family relations. One common pattern for married immigrants is for the husband to travel to the United States first to check things out. After arranging a place to live and getting a job, he sends for his wife. She arrives and also finds work. Any children remain behind, living with their grandparents. The result is that there are quite a large number of children in Governador Valadares whose parents are living in the United States.[5] Three *valadarenses* I met in New York City in the early 1990s pointed out another familial pattern. They estimated that about half of the fifty or so townspeople they know in New York send remittances back home, with perhaps one-third sending money expressly to support their spouses and children living there. These include married men and single mothers who are sustaining the wives and/or children they left behind. One Brazilian journalist reported on the poignant case of several men from Governador Valadares whose families stayed behind when they went to the United States; the men could not find work once they got there and had no money to pay for the return trip home (Caitano 2010a).

According to research by Ciaat, the local organization that supports immigrants and their families, 54 percent of families in Governador Valadares have at least one parent working abroad. Moreover, the study estimates that about 1,000 local marriages break up annually and suggests that emigration is the leading cause of marital separations and divorce. A therapist in town agrees that the absence of the immigrant family member is responsible for these breakups. She estimates that of the 60,000 families living in Governador Valadares, the "virus of separation" has led to the dissolution of 7,500 or more than 12 percent of marriages there (Scheller 2008b; see also Margolis 2002).

One concern of local educators is what they consider to be the lack of ambition among some children of immigrants, who see no reason to work hard in school or pursue a career because they too expect to immigrate to the United States. Despite the problems many immigrants encounter in the United States, the dream of immigrating there remains very much alive in the younger generation (Mineo 2006i; Duffy 2008).

A Snowflake Parable

A comic book titled *The Special Present* was published by the municipal government of Governador Valadares. Aimed at local children, it tells the story of a little boy whose parents are living and working in the United States. He is cared for by his grand-parents and does not remember his parents, who left for the United States when he was a baby.

The story is about the boy's request that his parents send him a snowflake as a present. After all, they have sent him all kinds of toys—even a talking soccer ball—in the past, so he cannot understand why they can't send him a snowflake as well. He makes fun of his best friend, whose parents can afford to buy him toys only at the Brazilian equivalent of a dollar store.

Meanwhile, a box arrives from his parents. It is full of water. They did indeed send him snowflakes, which had melted along the way.

The little boy has no interest in school since soon he will be old enough to go to America himself and earn lots of money, and eventually he does. He works long hours like his parents in the cold northern clime, to which he is unaccustomed.

But, back in Governador Valadares, his best friend goes to university, marries, and has children. And who, the cartoon booklet asks its young readers, is happier? (O Centro de Infor-mação e Assessoria Técnica n.d.)

The Making of a Transnational Community and the Return Home

In 1993, the *Diario do Rio Doce*, the principal newspaper of Governador Valadares, began publishing *States News*, which originally was a separate section in the paper's local edition. The new edition is a fine example of transnationalism because it is a weekly paper distributed to forty thousand people in both Brazil and the United States. It is written primarily for and by immigrants, but it is published in Governador Valadares and covers both the happenings in town and the doings of Brazilians living in various locales in the United States. Evidence of transnationalism—the idea that lives are lived across borders and between two nations—is ubiquitous in the city. For example, residents can tune into a local TV station to watch Catholic religious services broadcast from Somerville, Massachusetts, the site of a sizeable community of *valadarenses*, in order to catch a glimpse of relatives as they attend Mass. And another, slightly macabre example: a local funeral home allows citizens living abroad to view via the Internet the funerals of loved ones back home. "If the family desires we can transmit the audio with the sound of the funeral Mass, the funeral cortege in the streets of Governador Valadares and even the burial," said the director of the funeral home. Parenthetically, using similar technology, one maternity hospital in São Paulo and another in Victoria, Espírito Santo, allow distant family members to watch the birth of babies born to their relatives in Brazil. A stationary camera in the delivery room captures images of the birth. One woman living in Spain witnessed the birth of her niece at one of these hospitals (Millman 1997; quoted in Levitt 2001, 214; Herdy and Menezes 2010).

People also can be transnational. Sometimes referred to as "pendulums" (*pendulares*), these are individuals who, on a regular basis, live part of the year in Governador Valadares and part of the year in the United States. This is possible if one has a green card or has become an American citizen.[6] While the goal of most of those who can freely (and legally) travel back and forth between Brazil and the United States is to invest in the United States, especially in housing, many also invest in their hometown. Others return to Governador Valadares every year or two and may maintain a residence there, as well. One man, a native of the city, has divided his time between the United States and his hometown for decades. He remains in the United States for eight months and spends the rest of the year in Governador Valadares.

Still, an undetermined number of *valadarenses* never return to live. They rent out the apartments they purchased with their American-earned dollars and return home only for vacations. This was true of one woman I met at a restaurant in town. A native of Governador Valadares and a current resident of Danbury, Connecticut, she was in town for ten days visiting relatives and buying items for her store in Danbury, which caters to the Brazilian community there. She had no plans, she told me, to return to live permanently in Governador Valadares. Parenthetically, I was delighted when she asked me if I too planned to live permanently in the United States. She thought I was a Brazilian immigrant who, having lived in the United States for several years, acquired something of an American accent when speaking Portuguese!

This woman, however, may be an exception to the rule because many of her compatriots who have lived in the United States for fifteen, twenty, or more years still maintain an ideology of return. Of those who do return, supposedly "for good," some yo-yo back and forth between Brazil and the United States as many as three, four, even five times. The reason is that they simply cannot readjust to the exigencies of life in Brazil after years spent in the United States. Writes the sociologist Sueli Siqueira (2009b, 96), "The desire to stay [in Brazil] is strong but after working in the U.S., living in the rhythm of an industrialized society with access to consumer goods, even though on the periphery of that society, the immigrant fails to readapt, losing his place in his natal society." Sometimes it is small annoyances that cause unease. This was true of the son of a woman I met in town. On a recent visit home, her son, who had been living and working in New York City for several years, complained repeatedly that the electric shower in their apartment provided too little hot water and asked his mother how she could stand to take a shower with insufficient hot water.[7]

Some of the complaints made by returned emigrants in Governador Valadares are similar to those I heard from returnees I interviewed in Rio de Janeiro in the late 1990s. One common theme in the discourse of return is summed up in the remark of one returnee: "Brazil is disorganized. It's chaotic. It's a country that is poorly administered with too much bureaucracy." It is also needlessly complicated. Comments about having to "struggle" and "fight" to get things done were frequently heard. Another source of dissatisfaction was what was seen as the lack of law enforcement in Brazil and the impunity with which laws are broken. In contrast, in the United States, I was told, "the laws work" (*as leis functionam*). These remarks coalesced into a critique of the cloak of impunity that protects the Brazilian elite. In the United States, returnees say, laws are applied to everyone, no matter what one's station in life—a comment with which I would take issue. A final complaint concerned the meagerness of Brazilian wages. "Here you can work just as hard as in the United States, but you can't afford things," a number of returnees said. One pointed out that even though he worked as a waiter in the United States, he had an apartment and a car—an impossibility in Brazil (Margolis 2001a).

By the end of the first decade of the new millennium, only one-third of those former emigrants who had again taken up permanent residence in their hometowns felt that their lives had improved significantly after their return. Most other returnees had little or no hope for the future there and lamented the fact that they had failed to realize their dream of "doing America" (*fazendo América*). Still, for a significant percentage of these "failed" emigrants who had no prospect of returning to the United States, the vision of emigration remained alive and well—only this time the destination was Europe, with Portugal, Spain, and Germany the desired end points. While the European dream was not yet a "fever" of the sort that had sent many thousands to the United States, it was still flourishing among *valadarenses* and other residents of the Vale do Rio Doce well into the new millennium (Siqueira 2009b; Beraba 2007; Duffy 2008).

One new and unexpected development with regard to the town dates from 2008, when the financial crisis in the United States gripped the American economy. Believe it or not, some *valadarenses* began sending money to their hard-hit relatives living in the United States. One former resident of the town who had lived in the United States for two decades was about to lose his house to foreclosure when his family in Governador Valadares sold a property there and sent him part of the 350,000 *reais* they realized from the sale. Estimates suggest that, between 2008 and 2012, the amount of money sent monthly from the town to relatives in the United States increased by about 20 percent. Moreover, in contrast to earlier decades, by 2012 a majority—perhaps 65 percent—of *valadarenses* were going to the United States as actual tourists, not as would-be immigrants. The manager of a travel agency there said that, in earlier years, only 15 or 20 percent of those seeking tourist visas in fact wanted to go to the United States as tourists, while the rest, as we know, went there to seek their fortunes (Lobato 2012).

This, then, is a portrait of the best-known immigrant-sending community in Brazil. Now we turn once again to immigrant communities outside Brazil, more specifically to community-based institutions—or the lack thereof.

10

Faith and Community
Ties That Bind?

When you're in the United States you're a foreigner, and you live with the idea
that you're a foreigner 24 hours a day. . . . You feel like a fish out of water in this
country. So when you go to church, you can speak your language. You're entering
Brazil again. Language, food, gestures. . . . You forget you're in the U.S.

Brazilian immigrant in Boston (quoted in Levitt and de la Dehesa 1998)

The church is like my mother's house" (*A igreja é como a casa da minha
mãe*), declared a Brazilian immigrant living in Florida. Churches in
some Brazilian communities in the United States, including those in the
Atlanta area and in south Florida, have become important refuges for
Brazilians fearing arrest and deportation. It is the one place where they feel
safe. The importance of religion and ethnic churches among Brazilian
immigrants has been widely researched, and a number of scholars have
concluded that religious institutions are perhaps the strongest focal points
in these communities (Vasquez, Ribeiro, and Alves 2008).

To which religions do diasporic Brazilians belong? A random sample of
Brazilians in the Boston metropolitan area in the mid-2000s found that
more than one in three—37 percent—were Protestant; close to one in
two—48 percent—were Catholic; and most of the remaining 15 percent
claimed to have no religious preference. Thus, the proportion of Brazilian
immigrants, at least in the Boston area, who are Protestant is higher than it
is in Brazil. So it appears that Protestant churches, particularly evangelical
ones, occupy a greater space in the context of Brazilian emigration than
they do back home. However, these religious preferences do mirror other
shifts that have been taking place in Brazil itself. A survey conducted there
in conjunction with the 2010 census found that 68 percent of Brazilians

said that they were Catholic, down from 90 percent three decades earlier. As such, the move away from Catholicism and toward Protestantism, especially of the evangelical variety, is taking place both in Brazil and in Brazilian communities abroad (Marcelli et al. 2009; Freston 2008).

One issue on which all researchers agree is that a growing number of evangelical, "born-again" churches are serving Brazilian immigrant communities in many locales. In the greater New York metropolitan area, for example, there are more than one hundred Brazilian churches, with some forty-six in Queens alone, most but not all evangelical. Similarly, by the mid-2000s, there were at least fifty Brazilian churches in greater Boston, again, most often of the evangelical variety. In Atlanta, there are somewhere between thirty and forty churches, mainly evangelical, that conduct services in Portuguese. And, in a single county in south Florida, thirty-nine churches draw Brazilian believers. In all, there are an estimated eight hundred Protestant churches of various denominations serving Brazilian communities around the United States (D. Rodrigues 2010, 2012; Martes 2010; White 2008; Alves and Ribeiro 2002).

Many Brazilian immigrants—up to 40 percent—who were at least nominally Catholic in Brazil began frequenting Protestant churches after they arrived in the United States. This was the experience of one devout Catholic who became an adherent of Pentecostalism after visiting a Portuguese-language church in Astoria, Queens. There she "felt whole," she says. "This church is not a place we visit once a week. This church is where we hang around and we share our problems and we celebrate our successes, like we were family" (quoted in Santos 2008a, 33). A similar sentiment was expressed by an evangelical Brazilian in south Florida: "Those who don't have families here have the church, which is *our* family" (quoted in Vásquez 2009, 47). Thus, religious affiliations among Brazilian immigrants appear to be fluid. Many join evangelical churches when they first arrive and take advantage of the practical help these churches offer in finding jobs and housing; later some leave them after becoming more established in the United States (Pedroso 2008; Marcus 2008b).

As is evident from the quotation at the start of this chapter, one powerful lure of these churches is their ambiance of "Brazilianness" (*brasilidade*). The great majority of Brazilians who attend church do so in an explicitly Brazilian setting, that is, they rarely go to the church services of non-Brazilians. As a Brazilian bishop in Newark, New Jersey, put it: "There are things that can only be done in one's mother tongue, for example, praying" (quoted in Vásquez 2009, 44). Especially during the early years of emigration, newcomers find that the evangelical churches bestow an enveloping sense of belonging in an otherwise alien society where believers may not speak the language. These churches provide an ethnic cocoon of sorts for their flocks and, in so doing, help reinforce Brazilian identity in a country where it is otherwise submerged in a complex web of Latin American ethnicities. As a consequence, the traditional association between *brasilidade* and Catholicism is undermined by the rise of Protestant-based evangelicalism (Martes 1999, 2010; Freston 2008).

These churches also perform myriad social and economic roles for their followers. Says one evangelical pastor: "Our mission is to welcome the immigrant and be his [sic] guide and his support. If they need money to pay the rent, we'll raise the money for them. If they need work, we'll find them work" (quoted in Santos 2008a, 36). Then, too, they are a safe place to spend time when not working. One Pentecostal church in New York City offers a variety of activities—almost on a daily basis. Church services are held on Sunday and Thursday, and there are youth group meetings on Friday, Bible study on Wednesday, and all-night prayer vigils year-round. There are birthday and engagement parties and other celebrations to which all are invited. In essence, the church is both a house of worship and a community center. The pastor of this church contrasts these activities with the Portuguese-language Catholic Mass Brazilians attend in Queens. Soon after Sunday Mass is over at 8:30 in the morning, Brazilian churchgoers disperse to make way for the English Mass that follows (Margolis 1994a).

What is the specific attraction of evangelical churches over Catholic churches for the Brazilian immigrant community? The sociologist Ana Cristina Braga Martes studied three churches—Catholic, Baptist, and Presbyterian—in the Boston area, and her analysis is telling. Aside from religious services, all provide a variety of aid to immigrants: church employees serve as interpreters in hospitals, in schools, and in the judicial system and as sources of information on jobs and housing; they also distribute food and clothes, especially cold-weather items. She found, however, that, while the three churches offer similar assistance to immigrants, their ideological orientations are very distinct. The Catholic church is "collectively oriented," a collective identity that is built around consciousness of the "immigrant condition." The "immigrant worker" replaces the poor as the focus of compassion in local Catholic discourse. Catholic priests espouse a brand of liberation theology by situating it within the context of international migration. Their intent is to raise immigrants' consciousness of their social condition and, on this basis, unite them as a community. They also seek to elevate the social awareness of their parishioners should they return to Brazil. "The ideal is to transform the mass of immigrants into political actors," Martes writes (2010, 53).

Yet the Catholic emphasis on the "immigrant worker" is disturbing to many Brazilians. Identifying oneself as an immigrant worker is often rejected because a majority of Brazilians believe that their stay in the United States is temporary. "Brazilians don't identify with immigrants because . . . they see themselves in a condition of temporary workers." Their objective is to make as much money in the United States as possible in order to return to Brazil "and go from being an employee to a business owner," hardly the aim of individuals immersed in liberation theology (Martes 2010, 66).

For Protestants, on the other hand, identity is based on common religious faith, not on their shared condition as immigrants. Evangelical rhetoric is attractive to Brazilian immigrants because it suggests that worshipping God can bring financial and social benefits. Illness, addiction, and problems at work or at home can be "cured" through faith in God. This discourse also glorifies work and encourages social and economic mobility; personal success is applauded. "The desire to 'make money in America' . . . is welcomed and reinforced . . . in evangelical discourse as it directly encourages becoming wealthier as a sign of salvation," writes Martes, suggesting that the evangelical emphasis on worldly success coincides with immigrants' own aspirations (2010, 154). One example: Protestant pastors do not disapprove of the common practice among Brazilian immigrants of "selling jobs," while Catholic priests label it "un-Christian." These different stances toward the world of work and success are reflected in dress. Attendees at Protestant services tend to "dress up" for them; men wear suits and ties, for example, whereas the clothes worn to Catholic Mass are informal, everyday wear (Martes 1996a, 1996d, 1999; Gibson 2010).

The decentralized nature of the evangelical churches also gives them more flexibility than Catholic churches enjoy in adapting to the changing needs of their immigrant congregants. This decentralization, along with the self-financing of church structures by local members, affords evangelical churches more ability to expand as their followers grow in number. The monetary contributions of their parishioners pay the pastor's salary and support church buildings. Local Catholic churches, in contrast, are partially funded by the Church hierarchy, making it more difficult to expand into larger spaces. Because of its flexible, decentralized structure, one researcher has called evangelical Protestantism a "non-territorial religion that is made to travel." As such, it is "an ideal religion for transnational migrants" because it is not tied to a specific location or territory (Freston 2008). Indeed, the Brazilian Baptist church in Boston encourages its members to "evangelize transnationally," and some members have converted family members in Brazil through phone calls and videotapes. Moreover, evangelical churches do not rely on national religious structures like parishes and dioceses. As such, they are easily reproducible and far less dependent on religious specialists than are Catholic churches. Catholicism can establish a presence in a region, but it takes much more time to do so. This is undoubtedly one reason why the number of evangelical churches catering to the Brazilian immigrant community has far outpaced the number of Catholic churches (Levitt and de la Dehesa 1998).

Aside from being fewer in number, Catholic churches offer more limited services than their Protestant counterparts. For example, many evangelical churches provide day care when immigrant parents are at work; the Catholic church provides day care only during Mass. "Our church is prepared to help the Brazilian from the time he [*sic*] arrives," said one Protestant pastor, whose church offers free English classes, helps pregnant women get health care and infant gear, and provides food and assistance finding work when church members become unemployed (quoted in Martes 2010, 48).

As a result of all these services, the daily participation of Brazilian immigrants in church-related activities is greater among Protestants than among Catholics, who tend to socialize and get together for parties only on saints' days and other religious holidays. Then, too, the pastors of the evangelical churches are more involved in the lives and personal problems of their immigrant congregants—in issues like legalization and the decision whether to return to Brazil or stay in the United States—than are the Catholic priests serving the Brazilian community. Writes Martes (2010, 45): "The manner in which the Protestant churches become the primordial locus of immigrant sociability is important to an understanding of the success of these churches among Brazilian immigrants, the vast majority of whom were Catholic before they emigrated."

In a real sense, evangelicals set themselves apart and can be easily distinguished from Catholics and nonreligious Brazilians by their lifestyle and dress, especially the dress of women, who are expected to follow evangelical notions of modesty. Evangelical pastors exhort their congregants to avoid places where they might be tempted to drink alcohol or dance to music that is not related to the worship of God. Brazilians who are not evangelicals tend to view their compatriots who follow evangelical doctrine as "fanatics" because they spend their lives in church and do not dance or drink—or, from the point of view of traditional Brazilian norms, appear to have very much fun at all. It is also true that if one participates in all evangelical church activities, there is little or no time to socialize with nonevangelicals, and such mingling is discouraged in any case (Martes 1999; Gibson 2010; Rodrigues 2011).

The religious communities Martes studied in Boston and presumably elsewhere also provide a "captive market" and "customer base" for church members who own businesses. A Brazilian business owner who is part of a religious network has a ready-made clientele. This is especially true of evangelical business owners, who are more likely to draw customers from their own church network than are Catholic business owners. After all, business success is much admired in evangelical circles. This may be one reason that the percentage of evangelicals among Brazilian business owners in the greater Boston area is much higher than their share of the Brazilian population as a whole (Martes 2004).

Although I have relied on Martes's analysis of community-based religious institutions in the Boston area, there are also vibrant Brazilian religious communities in many other locations in the United States. Orlando, Florida, for example, with a sizeable Brazilian immigrant population, is home to the Downtown Baptist Church, a church that had more than four hundred Brazilian congregants by the mid-2000s, in which Christian hymns are sung in exuberant Portuguese. A growing influx of Brazilians to central Florida has sparked a small boom in church services in Portuguese. As one local pastor pointed out, historically churches in the United States have sent missionaries to Latin America: "Now the Brazilians are sending missionaries to America" (quoted in Pinsky 1997). Beginning in 1990, local Protestant churches have sponsored a number of new congregations, but, to date, Catholics in the Orlando area have only one monthly Mass in Portuguese—celebrated by an Irish priest who served as a missionary in Brazil—and there are still no regular Catholic services exclusively for Portuguese speakers. So, in central Florida, as in the Boston area, Baptist, Presbyterian, and Pentecostal services for Brazilians far outnumber those available to Catholics (Denman 2006; Bustos 1995).

Brazilian evangelicals in New York City—who spend a good deal of their spare time "spreading the word"—also have made their presence known. Beginning in the mid-1990s, large contingents of young believers participated in the annual Brazilian Independence Day Street Fair on West 46th Street, where they carried "Jesus Saves" signs and handed out literature for the Igreja Missionaria Cristiana (Missionary Christian Church) in

Queens. Another sizeable group of young *crentes* (believers) at the street fair touted the religious services of the Igreja Peniel, also in Queens.[1] They were followed by a third contingent, this time from the Igreja Missionaria Brasileira (Brazilian Missionary Church), who held placards aloft that read "repent and ye shall be saved." Congregants of the Igreja Adventista Luso-Brasileiro (Luso-Brazilian Adventist Church) also were present busily handing out religious flyers. At the same time, amid the street fair's noisy, dancing throngs, two representatives of the Catholic Church and one devotee of Brazilian Spiritism sat quietly at small tables on the sidewalk handing out literature about their respective spiritual campaigns.

Brazilian Believers Abroad

What of Brazilian religious participation outside the United States? Our knowledge about the religious beliefs and practices of Brazilian immigrants in specific locales abroad is uneven, but researchers in two countries with Brazilian communities of varying sizes—England and Australia—have provided some detail about this sphere of their lives. These data, in turn, point to some similarities between religion as practiced by Brazilians in those countries and religion as practiced in the United States.

In England, some of the contrasts between Catholic and evangelical churches are reminiscent of those in the United States. There are some seventy Brazilian evangelical churches in London, and by 2010 there were a total of four Brazilian priests celebrating Mass in Portuguese at eight churches in the greater London metropolitan area. Such statistics are telling; here, again, evangelical services far outnumber Catholic services.[2] Then, too, while in the past foreign missionaries went to Brazil in large numbers to spread the Christian message, this route has been reversed, with religious clergy from Brazil arriving in England to expand their mission to include diasporic immigrants (Souza 2010; Sheringham 2010b).

One notable difference between the discourse of evangelical and Catholic churches in London relates to immigrants' legal status. Here, too, the politics of these divergent stances is reminiscent of those in the United States. While evangelical pastors seem to agree that some doctrinal and practical flexibility is necessary to meet the needs of immigrants, they are less tolerant when it comes to the question of legal status. In contrast to the Catholic clergy, who are openly supportive of undocumented immigrants, evangelical pastors are very troubled by immigrants who are "irregular," and congregants are strongly encouraged to "regularize" their status. Yet, despite the church's hard line, undocumented immigrants are still welcomed to church services (Sheringham 2010b).

These contrasting attitudes concerning immigration status also are reflected in clerics' explanations of the political positions of their respective churches. One Catholic priest in London who ministers to Brazilians in the city expressed pride in the fact that the Catholic Church was a leader in the campaign for amnesty for undocumented immigrants, a position very much in line with the liberation theology espoused by Brazilian priests in Boston. In contrast, the evangelical churches preferred to maintain their distance from the political sphere because, as one senior pastor explained, "We feel that it is not part of our mission to get involved with politics. Jesus Christ called us to bring the Gospel." While they recognize that there may well be some "unjust" laws, the church's perspective was that "the Bible teaches that we must respect those who govern, whether we agree with them or not" (quoted in Sheringham 2010b, 192). Parenthetically, the apolitical stance of Brazilian evangelical churches outside Brazil contrasts with the active political involvement of some evangelical churches, most especially the Igreja Universal Reino de Deus (Universal Church of the Kingdom of God) within the country.

As in the United States, churches in England are viewed by Brazilians as welcoming places of refuge in an indifferent, alien culture. One Catholic priest who ministers to the Brazilian community in London said he was well aware that, in the context of emigration, many people go to church to address their practical needs more than their spiritual ones. "People come to church more here than in Brazil," he noted. "The majority come to church because they feel a lack, be it of a sense of 'Brazilianness' [or] of their language." Or, as another Catholic priest who serves London's Brazilian community explained, there are three things Brazilians have to do in their own language: "*brincar, xingar, e rezar*" — joke, swear, and pray (quoted in Sheringham 2010b, 190, 192). While leaders from both evangelical and Catholic churches felt it important for Brazilian immigrants to conduct their everyday lives in English, they considered their churches spaces where immigrants could come to relax, to replenish themselves, and to find solace.

While there is less information about religion as practiced by Brazilian immigrants in Australia, we do know that their religious affiliations reflect their position both in the local social hierarchy and in Brazil. Here the contrast is between evangelicals and followers of Spiritism. Among Brazilian immigrants in Australia, as in Brazil, evangelical sects tend to be the choice of the "disenfranchised." The adherents of Pentecostalism in Australia generally do not speak English and come from "the lower echelons of Brazilian society," and their class position is reflected in the geographical location of their churches—in lower-middle-class suburbs of Sydney. Conversely, most Brazilian followers of Spiritism in Australia, as in Brazil, belong to the educated middle and upper-middle class and live in upscale beach neighborhoods in Sydney. Those who are devotees of Spiritism are usually professionals who are fluent in English, and they often work with or are married to Australians. The two groups of Brazilians rarely interact (Rocha 2006, 149).

Are There Communities in the Brazilian Diaspora?

The division of Brazilians along class lines in Australia, the United States, and several countries in Europe points to an oft-noted characteristic of Brazilian immigrant communities: aside from religious institutions, their common ethnicity does not bind them in organized, cooperative associations. Again and again, observers of Brazilian communities outside Brazil, as well as members of those communities, have remarked upon their apparent disunity and lack of ethnic-based organizations. It has been suggested that one reason for the dearth of these organizations is that if immigrants dealt with local problems by participating in such groups, it would be an acknowledgment that they were unlikely to return home. "If we begin working to help the community here," said one immigrant, "it means admitting that we are here to stay" (quoted in Levitt 1997, 523; Resende 2005; Margolis 1994a, 1994b; Martes 2010).

Coupled with the discourse of disunity are allegations that Brazilian immigrants undermine and "bad-mouth" each other. Researchers have been regaled with claims about the lack of trust many Brazilian immigrants feel toward their compatriots; as one told me, "I can count my Brazilian friends on the fingers of one hand." "I am ashamed of my race here," confessed an immigrant in New York City. "Brazilians run from each other," said another. "People try to destroy each other," declared a Brazilian immigrant in Boston. "There is a joke here that the FBI knows that there will never be a Brazilian Mafia because every Brazilian is an egotist." This discourse also has been reported among Brazilians in south Florida, where one local heatedly declared, "I don't have nothing [sic] to do with the Brazilians you will meet here. . . . They are just different." Part of this discourse concerns not wanting to be identified as Brazilian. Or, as another immigrant in Florida told an anthropologist inquiring about his nationality, "I *was* Brazilian" (Magalhães 2004; Rosana Resende, personal communication).

Often these divisions are expressed in terms of those "other" Brazilians, that is, those purportedly "less desirable" Brazilians. Among some Brazilians in the United States, a distinction is made between "good Brazilians," mostly middle-class immigrants who arrived here by flying in on tourist visas, and "bad Brazilians," those more likely to be lower-middle or working class and who could not get visas and who came to the United States via Mexico. A researcher in New York City points to a similar division between what she calls "national" and "transnational " Brazilians. Transnationals are geared toward life in the United States, while nationals strive for "economic prosperity" intended for the return to Brazil and a new life there. Transnationals are generally better educated and are more likely to be legal than nationals. They visit Brazil once or twice a year but have no plans to live there again, while nationals talk of nothing but returning home. The two groups have an uneasy relationship, with nationals accusing transnationals of acting "too American" and transnationals rejecting nationals as materialists whose sole interest is making money (Strategier 2006).

As we know, Brazilians who arrived earlier in this migration stream were mostly middle class, while those who came after around 2000 usually have more humble roots. As such, many of the divisions described earlier appear to stem from differences in social class. Some additional examples illustrate this point. Several Brazilian immigrants expressed frustration at having to leave New York City because of its high cost of living and to "move to the other side of the river," that is, to New Jersey. Brazilians living in the Big Apple often refer pejoratively to Brazilians who live in Newark— most of whom are lower-middle and working class—and other areas considered less "*nobre*" (upscale) than New York. In the words of one Brazilian, "it was horrible to have to leave Manhattan and go live with that Brazilian gang [*brasileirada*] in Queens"; another said that since she moved back to Manhattan, she "had stopped having nightmares of having to live in Newark." Hence, "the other" here are those lower-status Brazilians who live in less desirable parts of the New York metropolitan area (quoted in Costa 2004a, 13).

Similar sentiments are reported for Brazilians on the west coast and in south Florida. Middle- and upper-middle-class Brazilian immigrants in the Los Angeles area avoid other Brazilians whom they consider of lesser rank. These Brazilians "generally think of 'community' as a synonym for low class people," writes one researcher. Moreover, they refuse to "publicly associate or to admit affiliation with other [Brazilian] citizens," believing that disassociation from their "lesser" compatriots will make their assimilation into American society easier and more complete (Beserra 2003, 74–75). Similarly, a researcher in Florida found little unity among Brazilian immigrants there; once again, it was along class lines that the divide appeared. "Without doubt," she notes, "the split among social classes has the major responsibility for the fragile unity of Brazilians in the region" (Oliveira 2003, 136).

To be sure, such fractures and the paucity of ethnic-based organizations are not unique to Brazilians in the United States; they have also been reported in England and Japan as well. In London, for example, there is a relative lack of formal secular institutions that represent and mobilize the Brazilian community there. Then, too, there have been unconfirmed reports of Brazilians denouncing each other to the Home Office, a serious breach for those without legal documents. Sometimes the purported denunciations are based on competition between Brazilians in the same business. As a consequence of these allegations and the fear of denunciation they create, Brazilians exhibit a certain reserve when first meeting one another (Sheringham 2010b; Torresan 1994).

In Japan, when Brazilian immigrants meet, the first questions they typically ask are "Where are you working" and "How much do you make?," and the foremost topics of conversation are hourly wages and the amount of overtime earned. But there, as in some immigrant communities in the United States, longer-term residents—those who have been in Japan for four, five, or more years—criticize this fixation on money. In fact, this is but one of the fault lines between new immigrants and longer-term Brazilian residents in Japan. There are those who plan to stay for a few more years and those who do not, those who know Japanese and those who do not, and those concerned that Brazilians follow the rules and make a good impression and those unconcerned about such matters. These fault lines, in turn, lead to an ambience of distrust. Says one observer of *nikkejin* in Japan: "One doesn't have to be a researcher to perceive that the coldness and the lack of solidarity among Brazilians comes from rivalry, greed, jealousy and the desire to have an advantage—or better, not to be at a disadvantage—with others." Or, as one Brazilian immigrant in Japan told this same observer, "I thank God because where I work there are few Brazilians" (Roth 2002; quoted in Chigusa 1994, 48–49).

Why the Fissures?

The sociologist Ana Cristina Braga Martes agrees with the researcher in Florida that social class is the primary explanation for these attitudes and behaviors. Differences in social class among Brazilian immigrants, she writes, "have as their point of reference divisions that already exist in Brazil." Shared national roots are not always sufficient for individuals to identify and socialize with each other. Within the setting of international migration, past practices are recontextualized and social roles are designed to follow preexisting social hierarchies that determine "inferiors" and "superiors" (Martes 2010, 163, 183).

Aside from social class, these divisions are also based, in part, on geographical origin in Brazil, as was noted in chapter 3. Evidence for this comes from another researcher in Florida who suggests that the key reason for the disunity of Brazilian immigrants he interviewed is regionalism. For example, even though immigrants from the state of Rondonia, in the western Amazon, often work alongside immigrants from Minas Gerais, especially those from Governador Valadares, trust is lacking between *rondonenses* and *mineiros* because the latter have a reputation as "bad risks," of not paying their debts, and of duping recent Brazilian émigrés. As a result, Brazilians from the northern part of the country—Rondonia and Acre—mostly hang out with one another after work and avoid contact with Brazilians from the southeast, especially those from Minas Gerais and Rio de Janeiro. *Cariocas* (natives of Rio) in particular are dismissed as "*malandros*" (rogues) who are best avoided. Such "us"-versus-"them" distinctions based on natal origin and urban as opposed to rural residence in Brazil also have been reported among Brazilians in Boston. Here the "us" is big-city residents from Rio de Janeiro and São Paulo, and "them" refers to "peasants," "*valadarenses*," and "*mineiros*," as in the statement "the majority of Brazilians [in Boston] are ignorant and come from the backwoods" (Pedroso 2008; quoted in Martes 1998).

Occasionally this divide occurs along the lines of citizenship. While a majority of Brazilian immigrants view Brazil as "*um país maravilhoso*" (a marvelous nation), a small minority, mostly those who have become American citizens, see it as a "horrible, corrupt place." Some of these Brazilian Americans attribute the same negative characteristics to Brazilian immigrants writ large that Brazilians in the United States often attribute to Hispanics—that they are "dirty, disorderly people." In other words, those who have become American citizens want to distance themselves from the less desirable Brazilian "other," particularly undocumented Brazilians working in menial jobs. Here a "generic identification" with American society often means "a concomitant depreciation of Brazilian society" (Costa 2004a; Martes 1998).

Another explanation for the negative perception Brazilian immigrants have of each other and of their community is that it may reflect a broader national discourse transposed to the immigrant milieu. Anyone who has spent time in Brazil (and speaks Portuguese) has often heard Brazilians say, "Brazil is not a serious country" or "Brazil doesn't work" or "Brazil is a country of the future, and it always will be." These are common refrains among Brazilians both in Brazil and in the United States. Just one example: when I did field research on returned emigrants living in Rio de Janeiro, they continually compared life in Brazil unfavorably to the life they had lived in the United States. Paraphrasing them here, they said that it is much easier to live in the United States, where you don't have to contend with the red tape, the bureaucracy, the corruption, the impunity with which laws are broken, the violence that is so rampant in Brazil. Or, as one Brazilian put it: "Brazilians are the first ones to speak badly of Brazil abroad" (Margolis 1998b).

A subtle and intriguing analysis concerning community and ethnic cohesion among Brazilian immigrants was suggested by Peter Brown in his undergraduate thesis at Harvard. He argues that Brazilians have experienced less fragmentation than "ethnic ambivalence, the simultaneous pull toward the celebration of national identity and push against fellow compatriots." He points to the concurrent celebration of "Brazilianness" by individuals and small groups and a feeling of "alienation" toward this same *brasilidade* when it comes to the Brazilian immigrant population writ large. The concept of ambivalence toward one's ethnic group is preferable to the notion of "fragmentation," which ignores the strong approval Brazilians feel toward one another in terms of what they view as their positive qualities. In a word, the same individuals express positive views of Brazilians individually and negative views of Brazilians collectively. As such, the Brazilian immigrant community is not categorically disunited but rather is conflicted and subtly ambivalent (Brown 2005b, 5).

Brazilians have high regard for themselves and their compatriots in terms of their strong work ethic and overall decency, but they have negative views of Brazilians as employers and community leaders. This is the reason that immigrants in the United States overwhelmingly say that they prefer American to Brazilian employers, who are said to be exploitative.

And this is also the reason they are usually reluctant to participate in events organized for the entire Brazilian community. It is true, of course, that there are striking exceptions, such as the wildly popular Brazilian Independence Day street fairs in New York and other cities. While Brazilians say their fellow nationals take advantage of and distrust one another, most of their interaction is, in fact, with other Brazilians; the social networks of the vast majority of Brazilian immigrants in the United States consist almost exclusively of other Brazilians (Margolis 2009).

Entwined with the notion of ethnic ambivalence is the distinctly Brazilian concept of "*jeitinho*," a way of doing things by circumventing rules and social conventions, a means of cutting red tape or finding a loophole. Because of the tortuous nature of bureaucracy in Brazil, doing things through official or legal channels is often extremely complicated, so Brazilians fall back on *jeitinhos* to get things done and overcome obstacles. On the one hand, a *jeitinho* may be used to help another Brazilian find a job or a place to live; on the other, a *jeitinho* may involve undermining or taking advantage of a compatriot. So the *jeitinho* functions as both a "social glue and social repellent for Brazilians" (Brown 2005b, 71).

As a consequence of its dual nature, the *jeitinho* is a source of profound ethnic ambivalence. In Brown's words, "Brazilians . . . celebrate their ingenuity, creativity and improvisation, forming fast friendships among those with whom they share personal relationships," but they also "feel uninterested in working with the average unknown Brazilian for fear of the very *jeitinho* that makes . . . Brazil and Brazilianness so unique." Thus, according to Brown, the Brazilian community is not a fragmented one but a deeply conflicted one, a community with highly polarized relations that are intensely social when it comes to family, close friends, and church networks and profoundly disconnected when it comes to the broader ethnic population (2005a, 9).

Contradictions: Evidence of Unity and Community

Two final questions about community remain. First, are Brazilians in some way unique among immigrant populations in their supposed anti-communitarianism? Second, are they truly lacking in secular organizations? The answer to both questions is a resounding no. I entirely agree with Manuel Vásquez, a scholar of religion who has written that "we should be careful not to 'pathologize' the Brazilian immigrant as uniquely anti-communitarian. Internal divisions and relations of exploitation among Brazilians bear strong similarities with Latino groups, such as Salvadorans, Colombians, Dominicans and Puerto Ricans" (2009, 38). Indeed, there is abundant evidence of internal discord among other immigrant populations, and, as in the case of Brazilians, many of these fissures are related to social class.

In a study of Latino immigrants in Washington, DC, the anthropologist Patricia Pessar found that solidarity had been inhibited by the heterogeneity of Latinos in terms of national origin, social class, race, and time of arrival. All of these variables contributed to "an ethos of distrust, suspicion, and social distance" among Latino populations in that city. Ethnic cohesion was particularly problematic for upwardly mobile immigrants who were wary of dissipating their resources "through the shared reciprocity and social leveling implied by ethnic solidarity" (Pessar 1995, 389, 391).

Ethnic entrepreneurship also can be an impediment to ethnic cohesion. Here it is often assumed that immigrants use common "ethnic resources"—that is, shared values, social ties, and identities—to establish successful ethnic economic enclaves. Evidence suggests, however, that the more immigrants depend on resources afforded by their social class over those bestowed by their ethnicity, the less likely they are to create cross-cutting ties based on their membership in a particular ethnic or national group. This is true, for example, among Latino immigrant entrepreneurs in Washington, DC. Immigrants who brought "class resources" with them to the United States or were able to amass such resources after they arrived relied far less on ethnic capital to set up businesses than did other, less privileged immigrants. Moreover, such differential access to social and financial resources can cause friction. To make my point: the familiar rhetoric that divides Brazilian immigrant communities was also heard in DC's Latino community. "We are our own worst enemies," said one Latino immigrant, commenting on the disunity among his co-ethnics (Pessar 1995, 387).

Similar divisiveness has been reported among Salvadoran immigrants living in Long Island, New York. Immigrants arrive there burdened by financial woes—the need to generate significant income not only for their own living expenses but also to pay off travel debts, send remittances to their families, and save money for the return home. Such financial pressures often lead to the suspension of the social ties that were integral to their lives prior to emigration. As such, immigrants come to the United States "expecting to find their old community solidarity, but encounter a competitive, aggressive sub-culture instead." The material motives that fuel the lives of new immigrants help explain complaints about their current circumstances. Many immigrants are "people divorced from a social setting, operating outside the constraints and inhibitions that it imposes, working totally and exclusively for money" (Mahler 1995, 30; Piore 1979, 55).

Here I think it is important to emphasize that, despite the loud allegations to the contrary—that Brazilians "bad-mouth" each other and talk of nothing but the disunity that is rife among their co-ethnics—most recognize the help they receive from their fellow Brazilians and realize that the shrill discourse about a community on the brink of implosion is vastly overstated. Scholars who have studied several Brazilian immigrant communities report on the assistance Brazilians receive from friends and relatives and on how their compatriots help them find jobs and places to live. Even long after they arrive in the United States or at other destinations, immigrant employment networks continue to operate. They help Brazilians who have lost jobs find other work or get new jobs with better wages or working conditions. Finally, while Brazilians may not have many friends within the immigrant community, the fact remains that all or nearly all of the friends they do have *are* Brazilian.

What about secular organizations in Brazilian immigrant communities? While not very numerous, they do indeed exist. In the random sample of Brazilians in the Boston metropolitan area mentioned earlier in this chapter, more than half—56 percent—of Brazilian adults claimed to have been involved in at least one type of civic, religious, or Internet-based group in the year prior to the study. More than one-third—36 percent—attended religious events or meetings, one-fifth were involved in web-based groups, and another 14 percent participated in youth, sports, parent-teacher, neighborhood, or other types of organizations. However, even though the vast majority of Brazilian immigrants—85 percent—were familiar with at least one of the three community-based associations that today serve Brazilian and other Portuguese-speaking populations in the region, a mere 5 percent have been affiliated in some capacity with one or another of these groups (Marcelli et al. 2009).[3]

The greater Boston area contrasts somewhat with the New York metropolitan region in that, over time, it has had several more secular organizations that serve Brazilian immigrants, including politically active ones.[4] One explanation is that Boston's Brazilian community is somewhat older than New York's, so ethnic-based associations have had more time to develop there. Then, too, Brazilians in Boston live in a few neighborhoods and small towns in the region, whereas the Brazilian population in New York is more dispersed; these residential patterns also may help or hinder the development of community-based organizations. Still, just as important is the fact that Brazilians are not the *only* Portuguese-speakers in Massachusetts; it is also home to sizeable numbers of immigrants from Portugal, the Azores, and Cape Verde; after Spanish, recall that, as mentioned in chapter 5, Portuguese is the most widely spoken foreign language in the Commonwealth (Martes 1995).

The oldest of these organizations is the Massachusetts Alliance of Portuguese Speakers (MAPS), a social service agency dating from 1970 that receives funding from various local, state, and federal programs. While the program is intended for the entire Portuguese-speaking community, most of its employees are Portuguese, while the majority of clients are Brazilians. Despite the growing presence of Brazilians in MAPS, it has been criticized by some members of the Brazilian community for not providing them with services specifically related to labor issues and their legal status as immigrants.

Aside from MAPS, two other major groups serve the Brazilian immigrant population in the state: the Brazilian Immigrant Center or BIC (Centro de Imigrante Brasileiro) with an office in Allston and the Brazilian Women's Group (Grupo Mulheres Brasileiras). BIC was started in 1995 by a Brazilian who had work-related problems. An activist organization, BIC is particularly attuned to workers' struggles around labor rights and immigration. It has had a conspicuous presence in actions protesting anti-immigration laws and has helped individual Brazilians with work-related issues.[5]

The Brazilian Women's Group, also founded in 1995, primarily addresses the concerns of immigrant women. It has held workshops on several issues of interest to the community, including workers' rights and legal information, and is perhaps best known for its Vida Verde program, which is directed at domestic-service workers and provides training on the risks of chemicals in some cleaning products and the use of natural products that protect employees and clients alike.

The Brazilian Alliance of the United States or ABE (Aliança Brasileira dos Estados Unidos), an organization serving Brazilian immigrants in Connecticut, was founded in 2003 and is based in Hartford. The organization offers English and computer classes, advises small business owners, has programs for children, and lobbies for immigration reform, especially for passage of the DREAM Act, which would allow a path to legalization for young undocumented immigrants who are in college or military service.[6]

In the early 1990s, in New York City, not a single secular organization served the Brazilian immigrant community there. The long-established Brazilian-American Chamber of Commerce focused on Brazilian businesses and American companies with interests in Brazil, but it had no engagement with Brazilian immigrants in the city. Today, however, there is a nonprofit organization that is geared to the needs of New York's Brazilians, the Brazilian Community Center of New York (Centro Comunitário Brasileiro de Nova Iorque), founded in early 2009. With offices in Astoria and a website, Global Citizen (Cidadão Global), the organization informs Brazilian immigrants, especially those working as housekeepers, of their rights with regard to immigration issues and employment; holds get-togethers for Brazilian teenagers; offers English, GED, and computer classes; lobbies for additional ESL classes and immigration reform; and encourages Brazilians to participate in the U.S. Census. In short, although small in number, Brazilian organizations in several sites in the United States and abroad have been organized with the intention of meeting the specific needs of diasporic Brazilians.[7]

A final word about the general lack of unity in Brazilian communities outside Brazil: it may, in part, result from the muddled notions of Brazilian ethnicity that prevail in many of the countries where Brazilians immigrate. It is these contested ways in which Brazilians classify themselves and they, in turn, are classified by others that is the subject of the chapter to follow.

11 |

What Does It Mean
to Be Brazilian?

I was Americanized when I lived in Brazil. It was when I started to live in
America that I started to learn about my own country . . . only then I became
Brazilianized.

Brazilian immigrant in Marietta, Georgia (quoted in Marcus 2011a, 62)

The Brazilian anthropologist Darcy Ribeiro ([1995] 2000), as noted
earlier, opined that "the Brazilian people see themselves as unique,
as singular," which explains how difficult it is for Brazilians to accept
inclusion in any other ethnic or cultural group. Brazilians insist on keeping
their unique identity—and some might add superiority—in many dimen-
sions, both at home and abroad. Witness Brazilians' annoyance if any one
dares to suggest that Diego Maradona, the Argentine soccer star, is a better
player than the enduring Brazilian icon Pelé or their irritation at the be-
nighted confusion of samba with salsa on the part of non-Brazilians.
Consider also the insistence that the singularity of Brazilian *cachaça* must
be recognized and not subsumed under the generic category "rum" as
made in other Latin American nations (Tosta 2004, 580; Benson 2004).[1]

So what, then, does it mean to be Brazilian, as the title of this chapter
asks or, more precisely, what does it mean to be a Brazilian immigrant living
in a foreign land? One issue that affects the answer is invisibility, the non-
recognition of Brazilians as a distinct national or ethnic group in many of
the countries to which they have immigrated. As is the case in the United
States, this occurs in common discourse when Brazilians are routinely
confused with or subsumed under existing cultural categories. A second
issue that impacts the characterization of Brazilians abroad is ignorance,
and, here again, the United States is at the forefront. Americans' scanty

knowledge of Brazil and their tendency to stereotype on the basis of what little they do know influences the reception Brazilians receive when they move abroad. Moreover, it is only in the past three decades or so that Brazilians have been immigrants, so their status as foreigners is a relatively new experience for them. Simply put, for many Brazilians, the novelty of being "foreign" is discomforting, and they do not yet know how they want to identify themselves or how they want others to identify them outside their *pátria amada* (beloved homeland).

Brazilian Invisibility

In the United States, the invisibility of Brazilians dates back at least two decades. From the 1990 U.S. Census on, Brazilians have been either largely invisible or, as we have seen, seriously underestimated in terms of their numbers. Since 1990, Brazilians have been defined as "non-Hispanic" on census forms, and in the 2000 U.S. Census they were also excluded from the "Latino" category. This is why the Brazilian Consulate in Miami advised Brazilians, in an ad in a local Brazilian newspaper, how to fill out the forms for the 2000 U.S. Census. The Consulate recommended that, to be properly counted and obtain the benefits of recognition, Brazilians should check the "Yes, other Hispanic/Latino" box when filling out the form and then write in "Brazilian" in the space next to this option. But this was no longer a viable choice in the most recent 2010 U.S. Census, where it was decided— in very specific terms—not only that Brazilians are *not* Latinos but that anyone who checked that box and wrote in "Brazilian" would not be counted as such (*Brazilian Sun* 2000; U.S. Census Bureau 2006).

Part of the invisibility of Brazilians in the United States stems from the fact that, although they are Latin Americans, they do not fit neatly into the common North American conception of what that term means. As a result of their confused ethnicity, one of the very first things a Brazilian immigrant learns to say when meeting an American is "I do *not* speak Spanish!" Most Americans simply fail to differentiate the language and culture of immigrants from various Latin American nations. As such, most Americans do not realize that Brazil is distinct linguistically and culturally from the rest of Latin America, which is one reason Brazilian identity is often turned into a hazy and contested category within the context of international migration.

Despite the growing number of Brazilians in the United States, in some American cities their disputed ethnicity has made them quite invisible as a distinct immigrant group. In New York, for example, few New Yorkers seem aware that there are Brazilians in their midst, and Brazilians are rarely mentioned in the media or in popular or academic works dealing with the city's diverse ethnic mix. Similarly, one of the few journalistic references to San Francisco's burgeoning Brazilian community came during the 1994 World Cup Finals, when local Brazilians could no longer be ignored as they wildly celebrated their nation's triumph in the city's streets. In Boston, in contrast, Brazilians have greater visibility, perhaps because they are more likely to be grouped with that city's sizeable Portuguese-speaking community from Cape Verde, the Azores, and Portugal than with its resident Hispanic population, And today in south Florida, Brazilians have finally achieved wide visibility as their wealthy compatriots have been busily snapping up houses and condominiums in such large numbers that they actually have had a positive impact on Miami's faltering real estate market (Ribeiro 1999; Barrionuevo 2012).

Brazilians are also seriously underestimated and nearly invisible in *The Newest New Yorkers 2000*, published by New York City's Department of City Planning. One reason is that the data include only lawful permanent residents and exclude undocumented immigrants. Brazilians show up in the New York metropolitan area as twenty-eighth out of thirty immigrant groups ranked by country of birth. And Brazilians are not listed at all among the top thirty immigrant groups in any of the five boroughs that make up New York City proper (Lobo and Salvo 2004).

Brazilians occasionally use this invisibility to their own advantage. Since Portuguese is very rarely studied as a second language in the United States, it can serve as a code language among Brazilian immigrants, as a boundary marker, when they do not want non-Brazilians to understand what is being said. Reports suggest, for example, that some gay Brazilians in the United States say they value the ability to speak freely and honestly and that this is why it is just as well that their American boyfriends do not learn too much Portuguese (Dunn 1999).

Another potential advantage of Brazilians' invisibility in the United States and their absence from or underestimation in official statistics and in studies of undocumented populations is this: if no one knows they are here, they will not be viewed as a group of "illegals" that authorities seek to deport. This affords them space to continue immigrating and working unhindered. Of course, if Brazilians are employed at construction sites, for example, along with large numbers of other immigrants who are undocumented, they may still be vulnerable to anti-immigrant actions by the authorities. Nevertheless, given this broad invisibility, they may be somewhat less threatened than other undocumented groups who are more visible and who are known to be present in large numbers. I think this analysis holds true in parts of the United States such as New York City and Los Angeles, where Brazilians are but one of dozens and dozens of immigrant populations, but in places like Danbury, Connecticut, and Framingham, Massachusetts, where Brazilians have reached a critical mass in terms of numbers, they are no longer invisible and, as we learned in chapter 5, may be subject to anti-immigrant rhetoric and harassment. In other words, invisibility, whether of individuals or institutions, can be useful as a survival tactic (Klein 2012).

American Ignorance

Latin America is often portrayed in the United States as a single culture arbitrarily divided into different nations. Or, as President Ronald Reagan declared in the early 1980s upon returning from a trip to Latin America, "You'd be surprised. They're all individual countries." During that same trip, at a state dinner hosted by the American Embassy in Brasília, Reagan offered a toast "to the people of Bolivia." Then there was the following remarkable exchange between former president George W. Bush and former Brazilian president Fernando Henrique Cardoso: "Are there blacks in Brazil? Do you have blacks too?" Bush asked an astonished President Cardoso. Bush's national security adviser, Condoleezza Rice, came to the rescue. Noticing how stunned Cardoso was, Dr. Rice quickly said to Bush, "Mr. President, Brazil has probably more blacks than the USA. It is the country with the most blacks outside of Africa." President Cardoso later diplomatically remarked that Bush was "still in training" on Latin America (Rohter 2012; Sims 1995).

A 2000 survey commissioned by the Brazilian Embassy in Washington, DC, to gauge Americans' knowledge (or lack thereof) of Brazil found rather astonishing ignorance on the part of Americans about this vast country. Just under 40 percent of those queried believed that Spanish is the official language of Brazil, nearly 25 percent thought that Buenos Aires is the Brazilian capital, fewer than 20 percent knew that Brasília is the capital of Brazil, and a mere 13 percent were aware that São Paulo is the nation's largest city and is, in fact, the third-largest city in the world after Tokyo and Mexico City. Given the size, location, and economic importance of Brazil, the surveyors were surprised to find that most Americans possess low levels of knowledge about the country and that even some influential opinion makers—members of the U.S. Congress and their staffs—lacked basic information about Brazil. Similarly, a professor at an elite New England college found from surveys he gave students in his Latin American history class that fewer than 60 percent of them knew that Brazilians speak Portuguese; the rest thought that Spanish is the language of Brazil and that Portuguese is spoken only in Portugal (Reynolds, Young, Shkolnik, and Pergmit 2000; Davis 1997).

Two more examples of American's ethnic benightedness: In a bank in Marietta, Georgia, a Spanish speaker was hired for the specific purpose of dealing with the bank's Brazilian clients. Then, in an interview on National Public Radio, a Miami businessman, after noting that Brazil is Florida's "largest trading partner," said with evident pride that it was wonderful that so many residents of south Florida "speak that country's language," referring, of course, to Spanish (Marcus 2008b)!

Still, Brazilian identity is a sensitive issue not only among Brazilian immigrants in the United States; it can also be contentious among Brazilians in Brazil. American ignorance about their country and the tendency to depict it in simplistic stereotypical terms have long infuriated Brazilians. This was evident in the national uproar over a 2002 episode of *The Simpsons*, the popular American television program about a politically incorrect cartoon family. In the episode, the Simpson family visits Rio de Janeiro, where one family member is kidnapped by a taxi driver, another visits a poor child she sponsors in the "Orphanage of the Filthy Angels," while a third gets hooked on a racy TV show, *Teleboobies*. The Simpsons also learn to do a new Brazilian dance, a successor to the lambada, called the "*penetrada*," and all get mauled by monkeys running amok on Copacabana Beach. Although the episode was not shown in Brazil, news of it filtered back through outraged Brazilians living in the United States. The result was a media frenzy in which the show was called a national insult; members of the foreign press were informed that Americans think Brazilians are "inferior, ignorant, perverted dirty animals"; and municipal authorities in Rio de Janeiro threatened boycotts and lawsuits (*Gainesville Sun* 2002).

The Making of Brazilian Identity
in the United States

"Brazuca" is a colloquialism for Brazilians living in the United States, although most Brazilians do not use this term, preferring to call themselves simply "Brazilian." As recent immigrants in this country, Brazilians for the first time in their lives find themselves in situations where they are viewed as an ethnic minority. "Brazilian" becomes a marked category within the context of international migration because it raises questions of identity with which Brazilians have had little or no prior experience or consciousness (Margolis 2007).

Identities are situational, and being Brazilian in Brazil has a different meaning from being Brazilian in the United States, Europe, or Japan. For immigrants, the meaning of "being Brazilian" shifts from belonging to a nationality to belonging to an ethnic group and from being in the majority to being a member of a minority. Moreover, in most cases, this is an identity imposed by the host society, since Brazilians, as well as other immigrant populations, at least when they first arrive, are far more likely to identify themselves by nationality than by local ethnic or racial categories (Jones-Correa and Leal 1998).

In Brazil, Brazilian national identity is taken for granted; it is an abstraction that is rarely a signifier, since all those one meets on a daily basis are likely to be Brazilian. Agreeing with the Brazilian immigrant quoted at the beginning of this chapter, two researchers opine that "Brazilians learn Brazil only after they come to the United States." Most bring with them regional cultural imagery that is superseded only by national symbols—the Brazilian flag, samba, *capoeira*, September 7 Independence Day celebrations—once they arrive in the United States or Japan or elsewhere abroad. One immigrant told me that she was never conscious of being Brazilian until she attended a Milton Nascimento concert in Boston, where she was made acutely aware of her nationality by the enthusiasm of her compatriots, who fervently cheered their fellow countryman (De Lourenço and McDonnell 2004).

Brazilian identity, then, means very different things within Brazil and outside Brazil. Typically, an individual's reference point in Brazil is not nationality but city or state of residence or social class. But, while national identity at home is a given and seldom noticed, Brazilians abroad are classified as foreigners from a distant and, to some, exotic land. As such, when Brazilian immigrants go to a *churrascaria* in New York or drink *caipirinhas* in a Brazilian nightclub in Lisbon or when Japanese Brazilians eat a *feijoada* in Nagoya, Japan, they are not just going out to eat and drink; they are going out to eat and drink *Brazil*—to take part in a conscious "reaffirmation . . . of their identities as displaced Brazilians."[2] Ponder the contrast between a restaurant in Brazil and a Brazilian restaurant in Japan or in the United States or in Italy. Brazilian restaurants abroad conspicuously extol *brasilidade* in their food, drink, and decor, but, in a restaurant in Brazil, "Brazilianness is unmarked"; it is a "non-issue" (Linger 2001b, 75; 1997, 3).

How is ethnic identity commonly constructed in immigrant communities? The noted scholar Frederick Barth defined ethnicity as a form of "social organization," as a way of arranging and classifying differences among social groups. The boundaries that mark such differences are ascribed to the group both from within—by members of the group itself—and by others, by outsiders. According to Barth, it is not the shared culture that defines the group as much as the *differences* between that group and other groups. Similarly, the Brazilian anthropologist Roberto Cardoso de Oliveira has called ethnic identity "an affirmation of us against the others [which] arises from opposition [and] is affirmed by negating the other." For this reason, ethnic identity is always relative and contextual. "It cannot be defined in absolute terms but rather in relation to a *system* of ethnic identities" (Barth 1998; Cardoso de Oliveira 1976, 8–9).

These observations help us understand the construction of identity among Brazilians-outside-Brazil since their identity is built in part on what I call a "we're not like them" perspective, a stance I first noted among Brazilians in New York City and one that has been observed by other researchers studying Brazilian communities in Boston, Atlanta, south Florida, and Los Angeles. "We're not like them" refers both to social class and to ethnicity; that is, "the other" can be other Brazilians who are purportedly of a lower social station and less education than the signifiers, or, more commonly, it can refer to other immigrant groups, most often Hispanics, Spanish speakers, and those of Spanish-speaking descent (Margolis 1994a; Sales 1999b; Fleischer 2002; Marcus 2004; Resende 2002; Beserra 2005).

In the United States, the rejection of an Hispanic identity is not limited to Brazilians. Immigrants from Argentina and Chile are more reluctant to embrace an "Hispanic" or "Latino" label than are immigrants from Mexico and Central America. Similarly, many Peruvian immigrants in the United States, particularly members of the middle and upper middle class, are loath to identify themselves as Hispanic or Latino. These Peruvians "find the category Hispanic problematic because it brackets them together with the predominant minority groups in the United States, homogenizes national and cultural diversities, and classifies them as marginalized and stigmatized Latin American immigrants." Then, too, a nationwide survey of Hispanic adults in the United States found that the terms "Latino" and "Hispanic" are not fully embraced even by Hispanics themselves. A majority—51 percent—said they most often identified themselves by their family's country of origin, with only 24 percent saying they preferred a pan-ethnic label (Marrow 2007; Paerregaard, 2005, 82; Taylor, Lopez, Hunter, and Velasco 2012).

To Brazilians in the United States, "the other" in terms of social class refers to Brazilians of lower social rank. When I interviewed Brazilian immigrants in New York City, I was often told about a local Brazilian cohort that was "uneducated" and "lacked manners" or that "were poor representatives of Brazilian society." Yet, when asked for specifics—who are these people? where do they live?—the response was always vague. "Well, I don't know any of them *personally*" was a common refrain, meaning, of course, I would never associate with such people and only know they're here because I hear them speaking mangled Portuguese on the street or in the subway (Margolis 1994a).

Such discourse involving the construction of social boundaries has been interpreted as an attempt by Brazilian immigrants to relocate themselves within the local pecking order. Although all are immigrants, many are undocumented and have limited English, and a majority hold low-level, unskilled jobs, such efforts obscure these commonalties and seek to re-create the sharp social distinctions of Brazilian society. Through the creation of boundary markers, the immigrant son of an elite family from Minas Gerais who is working as a dishwasher in Boston and the immigrant daughter of a middle-class family from Rio de Janeiro who cleans apartments in New York City and the university graduate from São Paulo who is a short-order cook in Miami can distinguish themselves from a vague but assuredly less desirable Brazilian "other" (Martes 1998, 2000).

This discourse also reflects the intense attention paid to class distinctions back home. The Brazilian anthropologist Roberto da Matta has called Brazil a society "preoccupied with authority and hierarchy . . . [with] a place for everything, and everything in its proper place." Most Brazilians are highly attuned to class differences and are quick to size up the social distance between themselves and others they meet. Yardsticks of such distance are general appearance, including dress, manner, and the "correctness" of a person's speech. The degree to which an individual's vocabulary and grammar are considered cultivated is used as a gauge of schooling and, thus, social standing (Da Matta 1991, 140–41; Margolis, Bezerra, and Fox 2001).

Social class is an important but particularly fraught issue in the construction of Brazilian immigrant identity for yet another reason. Because Americans do not differentiate Brazilian immigrants by social class, educational level, prior occupation, or geographical origin, Brazilians in the United States go out of their way to use the symbols of language and culture, as well as behavior, to separate themselves from others whom they deem lower on the social scale. In other words, Brazilians view themselves as law abiding and orderly, a people that does not "cause problems" unlike other immigrant populations, read "Hispanics." In comparing Hispanics unfavorably to Brazilians, one Brazilian immigrant had this to say: "Everybody knows Rio de Janeiro! The Hispanic has nothing. What city will he talk about that is universally known?" (quoted in Marcus 2008b, 282).

A flap centering around the departing remarks of Brazil's consul general in New York, as reported in the Brazilian press, demonstrates that the Brazilian desire to remain distinct from Hispanics apparently reaches the highest diplomatic levels. In a farewell meeting, the consul general cautioned leaders of New York's Brazilian community "not to get themselves mixed up with the *cucarachas* [cockroaches]," referring to Hispanics. "Leave the *cucarachas* to themselves," he went on. "Don't get involved with them." Following the uproar surrounding his comments, the "diplomat" asked forgiveness for using the word "*cucarachas*" to refer to New York's Hispanic population. He insisted his intention was "constructive." His only aim, he said, was to ensure that the Brazilian community remained separate from stigmatized communities that suffer discrimination. The consul general then went on to affirm that Brazilians are well known for being "law abiding and hard working," in contrast to "other communities that are rowdy and form gangs" (Suwwan 2005a, 2005b).

Social class and ethnicity sometimes coalesce in Brazilians' attempts to distinguish themselves from other immigrant groups. In her study of Brazilian housecleaners in Boston, Soraya Fleischer (2002) notes that Brazilians highlight their ethnic identity by praising their own work ethic and comparing it favorably to that of Hispanic women doing the same job. Brazilians, they claim, are harder working, more thorough, and more reliable than Hispanic housekeepers. By being extremely fastidious, Brazilian housecleaners attempt to undercut the "cultural misunderstanding" common among Americans that all housecleaners are simple, uneducated people. Or, as one immigrant put it, "the only way to show who you are, if you don't know how to speak English, the only way to express yourself is through work." In this construction, Brazilians are such "*um povo trabalhador*" (a hardworking people) that, once an American family has hired a Brazilian housekeeper, it will never settle for one of any other nationality (quoted in Menezes 2000, 61; Sales 2003).

It is not surprising that such "cultural misunderstandings" are particularly rife when it comes to employment as a domestic. Domestic service is especially difficult for Brazilian immigrants because of its low status and the low regard in which household workers are generally held in Brazil. These jobs more than any others are antithetical to immigrants' own lives and personal experiences back home. Newly arrived Brazilians enter this menial segment of the American job market and are quickly shorn of their earlier social selves. This disjunction between social roots and daily reality provides a crash course in downward mobility, one that Brazilians doggedly try to mediate by presenting themselves as superior to the "run-of-the-mill immigrant" (Margolis 1990; Fleischer 2002, 53).

In this regard, Brazilians are subscribing to some of the very same stereotypes of Hispanics held by many Americans—that they "do not like to work" and that they are involved in gangs, drug trafficking, and other criminal activities. Writes one researcher, "By appropriating stereotypes [of Hispanics] already existent in American society and using them as a mark of difference," Brazilians perpetuate a bigoted ideology that helps maintain the status quo (Sales 1999b, 2003). In order to distance themselves from such negative typecasting, Brazilians underscore their own distinct ethnicity by differentiating themselves from Hispanics in terms of their work ethic, their physical appearance, their social class, their education, their language, and their culture. This demarcation is supported by the fact that, like most Americans, Brazilians do not distinguish Hispanics by national origin, combining them into one undifferentiated mass, a singular "other" (Tosta 2004, 583).

Essentially, then, Brazilian immigrants in the United States are embracing not only American ethnic stereotypes but American ethnic hierarchies as well. They seek to distance themselves from the negatives commonly associated with the Hispanic-Latino rubric and, in doing so, give themselves a leg up on the ethnic ladder. But these attempts to differentiate themselves culturally and linguistically from other Latin Americans do not spring full blown from the experience of Brazilian immigrants in the United States. They are also a product of attitudes brought with them from Brazil, where feelings of cultural pride and a belief in the uniqueness of what they term the "Brazilian race" (*raça brasileira*) are pronounced. Such attitudes, in turn, can be traced back to Portugal, where tradition says that "neither good winds nor good marriages come from Spain." By vigorously citing their Lusitanian heritage, Brazilians have always kept themselves distinct from Spanish-speaking Latin Americans and are quite indifferent to the Iberian roots they share with their Latin neighbors. Or, as the Brazilian anthropologist Darcy Ribeiro put it, "Brazil and Spanish America [are] divided into two worlds, back to back to each other" (Riding 1992, 13; quoted in Riding 1989, 15).

Brazilians' sensitivity about their distinctiveness from the rest of Latin America and the Spanish-speaking world, in general, is illustrated by their anger at Telefónica, the Spanish-owned communications company that took over the inefficient state-run telephone monopoly in São Paulo. Most agreed that the company provided excellent service, but Brazilians were infuriated that, while the company is called Telefónica in Spanish, it should have been called Telefônica in Portuguese. Public disapproval was so great that the company had to apologize for the slight and quickly redesigned its logo with the appropriate accent mark (Smith 2003).

Nevertheless, because of certain cultural similarities between Brazilians and Hispanics in the United States, Brazilians' attempts to maintain a sharp distinction between themselves and Hispanics give way at times to a feeling of connection with other Latin Americans—in food and music, for example—an affinity that is rarely if ever felt in Brazil. This is particularly true in cities with large Latin American populations, such as Miami. There Brazilians can go to a fast-food restaurant catering to Hispanics and dine on their familiar rice and beans and tropical fruit juices. South Florida is also a desirable locale because of the relative ease of communicating in *portunhol*, a jumble of Portuguese and Spanish. Some Brazilians say they feel more at home in south Florida than in other parts of the United States because of the region's prevalent *latinidade*. Said one Brazilian resident in Miami, "I like it here because it has a Latin ambiance with American organization." And, for some Brazilians, living in Florida provides a new lens through which they perceive their own identity. Or, as one Brazilian in Miami put it, "We come to Florida and discover that we are Latino!" (Oliveira 2004; quoted in Oliveira 2003, 132; quoted in Resende 2002, 3).

Identifying as Latino or Hispanic and the advantages or disadvantages that those rubrics entail are clearly situational. In Miami they can increase one's social capital because Hispanics are thought to have significant economic and political power in that city. In contrast, being Hispanic in Massachusetts often translates into ethnic discrimination. In the first instance, then, the affiliation can be advantageous, while, in the second, with a few exceptions—the ability to participate in affirmative action programs reserved for Hispanics, for example—being Hispanic means losing one's distinctiveness and being subject to anti-Latino prejudice and possible ill treatment. Similarly, in New Orleans, Brazilians are said to distance themselves from the city's Latino population in order to shield themselves from the brunt of anti-immigrant discrimination. Nonetheless, as a researcher in Los Angeles points out, "in situations where access to resources is enhanced, Brazilians do not mind being identified with Latinos" (Martes 2010; Gibson 2010; Beserra 2003, 66).[3]

But this is an exception. Most Brazilian immigrants go to considerable lengths to demarcate and highlight their nationality, as evidenced in the 1990 U.S. Census, in which more than 90 percent of Brazilian immigrants classified themselves as "not Hispanic." Since nationality and ethnic labels are not necessarily mutually exclusive, Brazilians could easily identify themselves as Brazilians while still accepting, at least for some purposes, a Latino or Hispanic label. But it is undeniable that in most instances Brazilians, especially first-generation immigrants, do not do so; rather, they assert their national identity despite whatever pressure exists to adopt a pan-ethnic rubric (Marrow 2003; Wilson 1995).

Here is how one Brazilian immigrant in Atlanta distinguished his compatriots from the local Hispanic population: "Culturally, we are different: our *churrasco* [barbecue], our *pagode* [a Brazilian style of music] is just different." He went on: "We don't have a race category here in the United States: our race is Brazilian! We are not Hispanics or Latinos! No . . . only Brazilian! I am not black or white: I am Brazilian!" (quoted in Marcus 2011c, 216). This assertion illustrates the way the term "race" is used in Brazil. Its meaning is more fluid than it is in the United States; in Brazil "*raça*" can refer to phenotype, ethnicity, or nationality.

This rejection of Hispanic identity is, indeed, most pronounced in the first generation of Brazilian immigrants in the United States. Or, as one Brazilian put it, "being identified as Latino is only better than being Hispanic . . . when one cannot be Brazilian." Said another: "Of all the Americas the one with the most influence in Brazil is North America, that is, the United States. So how can we come to America and become 'Hispanic'? When one comes to America and has to give up being Brazilian, it is to become an American." Research suggests, in fact, that it is easier for young people of the second generation, who possess a better understanding of the local ethnic system, to declare their *latinidade* in contexts where it is advantageous to do so. This is why second-generation Brazilians are more willing than their parents to identify themselves as Latinos (Menezes 2000; quoted in Martes 2007, 243, 250; Marrow 2004).

Where do race and physical appearance fit into the complex web of Brazilian identity? After all, Brazilians come from a country where the so-called whitening of the race is a part of its history, a nation where "people of color" are in the majority and where the myth of Brazil as a "racial paradise" lives on. They then travel to a country where the category "nonwhite" replaces "mulatto" and "*pardo*," where a simplistic dual racial system reigns, and where the "one-drop" rule still prevails.[4] In terms of race, a majority of Brazilian immigrants describe themselves as "white," although in the United States they quickly learn that, because of the one-drop rule, not all Americans view them as such.[5] In fact, when asked to declare their racial identity, many Brazilians prefer the category "other," which has a multiracial ring to it and gives them an opportunity to avoid the "Hispanic" and "Latino" labels. Moreover, the category "other" most closely approximates Brazil's prevailing national ideology that Brazilians are indeed "a mixture of all the races" (Margolis 2008a; Martes 2007, 2010).

Brazilian Identity Elsewhere

Our hardware is Japanese, but our software is Brazilian.
Angelo Ishi, Japanese Brazilian journalist living in Japan
(quoted in Wehrfritz and Takayama 2000, 29)

We have a good deal of data about how Brazilian ethnicity plays out in Japan, both for the Japanese Brazilians (*nikkeijin*) themselves and for the Japanese. In fact, the biggest conundrum and the most-discussed aspect of Japanese Brazilians in Japan is their ethnic identity. In Brazil they are perceived—and in many instances see themselves—as Japanese rather than as Brazilians, but in Japan they are viewed as Brazilians. Having grown up as "*japones*" in Brazil, the unexpectedly cool reception they receive in their ancestral homeland undermines their sense of their own cultural identity. When they immigrate to Japan, their ethnic pride plummets as they realize they are regarded and are treated as inferior to "real" Japanese. To flee this stigmatized image, they eventually come to define themselves as foreigners—as Brazilians rather than as *nikkeijin* (Ishi 2003; Tsuda 2003; Yamanaka 1997).

Many *nikkeijin* feel a deep affinity for Brazil as a multicultural and multiracial society where a majority have prospered at least to some degree. At the same time, they hold a sentimental attachment to Japan, since most *nikkeijin* were raised in families that highlighted their distinctive Japanese ancestry and valued things Japanese. Although most had never visited Japan before immigrating there, they still maintained a Japanese sense of themselves through the food they ate, the traditional festivals they celebrated, and, for some, the Japanese-language classes they attended (Linger 2001a).

In spite of these cultural and ancestral roots, after the move to Japan, the Japanese identity that most *nikkeijin* enjoyed when living in Brazil gradually begins to fade. Instead of becoming more Japanese, they become *more* Brazilian; that is, they have a far stronger sense of their own Brazilian pedigree in Japan than they had in Brazil. The longer *nikkeijin* reside in Japan, the more they come to think of themselves as a distinct Brazilian minority living there. Because they have few social relationships with Japanese and remain isolated from many spheres of Japanese life, they begin to emphasize and celebrate markers of Brazilian identity such as the samba, to which most were indifferent in Brazil. One researcher found that more than 90 percent of the *nikkeijin* she interviewed who had identified as Japanese in Brazil shifted their identity in Japan, either becoming Nikkei Brazilian or, far more commonly, simply Brazilian (Roth 2002; Koyama 1998).

This turn of events was perhaps as surprising to the Japanese as it was to the *nikkeijin* themselves. After all, the latter are of Japanese descent and share physical features and ethnic names with native-born Japanese, so few Japanese doubted that these *nisei* and *sansei* would readily adopt Japanese ways. When this did not happen, the Japanese began vilifying the *nikkeijin* because of their legacy of ancestral emigration from Japan—only "failures" left the homeland—and because of the belief that the newcomers' status as recent immigrants meant they also had been failures in Brazil. Then, too, unlike Americans and western Europeans, Brazilians commanded little respect from the Japanese because they came from what is viewed as an underdeveloped tropical land, because few of them spoke Japanese, and because they had low social status as unskilled factory workers. In sum, they were treated as "second class or defective Japanese" (Koyama 1998; Tsuda 2003; Linger 1997, 16).

Feeling unwelcome and not fitting into Japanese society, many *nikkeijin* adopt an overtly Brazilian bearing. As one observer put it, they "perform a Brazilian counter identity" by wearing colorful Brazilian clothes, dancing in carnival parades—many for the first time in their lives—and speaking Portuguese in public for one and all to hear. Indeed, Angelo Ishi, the Japanese Brazilian journalist quoted at the beginning of this discussion, notes that the sting of downward mobility and the disparagement of their ethnicity impels *nikkeijin* to reassert their middle-class status through intense consumption and by socializing exclusively in Brazilian spaces, including bars, dance halls, shops, and restaurants. Given life's difficulties for *nikkeijin* in Japan, Brazilian restaurants and similar ethnic meeting places serve as a "green and yellow beacon of welcome" with their casual relaxed style, which Japanese Brazilians contrast with the strained formality of Japanese venues. In such places, *nikkeijin* can feel comfortable acting like Brazilians. This is why such locales provide a "paradoxical message—that *one is not in Brazil*, for Brazil itself is never so overtly, intensely Brazilian" (Tsuda 2003, 263, 82; Linger 1997, 15).

In short, many *nikkeijin* are deeply distressed by the irony of being regarded as Japanese in Brazil and then, once in Japan, discovering the profound differences between themselves and native-born Japanese. But their anguish also stems from other shifts in status: after being regarded positively in Brazil because of their Japanese heritage, they become unwelcome in Japan because of their Brazilian roots; from being middle class and white collar in Brazil, they turn into a derided underclass holding low-level blue-collar jobs in Japan (Rocha 2009).

When *nikkeijin* travel to Australia after having lived in Japan, their status improves to a degree because in Australia they are simply viewed as Asians. This means that, while they can strategically draw on their "Japaneseness" for purposes of employment and social networking, they still bear the brunt of Australia's traditional anxiety about Asia and Asians. Most Brazilian immigrants are attractive to Australians because of their cheerful, laid-back, and party-going ways, but Japanese Brazilians do not share in these positive attributes because they are perceived not as Brazilian but as Asian (Rocha 2009).

Evidence suggests, then, that non-*nikkeijin* Brazilians are generally viewed in a favorable light in Australia. But, for the immigrants themselves, their ethnicity, as in the United States, is partly built around "othering"—maintaining distinctions in temperament and personality, in this case from Anglo-Australians. That is, once again, Brazilian ethnicity is constructed around difference. Their experience as immigrants enhances their notion of Brazilianness as something distinct and special—warm, spontaneous, and affable, as distinct from what they typecast as the reserved frostiness of the Anglo-Australian (Duarte 2005).

What about Brazilian identity elsewhere? We know far less about how Brazilians fare in this respect in other countries where they now live, although, as we know from chapter 6, Portugal is an exception because Brazilian ethnicity there—obvious to all through speech and behavior—is at times lauded and at other times denigrated. We also know that in some locales—Canada, Italy, France, and Portugal—the occasional desire *not* to be identified as Brazilian stems from the thorough interrogation that a Brazilian passport signals upon entry into those countries.

Some research does touch on the notion of *brasilidade* in Spain and Italy, especially as it applies to Brazilian women. But in southern Europe it is sometimes difficult to tease out ideas about gender, sexuality, and race from notions of ethnicity and nationality. In Spain and Italy, Brazilian women are often stereotyped as having certain attributes—an outgoing personality, a cheerful disposition, a deeply sexual nature, and, equally important, an innate propensity for domesticity and motherhood. Foreign men appreciate their style of femininity, which is seen as joyful, caring, and intensely sexual. Research suggests that Italian and Spanish men are most attracted by what they perceive as the "tropical sensuality" of Brazilian women (Piscitelli 2011).

As in the United States and Japan, many Brazilians in England say they have become "more Brazilian" living abroad, despite some of the negative stereotypes directed at them. According to one Brazilian student in London, Brazilians are generally seen as neither "civilized" nor "barbarous" but as some sort of "neutral" type that is neither British nor European (Rezende 2010).

Brazilian Identity and Transnationalism

The transnational nature of much recent immigration also plays a role in identity formation. Transnationalism is a process in which international migrants maintain their ties to the home country, despite its geographical distance, while living in the country of settlement. The term "transnational" is used to indicate the ease with which people, objects, and ideas flow back and forth across international borders. Where immigration was once viewed as either a permanent break with the immigrant's homeland or a temporary stay in the host country for short-term economic gain, we now recognize that immigrants often are engaged in two societies at the same time. In essence, transnational migrants refuse to choose between two nations when each nation offers them valued resources (Glick Schiller, Basch, and Szanton Blanc 1992a, 1992b; Basch, Glick Schiller, and Szanton Blanc 1994).

Brazilians are no exception to this transnational stance. Because most Brazilian immigrants in the United States and elsewhere see themselves, at least initially, as sojourners rather than as settlers, they maintain strong ties to Brazil and, consequently, to their identity as Brazilians. Sojourners continue being oriented toward their own country; they are often little engaged with the host society and live for the day they can return home. As Brazilians in New York City often told me, "We are here, but our heads [or hearts] are in Brazil." Such dualism is rooted in Brazilian intentions. Again, at least at first, a majority come to the United States, Japan, or any of several European countries for the purpose of making a new life for themselves or their families *back in Brazil* (Margolis 2001b; Chavez 1988).

Brazilians are bifocal, a posture that allows them and other trans-nationals to view their world through different lenses and to adopt different identities simultaneously. Depending on the point of reference, such a bifocal stance reshuffles the relationships among local, regional, and national identities. Regional origin is often an important social marker in Brazil, but in the United States, where most Americans know almost nothing about Brazilian geography, being a *mineiro* or a *paulista* or a *carioca* or a *bahiano* (a native of Minas Gerais, São Paulo, Rio de Janeiro, or Bahia) means little. When Brazilians must deal with outsiders, they submerge their local and regional identities, which are of little significance in such encounters, although they usually remain important within the Brazilian immigrant community itself. For example, in the North American milieu, sophisticates from Rio de Janeiro are eager to distinguish themselves from Brazilians from small, provincial cities like Governador Valadares, whom they consider uneducated rubes. But local and regional identities lose their relative weight when "the other" is a foreigner, whether an American or a European. Still, locality remains important in the organization of the migratory experience where people from the same town may band together to help one another. Identity, once again, is situational; it varies depending on whether one is dealing with a fellow townsperson, another Brazilian, or a foreigner (Rouse 1991; Ribeiro 1997).

Thus, while living in the host society, not only are transnational migrants classified according to local ethnic rubrics but their sense of self also remains rooted in their own nation and even in a particular locale within it. These fluctuating identities are both self-imposed and decreed by the host society. As we have seen, the vast majority of Brazilians choose to self-identify to non-Brazilians by nationality, while in most instances American society pigeon-holes them into established ethnic categories such as Latino or Hispanic.

What does all of this mean for the future? There are two possibilities. Ultimately, the continuing rejection of pan-ethnic Latino and Hispanic labels that other groups—including Mexicans, Cubans, and Central Americans—embrace may diminish the ability of Brazilians to join in solidarity with other immigrants from Latin America and may reduce their political influence. If this is the path taken, Brazilian Americans in subsequent generations may create a discrete cultural and political identity and further disengage from any pan-ethnic organizations that emerge. Given this scenario, it is likely that Brazilians will maintain their distance from Hispanic-Latino lobbying and other political activities and will take no part in the discourse surrounding a so-called Hispanic-Latino "race." As a consequence and given the *requisite phenotype*, many Brazilian immigrants and their descendants may eventually become "white" as the Irish, Italians, and Jews did before them (Marcus 2008b; Brodkin 1998).

Still, it is also possible that if Brazilians remain in the United States through the second and subsequent generations—which, in fact, some are now doing—they will eventually succumb to American ethnic labeling and find the Latino or Hispanic designation less problematic than it was in the past. If this is the case, they will eventually merge with a larger and more diverse Latin American population. Nevertheless, ongoing transnationalism among Brazilians may dampen such assimilative forces, raising the question whether international migrants can, indeed, assimilate to their adopted lands while still retaining their unique national identities (Sales 2007).

What of the future writ large? Will Brazilians choose to stay in their host societies and eventually blend into the "mainstream," or will they become one of the distinct national minorities in the countries where they now live? Or will most eventually return to Brazil? How have changing economic conditions both at home and abroad affected such decisions? And what of the next generation? How are they faring in the adopted homelands of their parents? It is to this future and its possible ramifications that we finally turn.

12

Here Today and Gone Tomorrow?

Returning is more difficult than leaving.
A former Brazilian immigrant
in Governador Valadares
(quoted in Siqueira 2011, 447)

We Brazilians without Brazil
Ah, what pain in the debate to stay for good or not
And together we will laugh so much
That we will cry from homesickness with tears, so lost and lonely
Tears that resemble us
Because we are Brazilians without Brazil
Caldeira (1996)

What does the future hold for contemporary Brazilian immigrants and the next and subsequent generations of Brazilians outside Brazil? There are many factors involved in the decision to stay abroad or to return home. In the United States, one "push" toward home is the anemic condition of the American economy, including the unemployment rate, especially in construction and other segments of the labor market that employ large numbers of Brazilians. The same is true in Japan and some of the countries in Europe, including Spain, where Brazilians have settled. A potential "pull" toward Brazil is the state of that nation's economy in terms of the availability of jobs that pay decent wages. On the other hand, Brazil's cost of living, which by 2012 had risen dramatically, especially in the nation's large cities, can be seen as a disincentive for the return home. Then there is the exchange rate of the Brazilian currency vis-à-vis the U.S.

dollar, the euro, and the Japanese yen. If the *real* is strong, as it was in 2012, then the value of remittances sent back to Brazil necessarily declines, making the stay abroad less worthwhile.

For the undocumented, all these issues come into play, along with others unique to their unsettled legal status. In the United States, among the most troublesome is the difficulty obtaining a valid driver's license. Only two of the fifty American states will issue driver's licenses to immigrants without proof of legal status. Then there is the widespread alarm about local and federal attempts to clamp down on immigrants without papers, including the pervasive fear of deportation. The lack of geographical mobility—that is, the inability to go back to Brazil to see family and friends or tend to personal matters with the assurance that one can freely return to one's country of residence—also can plague the undocumented.

Before assessing the specific conditions that greet Brazilian immigrants both at home and abroad, it is helpful to analyze the actual behavior of immigrants in terms of the decision to stay or to go. Here I am indebted to Sueli Siqueira (2009b), who, after doing long-term research on return migration to Brazil, distinguishes four key outcomes. She based her scheme on the behavior she observed in Governador Valadares, but it has broader relevance and can help us understand the motives and behaviors of Brazilian immigrants writ large.

First, there are those who return to Brazil for brief visits but who view the United States, Japan, or other destinations as their home. These are the places where they live, work, and invest. They travel to Brazil on holidays and for family events and take their children there to visit relatives. Many still follow local news but no longer save money to invest in Brazil, although they may still send remittances to family members living there. In sum, these are people who, for all intents and purposes, no longer reside in their homeland. Of those interviewed in Governador Valadares, nearly 40 percent fit this profile (Siqueira 2009b).

A second outcome is characteristic of emigrants who return to Brazil purportedly "for good," invest their savings locally, and eventually lose everything because of inexperience in business matters or because they invested in a venture unsuited to local conditions. Or perhaps they simply are unable to readapt to life in Brazil. In any event, they re-migrate to the United States or to a destination in Europe or Japan. This is the "yo-yo migration" mentioned earlier, in which the departure and return may take place several times.

A good deal of evidence for this second scenario comes from Governador Valadares itself. Well over one-third of emigrants who returned to that city subsequently re-migrated to the United States because of failed investments, family problems, or the inability to readapt to life in town. And when travel to the United States was not possible, some chose to immigrate to Europe because they had relatives in Portugal, Spain, or Italy.

Like the immigrant quoted at the opening of this chapter, most of those interviewed said it is much more difficult to return to Brazil than to leave Brazil. An unwanted return is especially difficult for those emigrants who for several years had defined the United States as their home. In such cases, an unplanned return to Brazil to live represents an undoing of the dream built on long hours of hard work. When emigrants depart, they are full of hope for the future, but, when they return, they may have a sense of alienation from their hometown and from their old social universe. Simply put, they experience culture shock in reverse. When emigrants leave their country, they fully expect to feel alien and out of place, but, upon their return, many entertain the illusion that one simply has to step off the plane to feel at home. Says Siqueira about her findings, "It's the most perverse aspect of emigration when people come back home and feel like strangers in their own homeland. People feel lost, stuck in the middle, because in the United States, they also feel like foreigners. They become strangers in both lands" (Siqueira 2009a, 2009b; quoted in Mineo 2006h).

The third course is taken by those who go back to Brazil permanently and actually remain there. These are the emigrants who return home, have little difficulty readapting to life in Brazil, and have no plans to migrate again. Many of them are successful investors in local businesses and credit their time as emigrants, including the money they saved during their sojourns abroad, for their financial success. These are the individuals who fulfill the initial aspirations of the vast majority of Brazilian emigrants: to live and work in a foreign land for a few years in order to better one's life back home in Brazil.

The fourth path is followed by those who are true transnationals, those who actually live their lives in two nations. For example, there are Brazilians who reside in the United States and vacation in Brazil for one or two months every year. They own houses and cars in both countries and may have investments in both. They have close personal relationships in both places and are fully incorporated into each one. Such emigrants refuse to choose between two nations when both provide them with relationships and a way of life they value. As a consequence, their economic, political, cultural, and personal ties span international borders.

In the United States today, the last path—transnationalism—is possible only for Brazilians who have green cards or who have become American citizens. Since September 11, 2001, it has become increasingly difficult for immigrants of nearly all nationalities to be transnational, to easily travel back and forth between the United States and their home countries if they lack proper documents. The Brazilian Consulate's former liaison to the Brazilian community in New York City told me she received desperate phone calls from Brazilians who had been barred from re-entering the United States on their return from Brazil. In nearly all cases, they had previously worked and resided illegally in the United States, and when they returned, even with new visas or passports, they were stopped cold by U.S. immigration authorities (Costa 2004a).

Having a green card or American citizenship can play a critical role in the decision of some to return to Brazil. At first glance, this is counter-intuitive, since one would assume that having a green card or being a citizen and therefore being able to work legally would be an incentive for *staying* in the United States. But, in fact, a green card or U.S. passport provides immigrants with more options in that if they return to Brazil and regret the decision, they can easily re-migrate to the United States—within a year as a green card holder or at any time as a citizen. So having such options makes it easier to return home (Martes 2010).

Returning Home

Are Brazilian immigrants actually going back to Brazil? And, if so, how many and what is the specific evidence that they are doing so? According to the 2010 Brazilian census, in the five years between 2005 and 2010, almost 175,000 Brazilians returned to Brazil from abroad, twice as many as returned in the previous five-year period. Of these returnees, 52,000 had been living in the United States, 41,000 in Japan, 25,000 in Paraguay, and 21,000 in Portugal. Then, too, the 2011 American Community Survey found that the Brazilian population in the United States declined by a little over 8 percent between 2009 and 2011. The greatest decline was in Massachusetts, where, between 2005—its peak—and 2011, the Brazilian population fell by 22 percent.

There are also what I would characterize as "guesstimates" of the size of the returnee population provided by Brazil's Ministry of Foreign Affairs. The Ministry estimates that since the economic recession began in 2008, 20 percent of Brazilians living in the United States and a quarter of those in Japan have returned to Brazil. Similarly, the Center for Brazilian Immigrants in Boston suggests that some 15,000 to 20,000 of the state's 200,000 Brazilians left for home in 2008 and 2009 and expects additional departures in the future unless the economy improves and immigration reform allows the undocumented to work legally. Finally, from the perspective of the receiving end of this immigrant inflow, local officials in Governador Valadares estimate that about 10 percent of the local population living in the United States or up to 2,500 individuals returned to town during the early months of 2008, although some 30,000 *valadarenses* still live in the United States (Instituto Brasileiro de Geografia e Estatística 2012; TV Globo 2012a; Barnes 2009; Fornetti 2012b; Duffy 2008).

There are other, albeit indirect, indicators of this return, some from travel agents with a Brazilian clientele. One agent in Danbury, Connecticut, claimed that the number of Brazilians buying plane tickets for the return home increased after 2006 and that their profile changed, as well. "Before, it was men who supported their families in Brazil; now it is entire families" that are leaving, she said. Another in the Boston area said she had sold several thousand one-way plane fares to Brazil in 2007 alone, while a third travel agent in Newark, New Jersey, claimed to have sold 7,500 one-way return tickets to Brazil the following year. But the owner of another travel agency in Danbury insisted that some Brazilians bought one-way tickets to return home but later changed their minds. Why? "Bad here, worse there," they said (Siqueira, Assis, and de Campos 2010; quoted in Schreiber 2009).

Among the few businesses said to be booming in Brazilian communities across the United States are moving companies. Two months after opening its doors in Danbury in 2009, one moving company already had signed some fifteen or twenty contracts with local Brazilians to move their household effects back home. The manager of a moving company in New Jersey said the number of such contracts had increased by about 30 percent in 2009 compared to two years earlier, and the owner of a third company in Framingham, Massachusetts, also noted a large increase.[1] Personnel at the Brazilian Consulate in Miami estimate that, on the basis of data from moving companies in the area and one-way airline tickets sold by local travel agents, the number of Brazilians returning home has tripled since 2007. Moreover, when Brazilians decide to return home after residing abroad, they have to fill out a form for Brazilian customs declaring what property they are taking with them. The Brazilian Consulate in Miami reports that it processed about five of these forms a day in 2007 but that by 2010 it was processing around fifteen forms daily (Siqueira, Assis, and de Campo 2010; Schreiber 2009; Godoy 2007; BBC Brasil 2007).

Another indicator is the decline in other businesses that traditionally cater to Brazilians, and, indeed, owners of remittance agencies and other small enterprises that serve Brazilians are fearful of a drop in clients as Brazilian immigrants return home. This worry has been especially strong since 2008, when the financial crisis hit the American economy. "Over the last four years business has fallen off drastically. Many people are returning [to Brazil]," said a clerk at the Padaria Brasileira (Brazilian Bakery) in Newark, which recently reduced its space to adjust to the loss of business. Sales at a jewelry store in Framingham were down 75 percent, and the owner says she may have to close. "Once shops like mine won't make it through, they will realize what they lost," she said of local residents. Still, very few Brazilian businesses in that city have actually closed, although some new ones that send personal belongings back to Brazil may indicate an uptick in returns there (Fornetti 2012a; Ryssdal 2008; Skorczeski 2009).

Those "Push" Factors

What, then, are the specific "push" factors that have led Brazilians to abandon their host nations and return home? From 2007 on, the single leading catalyst for the return to Brazil has been the economic crisis in the United States, several countries in Europe, and Japan. A study of nearly four hundred Brazilians who left the United States for Governador Valadares over that period found that more than 40 percent returned to Brazil because they were working less and therefore earning fewer dollars. Prior to the economic meltdown, some townspeople held up to three jobs and earned as much as $20 an hour. But, with the onset of these economic woes, many were earning only $9 an hour, and they deemed remaining in the United States simply not worth the sacrifice (Siqueira, Assis, and de Campo 2010; Caitano 2010a; Máximo and Faleiros 2010).

In Newark, New Jersey, Mount Vernon, New York, Pompano Beach, Florida, and elsewhere, Brazilians have been leaving for home by the hundreds because of a decline primarily in construction and housekeeping jobs.[2] In a single month in 2009, some fifty Brazilian families in Newark—including many who owned real estate there and had not planned to leave—pulled up stakes and headed home. As a consequence, the number of patrons in local restaurants, grocery stores, hair salons, and other businesses owned by and catering to Brazilians is down. According to the editor of Newark's Brazilian newspaper, while many Brazilians are indeed leaving the area because of lack of jobs, not all are returning to Brazil. Several are traveling to other states—he gave Florida and California as examples—in search of employment. Some men in Newark are leaving their spouses and children behind to seek work elsewhere in the United States (Bernstein and Dwoskin 2007; Buechler 2010; Francisco Sampa, personal communication).

One unexpected outcome of the economic downturn in the United States is that both documented and undocumented immigrants are being deeply impacted by it. Almost 40 percent of those interviewed in Governador Valadares had been in the United States legally but nonetheless had returned to Brazil because of the economic difficulties they encountered in their adopted country. Still, many Brazilians who have green cards or who have become American citizens—about 25 percent of those returning home in one sample—hoped the crisis would pass and that they would then be able to return to the United States and find work. Thus, they saw themselves living in Brazil "temporarily." Should the U.S. economy improve, they would consider returning to their adopted land (Martes 2010).

Not only are more Brazilians going home because of the weak U.S. economy, but also fewer are arriving in the first place. "Zero. Zero. Zero. No one is coming from Brazil," says a Brazilian in Framingham as he counts the handwritten entries in his notebook, which is used to register immigrants who are looking for work. The director of the Bom Samaritano social services center in town says he now gets at most a handful of inquiries each day. This has happened because word of the crisis has indeed traveled back to Brazil. In 2008, potential emigrants there told an inquiring researcher that, while they would still like to go to the United States, they were afraid to make the journey because they knew many people who were unemployed there. This shows that transnational connections to friends and relatives living in this country influence decisions to stay home or go to join them. It also tells us that, with the onset of the economic crisis, Brazilian narratives that view the United States as a land of milk and honey have begun to fray (Siqueira 2009b; Gibson 2010).

I began work as a shoeshine man in 2004 when a Brazilian friend left for Florida. He sold me his shoeshining kit, and I took over his business and some of his regular clients. I did well for a few years. I'd take my shoeshine kit to offices in Manhattan, Queens, and Long Island.

My best clients were guys at the mortgage companies. I used to go by several mortgage and brokerage offices—in Midtown Manhattan, in Queens. Most of the guys who worked there were young, and they gave good tips.

My problems started in 2007 when the mortgage crisis hit. I asked my friends who also work as shoeshiners because I was thinking maybe it's just me, but they said it was happening to them, too.

At first people just started cutting back a little. Clients who usually got a shine every week now had a shine every two weeks. You think it's not much because a shoeshine costs only $5 with maybe a $1 tip. But when everybody starts spending less, it really hits home.

Then, in 2008, the mortgage offices began closing down. I used to have a route of ten different mortgage offices, but in the last year nine of the ten closed. I had been making $4,000 a month, but now I barely take home $2,400 or $2,500 a month. (cont. p. 211)

In the United States, another "push" toward home has been the crisis in the real estate market. Brazilians, along with other immigrants, were targets of subprime-mortgage lenders since most lacked good credit histories or proof of employment and income. Moreover, their immigration status apparently was of no consequence to these lenders. Some mortgage companies offered financing to Brazilians and other immigrants without requiring documentation of any kind. As a result, beginning around 2007, many Brazilians—documented and undocumented—in Framingham, Newark, and other Brazilian communities in the United States were able to buy houses with subprime loans. Because of easy credit, many deemed this a good deal because their mortgage, at least initially, cost only a little more than what they were paying for rent. Moreover, they could divide their houses into two or three separate living units, one for their own family and the others to rent out. The rent money, in turn, would help pay off the mortgage.

All of this changed once higher interest rates kicked in. The mortgage of one Brazilian family in the Boston area, for example, increased from $1,500 to $2,600 a month—and this at a time when, because of the weak economy, the husband, who had a job in construction, was working fewer hours and his wife, who cleaned thirty houses, lost more than one-third of her clients. As a subprime, high-risk borrower, the family had to pay an interest rate on the mortgage that suddenly rose to 12 percent annually. Not having paid much attention to the details in the mortgage contract, the family became aware of the problem only once monthly payments skyrocketed (Siqueira 2009b).

This scenario was not uncommon. According to the founder of the Brazilian Immigrant Center in Massachusetts, about thirty thousand Brazilians in the state own their own homes, and many are having trouble paying their mortgages. "Everyday," he said, "I get calls from 20 people who have difficulties paying for their houses. When a person has a large debt and also owes a lot on credit cards, we counsel them to declare personal bankruptcy" (quoted in *O Globo* 2007). Likewise, it is estimated that 30 percent of homes owned by Brazilians in the Newark area went into foreclosure; all had subprime mortgages. As an upshot of these events, some Brazilians simply despaired and abandoned everything; they shut the doors to their homes, left the keys behind, and departed for Brazil. One calculation is that as many as five thousand Brazilians have left the United States because of such mortgage debts and the concomitant difficulty of finding employment to help pay them off (Siqueira, Assis, and de Campo 2010).

The exchange rate between the Brazilian *real* and the currencies of the nations to which Brazilians immigrate is another salient "push" factor in the equation of return. Researchers agree that when foreign currencies are weak vis-à-vis the Brazilian *real*, making sending remittances to Brazil much less attractive, the desire to remain abroad and keep working in order to send money home is diminished. In mid-2007, the *real* reached a high of $1.94 against the dollar, and it has remained strong ever since. Similarly, one catalyst for the return home of Brazilians who had been living in

(Cont. from p. 210)

Last year me and my wife started talking about going back to Brazil. The economy there is much more stable than when we left. Back in Brazil I'd look for a job as a mechanic, which I'm trained for. All my brothers and sisters are there, and I've been away for so long. . . .

Our biggest problem now is that we can't save anything anymore. We're barely making enough to make ends meet. To live away from your own country . . . for what? You can't save anything. It just doesn't make sense. We had planned to wait until the end of the year, but things are just getting worse. Now we are thinking of leaving sooner. (Huff-Hannon 2009)

England is the weakness of the pound sterling in relation to the *real*. The consequences of a strong Brazilian currency back home are very real. Some twenty-five towns and cities in the region of Governador Valadares, for example, felt the economic impact and experienced a significant drop in real estate and other local investments because of the strength of the *real* (Marcus 2008; Máximo and Faleiros 2010; Moreira 2007).

Far harder to quantify is the role that fear plays in the return home, but there is little doubt that it is a significant one. In one survey of returnees, fully 37 percent said they left the United States because of the crackdown on undocumented immigrants and the risk of arrest and deportation. The stress of being undocumented, of receiving daily reports of people being stopped for minor traffic violations and running the risk of being detained and deported, are everyday narratives that cause high anxiety in Brazilian communities across the United States. In south Florida, the expiration of a driver's license is often a turning point for families already suffering from the slump in construction jobs. "There's no public transportation here in Florida, so people drive to work in fear and trembling," said one resident familiar with conditions there. But even with a driver's license many become fearful at the sound of a police siren.[3] Some Brazilians have simply given up and said, 'I've had enough'" (Siqueira, Assis, and de Campo 2010; quoted in Bernstein and Dwoskin 2007).

The vice consul at the Brazilian Consulate in Miami said one reason for the exodus from south Florida is the fear that gripped undocumented Brazilians as the number of their undocumented compatriots who were imprisoned and deported rose sharply. In his consular district alone, more than 150 Brazilians were deported in the last five months of 2007, and, according to a Baptist pastor in Pompano Beach, perhaps the largest Brazilian community in the state, "this is the worst crisis confronting the Brazilian community in the U.S. in the last seventeen years. I never heard as many of my compatriots deciding to return to Brazil" (BBC Brasil 2007).

The Brazilian owner of a jewelry store in Framingham who has lived there for sixteen years and is an American citizen takes credit for helping to revitalize the city's downtown. Still, Framingham officials have turned "hostile" to the local Brazilian community, she claims. Police have begun to demand documentation, and city officials have stopped returning calls. "We felt at home," she says, "but it has changed. I feel violated. I tried to be a voice for my community," but now "there is no one out there listening. Their agenda is being fulfilled. We are disappearing by the minute" (quoted in Ryssdal 2008).

Such is the level of anxiety among undocumented Brazilians that many have prepared themselves in case they are caught in the vise of ICE—the acronym for U.S. Immigration and Customs Enforcement. "They're sending their belongings to Brazil because they don't want to lose everything they bought here if they're caught," said one merchant in Massachusetts who says he is selling shipping containers like hotcakes. "They want to be caught with the minimum, with only the clothes they have on" (quoted in Mineo 2007).

All sorts of other precautions are being taken. In recent years, the size and number of Brazilian flags displayed in Boston and in other Brazilian communities in the United States has been reduced. Not only are such signs of "foreignness" less likely to appear on cars or poking out of apartment windows, but even Brazilian-owned businesses are more reluctant to call attention to their ethnicity. Some stores that cater to Brazilians now conspicuously display only American flags. This is a strong sign that Brazilians are not untouched by the virulent anti-immigrant rhetoric heard in some quarters of this country. Then, too, Brazilians, along with other immigrants, were extremely disappointed when the U.S. Congress failed to pass immigration reform in 2007 and when the DREAM Act was similarly shot down three years later. "Brazilians who . . . became tired of waiting for immigration reform are also leaving the country. You can't spend your entire life waiting to be legal," said one undocumented immigrant (quoted in Bernstein and Dwoskin 2007).

To illustrate how important the politics of immigration reform and fear of detention and deportation are in the calculus of the future plans of Brazilian immigrants in the United States, I offer quotations from two researchers studying Brazilians in this country, the first in New Orleans and the second in New York City:

> I get asked about what I think Obama will do about immigration almost daily here in New Orleans. I also met a recently arrived immigrant (on his second trip) who decided to come back to NOLA because Obama was in power and he wanted to be here in case of amnesty.

And in New York City:

> So far what I am finding out is that many decided to stay after Obama won (Gibson 2012; Daniela Medina, personal communication).

Other Returns: England, Europe, and Japan

The economic crises in other immigrant destinations also have some Brazilians packing their bags and heading home. While we know this exodus is taking place, we know less about what it has meant for the locales they left behind. Ericeira, a small Portuguese city fifty kilometers from Lisbon and a redoubt of Brazilian immigrants, may indicate a more general pattern. Early in the millennium the number of Brazilians living there reached four thousand out of a population of thirteen thousand but by 2012 barely fifteen hundred remained. And of the Brazilians still there, 35 percent have said they will return home sometime in the near future. As a result, the sales in local supermarkets are down by 60 percent, many real estate offices have closed, restaurants are empty, and small shopping centers have been abandoned. "Some months back representatives of a Spanish construction company arrived here and recruited unemployed Brazilians to work on construction projects for the 2014 World Cup in São Paulo. Everyone left," said the owner of a bar in town, who measures the financial crisis by the volume of drinks he sells. In 2006 he sold twenty kegs of beer a day, while six years later he was barely selling two kegs daily (Belchior 2012).

What are the conditions that led to this exodus? In England, working conditions have worsened since the financial crisis began as lower wages forced immigrants in unskilled jobs to look for more than one position. The earnings of a Brazilian who had been in London for five years and who worked as a "*motoboy*," a courier who delivers documents to business offices, fell from £500 to £350 ($790 to $553) a week. For new arrivals who can find no work, "that's a good excuse to return home," said the founder of the Casa do Brasil, an NGO in London. Even though some complain, the majority of Brazilians still see England as a land of opportunity. "Here hours might be cut, but not jobs like in Spain and Italy. The Brazilian who arrives here and wants to work finds work the same day," he said (quoted in Máximo and Faleiros 2010).

As late as 2007, more Brazilians appeared to be arriving in London than were leaving for Brazil. One observer suggests that, thus far, the economic downturn in Britain and the growth of the Brazilian economy have not created a large exodus of immigrants. According to one study, while most Brazilians in London—nearly 60 percent—eventually want to return home, their plans are on hold because of the reasons that brought them to England in the first place. "Many came for economic reasons or because they had family here. This makes them think twice before returning," writes one researcher. More middle-class immigrants, she notes, tended to be leaving for Brazil, perhaps attracted by good job prospects there. For poorer immigrants, making money in Britain is not as easy as it once was. People who work as housecleaners and in restaurants are complaining because, whereas ten years ago £1 bought six *reais*, now it buys only three (Pinto 2012; Pereira 2008a).

Although the numbers are uncertain, a decline in the Brazilian population in London has been reported by merchants who cater to them. "The Brazilians have disappeared. We are trying to hire someone who is fluent in English to attract more than just Brazilians," said one shop owner, who continued, "In every ten clients we had, six left for Brazil." The owner of a store selling Brazilian products near Victoria Station believes that many Brazilians decided to return home in late 2009, and, as a result, she lost a number of good customers. Late in the year in London, when it gets cold and dark at 4:00 in the afternoon, the "tropical immigrants" get depressed and head home, she said (Pinto 2012; quoted in Máximo and Faleiros 2010).

Some Brazilians have gone back to Brazil but then re-migrated to the continent, saying they were disenchanted with the Brazilian boom and that the quality of life still remains better abroad. One Brazilian is back in London after spending six months in Brazil. He first arrived in England in 2009 after living in Portugal for eight years. "When the situation got worse in Portugal, I thought about going back to Brazil, but then I decided to take a chance and learn English in London," he said. Like him, some Brazilians move from country to country in Europe, leaving those locales where the economic crisis has had a greater impact and heading instead to places like London, where they say there is still the promise of a better financial future (Pinto 2012).

One observer of the London scene explains the situation this way: while unemployment in Brazil is at a record low, most available jobs are either for highly qualified workers or for those with only a basic education. Workers in the middle—people who have spent some ten years in school but who do not have university or professional qualifications—struggle to find work. And it is these "middle-level" workers who make up a large proportion of the Brazilian community in London. "Brazil is great for those with qualifications," he said, "but that's not my case. I want to go back one day, but not now" (quoted in Pinto 2012).

Finally, as in the United States, the threat of arrest and deportation in Great Britain contributes to the uncertainty about the future for undocumented immigrants because, to some degree, they lose control of it. If they encounter an immigration problem, they may be suddenly and forcibly removed from the country and returned to Brazil. And, as we observed in chapter 6, Brazil led all other nationalities in the number of its citizens denied entry to England in the first place.

As we know from newspaper headlines, the Irish Republic and Spain have suffered severe economic downturns in recent years, making them far less attractive to Brazilian immigrants. In the case of Ireland, the evidence is strong that Brazilians are leaving for home. In Gort, the quintessential "Brazilian" town in the Irish Republic, an estimated two-thirds of Brazilians have left as a result of job shortages and declining economic opportunities. The meatpacking plant in town closed, and many workers sought work in construction, a particularly hard-hit sector. "Since construction has stopped, there are no jobs," said one Brazilian. Several Brazilian businesses closed their doors, and their owners left town. In the town plaza, only about twenty Brazilians a day arrive looking for work, a far cry from earlier years. One Brazilian who had worked in construction opened a travel agency and began selling flights to Brazilians returning home. Some of those leaving also point out that the economic situation in Brazil is improving, yet another reason for their departure (Dowd 2009; Cade 2010; Sheringham 2009).

After Greece, Spain is the basket case of Europe, with an unemployment rate in 2012 that approached 25 percent, the highest on the continent, and more than half of those under thirty were out of work. Since 2008, Brazilians, especially men, have been profoundly affected by the economic crisis there, primarily because many worked in construction. Although, as elsewhere, most Brazilians in Spain have always viewed their stay as temporary, a report on TV Globo suggests that now even some long-term residents are leaving for Brazil (Masanet and Baeninger 2010, 2011; Daley 2012; TV Globo 2012b).

As the effects of the financial crisis and unemployment took hold in 2008, Spain, Portugal, Japan, and other countries adopted "pay-to-go" policies that offer cash payments to immigrants willing to return home voluntarily. However, some observers question the efficacy of such programs. In Spain, for example, with an estimated 100,000 unemployed immigrants, fewer than 10,000 have taken advantage of the "pay-to-go" program, which has been in place since 2008. And, of the more than 150,000 Brazilians in the country, only 186 used the program to finance their return home. One problem is that the policy has restrictions on immigration, making it more difficult for former immigrants to return in the future. Similarly, the Portuguese government has a program to help unemployed immigrants, including Brazilians, finance the return home, but the policy has several restrictions. As a result, some who do not qualify for the program and who do not have enough money to pay for the return to Brazil themselves have been selling their jewelry and other valuables to raise money for the airfare home (Máximo and Faleiros 2010; TV Globo 2012b).

Japan's "pay-to-go" program appears to be more successful than those in other countries. Perhaps one reason is that the situation of unemployed *nikkeijin* is different from that of immigrants elsewhere. In Japan, if a Japanese Brazilian loses a job, there is very little chance of finding other work, and the only alternative is to return to Brazil. In contrast, an unemployed Brazilian in the United States can move to another state; someone who loses a job in Florida may be able to find work in Georgia or in post-Katrina New Orleans (Ribeiro 2009).

After thousands of Brazilians and Peruvians of Japanese ancestry lost their jobs—mostly in the automotive and electronics industries—Japan's "pay-to-go" program was instituted. It applies only to immigrants of Japanese ancestry who received special visas to enter the country to work in manufacturing plants. The government offered 300,000 yen (about $3,000) to an unemployed foreigner and 200,000 yen (about $2,000) to each family member. However, the catch was that, by accepting the money, the immigrant became ineligible to return to Japan. Some sixty thousand *nikkeijin* did, in fact, go back to Brazil, about one-third through the government's "pay-to-go" program (Tabuchi 2009; Máximo and Faleiros 2010).

The flights from Japan to Brazil are said to be full, and there have been large increases in the sale of one-way tickets home. As a consequence, many Brazilian schools in Japan have closed, either because the students returned to Brazil with their parents or because their unemployed parents could no longer afford tuition. One school that opened in 2007 and had as many as eighty-five students before the economic crisis hit finally closed its doors at the end of 2009, when only thirty-one students enrolled. To be sure, not all *nikkeijin* were heading home; an estimated 110,000 Brazilians in Japan have established permanent residence there (Sasaki 2010).

Despite the economic difficulties I have outlined, several factors keep Brazilians anchored in the United States and in other immigrant destinations. One anchor in the United States is immigrants' desire for their children to have access to good public schools, schools that are considered far superior to those in Brazil.[4] Then, too, Brazilians who have close relatives living in the United States, Japan, or another destination or who are married to natives of those countries think twice about returning home. Other Brazilians have jobs as teachers, interpreters, and social workers and work with their compatriots. These are generally considered good jobs that are based on the ongoing presence of a local Brazilian community. The same is true of Brazilians who have small businesses that cater to their ethnic cohort (Martes 2010).

Brazilians in various locales often mention the high rate of crime in Brazil and the fear that it induces as a reason for their reluctance to return home. "I would have a maid in Brazil," said one Brazilian living in south Florida. "Here I clean houses. But I feel safe. In São Paulo we never wore jewelry and we never went out at night." Said another living in Boston, "One of the things I like about this country is the security from violence." Similarly, in Ireland, while some Brazilians complained about the lack of leisure activities, this was nearly always counterbalanced by the more important issue of safety and security, particularly for their children. And, in Portugal, despite problematic economic conditions, the absence of urban violence made some Brazilians living there reluctant to consider returning home (quoted in Brinkley-Rogers 1998; Sheringham 2009; França 2010).

The Return Home: Problems

In 2010, Brazil's Ministry of Foreign Affairs issued the *Guia de Retorno ao Brasil*, the *Return to Brazil Guide*, published in Portuguese and English and intended as "a tool for Brazilian consular agents, for the staff of assistance organizations abroad as well as for voluntary workers, enabling them to better inform returning Brazilian nationals on how to benefit from the many available programs and services in Brazil in the areas of health, education, work and housing. . . . Thus, we hope that the return to Brazil won't be the end of a dream, but a new beginning" (Ministério das Relações Exteriores 2010).

The guide goes on to list many existing federal programs and services for health, education, family welfare, gender equity, micro-credit, and so on. None of these are specifically designed for returned migrants, and some such as the *bolsa família* (family grant), a program that provides financial assistance to the poorest of poor Brazilian families who have children in school, is a program for which returned migrants are very unlikely to qualify. Nevertheless, the publication of the guide indicates that the Brazilian government is at least aware that emigrants are returning to Brazil and that some may be having problems upon the return home.

I have already alluded to a few of the difficulties faced by returned emigrants and the feeling of many that it is more difficult to return home than to leave. "The return is a new immigration," says the Brazilian psychologist Sylvia Dantas DeBiaggi, who has studied Brazilian immigrants in Boston and their return to Brazil (TV Globo 2012a). What is called the "regression syndrome" was first identified by a psychiatrist in São Paulo who posited such a condition after dealing with the frustrations of Brazilians returning home from Japan. He characterizes it as a "spiritual jet lag" that afflicts former emigrants. Professionals in contact with returnees and returnees themselves report feelings of being uprooted, of having lost their ties, of being outside and apart from "what we should know like the palm of our hand" (Lourenço and Cunha 2012).

Those who suffer from "regression syndrome" are often considered "snobs" by relatives and friends who have little patience for returnees who complain about crime, garbage in the streets, lack of rights and respect for the law, and what they say is the "disorganization" of Brazilian society. Returnees also impact those left behind. Some harbor feelings of abandonment, resentment, and jealousy, according to Dr. DeBiaggi. Nor are these reactions fleeting. "The adaptation to a new country usually takes about six months but the readaptation to one's natal country can take as long as two years," writes one expert observer. In simple terms, the place they left is not the same as the place they return to (quoted in Lourenço and Cunha 2012).

On the basis of her study of former emigrants in Governador Valadares, Sueli Siqueira notes that the region is receiving "an influx of frustrated returnees," many without hope for the future and with a very negative view of their hometown. After living in the United States for years, returned emigrants want everyone to know about their successes abroad. For those whom success has eluded, the greatest humiliation is to return home and have to work for someone else. Once back in Brazil, they do not want to be employees; they want to be employers and to be masters of their own fate (Siqueira et al. 2010; Marcus 2008).

Such feelings of estrangement are by no means limited to Brazilians arriving home from the United States and Japan. A Brazilian woman who had lived in Australia now says: "A short time after returning to Brazil I realized that I should have made my life in Australia. I no longer enjoyed the people or the places I knew before I left. I only talk to Brazilians who I knew abroad" (quoted in Lourenço and Cunha 2012).

The lifestyle of a majority of returnees is in some ways inferior to what they had abroad. One researcher who interviewed former emigrants in Brazil believes that achieving their economic goals in the United States or elsewhere rarely results in a fundamental change in one's social and economic position in Brazil. The money earned in the United States is enough to complete certain projects back home—building a house, paying for a child's education, buying land or cattle, or paying off a debt. Unless they are able to start a successful business, returnees find that the jobs they held before immigrating to the United States rarely are appreciably different from those they can get after the return home. For several months following their homecoming, emigrants benefit from economic stability because most have a cash reserve, but life soon returns to a standard rhythm much like what it was before they emigrated (Gibson 2010).

While it is possible to return to the place one leaves, it is not possible to return to an earlier time. For many Brazilian women, the experience of emigration is transformational; for the first time, they see themselves as capable of managing their own lives. This explains why many complain about the resurrection of traditional gender roles once they arrive back home. Women emigrants are often dismayed by the return to the old way of doing things, much preferring the arrangements they had had with their husbands or partners when they lived abroad. During emigration, it was more acceptable to many Brazilian men to divide domestic responsibilities because it was seen as provisional. After all, Brazil is the place where *real* life is lived, a place where, for some, such an equitable division of labor is unthinkable. This stance is unacceptable to many women who refuse to give up the independence they enjoyed as immigrants. In time, some couples separate or divorce because women will no longer tolerate being the sole caretakers of hearth and home (Siqueira 2011).

This is but one example of the conflicts that arise post-migration. A sociologist who runs a government program to aid families of Brazilian immigrants notes that returnees often think they can forge a life that combines the best of both worlds, but they usually wind up frustrated. "Immigrants can tell you what's good here in Brazil, and what is good in the United States, but there's no way to achieve that middle ground that they're always looking for, bringing what's good there back here" (quoted in Kugel 2009).

And Those "Pull" Factors?

Brazil may be an exception to the following rule: despite the financial crises in Western nations and high rates of unemployment, international immigrants are not returning home in large numbers. One reason that Brazil is an exception is that in 2010 Brazil's economy grew by 7.5 percent—the highest growth in 25 years—and, although it slowed to 3.5 percent growth the following year, Brazil's unemployment rate was 5.4 percent in 2012, a figure the Obama administration would surely envy (Biller and Colitt 2012).[5] Oil discoveries, a commodities boom, political stability, relatively low inflation, the World Cup in 2014, and the Olympics in 2016 all coalesce to make a mockery of the timeworn joke that "Brazil is a country of the future, and it always will be." While many international migrants are suffering economically as the recession deepens, Brazilians are among the few who have the option and incentive to return home (Barrionuevo 2011b; Huff-Hannon 2009).

Does this good news about Brazil translate not only into return but into improved economic prospects for returnees? The few hard data that exist on this are mixed, and two data points need to be considered: actual salaries and the cost of living in Brazil. There is no question that, unlike the situation in the United States, Brazil's income gap is slowly closing.[6] Some 35 million people entered the middle class between 2003 and 2011, while the size of the Brazilian middle class rose from 37 percent of the population in 2003 to 55 percent by 2010. By 2012 some 25 percent of Brazilians were middle class by global standards. Then, too, in recent years, the average Brazilian's purchasing power has increased by more than 40 percent, lifting around forty million people out of poverty (Barrionuevo 2011a; Trebat 2011; Global Property Guide 2011).

While clearly an outlier, Brazil's economic boom has meant that nannies working for very wealthy families can earn as much as $3,000 a month in cities like Rio de Janeiro and São Paulo, can afford to buy homes of their own, and can join the middle class. Many are demanding salaries two to five times greater than those they earned just five years earlier. The income of domestic employees, in fact, including nannies and maids, rose 34 percent between 2003 and 2009, more than twice the increase for all Brazilian workers (Barrionuevo 2011a).

This is an indication that, because of the vibrant Brazilian economy and the economic crisis in rich countries, something is happening in Brazil that was unimaginable even a few years ago; the salaries of workers in some areas—from executives and managers to engineers and IT professionals—are actually higher than those in Europe and the United States. Weekly income is as much as 85 percent higher in a handful of jobs. Some examples: A senior electrical engineer who can earn $9,000 a month at a large Brazilian company would be paid about $4,850 in Spain, a difference of more than 85 percent. One survey found that commercial managers in Brazil were earning 79 percent more than their peers in the United States—almost $11,000 in Brazil versus $6,000 in the United States. A commercial director in Brazil earns at least $17,000—more than 13 percent more than the pay ($15,000) for a similar position in Great Britain. In Brazil in 2011, the salary of a recent engineering graduate was about $3,400 a month, and it is not difficult to find starting salaries up to $4,850 a month, about what experienced engineers earn in Portugal. Some systems analysts make as much as $12,000 a month in Brazil. These figures illustrate the fact that, with every additional year of education, Brazilians' incomes increase an average of 12 percent. Aside from the robust Brazilian economy and the economic crisis abroad, these differentials also point to what many see as the overvaluation of Brazil's currency and the labor shortage in several fields there. Moreover, this phenomenon is likely to continue, impacting more professions and spreading to more technical and administrative positions (Batista 2011; Trebat 2011).

Such generous salaries are bringing a certain number of expatriates back home and are attracting some Americans and Europeans to the country, as well. A Brazilian journalist told me that at least three highly educated Brazilian couples she knows in New York City who have been living in the United States for a decade or more—people she thought would *never* return to Brazil to live—are now planning to move back home after they secured high-paying jobs in Rio de Janeiro and São Paulo. There is even some evidence that a few of the very well-educated children of Brazilian immigrants in the United States are returning to Brazil for jobs (Colitt 2012; Semple 2012).

Not all highly educated Brazilians are benefiting from such financial largess. A woman who had previously lived in the United States and New Zealand sent me an e-mail saying that she is considering leaving Brazil again because "the situation continues to be the same." She works as a journalist in an advertising agency and writes, "I only earn enough to pay my bills. As I see it the country hasn't changed. Even for a person like me, a university graduate who speaks English and Spanish, the situation is not easy. I'm thinking of going to Canada where legalization is faster. But it's a decision I will make in a few months. For the time being, I'll stay in Brazil."

Then, too, the standard of living in some parts of Brazil that sent emigrants to the United States such as Pará, the home state of a number of Brazilians in New Orleans, is still quite basic. Parts of the region appear to be particularly isolated from the economic prosperity enjoyed by other areas of the country, prosperity that might deter local citizens from emigrating in the future. One researcher interviewed three returned migrants living in Pará, all of whom had been unemployed for more than a year since arriving home from the United States (Gibson 2010).

The second data point is the high cost of living in Brazil, especially in the nation's large urban areas, which attract most of the well-educated returnees. A case in point: A 30-year-old man has been living in Brazil for several months and is earning 30 percent more than he earned in Portugal. Despite the generous salary, he is not upbeat: "The cost of living is much higher in Brazil," he says. "I live in São Paulo where rent is double what it is in Portugal. Food, everything is more expensive so we can save less." Brazilian emigrants returning from the United States expressed dismay at the high prices at home. "Seven *reais* [about $4.25] for a glass of orange juice!" one shocked emigrant exclaimed upon arriving in Brazil. São Paulo and Rio de Janeiro are respectively the tenth and twelfth most expensive cities in the world, according to research that classified more than two hundred metropolitan areas. Living in such cities means higher costs for transportation, food, clothing, and entertainment, and the cost of housing, in particular, is often cited as a problem. Prices are indeed extremely high in Brazil; as one long-time foreign observer put it, "An ordinary Chilean red may go for $100 and brand-name sneakers for $350. Paris and New York seem like a steal" (Batista 2011; TV Globo 2012b; Cohen 2012).

The challenges resulting from Brazil's high cost of living may well recede over time, assuming that both real wage growth and low unemployment continue. Brazilian middle-class salaries today are still far below those in the West. The average salary for a middle-class family in Brazil is around $1,400 a month, or some $18,250 a year, including the "thirteenth-month bonus" salary. This would be less of an issue were it not for how much things cost in Brazil, especially in its major cities. Moreover, Brazil's gross domestic product per capita has a good way to go before it matches the level found in developed countries. It now stands at about one-third of the European average (Trebat 2011; Freedman 2012).

For now, the good news about the growth of the Brazilian economy furthers the hope that, when emigrants return home, their financial situation will be better than it was before they left. According to the founder of the Center for Brazilian Immigrants in Massachusetts, the expansion of Brazil's economy may come into play in a few years as the major reason for the return home, but, for now, the "push out" because of unemployment and other problems in destination countries is a better explanation for the return than the "pull in" of the improved Brazilian economy (Pereira 2008a).

One of the most notable trends among Brazil's expanding middle class is international travel, a trend that, as we will see, may eventually impact would-be immigrants, especially those who want to go to the United States. Now more than ever, Brazilians are traveling abroad and are spending billions of dollars while doing so. In 2011, 1.5 million Brazilians visited the United States, injecting $5.9 billion into the American economy. Brazilian travelers to the United States now spend more per capita than do visitors from any other country, an average of some $5,400. Ski resorts in Vermont are scrambling to hire Portuguese-speaking ski instructors to meet the unexpected and rapidly growing demand from thousands of adventurous Brazilians. Brazilians are such avid shoppers that, it is said, TAM, Brazil's major international airline, has had to carry extra fuel on flights originating in the United States to accommodate the mounds of luggage brought on board by Brazilian passengers heading home with their purchases. Remarks Thomas Shannon Jr., U.S. Ambassador to Brazil, "Brazilians travel with almost fanatical zeal to the U.S." (Rogers 2011; quoted in Glickhouse 2011).

The numbers are only expected to increase. By 2013, estimates suggest that 1.8 million U.S. tourist visas will be issued to Brazilian travelers. Brazilians' economic impact is so powerful that the American travel, restaurant, lodging, and retail industries, along with the U.S. Chamber of Commerce, have been lobbying Washington to allow Brazilians to travel to the United States without tourist visas. Responding to these demands, President Obama announced in 2012 in a speech in Orlando, Florida—a hotbed of Brazilian tourism—that the U.S. government would begin "facilitating" visas for Brazilians to enter the country. The State Department has been instructed to process 40 percent more visa applications for Brazilians and to open two additional American consulates in Brazil by 2013, one in Belo Horizonte and the other in Porto Alegre (Salomon and Barchfield 2012; Alvarez 2011; Barbosa 2012).

During a visit to the United States in April 2012, Brazilian president Dilma Rousseff and President Obama promised to work toward the elimination of tourist visas altogether, both for Brazilians traveling to the United States and for Americans traveling to Brazil. When the rate of rejection for tourist visas for a country is less than 5 percent, that country can enter the Visa Waiver Program, in which tourist visas are no longer required for travel to the United States. But as we noted in chapter 4, it is difficult to believe data purporting to show that only 5 percent of Brazilians applying for tourist visas to enter the United States are turned down. Nonetheless, should such a program for Brazilians be established, my guess is that this may encourage a resurgence of immigrants, particularly if the Brazilian economy ceases to be the goose that is laying the golden egg.

The New Generation

When I did my original research in the early 1990s, the issue of second-generation Brazilians in the United States did not come up, because a majority of the Brazilian immigrants I interviewed were young and unmarried, and very few had children. According to the 1990 census, nearly 94 percent of Brazilians in the United States were foreign born, reflecting how recent this migration stream was. Now, with the passage of time, scholars are making their first forays into research on this new generation of Brazilians in the United States, many of whom can be more precisely described as the "1.5 generation," that is, Brazilians who came to this country as young children and are now adolescents or young adults. What relatively little information we do have about this generation of Brazilians comes entirely from research done in the United States (Marrow 2003; Portes 1990).

So what is it telling us about this new generation? We know that concerns for children's welfare play an important role in parents' decision to remain in the United States and perhaps other destinations, as well. The appeal of a good education and a decent quality of life are major motives cited by immigrants for their decision to stay. In short, having an American-born child redefines the expectation of temporariness. Children also appear to make immigrants feel more integrated into U.S. society. Many baptize their U.S.-born children with American names; Michael, Anthony, Jennifer, John, and Linda are all popular among Brazilian families in Danbury, Connecticut. The sociologist Teresa Sales, who has done research on the new Brazilian generation in Boston, writes, "With an American citizen in the family, the immigrant begins to feel like a genuine participant in American society, in contrast with the first wave's almost exclusive focus on making money to take back to Brazil" (Menezes 2003; Sales 1999b, 2003, 132).

Brazilians are indeed procreating abroad. A purported "baby boom" among Brazilian immigrants in Massachusetts occurred as the turn of the new millennium approached, when the number of children born to Brazilian mothers there increased by 140 percent over the number born earlier in the decade. This may indicate that Brazilians were putting down roots in the United States, since the baby boom coincided with Brazilians buying 30 percent of all houses sold to immigrants in the state, perhaps signs that the community had become less transitory and more stable (Maisonnave 2005g).

We do not know how many children have been born in the United States to Brazilian parents or how many Brazilian-born children have accompanied their parents to the United States. We do know that an unknown number of Brazilian children have been reunited with their parents in the United States using the services of *coyotes* who were paid to smuggle them in through Mexico. Parents arrived in the United States first, took jobs, and saved their wages to pay for their children's later passage. Other Brazilian-born children were brought to this country by their grandparents under the guise of a visit to Disney World and were then reunited with their parents who were already here. A "fake grandparents" scheme also surfaced. Here the purported "relatives" in Brazil were paid to accompany "their grandchildren" to Disney World, once again to reunite them with their parents. Child travel has taken place in the other direction as well, with some undocumented Brazilians, unable to travel to Brazil themselves, arranging to have their American-born children brought to Brazil by documented Brazilian friends for visits with relatives there (Siqueira, Assis, and de Campo 2010).

These arrangements highlight the fact that children's legal status shapes their lived experience in the United States. For American-born children who, by virtue of their place of birth, are U.S. citizens, this is not an issue, although some Brazilians erroneously believe that their American-born children are the key to their own legalization. Above all, legal status impacts opportunities for higher education and subsequent employment. An example of how it does so: during a visit to Danbury, Connecticut, I met a twenty-year-old Brazilian-born woman who had been brought to the

United States by her parents at the age of twelve. She spoke unaccented English and had graduated from high school with good grades and SAT scores but had been unable to go to college because of her undocumented status. Although admitted to the University of Florida, the University of Miami, and elsewhere, she was ineligible for scholarships or loans; even in Connecticut, where she had lived since arriving in the United States, she would have had to pay out-of-state tuition because of her irregular status. She spent her days at a series of low-level jobs and told me that she prays for the passage of the DREAM Act, which would allow her to get on with her life (Menezes 2000).

She is hardly alone. In 2009, of the estimated sixty-five thousand un-documented immigrants who graduated from American high schools, only 5 percent went on to four-year colleges. For most of them, the costs were simply too high. Not only are they ineligible for federal financial aid but only ten states allow them to pay the far cheaper in-state tuition. As with the woman from Danbury, their only hope for the future and a path to legalization is passage of the DREAM Act. In fact, in a surprise move, in June 2012, President Obama announced what might be termed a "mini-DREAM Act" through which undocumented youth under the age of thirty who were brought to the United States as children would be allowed to remain in this country and receive two-year work permits that would be renewable in two-year increments (Berger 2010; Preston and Cushman 2012).

Still, even prior to this shift in policy, some young Brazilians had managed to find a way around the albatross of their undocumented status. While undocumented and quasi-legal adolescents—those who have applied to regularize their legal status but have not yet obtained it—face financial barriers to higher education, some are able to surmount them. They do this by attending community colleges or night classes and working during the day. However, young people seek to become documented not just to better their educational and future job prospects but also as part of an attempt to regain the social status many of them and their parents had in Brazil. In this sense, acquiring documentation—becoming legal—is a strategy for distinguishing themselves from what they perceive as lower-status Latino immigrants, with whom they are often confused. Simply put, they recognize that being "out-of-status" limits their social mobility, which, indeed, is the case (Cebulko 2009; Assis 2007).

Without higher education and legal papers, many 1.5-generation Brazilians have no choice but to take the same low-level jobs their parents have long held. This is why it is not uncommon for undocumented youth to drop out of high school. Because of their irregular status, they know that a diploma will not lead to better job prospects. Since parents usually have low-paid jobs, their son's or daughter's wages may become important in sustaining the family. In one survey in Massachusetts, the vast majority of young Brazilians—80 to 85 percent—had full- or part-time jobs while attending high school. And they can be pressured to keep working even if it conflicts with their schooling because their jobs may account for as much as one-third of a family's income. And so it has been suggested that work, more than anything else, is what distinguishes the lives of young Brazilians in the United States from their lives back home in Brazil. As children in Brazil, they went to school and likely experienced a traditional childhood surrounded by parents and a circle of relatives; in the United States, in contrast, from early on they are pulled into the adult world, into the world of work (Fritz 2011; Sales and Loureiro 2008).

What is striking about this is the degree to which some members of the new generation reproduce the parental generation in terms of employment and values; a paid job is central to their daily lives. What is more, their work is very similar to that of their parents; they have jobs in supermarkets, restaurants, or construction and work as housecleaners and babysitters. Work, in turn, opens up the world of consumerism to these young people. In one study in Boston, about half of the respondents used their earnings to help support their families; the rest worked not out of necessity but to have their own spending money to do with as they pleased. They were also aware that, more than anything else, their ability to work and consume was what distinguished them from their peers in Brazil. The opportunities for employment and consumption afforded by the American economy also shaped their future plans; these were cited as the most common reasons for wanting to remain in the United States (Sales 2007).

The willingness of many of these adolescents to work very long hours with little complaint impressed researchers studying the new Brazilian generation. Acknowledging the sacrifices their parents had made to come to the United States, many expressed an obligation to follow in their foot-steps and to work hard to earn money. Within this environment, school was often secondary, and parents who worked long hours had little time or inclination to oversee their children's schooling. Education was viewed instrumentally, as a way to learn English in order to earn money, rather than as an end in itself. Very few saw it as preparation for moving up the employment ladder. Consequently, the future of this group of young people in terms of their insertion in the labor market looks very much like that of their parents. While with experience they may eventually get somewhat better-paying jobs, they are likely to remain confined to the unskilled secondary sector of the U.S. labor market (Sales 2007; Scudeler 1999).

In addition to contributing to family income, the new generation often serves as a link between their parents and American society. Virtually all of the 1.5- and second-generation Brazilians are bilingual in English and Portuguese, but many first-generation parents speak little English. They may work in immigrant settings and shop in Brazilian-owned stores, so they usually can get by with what little English they do know. But when it comes to having a medical appointment, renting an apartment, buying a car, or dealing with a bank or a government agency that requires interacting with Americans, their children become essential as interpreters and guides. Sometimes the child's voice is recorded on the family's answering machine, and at home children often take phone calls in lieu of their parents (Menezes 2003).

So members of this new generation act as a bridge between their parents and American society. Does this impact their sense of identity, that is, how they identify themselves in terms of ethnicity and race? First, this generation has to self-identify in accordance with the U.S. system of classification because they are more immersed in American institutions than are their parents. As students in school, for example, their national, ethnic, and racial origins come to the fore when they are required to fill in forms asking about their personal history. Then, too, they are usually more knowledgeable than their parents about issues surrounding race and ethnicity in the United States (Martes 2010).

This new generation not only speaks English but also grew up in a multicultural environment and is likely to have friends and acquaintances outside the Brazilian community. Yet, as we have seen, their parents—as first-generation Brazilians—almost always emphasize their nationality while rejecting other ethnic labels such as Hispanic and Latino. However, their U.S.-born and 1.5-generation children often have Latino friends and, unlike their parents, usually do not mind being identified with them. Moreover, those that have been sufficiently "Americanized" may actually benefit from this identification, since they know that, in certain contexts, *latinidade* can be advantageous. Nevertheless, at least one observer believes that the new generation eventually will follow the lead of their parents and ultimately identify themselves as Brazilian Americans (Fritz 2011; Menezes 2003; Martes 2010).

The case of the new generation of Afro-Brazilians is more complicated. Because of the one-drop rule in the United States, Brazilians of color learn to see themselves as having only one option, assimilation as African Americans, an option they generally reject. They prefer to be called Brazilians since, by doing so, they can avoid the one-drop rule and, therefore, being identified as "just black." Writes a researcher who has studied this issue: "The desire is to become American but if America cannot include them without classifying them as African-Americans, they then try to remain Brazilian-Americans or simply . . . Brazilians" (Fritz 2011, 110).

Finally, what is the stance of members of the new generation regarding their future? Many adolescents having grown up in the United States express fondness for this country, view it as more egalitarian than Brazil, and believe that it offers them more opportunities than Brazil. However, whether U.S. born or members of the 1.5-generation, most of these young Brazilians have, in the words of one researcher, an "extremely superficial knowledge of Brazil" (Martes 2010, 236). Those who left as young children have only vague memories of their natal land, and, if their parents remain undocumented, they are unlikely to have been to Brazil for a visit. Still, problems can arise when "parents want to go back to Brazil and their children want to stay here," said a Brazilian psychologist. "I know a girl who wants to stay here, but her family wants to go back. She's dominant in English, she can't function there" (quoted in Mineo 2004). There is also the example of how different the experiences of two Brazilian-born teenagers are in adapting to the United States. One is very content with her life in this country and plans to remain here permanently, while the other, who was forced to give up a scholarship when her mother moved to Boston, resents the move and has definite plans to return to Brazil to live (Braga 2007).

Aside from children born in the United States to Brazilian parents, there are other Brazilian Americans, as well: Brazilian immigrants who have become American citizens or who have *"jurado a bandeira"* (sworn to the flag), as they describe naturalization. After Brazil passed legislation in 1996 permitting dual nationality, the rate of naturalization among Brazilians in the United States doubled, and, between 2000 and 2010, close to fifty-five thousand Brazilians became naturalized American citizens. While this is not a large number, it does contrast with earlier years; in the mid-1990s, in Framingham, Massachusetts, for example, not a single Brazilian was a U.S. citizen. A few years later, Representative Joe Kennedy accepted an invitation to speak to the Brazilian community there, demonstrating the growing political potential of this population (Jones-Correa 2001; Sales 1998b).

Final Thoughts

As I was completing this book, news broke in the U.S. media that Eduardo Saverin, a cofounder of Facebook, had renounced his U.S. citizenship. The Brazilian-born Saverin was brought to Miami from São Paulo in 1992 at age thirteen, when his wealthy parents feared a kidnapping threat. He became an American citizen in 1998. Saverin renounced his citizenship, allegedly to avoid paying millions of dollars in U.S. taxes when Facebook went public, in May 2012. He plans to continue living and working in Singapore, where there are no taxes on capital gains (Whitaker 2012).

Saverin's actions created quite a stir in the United States. "Mr. Saverin has decided to 'defriend' the United States of America just to avoid paying his taxes," fumed Senator Charles Schumer of New York. His decision to renounce his U.S. citizenship, purportedly to avoid a large tax payment, almost certainly means that he will not be able to return to the United States again. "There's a specific provision of immigration law that says that a former citizen who officially renounces citizenship, and is determined to have renounced it for the purpose of avoiding taxation, is excludable," according to the Director of the American Immigration Lawyers Association. The only way Savarin could visit or live in the United States again would be to convince the authorities that his decision was not based on avoiding taxes, a highly unlikely event (Weisman 2012; Kapur 2012).

As I read this news, I thought about how Brazilian immigrants in the United States would react to it. I imagine that the vast majority of Brazilians in this country would greet Saverin's decision with utter disbelief. Whether they remain in the United States or eventually return to Brazil, nearly all of them have made enormous sacrifices to come here, and I believe they would be astounded that someone—a fellow compatriot no less—would *voluntarily* give up the right to live in this country or to come and go from it as he pleased. My guess is that the near universal reaction would be: "What was he thinking? How could he do such a thing? How could he simply abandon what so many of his co-nationals had given up so much to achieve: to live and work in the United States at least for a time?"

Notes

Preface and Acknowledgments

1. Brazilians regularly refer to their presidents by their first names (Romero 2012b).
2. As of 2012, some areas of this country with a significant Brazilian presence—Philadelphia, Chicago, and Houston are examples—remain terra incognita in terms of research.
3. Itinerant consulates regularly travel to smaller cities and towns that have significant Brazilian immigrant populations. While there, consular personnel service the needs of the local Brazilian community.

Chapter 1. The Boys (and Girls) from Brazil

1. According to the most recent data available, 51 percent of Brazilians in the United States are women and 49 percent are men, and over half—56 percent—are married (Lima 2009).
2. By 2016, Brazil is expected to become the world's fifth-largest economy. Still, its gross domestic product (GDP) per capita ranks seventieth in the world (Whitefield 2011).
3. *Coyotes* are individuals paid to smuggle immigrants into the United States, most often from Mexico.
4. The term "1.5 generation" refers to those who immigrated to the host country as young children; "second generation" refers to those who were born there.

Chapter 2. Why They Go

1. The U.S. "seduction" of Brazil, which began during World War II, is amply documented in Tota (2009).
2. Some economists have suggested that the *Real* Plan benefited the working class and the poor more than the middle class. The poor no longer had to deal

with inflation that robbed them of 30 to 40 percent of their monthly income. Between July 1994 and July 1995, the basic market basket did not increase in price, while, at the same time, the minimum wage rose by 10 percent (Klagsbrunn 1996; *Veja* 1995).

3. In mid-2012, the national minimum monthly wage in Brazil was 622 *reais*, around US$360; it was projected to be 667 *reais* by 2013.

4. Far more research exists on Brazilians' immigration to the United States and Japan than on their immigration to other destinations, which is reflected in the employment data cited here.

5. A samba school is a club devoted to practicing and exhibiting samba. The schools, traditionally associated with a particular neighborhood in Rio de Janeiro, have various events throughout the year, the most important of which are rehearsals for the main event, the yearly samba parade during Brazil's Carnaval.

6. *Batucada* is Afro-Brazilian percussion music often associated with the Brazilian Carnaval.

7. Since virtually all money sent home by Brazilians living in Japan is sent through banks, remittance figures for that country are thought to be far more accurate than figures for other countries.

8. Similar ID cards were first issued by Mexican consulates across the United States.

Chapter 3. Who They Are

1. By 2009, just over 11 percent of Brazilians were university graduates.

2. The 2000 census also found that in New York City, 31 percent of Brazilians had college or graduate degrees, whereas only 7 percent of Mexicans and 9 percent of Ecuadorians had these credentials (Berger and Santos 2005).

3. In 2009 Brazil's Foreign Ministry opened a consulate in Hartford, Connecticut, to serve the large population of Brazilian immigrants living in the state. Earlier they were served by the Brazilian Consulate in New York City.

4. After 2000, there were more people of color in the Brazilian community in Boston than earlier, probably caused by a shift in the social class of immigrants (Martes 2010).

5. Belo Horizonte, the third-largest city in Brazil, is the capital of the state of Minas Gerais.

6. Officials in Goiás estimate that 10 percent of the state's population—between 400,000 and 500,000 of its 4.5 million residents—live abroad and that they send more than $1 billion a year to Brazil (Mineo 2008). Goiás is also the home state of many Brazilian immigrants living in the Republic of Ireland, discussed in chapter 6.

7. Brazilians who can prove Italian ancestry can acquire Italian passports. This is discussed further in chapter 6.

Chapter 4. How They Arrive

1. A federal district court judge ruled in the complainant's favor and found that the visa policies at the American consulate in São Paulo were illegal (Shenon 1998).

2. This is a policy according to which nationality or citizenship is not determined by place of birth but is based on whether one has an ancestor who was a national or citizen of that particular country.

3. The most common estimate among specialists is that for every immigrant caught, three make it safely over the border.

4. Prices to final destinations in the United States were sometimes as high as $15,000 (Bautzer and Moreira 2003).

5. Some Brazilians from the Amazon region enter the United States clandestinely via Panama. They are stowaways or work as stevedores on boats headed for U.S. ports (Pedroso 2008).

6. One-third of immigrants from Governador Valadares entered the United States via Mexico (Siqueira 2009b).

7. New York City has a policy of "don't ask, don't tell" in regard to undocumented immigrants. Personnel in hospitals, schools, and other municipal institutions are prohibited from asking immigrants about their legal status, allowing them access to city services. Because of the city's policy, one Brazilian said to me, "I'm illegal, but I feel so much more like a citizen."

Chapter 5. "Doing America": Big Cities and Small

1. Long Branch's hardwood floor industry is dominated by Brazilian laborers (Donohue 2005).

2. Portuguese is the first language of just under 10 percent of students in Massachusetts and is the second-most commonly spoken foreign language in the state after Spanish.

3. Since the late 1990s, there has been a considerable influx of Brazilians to Framingham from Goiás, in Brazil's central west (Mineo 2008).

4. The increase in the size of the Brazilian population on Martha's Vineyard is such that Brazilian immigration will be included in the new exhibits being planned for the island's historical museum. I have been serving as a consultant for this exhibit.

5. Although arrests and deportation proceedings are supposed to be brought only against those accused of serious crimes, in Cobb County, almost 80 percent of those so detained were guilty of little more than traffic violations (Preston 2011a).

6. By 2012 Argentines had overtaken Brazilians as the most important foreign buyers of real estate there (Barrienuevo 2012).

Chapter 6. Other Destinations: Europe, England, and the Republic of Ireland

1. The Brazilian *real* appreciated nearly 50 percent against the U.S. dollar between December 2008 and early 2011 (Jordan and Trevisani 2011).

2. The Portuguese *escudo* was not viewed as a strong currency before the introduction of the euro to Portugal in the late 1990s.

3. This does not imply that all Brazilians have easy entry. In 2004, Brazil was the country with the largest number of citizens barred from entering Great Britain by immigration authorities (*Folha de São Paulo* 2005).

Chapter 7. Other Destinations: Pacific Bound

1. In one study in São Paulo, every Japanese Brazilian interviewed had at least one family member, either currently or in the past, working in Japan (Nishida 2009).

2. Of course, not all such marriages followed this pattern; some were true love matches.

3. In Peru, cases have been reported of non-Japanese Peruvians having eye surgery in order to pass themselves off as having Japanese ancestry so that they could obtain work in Japan (Sasaki 1995).

4. This changed in 2009; due to rising unemployment, the Japanese government began offering to pay for *nikkejins'* travel to Brazil if they promised not to return to Japan for ten years. This policy is discussed in chapter 12.

5. Spiritism is also referred to in Brazil as *Kardecismo*, a reference to Alain Kardec, a Frenchman whose ideas had a major impact on Spiritism, a religion with a significant middle-class following in Brazil (Bezerra 2002).

Chapter 8. Other Destinations: And for the Poor

1. From 1967 on, foreigners were permitted to buy land along this border region of Paraguay (Wilson, Hay, and Margolis 1989).

2. Day laborers are often called *boia fria* (literally "cold lunch") because, by the time they eat the hot lunch they carried with them to the fields in the morning, it is cold.

3. Between 1970 and 1990, an estimated seventy thousand children were born to Brazilian parents in Paraguay (Alves 1990).

4. Approximately ten thousand Yanomami live in the far northern Brazilian state of Roraima, and another twelve thousand live in southern Venezuela.

5. More recently, similar incursions by Brazilian miners into Indian lands in Venezuela led to unconfirmed reports of a massacre in a Yanomami village (Neuman and Diaz 2012).

Chapter 9. Quintessential Emigrants: *Valaldarenses*

1. Today the company, now known as CVRD, is the third-largest mining company in the world (Rohter 2012).

2. Four percent of *valadarenses* go to Canada, just under 3 percent go to Europe, and the rest go to Japan and Australia.

3. In a 1989 random sample of *valadarense* emigrants, 61 percent said they had trouble getting a tourist visa to the United States; this is the reason that 44 percent of those questioned had arrived there via Mexico. More than 75 percent of those who arrived in the United States after 2000 entered illegally using false passports or entry via Mexico (Goza 2003; Siqueira 2009b).

4. In towns and villages outside Governador Valadares in the Vale do Rio Doce, about two-thirds of returnees invested in cattle and farmland.

5. In the most exclusive private girls' school in town, 15 percent of the students have parents who live abroad. The girls are being raised by grandparents (Mineo 2006i).

6. Estimates are that, by 2009, nearly 60 percent of *valadarenses* remained undocumented, some 20 percent had green cards, and another 15 percent were American citizens (Siqueira 2009b).

7. In many homes in Brazil that lack separate hot-water heaters, an electric showerhead (*chuveiro electrico*) is the most common way of heating shower water.

Chapter 10. Faith and Community: Ties That Bind?

1. *Creente*, meaning "believer" in Portuguese, is the common term used to refer to evangelical Protestants in Brazil.

2. Similarly, in the Republic of Ireland, in the small town of Gort, there are six evangelical churches established by Brazilians and one Catholic Mass celebrated weekly in Portuguese (Sheringham 2010b).

3. A study of Boston labor unions' efforts to recruit Brazilians suggests that, despite the general weakness of community organizations, they may be ripe for unionization (Kirshner 2008).

4. At one time or another, Boston has had as many as seven associations serving the Brazilian community, but some have closed, and by 2012 only three were still in operation.

5. Similar organizations, both called Centro Comunitário Brasileiro, serve the Brazilian populations in San Francisco and south Florida.

6. U.S. Senator Richard Durbin of Illinois was purportedly inspired to write the DREAM Act legislation by a young undocumented Brazilian, a gifted concert pianist, brought to Chicago by her parents as a young child (Ezabella 2012).

7. In London two organizations, ABRAS founded in 2007 and Casa do Brasil in 2009, provide support services for Brazilian immigrants (Sheringham 2010b).

Chapter 11. What Does It Mean to Be Brazilian?

1. One result of the April 2012 meeting between President Obama and Brazilian President Dilma Rousseff at the White House was that the United States will recognize *cachaça* as a distinct product and will stop calling it "Brazilian rum" and applying tariffs intended to shield Caribbean rums from competition (*Economist* 2012).

2. A *churrascaria* is a barbecue restaurant; a *caipirinha* is an alcoholic drink made of *cachaça*, muddled limes, and sugar; and a *feijoada* is Brazil's national dish consisting of meats cooked in black beans and accompanied by rice, greens, and fresh orange slices.

3. Some Brazilians in Los Angeles are said to prefer being stereotyped as "exotics" to being included in the stigmatized and racialized stereotype of "Hispanic" (Beserra 2005).

4. The term *pardo* is used in the Brazilian census to identify someone of mixed racial ancestry.

5. White Brazilians appeared to be in the majority in the United States until about 2000, after which immigrants from Brazil became more racially diverse (Martes 2010).

Chapter 12. Here Today and Gone Tomorrow?

1. For $3,000, one moving company was offering a large shipping container for sending household goods to Brazil, along with two airline tickets to fly there.

2. Between 2007 and 2008, 700,000 jobs were lost in construction in the United States.

3. The driver's license issue is much less important in New York City because of its vast public transportation network. A car is unnecessary there, unlike so many other places where Brazilians have settled.

4. Public schools in Brazil are notoriously weak, and parents who can possibly afford it send their children to private schools.

5. During the first trimester of 2012, however, Brazil's economy only grew by a very disappointing 0.2 percent and by only 1 percent for all of 2012 (Leitão 2012; Romero 2012c).

6. Brazilian workers who made up the lowest 10 percent of the labor force in terms of income had higher salary increases than the remaining 90 percent of Brazilian workers but national per capita income was still only $12,000 (Rapoza 2012a, 2012b).

References

Abraham, Yvonne. 2005. "Immigrant Labor Force Booming." *Boston Globe*, June 19.

Abud, Tatiana Diniz. 2010. "El Brasil de Francia: Representación de la cultura brasileña, la imagen del país y la conservación de estereotipos." In *1º seminário de estudos sobre imigração brasileira na Europa*, edited by Flávio Carvalho, Maria Badet Souza, Manuella Callou, and Mar Rubiralta, 265–72. Barcelona: Universitat de Barcelona.

Albuquerque, José Lindomar C. 2009. "A dinâmica das fronteiras: Deslocamento e circulação dos 'brasiguaios' entre os limites nacionais." *Horizontes Antropológicos* 15, no. 31: 137–66.

Almeida, Marcony. 2010. *I Came through Mexico.* Lexington, KY: Portuguese Review.

Almeida, Marta. 1994. "Brazilian Immigration in Dade and Broward Counties." Mimeo. Florida/Brazil Institute, University of Florida, Gainesville.

Alvarez, Lizette. 2011. "Miami Has a Hearty Oi (Hello) for Free-Spending Brazilians." *New York Times*, December 28, p. 11.

Alves, José Claudio Souza, and Lúcia Ribeiro. 2002. "Migração, religião e transnaionalismo: O caso dos brasileiros no sul da Flórida." *Religião e Sociedade* 22, no. 2: 65–90.

Alves, José Luis. 1990. *Brasiguaios: Destino incerto.* São Paulo: Global Editora.

Amaral, Rubem Guimarães. 2005. "Perfil da comunidade brasileira no exterior." Departamento das comunidades brasileiras no exterior, Ministério das Relações Exteriores, Brasília.

American Community Survey. 2007–9. http://www.census.gov/acs/www/data_documentation/2009_release/.

———. 2011. http://www.census.gov/acs/www/data_documentation/2011_release/.

Amorim, Lucas. 1997. "Consulados brasileiros." Presentation at the Primeiro Simpósio Internacional sobre a Emigração Brasileira, Lisbon, October 23–25.

Araújo, Ledice. 1995. "Serviços: Altas de até 200% são difíceis de engolir." *O Globo*, July 1, p. 4.

Assis, Glaúcia de Oliveira. 2003. "De Criciúma para o mundo—Os novos fluxos da população brasileira: Gênero e rearranjos familiares." In *Fronteiras cruzadas: Etnicidade, gênero e redes sociais*, edited by Ana Cristina Braga Martes and Soraya Fleischer, 199–230. São Paulo: Editora Paz e Terra.

———. 2007. "A segunda geração de emigrantes brasileiros nos EUA: Gênero, etnicidade e preconceito." Paper presented at the meeting of the Latin American Studies Association, Montreal, September 5–8.

———. 2011. "Entre dois lugares: As experiências afetivas de mulheres imigrantes brasileiras nos Estados Unidos." In *Gênero, sexo, amor e dinheiro: Mobilidades transnacionais envolvendo o Brasil*, edited by Adriana Piscitelli, Gláucia de Oliveira Assis, and José Miguel Nieto Olivar, 321–62. Campinas: Núcleo de Estudos de Gênero, Universidade Estadual de Campinas.

Assumpção, João Carlos. 1997a. "Concessão de visto para EUA é discriminatória, diz diplomata." *Folha de São Paulo*, May 15.

———. 1997b. "Consulado adota ação itinerante." *Folha de São Paulo*, July 27.

Assunção, Viviane. 2011. "Onde a comida não tem gusto: Estudo antropológico das práticas alimentares de imigrantes brasileiros em Boston." PhD dissertation, Universidade Federal de Santa Catarina, Florianópolis.

Badet Souza, Maria. 2010. "Mass media, género y construcción de imaginarios sociales: Un análisis de la representación mediática de Brasil en España." In *1º seminário de estudos sobre imigração brasileira na Europa*, edited by Flávio Carvalho, Maria Badet Souza, Manuella Callou, and Mar Rubiralta, 137–44. Barcelona: Universitat de Barcelona.

Badgley, Ruey T. 1994. "Brazucas in Beantown: The Dynamics of Brazilian Ethnicity in Boston." Senior honors thesis in Anthropology, Connecticut College, New London, Connecticut.

Barbosa, Flávia. 2012. "Brasil e EUA vão trabalhar para abolir visto." *O Globo*, April 10, p. 5.

Barnes, Taylor. 2009. "No Place Like Home: Brazilian Immigrants Leave U.S. for Better Job Prospects." *Christian Science Monitor*, September 24. http://www.csmonitor.com/Business/2009/0924/no-place-like-home-brazilian-immigrants-leave-us-for-better-job-prospects.

Barrionuevo, Alexei. 2008. "Left-Leaning President's Election Gives Hope to Landless Paraguayans." *New York Times*, October 14, p. 6.

———. 2011a. "Upwardly Mobile Nannies Move into the Braziian Middle Class." *New York Times*, May 20, p. 7.

———. 2011b. "After a Year in Economic Overdrive, Brazil Hopes to Elude Pitfalls." *New York Times*, October 9, p. 10.

———. 2012. "Argentines Turn Cash into Condos in Miami." *New York Times*, September 13, p. RE1.

Barry, Dan. 2008. "Does the Real Ireland Still Exist?" *New York Times*, May 18, Travel, pp. 1, 8.

Barth, Frederick. 1998. *Ethnic Groups and Boundaries: The Social Organization of Cultural Difference*. Prospect Heights, IL: Waveland Press.

Basch, Linda, Nina Glick Schiller, and Cristina Szanton Blanc. 1994. *Nations Unbound: Transnational Projects, Postcolonial Predicaments, and Deterritorialized Nation-States*. Langhorne, PA: Gordon and Breach.

Batista, Henrique Gomes. 2011. "Remuneração no Brasil chega a ser 85% maior do que em países ricos." *O Globo*, December 3.

Bautzer, Tatiana, and Ivana Moreira. 2003. "Endurecimento americano atinge brasileiros." *EU and Valor Econômico*, June 13, pp. 12–13.

BBC Brasil. 2007. "Ilegais brasileiros estão voltando para casa, diz jornal de Miami." BBC Brasil, December 17. http://www.bbc.co.uk/portuguese/reporter bbc/story/2007/12/071217_pressmiamiheraldrw.shtml.

Belchior, Luiza. 2012. "Volta de brasileiros para casa enxuga economia em Portugal." *Folha de São Paulo*, July 15, p. 14.

Beleli, Iara. 2010. "Imagens de brasileiros/as no atravessar das fronteiras: (Des)organizando imaginários." In *1º seminário de estudos sobre imigração brasileira na Europa*, edited by Flávio Carvalho, Maria Badet Souza, Manuella Callou, and Mar Rubiralta, 121–28. Barcelona: Universitat de Barcelona.

Belson, Ken, and Jill P. Capuzzo. 2007. "Towns Rethink Laws against Illegal Immigrants." *New York Times*, September 26, pp. 1, 23.

Benson, Todd. 2004. "If You Hear 'Cachaça,' Don't Think of Rum." *New York Times*, December 24, pp. W1, 4.

Beraba, Marcelo. 2007. "Os que voltam não têm trabalho nem dinheiro, afirma socióloga." *Folha de São Paulo*, December 9.

Berger, Joseph. 2010. "Whither the Dream." Education Life, *New York Times*, January 3, p. 29.

Berger, Joseph, and Fernanda Santos. 2005. "Trading Status for a Raise." *New York Times*, December 26, pp. B1, 7.

Bernstein, Nina, and Elizabeth Dwoskin. 2007. "For Many Brazilians Here Illegally, the Promised Land Has Lost Its Promise." *New York Times*, December 4, p. 32.

Beserra, Bernadete. 2003. *Brazilian Immigrants in the United States: Cultural Imperialism and Social Class*. New York: LFB Scholarly Publishing.

———. 2005. "From Brazilians to Latinos? Racialization and Latinidad in the Making of Brazilian Carnival in Los Angeles." *Latino Studies* 3, no. 1: 53–75.

Beting, Joelmir. 1997. "Saudades de feijão." *O Globo*, March 2, p. 54.

Bezerra, Neda. 2002. "The Road to Spiritism." PhD dissertation, University of Florida, Gainesville.

Biller, David, and Raymond Colitt. 2012. "Brazil Record-Low Unemployment

Creating Scarcity of Maids." *Bloomberg*, November 20. http://www.bloom
berg.com/news/2012-11-21/brazil-record-low-unemployment-creating-
scarcity-of-maids.html.

Bógus, Lúcia Maria Machado. 1995a. "Brasileiros em Portugal: Novos movimentos
migratórios ou volta às origens? *Travessia: Revista do Migrante* 21 (January–
April): 16–19.

———. 1995b. "Migrantes brasileiros na Europa occidental: Uma abordagem
preliminar." In *Emigração e imigração no Brasil contemporânea*, edited by
Neide Lopes Patarra, 111–21. Campinas: Programa Interinstitucional de
Avaliação e Acompanhamento das Migrações Internacionais no Brasil.

Bógus, Lúcia Maria Machado, and M. Silvia B. Bassanesi. 2000. "Brasileiros na
Itália: Movimentos migrátorios e inserção social." Paper presented at the
meeting of the Latin American Studies Association, Miami, March 16–18.

Botelho, Vera Lucia. 1998. "Towards Transnationalism: A New Pattern in International Migration: Case Study on Brazilian Immigration to British Columbia." Mimeo.

Braga, Leticia J. 2007. "Becoming Brazuca? A Tale of Two Teens." *Revista, Harvard
Review of Latin America* (Spring): 42–45.

Braga, Paulo. 2003. "A geografia do matrimônio." *EU and Valor Econômico*, June
13, p. 15.

Brasch, Katherine. 2007. "Finding Their Place in the World: Brazilian Migrant
Identitites in an Interconnected World." PhD dissertation, University of
Toronto.

Brazilian Sun. 2000. Census 2000. No. 34, March, p. 1.

Brightwell, Graça. 2010. "Saboreando o Brasil em Londres: Comida, imigração e
identitidade." *Travessia: Revista do Migrante* 66 (January–June): 21–31.

Brinkley-Rogers, Paul. 1998. "The Brazilians among Us." *Miami Herald*, July 11,
p. 1.

Brodkin, Karen. 1998. *How Jews Became White Folks: And What That Says about
Race in America*. New Brunswick, NJ: Rutgers University Press.

Brooke, James. 1990. "A New Assault on Brazil's Woes." *New York Times*, March
15, pp. C1, 16.

———. 1991a. "As Collor Completes First Year, Brazilians Write Off Their Highest
Hopes." *New York Times*, March 14, p. 3.

———. 1991b. "Brazil's Fresh Young President Has Grown Old Fast." *New York
Times*, October 20, p. C4.

———. 1991c. "In Brazil, Pessimism Starts to Keep Pace with Inflation Rate." *New
York Times*, December 1, p. 11.

———. 1991d. "Landless Fret about Brazilians in Paraguay." *New York Times*, April
25, p. 10.

———. 1992. "Venezuela's Policy for Brazil's Gold Miners: Bullets." *New York
Times*, February 16.

———. 1993. "In Brazil Wild Ways to Counter Wild Inflation." *New York Times*, July 25, p. 11.

———. 1994a. "Economy Dampens Ardor of Brazilians." *New York Times*, January 5, p. C11.

———. 1994b. "Brazilians Get Serious on Inflation and Deficit." *New York Times*, March 3, p. D2.

———. 2001."Sons and Daughters of Japan: Back from Brazil." *New York Times*, November 27, p. 4.

Brown, Peter. 2005a. "Understanding Brazuca 'Fragmentation': A Qualitative Study of Brazilian Immigrants and Their Community in Boston, Massachusetts." Paper presented at National Congress on Brazilian Immigration to the United States, David Rockefeller Center for Latin American Studies, Harvard University, Cambridge, MA, March 18–19.

———. 2005b. "The Ambivalent Immigrants: Brazilians and the Conflict of Ethnic Identity." Senior honors thesis, Harvard University, Cambridge, MA.

Buarque, Daniel. 2009. "Comunidade brasileira nos EUA se mobiliza para participar do censo do país." *O Globo*, August 16.

Buechler, Simone J. 2010. "Suffering the Burst Bubble: Brazilian Immigrants in Newark, NJ." Paper presented at the meeting of the Latin American Studies Association, Toronto, October 6–9.

Bush, George W. 2005. "President Discusses Border Security and Immigration Reform in Arizona." Speech, Department of Homeland Security, Davis-Monthan Air Force Base, Tucson, AZ, November 28. http://georgewbush-whitehouse.archives.gov/news/releases/2005/11/20051128-7.html.

Bustos, Sergio R. 1995. "South Florida Becomes Haven for Brazilians." *Fort Lauderdale Sun Sentinel*, February 12, pp. 1, 11.

Butterman, Steven F. 2008. "Performing Positively or Performing Positivism? A Critical Assessment of the First Decade of the Brazilian International Press Award." Paper presented at Brazilian-Americans in Georgia and Beyond: A Multi-Disciplinary Symposium, University of Georgia, Athens, and Georgia State University, Atlanta, April 25–26.

Cade, Jamil. 2010. "Brasileiros fazem as malas na Irlanda." *O Estado de São Paulo*, November 15.

Caitano, Adriana. 2010a. "O sonho americano ficou para trás." *Veja*, September 5.

———. 2010b. "Quando morar nos Estados Unidos era moda." *Veja*, September 5.

Caldeira, Paulo. 1996. "Nós os brasileiros SEM BRASIL." *The Brasilians*, May, p. 7.

Câmara dos Deputados. 2008. "Deputados apóiam criação do 'estado do emigrante.'" Agência Câmara, June 17. http://www2.camara.gov.br/agencia /noticias/123602.html.

Campell, Alexia. 2010. "Two Charged with Human Smuggling." *Orlando Sun Sentinel*, October 15. http://www.thechronicleherald.ca/canada/96745-two-charged-with-human-smuggling.

Capuzzo, Jill P. 2006. "Town Battling Illegal Immigration Is Emptier Now." *New York Times*, July 28, pp. B1, 6.

———. 2007. "Town Pulls Back on Immigration Law." *New York Times*, September 19, p. 24.

Cardoso de Oliveira, Roberto. 1976. *Identitdade, etnia e estructura social*. São Paulo: Livraria Editora Pioneira.

Cariello, Rafael. 2008. "Brasil lidera deportações no Reino Unido." *Folha de São Paulo*, February 24.

Catholic Social Services of the Diocese of Fall River (CSS) and the Brazilian Immigrant Association of Cape Cod and the Islands (BIACCI). 2001. "Brazilian Survey Project, Cape Cod and the Islands." Mimeo.

Cavalcanti, Leonardo. 2005. "Rethinking the Social Construction of the Immigrant: Reflections on the Urban Experience of Brazilians Living in the United States and Spain." Paper presented at the National Congress on Brazilian Immigration to the United States, David Rockefeller Center for Latin American Studies, Harvard University, Cambridge, MA, March 18–19.

———. 2007. "El papel de la actividad empresarial de los migrantes en los procesos de movilidad social y (re)construcción de la categoría 'inmigrante' en España: Un acercamiento al caso brasileño en las ciudades de Madrid y Barcelona." Paper presented at the meeting of the Latin American Studies Association, Montreal, September 5–8.

———. 2008. "Breves comentários sobre a imigração brasileira em Barcelona." In *Travessias na desordem global: Fórum Social das Migrações*, edited by Serviço Pastoral dos Migrantes, 112–22. São Paulo: Ediçoes Paulinas.

Cebulko, Kara. 2009. "Documented, Undocumented and 'Somewhere in-Between': Documentation Status and the Lives of Children of Brazilian Immigrants." PhD dissertation, Indiana University, Bloomington.

Chavez, Leo R. 1988. "Settlers and Sojourners: The Case of Mexicans in the United States." *Human Organization* 47, no. 2: 95–107.

Chigusa, Charles Tetsuo, ed. 1994. *A quebra dos mitos: O fenômeno dekassegui através de relatos pessoais*. Mizuhiki, Japan: IPC Produção and Consultoria.

Chock, Phyllis. 1995. "Ambiguity in Policy Discourse: Congressional Talk about Immigration." *Policy Sciences* 28:165–84.

Clark, Sara K. 2010. "Brazilians Are a Growing Market for U.S. Tourism." *Orlando Sentinel*, June 20.

Clendenning, Alan. 2005. "Brazil Cracks Down on Illegal Immigration." Associated Press, September 14. http://www.highbeam.com/doc/1P1-113141360.html.

Cohen, Roger. 1988. "Brazil's Price Spiral Nears Hyperinflation." *Wall Street Journal*, December 8, pp. 1, 19.

————. 2012. "In Search of Sustainable Swagger." *New York Times*, April 2, p. 22.

Colitt, Raymond. 2012. "Foreign Workers Flooding Brazil as Salaries Rise: Jobs." *Bloomberg*, May 30. http://www.bloomberg.com/news/2012-05-30/foreign-workers-flooding-brazil-as-tight-market-lifts-pay-jobs.html.

Comunidade News. 2007. "Brasileiros dão adeus ao sonho americano." *Comunidade News*, August 7–13, p. 32.

————. 2008. "Mesmo com todos os perigos, brasileiros continuam a atravessar a fronteira." *Comunidade News*, June 11.

————. 2009a. "Abaixo-assinado pede eleição de deputados no exterior." *Comunidade News*, March 24.

————. 2009b."Banco do Brasil inicia atividades nos EUA com empresas de remessas." *Comunidade News*, July 8.

Corrêa, Alessandra. 2010. "'Brasileiros tiveram papel central na reconstrução de Nova Orleans,' diz pesquisadora." BBC Brasil, August 30. http://www.bbc.co.uk/portuguese/noticias/2010/08/100830_nova_orleans_brasileiros_ale_rw.shtml.

Corrêa, Marcos Sá. 1994. "O Brasil se expande." *Veja*, September 7, pp. 70–77.

Cortêz, Cácia. 1994. "Brasiguaios." *News from Brazil*, no. 133, p. 1.

Costa, Célia, and Marcelo Dutra. 2006. "PF prende 3 em operação contra imigração ilegal." *O Globo*, March 8, p. 8.

Costa, Maria Teresa Paulino da. 2004a. "Algumas considerações sobre imigrantes brasileiros na jurisdição do consulado brasileiro de Nova York." Mimeo. Consulado Brasileiro, New York.

————. 2004b. Presentation at the Conference on Brazilians in the U.S.: Another Invisible Latino Diaspora. Aliança Brasileira nos Estados Unidos, Central Connecticut State University, New Britain, April 16.

Cristina, Léa. 1995. "Brasil supera EUA nos preços." *O Globo*, July 1, p. 4.

Cypriano, Tania. 2007. *Grandma Has a Video Camera*. Film. New York: Viva! Pictures.

Daley, Suzanne. 2012. "Spain Recoils as Its Hungry Forage Trash Bins for a Next Meal." *New York Times*, September 25, p. 1.

Da Matta, Roberto. 1991. *Carnivals, Rogues, and Heroes: An Interpretation of the Brazilian Dilemma*. Translated by John Drury. Notre Dame, IN: University of Notre Dame Press.

Dantas, Iuri. 2005. "Bush elogia 'remoção rápida' de brasileiros." *Folha de São Paulo*, November 30.

Dávila, Sérgio. 2005. "'Revolta dos brasucas' agita cidade dos EUA." *Folha de São Paulo*, November 17.

Davis, Darién. 1997. "The Brazilian-Americans: Demography and Identity of an Emerging Latino Minority." *Latin Review of Books* (Spring/Fall): 8–15.

De Almeida, Alfredo Wagner Berno. 1995. "Exportação das tensões sociais na

Amazônia: Brasivianos, brasuelanos e brajolas-identidades construídas no conflito." *Travessia: Revista do Migrante* 21 (January–April): 28–36.

DeBiaggi, Sylvia Duarte Dantas. 1996. "Mudança, crise e redefinição de papéis: As mulheres brasileiras lá fora." *Travessia: Revista do Migrante* 26 (September–December): 24–26.

———. 2002. *Changing Gender Roles: Brazilian Immigrant Families in the U.S.* New York: LFB Scholarly Publishing.

De Carvalho, José Alberto Magno. 1996. "O saldo dos fluxos migratórios internacionais do Brasil na década de 80—Uma tentativa de estimação." *Revista Brasileira de Estudos de População* 13, no. 1: 3–14.

De Jesus, Sonia Melo. 2003. "Protagonistas de um Brasil imaginário: Faxineiras brasileiras em Boston." In *Fronteiras cruzadas: Etnicidade, gênero e redes sociais*, edited by Ana Cristina Braga Martes and Soraya Fleischer, 99–114. São Paulo: Editora Paz e Terra.

De Lourenço, Cileine, and Judith McDonnell. 2004. "The Politics of Identity: Brazilian Women Workers in Massachusetts." Paper presented at the meeting of the Latin American Studies Association, Las Vegas, October 6–8.

De Moura Castro, Claudio. 1989. "What Is Happening in Brazilian Education?" In *Social Change in Brazil, 1945–1985*, edited by Edmar L. Bacha and Herbert S. Klein, 263–309. Albuquerque: University of New Mexico Press.

Denman, Barbara. 2006. "Orlando Brazilian Church Finds God's Presence." *Florida Baptist Witness*, August 15.

De Oliveira, Elza. 1995. "Brasileiros podem ser expulsos do Paraguai." *O Globo*, July 3, p. 5.

De Oliveira, Renan Antunes. 1996a. "Framingham é capital dos 'brazucas' nos EUA." *O Estado de São Paulo*, October 13, p. C1.

———. 1996b. "Brasileiros mantêm hábitos em Framingham." *O Estado de São Paulo*, October 13, p. C5.

Donohue, Brian. 2005. "Brazilian Influx: As Mexico Border Crossings Increase, New Arrivals Fill Jersey Trades." *Star-Ledger* (Newark), November 14, p. 1.

dos Santos, Gislene Aparecida. 2001. "O caso dos migrantes da cidade de Criciúma Brasil para os Estados Unidos." *Scripta Nova. Revista Electrónica de Geografía y Ciencias Sociales, Universidad de Barcelona* 94, no. 13. http://www.ub.edu /geocrit/sn-94-13.htm.

———. 2006. "Catarinenses na fronteira México-Estados Unidos." *Travessia: Revista do Migrante* 55 (May–August): 23–31.

dos Santos, José Rebelo, Maria Filomena Mendes, Conceição Rego, and Maria da Graça Magalhães. 2010. "Imigrantes brasileiros em Portugal: Integração e sua percepção em relação aos portugueses." In *1º seminário de estudos sobre imigração brasileira na Europa*, edited by Flávio Carvalho, Maria Badet Souza, Manuella Callou, and Mar Rubiralta, 170–77. Barcelona: Universitat de Barcelona.

Dowd, Vincent. 2009. "Ireland's Brazilians Pack Their Bags." BBC, October 5. http://news.bbc.co.uk/2/hi/business/8280276.stm.

Duarte, Fernanda. 2005. "Living in 'the Betweens': Diaspora Consciousness Formation and Identity among Brazilians in Australia." *Journal of Intercultural Studies* 26, no. 4: 315-35.

Duarte, Karla Faria, Aparecida Amorim, Carlos Alberto Dias, and Sueli Siqueira. 2008. "Emigração e protestantismo: Vivência religiosa de fiéis evangélicos em contexto emigratório." In *Anais do XIII seminário sobre a economia mineira*, 1-22. Belo Horizonte: UFMG/Cedeplar.

Duffy, Gary. 2008. "Brazilians Shun 'American Dream.'" BBC, March 25. http://news.bbc.co.uk/2/hi/business/7312408.stm.

Dunn, Ashley. 1995. "In Newark, Immigration without Fear." *New York Times*, January 17, p. 11.

Dunn, Cyndi. 1999. "How Native Speakers See Us." *Anthropology News*, December, p. 11.

Economist. 2009. "Brazil Takes Off." *Economist*, November 12, p. 1.

———. 2012. "One Step at a Time." *Economist*, April 14.

Epstein, Aaron. 1997. "Codes Conceal U.S. Visa-System Bias, Suit Claims." *Miami Herald*, June 5, p. 1.

Espinoza, Rudolfo. 1994. "El sud." *News from Brazil*, January, pp. 17-18.

Evans, Yara. 2010. "Brasileiros em Londres: Um perfil socioeconômico." *Travessia: Revista do Migrante* 66 (January–June): 9-19.

Evans, Yara, Tánia Tonhati, Gustavo Tenoni Dias, Maria das Graças Brightwell, Olivia Sheringham, Ana Souza, and Cleverson Souza. 2011. *For a Better Life: Brazilians in London, 2010.* London: Grupo de Estudos Sobre Brasileiros no Reino Unido.

Evans, Yara, Jane Wills, Kavita Datta, Joanna Herbert, Cathy McIlwaine, Jon May, José Osvaldo de Araújo, Ana Carla França, and Ana Paula França. 2007. "Brazilians in London: A Report for the *Strangers into Citizens Campaign*." Queen Mary College, University of London. http://www.geog.qmul.ac.uk /globalcities/reports/docs/brazilians.pdf.

Ezabella, Fernanda. 2012. "Notas de um sonho americano." *Folha de São Paulo*, June 27, p. 20.

Fernandes, Adriana. 2008. "Caixa lança linha de crédito imobiliário para emigrantes." *O Estado de São Paulo*, November 25.

Fernandes, Daniela. 2003. "Comunidade pequena em Paris." *EU and Valor Econômico*, June 13, pp. 14-15.

Fernandes, Duval Magalhães, and José Irineu Rangel Rigotti. 2008. "Os Brasileiros na Europa: Notas introdutórias." Paper presented at Seminário Brasileiros no Mundo, Rio de Janeiro, July 17-18.

Ferraz, Silvio. 1996. "Acima do equador." *Veja*, July 10, pp. 54-55.

Fleischer, Soraya. 2002. *Passando a América a limpo: O trabalho de housecleaners brasileiras em Boston, Massachusetts.* São Paulo: Annablume Editora.

Folha de São Paulo. 1989. "Consulado dos EUA no Rio nega visto a mineiros." *Folha de São Paulo,* July 23, p. 4.

———. 1990. "Cresce o numero de Brasileiros que não querem mas ser brasileiros." *Folha de São Paulo,* March 18, p. C1.

———. 1997a. "America" é símbolo de progresso." *Folha de São Paulo,* January 26, p. 6.

———. 1997b. "Desejo de sair ainda existe." *Folha de São Paulo,* January 26, p. 6.

———. 2005a. "Captura de brasileiros nos Estados Unidos decuplica." *Educação,* May 5. http://educacao.uol.com.br/atualidades/imigracao-ilegal-captura-de-brasileiros-nos-estados-unidos-decuplica.jhtm.

———. 2005b. "Inglaterra estuda pedir visto de brasileiro." *Folha de São Paulo,* January 12.

Forjaz, Maria Cecilia Spina. 1993. "Os exilados da década 80: Imigrantes brasileiros nos Estados Unidos." *Revista de administração de empresas* 33 (January–February): 66–83.

Fornetti, Verena. 2011. "Cresce 9% nos EUA total de brasileiros deportados no ano." *Folha de São Paulo,* November 24.

———. 2012a. "Brasileiros fecham seus negócios nos EUA." *Folha de São Paulo,* February 22.

———. 2012b. "Cadê os brasileiros?" *Folha de São Paulo,* April 13.

Fox, Jason. 1997. "Little Burajiru: Brazilians of Non-Japanese Descent in Japan." Research proposal, Department of Anthropology, University of Florida, Gainesville.

França, Thais. 2010. "Excluindo sexo, raça e etnia: Mulheres brasileiras trabalhadoras em Portugal." In *1º seminário de estudos sobre imigração brasileira na Europa,* edited by Fláavio Carvalho, Maria Badet Souza, Manuella Callou, and Mar Rubiralta, 101–11. Barcelona: Universitat de Barcelona.

Frangella, Simone. 2010. "O made in Brasil em Londres: Migração e os bens culturais." *Travessia: Revista do Migrante* 66 (January–June): 33–43.

Freedman, Jennifer M. 2012. "Brazil's Future Less Bright amid Slowdown, De Gucht Says." *Bloomberg Businessweek,* May 7. http://www.businessweek.com/news/2012-05-07/brazil-s-future-less-bright-amid-slowdown-de-gucht-says.

Freston, Paul. 2008. "The Religious Field among Brazilians in the United States." In *Becoming Brazuca: Brazilian Immigration to the United States,* edited by Clémence Jouët-Pastré and Leticia Braga, 255–68. David Rockefeller Center Series on Latin American Studies. Cambridge, MA: Harvard University Press.

Fries, Laura. 2005. "Feliz ano novo!" *Creative Loafing,* January 12. http://tampa.creativeloafing.com/gyrobase/feliz_ano_novo_/Content?oid=4975.

Fritz, Catarina. 2011. *Brazilian Immigration and the Quest for Identity.* New York: LFB Scholarly Publishing.

Fussell, Elizabeth. 2007. "Brazilian Mobile Consulate Survey, New Orleans, LA." Mimeo.

———. n.d. "Hurricane Chasers in New Orleans: Latino Immigrants as a Source of a Rapid Response Labor Force." Mimeo. Department of Sociology, Washington State University.

Gainesville Sun. 2002."'Simpsons' Spoof Hits Raw Nerve in Brazil." *Gainesville Sun,* April 17, p. 5.

Galvão, Heloisa Maria. 2005. *As viajantes do século vinte.* Rio de Janeiro: HP Comunicação Editora.

Galvão, Vinicius Queiroz. 2005. "Ameaçados, brasileiros fogem nos EUA." *Folha de São Paulo,* August 21.

———. 2011. "Para EUA, candidato a visto é dividido em "bom," "mau" e "feio." *Folha de São Paulo,* February 1.

Gerson, Daniela. 2004. "Immigration Comes to Martha's Vineyard: Celebrity Getaway Hit with Big City Problems." *New York Sun,* July 12, p. 1.

———. 2005. "Swapping Caipirinhas for Currywurst: Immigration from Brazil to Germany Is on the Rise." *Der Spiegel,* September 9.

———. 2009. "How Migration Transformed Martha's Vineyard." *Financial Times,* August 15.

Gibson, Annie McNeill. 2008. "Brazucas in NOLA: A Cultural Analysis of Brazilian Immigration to New Orleans Post-Katrina." Paper presented at the meeting of the Brazilian Studies Association, New Orleans, March 27–29.

———. 2010. "Immigrating to New Orleans Post-Katrina: An Ethnographic Study of a Brazilian Enclave." PhD dissertation, Tulane Univesity, New Orleans.

———. 2012. *Post-Katrina Brazucas: Brazilian Immigrants in New Orleans.* New Orleans: University of New Orleans Press.

Glickhouse, Rachel. 2011. "Brazilians' 'Fanatical' Travel to U.S. Helps Drive Brazil's Economic Boom." *Christian Science Monitor,* August 11.

Glick Schiller, Nina, Linda Basch, and Cristina Szanton Blanc, eds. 1992a. *Towards a Transnational Perspective on Migration: Race, Class, Ethnicity and Nationalism Reconsidered.* Vol. 645. New York: Annals of the New York Academy of Sciences.

———. 1992b. "Transnationalism: A New Analytic Framework for Understanding Migration." In *Towards a Transnational Perspective on Migration: Race, Class, Ethnicity and Nationalism Reconsidered,* edited by Nina Glick Schiller, Linda Basch, and Cristina Szanton Blanc, 645:1–27. New York: Annals of the New York Academy of Sciences.

Global Property Guide. 2011. "Brazilian Rent Prices Booming, Analysts Fear Bust." *NuWire Investor,* June 14. http://www.nuwireinvestor.com/articles /brazilian-rent-prices-booming-analysts-fear-bust-57389.aspx.

Godoy, Denyse. 2007. "Brasileiros contam por que deixaram os EUA para trás." *Folha de São Paulo,* December 9.

Gomide, Raphael. 2009. "3 milhões de brasileiros vivem no exterior." *Folha de São Paulo Cotidiano,* October 16.

Goodnough, Abby. 2010. "Immigrants' Pilot Lessons Spur Inquiry by the U.S." *New York Times*, November 6, p. 17.

Goyette, Jared. 2008. "Back to Brazil." *Charleston City Paper*, February 20, p. 1.

Goza, Franklin. 1994. "Brazilian Immigration to North America." *International Migration Review* 28, no. 1: 136–52.

———. 1999. "Brazilian Immigration to Ontario." *International Migration* 37, no. 4: 765–89.

———. 2003. "Redes sociais e a integração de brasileiros no Canadá e nos Estados Unidos." In *Fronteiras cruzadas: Etnicidade, gênero e redes sociais*, edited by Ana Cristina Braga Martes and Soraya Fleischer, 263–88. São Paulo: Editora Paz e Terra.

———. 2005. "EUA representam a terra prometida." *Folha de São Paulo*, January 16.

Grand, Desiree, and Franziska Castillo. 2004. "Little Brazil Emerges." *Journal News* (Westchester County, NY), May 8, p. 1.

Green, James N. 2010. *We Cannot Remain Silent: Opposition to the Brazilian Military Dictatorship in the United States*. Durham, NC: Duke University Press.

Grieco, Elizabeth M., and Edward N. Trevelyan. 2010. "Place of Birth of the Foreign Born Population: 2009." American Community Survey Briefs. Washington, DC: U.S. Census Bureau.

Guedes, Luisa. 2007. "Brasileiros denunciam dificuldades e maus-tratos ao tentarem entrar em outros países." *O Globo*, October 18.

Hasenbalg, Carlos, and Alejandro Frigerio. 1999. *Imigrantes brasileiros na Argentina: Um perfil sociodemográfico*. Serie Estudos no. 101. Rio de Janeiro: Instituto Universitário de Pesquisas do Rio de Janeiro.

Healy, Claire. 2008. "Carnaval do Galway: The Brazilian Community in Gort, 1999–2006." *Irish Migration Studies in Latin America* 4, no. 3: 150–53.

Henley, Jon. 2000. "Chic Parisians Find Hookers a Drag." *Guardian*, January 25.

Herdy, Thiago, and Maiá Menezes. 2010. "Em Governador Valadares, enterro agora é exibido para os Estados Unidos." *O Globo*, November 20.

Higuchi, Naoto. 2001. "Migration Process of Nikkei Brazilians." Paper presented at the International Symposium on Latin American Emigration, National Museum of Ethnology, Osaka, Japan, December 11–13.

Hisayasu, Alexandre. 2005. "Brasil prende quadrilha de imigração ilegal." *Folha de São Paulo*, November 30.

Hoefner, Michael, Nancy Rytina, and Bryan C. Baker. 2009. "Estimates of the Unauthorized Immigrant Population Residing in the United States: Jan. 2008." Office of Immigration Statistics, Department of Homeland Security Population Estimates, Washington, DC.

Huamany, Walter. 2004. "Primeiros repatriados dos EUA chegam ao país." *O Globo*, January 29, p. 8.

Huff-Hannon, Joseph. 2009. "Hard Days for a Buff and Shine Man." *New York Times*, February 6, p. C7.

Hurdle, Jon. 2006. "New Jersey Protestors Clash over Illegal Immigration." Reuters, August 20. http://www.redorbit.com/news/general/624634/new_ jersey_protestors_clash_over_illegal_immigration/.

Ikegami, Shigehiro. 2001. "Brazilians and Local Industrailization in Hamamatsu: A Case of an Industrial City in Japan." Paper presented at the International Symposium on Latin American Emigration, National Museum of Ethnology, Osaka, Japan, December 11–13.

Infante, Anelise. 2008. "Estudantes brasileiros barrados na Espanha embarcam para o Brasil." *Folha de São Paulo*, July 3.

Inman, Philip. 2011. "Brazil Overtakes UK as Sixth-Largest Economy." *Guardian*, December 25.

Instituto Brasileiro de Geografia e Estatística (IBGE). 2012. "Para IBGE, crise internacional atraiu mais imigrantes ao Brasil." *Notícias*, April 27.

———. 2011. *Censo Demográfico 2010*. Rio de Janeiro. http://www.ibge.gov.br /home/estatistica/populacao/censo2010/default.shtm.

Ishi, Angelo. 2003. "Searching for Home, Pride, and 'Class': Japanese Brazilians in the Land of the Yen." In *Searching for Home Abroad: Japanese Brazilians and Transnationalism*, edited by Jeffrey Lesser, 75–102. Durham, NC: Duke University Press.

———. 2004. "Social and Cultural Aspects of Brazilians in Japan." IDB Migration Seminar, Migration and Remittances in the Context of Globalization: The Case of Japan and Latin America. http://idbdocs.iadb.org/wsdocs/get document.aspx?docnum=556433.

Jones-Correa, Michael. 2001. "Under Two Flags: Dual Nationality in Latin America and Its Consequences for the United States." *International Migration Review* 35, no. 4: 997–1029.

Jones-Correa, Michael, and Diana Leal. 1998."Becoming 'Hispanic': Secondary Panethnic Identifications among Latin American-Origin Populations in the United States." *Hispanic Journal of Behavioral Sciences* 18:214–54.

Jordan, Miriam, and Paulo Trevisani. 2011. "Buoyed by Recovery, Migrants Send Home More Money." *Wall Street Journal*, March 14.

Jornal do Brasil. 1997a. "Consulado barra atleta mulato." *Jornal do Brasil*, March 15, p. 21.

———. 1997b. "Consulado americano nega visto a prefeitinho." *Jornal do Brasil*, April 15, p. 18.

Jouët-Pastré, Clémence, and Leticia J. Braga, eds. 2008. *Becoming Brazuca: Brazilian Immigration to the United States*. David Rockefeller Center Series on Latin American Studies. Cambridge, MA: Harvard University Press.

Kammer, Jerry. 2002. "Flow of Brazilians to U.S.: A Growing Trend." *San Diego Union-Tribune*, August 5, p. 1.

———. 2005. "Loophole to America." *San Diego Union-Tribune*, June 4, p. 1.

Kapur, Sahil. 2012. "Facebook's Eduardo Saverin Likely Barred From Re-Entering

U.S." Talking Points Memo, May 17. http://tpmdc.talkingpointsmemo.com /2012/05/facebook-eduardo-saverin-ipo-citizenship-singapore-immigration.php ?ref=fp.

Kaste, Martin. 2006. "For Poor Brazilians, a Perilous, Illegal Journey to U.S." *Reporter's Notebook*, National Public Radio, April 16. http://www.npr.org /templates/story/story.php?storyId=5342957.

Kashiwazaki, Chikako. 2002. "Japan's Resilient Demand for Foreign Workers." Migration Policy Institute, May. www.migrationinformation.org/feature /display.cfm?ID=8.

Kershaw, Sarah. 2010. "Immigration Crackdown Steps into the Kitchen." *New York Times*, September 8, p. D3.

Kirshner, Joshua. 2004. "*A União Tem Força*? A Comparative Study of Labor Union Outreach to Brazilian Immigrant Workers in Boston." Paper presented at the Association of Collegiate Schools of Planning Annual Conference, Portland, Oregon, October 21–24.

———. 2008. "An Analysis of Three Labor Unions' Outreach to Brazilian Immigrant Workers in Boston." *Journal of Labor and Society* 11 (June): 255–75.

Klagsbrunn, Victor Hugo. 1996. "Globalização da economia mundial e mercado de trabalho: A emigração de brasileiros para os Estados Unidos e Japão." In *Migrações internacionais: Herança XX, Agenda XXI*, edited by Neide Lopes Patarra, 33–48. Campinas: Programa Interinstitucional de Avaliação e Acompanhamento das Migrações Internacionais no Brasil.

Klein, Misha. 2012. *Kosher Feijoada and Other Paradoxes of Jewish Life in São Paulo*. Gainesville: University Press of Florida.

Klintowitz, Jaime. 1995. "O país pula a cerca." *Veja*, July 19, pp. 60–67.

———. 1996. "Nossa gente lá fora." *Veja*, April 3, pp. 26–29.

Kocian, Lisa. 2005. "Tempest over Illegal Immigrants Roils Town." *Boston Globe*, May 19.

Kottak, Conrad Phillip. 2009. *Prime-Time Society: An Anthropological Analysis of Television and Culture*. Updated edition. Walnut Creek, CA: Left Coast Press.

Koyama, Chieko. 1998. "Japanese-Brazilians: The Transformation of Ethnic Identity in the Country of Their Ancestors." MA thesis, University of Florida, Gainesville.

Kugel, Seth. 2009. "Longing for Ginger Ale." *GlobalPost*, April 18. http://www .globalpost.com/dispatch/brazil/090414/longing-ginger-ale.

Langevin, Mark S. 2010. "Gravity and Turbulence: United States-Brazil Relations under Obama and Lula." *American Diplomacy*, June. http://www.unc.edu /depts/diplomat/item/2010/0406/comm/langevin_brazil.html.

Larimer, Tim, and Hiroko Tashiro. 1999. "Battling the Bloodlines." *Time*, August 9.

Leitão, Miriam. 2012. "Perto do zero: O Brasil parou de crescer." *O Globo*, September 10.

Levitt, Peggy. 1997. "Transnationalizing Community Development: The Case of Migration between Boston and the Dominican Republic." *Nonprofit and Voluntary Sector Quarterly* 26, no. 4: 509–26.

———. 2001. *The Transnational Villagers*. Berkeley: University of California Press.

Levitt, Peggy, and Rafael de la Dehesa. 1998. "The Role of the State in Shaping Transnational Political Participation." Paper presented at the meeting of the Latin American Studies Association, Chicago, September 24–26.

Lima, Alvaro. 2009. "Brasileiros na América." http://www.digaai.org/wp/pdfs /Brazilians_in_the_US_portugues.pdf.

Lima, Alvaro, and Eduardo Siqueira. 2007. *Brazilians in the U.S.: A Demographic and Economic Profile*. Boston: Mauricio Gaston Institute, University of Massachusetts.

Linger, Daniel T. 1997. "Brazil Displaced: Restaurante 51 in Nagoya, Japan." *Horizontes Antropológicos* 5:181–203.

———. 2001a. *No One Home: Brazilian Selves Remade in Japan*. Durham, NC: Duke University Press.

———. 2001b. "The Identity Path of Eduardo Mori." In *History in Person*, edited by Dorothy Holland and Jean Lave, 217–44. Santa Fe, NM: School of American Research Press.

Lobato, Paulo Henrique. 2012. "Dinheiro de Valadares salva negócios nos EUA." *Estado de Minas*, April 15, p. 1.

Lobo, Arun Peter, and Joseph J. Salvo. 2004. *The Newest New Yorkers 2000*. Population Division, New York City Department of City Planning, New York. http://www.nyc.gov/html/dcp/html/census/nny.shtml.

Longa, Lyda. 1994. "Brazilian Investors Claim Florida as Their Home Away from Home. *Wall Street Journal*, November 16, pp. F1, 3.

Lourenço, Amanda, and Juliana Cunha. 2012. "De volta ao país, brasileiros sofrem 'síndrome do regresso.'" *Folha de São Paulo*, March 6.

Luis, Emerson. 1993. "Sabot Policy." *News from Brazil* 87 (March): 16.

Luna, Alfons. 2005. "Brasil é o segundo destino de remessas de emigrantes no mundo." *UOL Economia*, March 22. http://noticias.uol.com.br/economia /ultnot/2005/03/22/ult35u40080.jhtm.

Machado, Igor José de Renó. 2003. "CÁRCERE PÚBLICO: Processos de exotização entre imigrantes brasileiros no Porto, Portugal." PhD dissertation, Instituto de Filosofia e Ciências Humanas, Universidade Estadual de Campinas, Campinas, São Paulo.

———. 2006. "Imigração em Portugal." *Estudos Avançados* 20, no. 57: 119–35.

Machelor, Patty. 2002. "Brazilian Entrants More Common." *Arizona Daily Star*, August 1.

Magalhães, Valéria Barbosa de. 2004. "Diversity among the Brazilians in South Florida: The Case of the Gays and Lesbians." Paper presented at the meeting of the Latin American Studies Association, Las Vegas, October 6–8.

Mahler, Sarah J. 1995. *American Dreaming: Immigrant Life on the Margins.* Princeton, NJ: Princeton University Press.

Maia, Suzana, 2012. *Transnational Desires: Brazilian Erotic Dancers in New York.* Nashville: Vanderbilt University Press.

Maisonnave, Fabiano. 2005a. "Explode número de brasileiros presos nos EUA." *Folha de São Paulo,* January 16.

———. 2005b. "Prisões também aumentam do lado mexicano." *Folha de São Paulo,* January 16.

———. 2005c. "Captura de brasileiros nos EUA decuplica." *Folha de São Paulo,* May 5.

———. 2005d. "EUA tem recorde de detidos brasileiros." *Folha de São Paulo,* October 5, p. 35.

———. 2005e. "Comunidade da região vive 'baby boom.'" *Folha de São Paulo,* December 4.

———. 2005f. "Empresário emprega outros 30 brasileiros." *Folha de São Paulo,* December 4.

———. 2005g. "Pesquisa mapeia os brasileiros de Boston." *Folha de São Paulo,* December 4.

Maisonnave, Fabiano, and Thiago Guimarães. 2005. "Rota do tráfico na Guatemala é o novo caminho para atingir EUA." *Folha de São Paulo,* November 30.

Marcelli, Enrico, Louisa Holmes, David Estella, and Fausto da Rocha. 2009. "Visible Migrants: The Health and Socioeconomic Integration of Brazilians in the Boston Metropolitan Area." Brazilian Immigrant Center and San Diego State University, San Diego.

Marcus, Alan P. 2004. "Brasileiros em Massachusetts, E.U.A.: A identidade étnica de uma minoria invisivel." Paper presented at the meeting of the Brazilian Studies Association, Rio de Janeiro, June 9–12.

———. 2008a. "New Immigrant Settlements in the U.S. South: Brazilians in Marietta, Georgia." Paper presented at the meeting of the Brazilian Studies Association, New Orleans, March 27–29.

———. 2008b. "The Contexts and Consequences of Brazilian Transnational Migration Processes: An Ethnic Geography in Two Countries." PhD dissertation, University of Massachusetts, Amherst.

———. 2009a. "Back to Piracanjuba and Governador Valadares: Returnees, Geographical Imaginations and Its Discontents." Paper presented at the meeting of the Latin American Studies Association, Rio de Janeiro, June 11–14.

———. 2009b. "(Re)creating Places and Spaces in Two Countries: Brazilian Transnational Migration Processes." *Journal of Cultural Geography* 26, no. 2: 173–98.

———. 2009c. "Brazilian Immigration to the United States and the Geographical Imagination." *The Geographical Review* 99, no. 4: 481–98.

———. 2011a. "Experiencing Ethnic Economies: Brazilian Immigrants and Returnees." *Journal of Immigrant and Refugee Studies* 9:57–81.

———. 2011b. *Towards Rethinking Brazil: A Thematic and Regional Approach.* Hoboken NJ: John Wiley.

———. 2011c. "Racial Self-identification among Brazilian Immigrants in the U.S. and Returnees in Brazil." In *Race, Ethnicity, and Place in a Changing America,* 2nd ed., edited by John W. Frazier and Eugene L. Tettey-Fio, 197–209. New York: SUNY Press.

Margolis, Maxine L. 1973. *The Moving Frontier: Social and Economic Change in a Southern Brazilian Community.* Gainesville: University of Florida Press.

———. 1990. "From Mistress to Servant: Downward Mobility among Brazilian Immigrants in New York City." *Urban Anthropology* 19, no. 3: 1–17.

———. 1992. "Women in International Migration: The Case of Brazilians in New York City." Conference Paper No. 66. Changing Perspectives on Women in Latin America and the Caribbean, Columbia University–New York University Consortium for Latin American and Caribbean Studies, New York, April 24.

———. 1994a. *Little Brazil: An Ethnography of Brazilian Immigrants in New York City.* Princeton, NJ: Princeton University Press.

———. 1994b. "A House Divided: The Absence of Community Organization among Brazilian Immigrants in New York City." Paper presented at the meeting of the American Anthropological Association, Atlanta, November 30–December 4.

———. 1995a. "Brazilians and the 1990 United States Census: Immigrants, Ethnicity and the Undercount." *Human Organization* 54, no. 1: 52–59.

———. 1995b. "Transnationalism and Popular Culture: The Case of Brazilian Immigrants in the United States." *Journal of Popular Culture* 29, no. 1: 29–41.

———. 1998. "We Are *Not* Immigrants: Contested Categories among Brazilians in New York City and Rio de Janeiro." In *Diasporic Identity,* edited by Carol A. Mortland, 30–50. Selected Papers on Refugees and Immigrants, vol. 6. Arlington, VA: American Anthropological Association.

———. 2001a. "With New Eyes: Returned International Immigrants in Rio de Janeiro." In *Raízes e rumos: Perspectivas interdisciplinares em estudos americanos,* edited by Sonia Torres, 239–44. Rio de Janeiro: Editora 7 Letras.

———. 2001b. "Notes on Transnational Migration: The Case of Brazilian Immigrants." In *Negotiating Transnationalism,* edited by MaryCarol Hopkins and Nancy Wellmeier, 202–22. Selected Papers in Refugees and Immigrants, vol. 9. Arlington, VA: American Anthropological Association.

———. 2002. "Separation and Divorce in Brazilian Immigrant Families." In *Contemporary Ethnic Families in the United States: Characteristics, Variations, and Dynamics,* edited by Nicole V. Benokraitis, 319–21. New York: Prentice Hall.

———. 2003. Forum on Brasphobia, sponsored by the Brazilian Rainbow Group, Hunter College–CUNY, New York.

———. 2007. "Becoming Brazucas: Brazilian Identity in the United States." In *The Other Latinos: Central and South Americans in the United States*, edited by José Luis Falconi and José Antonio Mazzotti, 210–27. David Rockefeller Center Series on Latin American Studies. Cambridge, MA: Harvard University Press.

———. 2008a. "Race in Brazil." In *Encyclopedia of Race and Racism*, vol. 1, edited by John H. Moore, 245–49. Detroit: Macmillan Reference USA.

———. 2008b. "September 11 and Transnationalism: The Case of Brazilian Immigrants in the United States." *Human Organization* 67, no. 1: 1–11.

———. 2009. *An Invisible Minority: Brazilians in New York City*. Revised and updated edition. Gainesville: University Press of Florida.

Margolis, Maxine L., Neda Bezerra, and Jason Fox. 2001. "Brazil." In *Countries and Their Cultures*, edited by Melvin Ember and Carol R. Ember, 282–301. New York: Macmillan Reference.

Marrow, Helen B. 2003. "To Be or Not to Be (Hispanic or Latino): Brazilian Racial and Ethnic Identity in the United States." *Ethnicities* 3:427–64.

———. 2004. "Coming to Grips with Race: Second-Generation Brazilians in the United States." Paper presented at the meeting of the Brazilian Studies Association, Rio de Janeiro, June 9–12.

———. 2007. "Who Are the Other Latinos, and Why?" In *The Other Latinos: Central and South Americans in the United States*, edited by José Luis Falconi and José Antonio Mazzotti, 39–77. David Rockefeller Center Series on Latin American Studies. Cambridge, MA: Harvard University Press.

———. 2012. "In Ireland 'Latin Americans Are Kind of Cool': Evaluating a National Context of Reception with a Transnational Lens." *Ethnicities*. Prepublished October 17, doi:10.1177/1468796812463188.

Martes, Ana Cristina Braga. 1996a. "Solidariedade e competição: Acesso ao mercado de trabalho e atuação das igrejas entre os imigrantes brasileiros na área de Boston." Mimeo.

———. 1996b. "Social Remittances: Brazilians in Boston." Mimeo.

———. 1996c. "Trabalhadoras brasileiras em Boston." *Travessia: Revista do Migrante* 26 (September–December): 19–23.

———. 1996d. "A atuação das igrejas entre os imigrantes brasileiros nos Estados Unidos." *Multiciência* 1, no. 1: 109–17.

———. 1997. "Respeito e cidadania: O ministerio das relações exteriores e os imigrantes brasileiros em Boston." Paper presented at the First Symposium on Brazilian Emigration, Lisbon, October 23–25.

———. 1998. "Citizenship and Solidarity: The Construction of Identities among Brazilian Immigrants in Massachusetts." Paper presented at the meeting of the Latin American Studies Association, Chicago, September 24–26.

———. 1999. "Os imigrantes brasileiros e as igrejas em Massachusetts." In *Cenas do Brasil migrante*, edited by Rosana R. Reis and Teresa Sales, 87–122. São Paulo: Boitempo.

———. 2000. *Brasileiros nos Estados Unidos: Um estudo sobre imigrantes em Massachusetts.* São Paulo: Editora Paz e Terra.

———. 2004. "Brazilian Immigration: Historical Perspective and Identity." In *Giving Voice to a Nascent Community: Exploring Brazilian Immigration to the U.S. through Research and Practice*, edited by Clémence Jouët-Pastré, Megwen Loveless, and Leticia Braga, 38–41. Working Paper No. 04/05-2, David Rockefeller Center for Latin American Studies, Harvard University.

———. 2007. "Neither Hispanic Nor Black: We're Brazilian." In *The Other Latinos: Central and South Americans in the United States*, edited by José Luis Falconi and José Antonio Mazzotti, 231–56. David Rockefeller Center Series on Latin American Studies. Cambridge, MA: Harvard University Press.

———. 2008. "The Commitment of Return: Remittances of Brazilian Emigrés." In *Becoming Brazuca: Brazilian Immigration to the United States*, edited by Clémence Jouët-Pastré and Leticia Braga, 125–50. David Rockefeller Center Series on Latin American Studies. Cambridge, MA: Harvard University Press.

———. 2010. *New Immigrants, New Land: A Study of Brazilians in Massachusetts.* Gainesville: University Press of Florida.

Martes, Ana Cristina Braga, and Weber Soares. 2006. "Remessas de recursos dos imigrantes." *Estudos Avançados* 20, no. 57: 41–54.

Martins, Rui. 2010. "Padres, pastores, comerciantes, viva o conselho de emigrantes." *Correio do Brasil*, November 14.

Masanet, Erika, and Rosana Baeninger. 2010. "Os impactos laborais da crise econômica sobre a população brasileira na Espanha." In *1º seminário de estudos sobre imigração brasileira na Europa*, edited by Flávio Carvalho, Maria Badet Souza, Manuella Callou, and Mar Rubiralta, 205–12. Barcelona: Universitat de Barcelona.

———. 2011. "Brasileiros e brasileiras na Espanha: Mercado de trabalho, seguridade social e desemprego." *Revista Paranaense de Desenvolvimento* 121:65–89.

Massey, Douglas S. 1988. "Economic Development and International Migration in Comparative Perspective." *Population and Development Review* 14, no. 3: 383–411.

———. 1990. "Social Structure, Household Strategies, and the Cumulative Causation of Migration." *Population Index* 56, no. 1: 3–26.

Massey, Douglas S., J. Arango, G. Hugo, A. Kouaouci, A. Pellegrino, and J. E. Taylor. 1998. *Worlds in Motion: Understanding International Migration at the End of the Millennium.* Oxford: Clarendon Press.

Massey, Douglas S., Rafael Ailrcon, Jorge Durand, and Humberto Gonzales. 1987. *Return to Aztlan.* Berkeley: University of California Press.

Máximo, Luciano, and Gustavo Faleiros. 2010. "Crise traz de volta ao país 400 mil 'expatriados.'" *EU and Valor Econômico*, May 24.

McDonald, Dan. 2010. "Framingham's Jim Rizoli Plans Challenge of Rep. Richardson." *MetroWest Daily News*, February 12.

Meihy, José Carlos Sebe Bom. 2004. *Brasil fora de si*. São Paulo: Parábola.

Meirelles, José Passos. 2005. "Triplica número de brasileiros detidos nos EUA." *Sindicato Mercosul*, April 25.

Menai, Tania. 1999. "Em Nova York mas com dinheiro." *Veja*, December 1, pp. 23, 60–63.

———. 2007. *Nova York: Do oiapoque ao chuí*. Rio de Janeiro: Casa da Palavra.

Menconi, Darlene. 2004. "O verde contra ataca." *Isto É*, June 9, pp. 92, 97.

Menezes, Gustavo Hamilton. 2000. "Filhas da emigração: Sobre a segunda geração de brasileiros nos EUA." MA thesis, Universidade de Brasília, Brasília.

———. 2003. "Filhos da imigração: A segunda geração de brasileiros em Connecticut." In *Fronteiras cruzadas: Etnicidade, gênero e redes sociais*, edited by Ana Cristina Braga Martes and Soraya Fleischer, 157–73. São Paulo: Editora Paz e Terra.

Millman, Joel. 1997. *The Other Americans: How Immigrants Renew Our Country, Our Economy and Our Values*. New York: Viking.

———. 2006. "Immigrant Group Puts a New Spin on Cleaning Niche." *Wall Street Journal*, February 16, p. 1.

Mineo, Liz. 2004. "Second Generation Breaks from Traditions." *Milford Daily News*, January 22.

———. 2005a. "Ministers Discourage Illegal Journey." *Milford Daily News*, July 10, p. 1.

———. 2005b. "Brazilian Commission: Group Visits MetroWest, Boston to Deal with Immigrant Issues." *Milford Daily News*, October 23, p. 1.

———. 2006a. "Streets Paved with Dollars." *MetroWest Daily News*, December 17.

———. 2006b. "Climbing the Social Ladder." *MetroWest Daily News*, December 17.

———. 2006c. "Empty Villages Left Behind." *Milford Daily News*, December 17.

———. 2006d. "A Newspaper Connects Two Communities." *MetroWest Daily News*, December 17.

———. 2006e. "Smugglers Trade in Dreams." *MetroWest Daily News*, December 17.

———. 2006f. "Long Odds Don't Deter Immigrants." *MetroWest Daily News*, December 17.

———. 2006g. "Brazilian Congress Takes Tougher Stance on Smuggling." *Milford Daily News*, December 20.

———. 2006h. "Strangers in Two Lands." *MetroWest Daily News*, December 19.

———. 2006i. "Emigration Disturbs Schools, Students." *MetroWest Daily News*, December 20.

———. 2006j. "A Shaky Economy Driven by Dollars from Illegal Immigration." *MetroWest Daily News*, December 19.

———. 2007. "Brazilians Getting One-Way Ticket Home." *MetroWest Daily News*, October 2.

———. 2008. "New Trends Show Many Brazilians in Region Hail from Goias." *Milford Daily News*, January 13.

Ministério das Relações Exteriores. 2010. "Guia de Retorno ao Brasil." Brasília. http://www.portalconsular.mre.gov.br/avisos/guia-de-retorno-ao-brasil.

———. 2011. "Brasileiros no Mundo Estimativas." 3rd edition. Brasília. http://tinyurl.com/BrasileirosEstimativas.

Moeller, Susan. 2003. "Dreams Dashed as Visas Denied." *Cape Cod Times*, February 24.

Moreira, I. 2007. "Dolar a R$2 gera crise em cidade de MG." *EU and Valor Econômico*, August 28, p. 16.

Moroz, Jennifer. 2005a. "A New Jersey Town, a Brazilian Deluge, Diverging Hopes." *Philadelphia Inquirer*, October 9, p. 1.

———. 2005b. "Flight to the U.S. Brings Brazilians Pain and Promise." *Philadelphia Inquirer*, October 10, p. 6.

———. 2005c. "A Struggle to Find Common Ground on Unfamiliar Turf." *Philadelphia Inquirer*, October 10, p. 1.

———. 2005d. "A Struggle to Plant Roots While Living in Constant Fear." *Philadelphia Inquirer*, October 11, p. 1.

Motta, Felipe. 2010. "'Ele queria melhorar de vida,' diz prima de brasileiro morto no México." *Folha de São Paulo*, August 30.

Moura, Fernando. 2010. "Pororoca no tejo." *EU and Valor Econômico*, August 20–22, pp. 20–22.

Mugnatto, Sílvia. 1997. "Brasileiro confia menos no real." *Jornal do Brasil*, June 11, p. 14.

Munoz, Lorenza. 1995. "Southland Samba: Immigrant Community's Diverse Culture of Art, Music, Cuisine and Religion Is Alive on Westside." *Los Angeles Times*, July 13, p. J12.

Musante, Fred. 1996. "New Takes on the Melting Pot." *New York Times*, Connecticut Weekly, March 31, pp. 1, 12.

Nascimento, Solano. 2005. "A cidade goiana das 'espanholas.'" *Veja*, March 2, pp. 52–53.

Neto, João Sorima, and Ernesto Bernardes. 1996. "A Miami do Brasil." *Veja*, July 17, pp. 50–65.

Netto, Vladmir. 1997. "Torneira fechada." *Veja*, July 2, p. 54.

Neuman, William, and Maria Eugenia Diaz. 2012. "Venezuela to Investigate Report That Brazilian Miners Massacred Indian Village." *New York Times*, August 30, p. 7.

New York Times. 1995. "Soccer in the Mah-Jongg Belt: Brazilian Resort Workers Form an Unlikely Catskills Colony." *New York Times*, October 21, p. 16.

Nidecker, Fernanda. 2008. "Em 2006, três países 'expulsaram' mais de 20 mil brasileiros." BBC Brasil, March 25. http://www.bbc.co.uk/portuguese/reporter bbc/story/2008/03/080320_imigracaodevolvepaisesricos_fp.shtml.

Nishida, Mieko. 2009. "Why Does a Nikkei Want to Talk to Other Nikkeis? Japanese Brazilians and Their Identitites in São Paulo." *Critique of Anthropology* 29, no. 4: 423–45.

Noguera, Mari Carmem, and Luciana Coelho. 2005. "Espanha legaliza 700 mil imigrantes." *Folha de São Paulo*, June 3.

Nolan, Bruce. 2008. "Many Brazilians Settling in N.O., but for How Long?" *Times-Picayune* (New Orleans), January 19.

Nublat, Johanna. 2010. "Pleito para conselho do Itamaraty move líderes 'brasucas.'" *Folha de São Paulo*, August 30.

O Centro de Informação e Assessoria Técnica (CIAAT). n.d. *Um presente especial.* Governador Valadares, Minas Gerais. http://www.ciaatgv.com.br/.

O Globo. 1995. "Class média passou logo da euforia à inadimplência." *O Globo*, July 1, p. 4.

———. 2001. "Guia de salário." *O Globo*, March 2, p. 22.

———. 2007. "Crise do crédito atinge brasileiros nos EUA." *O Globo*, August 8.

———. 2010. "Pré-candidatos buscam voto de brasileiros no exterior." *O Globo*, April 22.

O'Leary, Mary E. 2005. "Danbury March Shows Support for Immigrants." *New Haven Register*, June 13, p. 1.

Oliveira, Adriana Capuano de. 2003. "O caminho sem volta: Classe social e etnicidade entre os brasileiros na Flórida." In *Fronteiras cruzadas: Etnicidade, gênero e redes sociais*, edited by Ana Cristina Braga Martes and Soraya Fleischer, 115–38. São Paulo: Editora Paz e Terra.

———. 2004. "Bienvenido a Miami: A inserção dos imigrantes brasileiros através da América Latina." PhD dissertation, Universidade Estadual de Campinas, Campinas, São Paulo.

Olmsted, Ana Santos. 2010. "A comunidade brasileira em Atlanta." Paper presented at the meeting of the Brazilian Studies Association, Brasília, July 22–24.

Onishi, Norimitsu. 2008. "Enclave of Brazilians Tests Insular Japan." *New York Times*, November 2, p. 9.

Organização Internacional para as Migrações. 2010. *Perfil migratório do Brasil 2009.* Geneva. http://publications.iom.int/bookstore/free/Brazil_Profile2009.pdf.

Padilla, Beatriz. 2007. "A imigrante brasileira em Portugal: Considerando o gênero na análise." In *Imigração brasileira em Portugal*, edited by Jorge Malheiros, 113–34. Lisbon: Observatório da Imigração.

Padilla, Beatriz, Mariana Selister, and Gleiciani Fernandes. 2010. "Ser brasileira em Portugal: Imigração, gênero e colonialidade." In *1° seminário de estudos sobre imigração brasileira na Europa*, edited by Flávio Carvalho, Maria Badet Souza, Manuella Callou, and Mar Rubiralta, 113–20. Barcelona: Universitat de Barcelona.

Paerregaard, Karsten. 2005. "Inside the Hispanic Melting Pot: Negotiating National and Multicultural Identities among Peruvians in the United States." *Latino Studies* 3, no. 1: 76–98.

Paiva, Esdras. 1997. "Tudo pelo visto." *Veja*, April 2, p. 79.

Paiva, Paulo. 2001. "Remessas ajudam nas contas do pais." *Gazeta Mercantil*, August 13, p. 1.

Paoletti, R. 1987. "Enclave brasileiro." *Isto É* 560:58–59.

Patarra, Neide Lopes, and Rosana Baeninger. 1995. "Migrações internacionais recentes: O caso do Brasil. In *Emigração e imigração no Brasil contemporânea*, edited by Neide Lopes Patarra, 78–88. Campinas: Programa Interinstitucional de Avaliação e Acompanhamento das Migrações Internacionais no Brasil.

Pedroso, Elias. 2008. "Imigrantes da Amazônia ocidental no estado da Flórida." Honors thesis, Universidade Federal do Acre, Rio Branco.

Peixoto, Fabrícia. 2010. "Remessas de brasileiros no exterior têm maior queda em 11 anos." BBC Brasil, February 3. http://www.bbc.co.uk/portuguese/noticias /2010/02/100203_remessasbrasileiros_fp.shtml.

Peixoto, Paulo. 2007. "Governador Valadares ainda tenta se adaptar." *Folha de São Paulo*, December 9, p. C29.

Pereira, Mariana Cunha. 2006. "Processos migratórios na fronteira Brasil-Guiana." *Estudos Avançados* 20, no. 57: 209–19.

Pereira, Néli. 2008a. "Boom ainda não atrai imigrantes de volta ao Brasil." BBC Brasil, March 24. http://www.bbc.co.uk/portuguese/reporterbbc/story /2008/03/080319_imigracaoboomeconomia_np.shtml.

———. 2008b. "Alta do real força aumento de jornada de trabalho de imigrantes." BBC Brasil, March 24. http://www.bbc.co.uk/portuguese/reporterbbc /story/2008/03/080320_imigracaoaltareal_np.shtml.

Pereira, Néli, and Sylvia Salek. 2008. "Êxodo de brasileiros continua após três décadas." BBC Brasil, March 24. http://www.bbc.co.uk/portuguese/reporter bbc/story/2008/03/080318_imigracao25anosexodo.shtml.

Perroud, Mélanie. 2007. "Migration retour ou migration détour? Diversité des parcours migratoires des brésiliens d'ascendance japonaise." *Revue Européenne des Migrations Internationales* 23, no. 1: 49–70.

Pesquisa Nacional por Amostragem de Domicílio. 2009. Bahia: Instituto Brasileiro de Geografia e Estatística.

Pessar, Patricia R. 1995. "The Elusive Enclave: Ethnicity, Class and Nationality among Latino Entrepreneurs in Greater Washington, DC." *Human Organization* 54, no. 4: 383–92.

Pickel, Mary Lou. 2000. "Brazilians Catch Wave to Atlanta." *Atlanta Constitution*, September 18, p. B1.

Pinho, Ana Filipa Antunes. 2010. "Dos "Brasis" para os "Portugais": Trans-formações da emigração brasileira nos últimos 20 anos." In *1° seminário de estudos sobre imigração brasileira na Europa*, edited by Flávio Carvalho, Maria Badet Souza, Manuella Callou, and Mar Rubiralta, 197–204. Barcelona: Universitat de Barcelona.

Pinsky, Mark I. 1997. "Brazilian Rhythms Stirring Church Services in Orlando." *Orlando Sentinel*, September 27, p. 1.

Pinto, Rodrigo. 2012. "Is Brazil's Economic Growth Enough to Draw Emigrants Home?" BBC Brasil, March 6. http://www.bbc.co.uk/news/uk-17272698.

Piore, Michael J. 1979. *Birds of Passage: Migrant Labor and Industrial Societies*. New York: Cambridge University Press.

Pires, Bianka André. 2010. "Brasileirinhos em Barcelona: Resultados do processo de integração socioeducativa em verde, amarelo e vermelho." Paper presented at the meeting of the Brazilian Studies Association, Brasília, July 22–24.

Piscitelli, Adriana. 2008. "Transits: Brazilian Women Migration in the Context of the Transnationalization of the Sex and Marriage Markets." *Horizontes Antropológicos* 4:101–36.

———. 2009. "Migración y sexualidad: De Brasil a Europa." Paper presented at the Diálogo Latinoamericano sobre Sexualidad y Geopolítica, Observatorio de Sexualidad y Política, Rio de Janeiro, August 19.

———. 2011. "Actuar la *brasileñidad*? Tránsitos a partir del mercado del sexo." *Etnográfica* 15, no. 1: 5–29.

Porter, Eduardo, and Elizabeth Malkin. 2005. "Way North of the Border." *New York Times*, September 30, pp. C1–2.

Portes, Alejandro, ed. 1990. *The New Second Generation*. New York: Russell Sage Foundation.

Powell, Michael. 2005. "New Tack against Illegal Immigrants: Trespassing Charges." *Washington Post*, June 10, p. 1.

Prada, Paulo. 2010. "For Brazil It's Finally Tomorrow." *Wall Street Journal*, March 29.

Preston, Julia. 2011a. "Napolitano Accuses Critics of Politicizing Border Issues." *New York Times*, February 1, p. 17.

———. 2011b. "Resistance Widens to Obama Initiative on Criminal Immigrants." *New York Times*, August 13, pp. 11, 15.

Preston, Julia, and John H. Cushman Jr. 2012. "Obama to Permit Young Immigrants to Remain in U.S." *New York Times*, June 16, pp. 1, 16.

Raijman, Rebeca. 2001. "Mexican Immigrants and Informal Self-Employment in Chicago." *Human Organization* 60, no. 1: 47–55.

Rapoza, Kenneth. 2012a. "In Brazil: The Poor Get Richer Faster." *Forbes*, September 25.

———. 2012b. "Brazil Economy Not What It Once Was." *Forbes*, December 4.

Reel, Monte. 2006. "Losing Its Young to an American Dream." *Washington Post*, November 14, p. 22.

Resende, Rosana. 2002. "Tropical Brazucas: A Preliminary Study of Brazilians in South Florida." Paper presented at the mini-seminar Brazilians outside Brazil: Brasileiros Fora do Brasil, University of Miami, Coral Gables, April 5.

———. 2005. "Fragile Threads." *Hemisphere* 15 (Summer): 4–6.

———. 2009. "Tropical Brazucas: Brazilians in South Florida and the Imaginary of National Identity." PhD dissertation, University of Florida.

Rey, Valquíria. 2008a. "Fila para cidadania italiana tem 500 mil brasileiros." *O Globo*, March 25.

———. 2008b. "Goiana já levou mais de 50 parentes para a Itália." *O Globo*, March 26.

———. 2008c. "Paulistana troca faxinas por prostituição." BBC Brasil, March 27. http://www.bbc.co.uk/portuguese/reporterbbc/story/2008/03/080319_imigracaodomesticaprostituta.shtml.

Reynolds, Michael, Clifford Young, Jamie Shkolnik, and Michel Pergmit. 2000. "A Public Opinion Poll on Brazil's Image in the United States of America." Report submitted to the Brazilian Ministry of Foreign Relations. National Opinion Research Center (NORC), University of Chicago, Chicago.

Rezende, Claudia Barcellos. 2010. "Ver-se nos olhos do outro: Gênero, raça e identitidade brasileira no estrangeiro." *Travessia: Revista do Migrante* 66 (January–June): 65–76.

Ribeiro, Darcy. [1995] 2000. *The Brazilian People*. Translated by Gregory Rabassa. Gainesville: University Press of Florida.

Ribeiro, Gustavo Lins. 1996. "Brazilians Are Hot, Americans Are Cold: A Non-structuralist Approach to Brazilian Bodies and Culture in San Francisco." Paper presented at the meeting of the American Anthropological Association, San Francisco, November 20–24.

———. 1997. "Street Samba: Carnaval and Transnational Identities in San Francisco." Paper presented at the meeting of the Brazilian Studies Association, Washington, DC, November 13–15.

———. 1998. "Goiania, California: Vulnerabilidade, ambiguidade e cidadania transnacional." Série Antropologia 235, Departamento de Antropologia, Universidade de Brasília, Brasília.

———. 1999. "O que faz o Brasil, *Brazil*: Jogos identitários em San Francisco." In *Cenas do Brasil migrante*, edited by Rosana Rocha Reis and Teresa Sales, 45–85. São Paulo: Boitempo.

Ribeiro, Valéria. 2009. "Crise reduziu envio de recursos de imigrantes brasileiros para suas famílias." *Comunidade News*, June 25.

Riding, Alan. 1989. "Aloof Giant, Brazil Warms to Neighbors." *New York Times*, February 21, p. 15.

———. 1992. "Bedfellows with Spain, Lisbon Won't Cuddle." *New York Times*, June 14, p. 13.

Rocha, Cristina. 2006. "Two Faces of God: Religion and Social Class in the Brazilian Diaspora in Sydney." In *Relgious Pluralism in the Diaspora*, edited by R. Pratap Kumar, 147–60. Boston: Brill.

———. 2009. "Triangular Transnationalism: Japanese Brazilians on the Move between Japan, Australia and Brazil." Mimeo.

———. 2010. "Conexiones sur-sur: Vivir entre Australia y Brasil." In *Nuevos retos del transnacionalismo en el estudio de las migraciones*, edited by Carlota Solé, Sonia Parella, and Leonardo Cavalcanti, 115–29. Madrid: Ministerio de Trabajo e Inmigración.

Rodrigues, Alan, and Sonia Filgueiras. 2005. "Guerra ao tráfico humano." *Isto É*, March 9, p. 53.

Rodrigues, Donizete. 2010. "Brazilian Immigrants and Pentecostalism in New York City." Joint Brazil and Religion Seminar, Columbia University, April 12.

———. 2012. "The Brazilianization of New York City: Brazilian Immigrants and Evangelical Churches in a Pluralized Urban Landscape." In *Ecologies of Faith in New York City*, edited by Richard Cimino, Nadia A. Mian, and Weishan Huang, 120–41. Bloomington: Indiana University Press.

Rodrigues, Elsa. 2010. "Do *Brasil-Palhaço* ao *Portugal-Europa:* A importância do '*onde se vem*' na construção do '*para onde se vai*' nas estratégias de imigrantes femininas brasileiras em Portugal." In *1º seminário de estudos sobre imigração brasileira na Europa*, edited by Flávio Carvalho, Maria Badet Souza, Manuella Callou, and Mar Rubiralta, 129–36. Barcelona: Universitat de Barcelona.

Rodrigues, Francilene. 2006. "Migração transfronteiriça na Venezuela." *Estudos Avançados* 20, no. 57: 197–207.

Roett, Riordan. 2010. *The New Brazil*. Washington, DC: Brookings Institution Press.

Rogers, Tim. 2011. "Let Them In: How Brazilians Could Help the U.S. Economy." *Time*, June 3.

Rohter, Larry. 2001. "Local Cry: An Awful Lot of Brazilians in Paraguay." *New York Times*, June 12, p. 4.

———. 2002. "South American Trading Bloc Frees Movement of Its People." *New York Times*, November 24, p. 4.

———. 2005. "Brazilians Streaming into U.S. through Mexican Border." *New York Times*, June 30, p. 3.

———. 2012. *Brazil on the Rise: The Story of a Country Transformed*. New York: Palgrave Macmillan.

Romero, Simon. 2000. "Guyana: Caught in Brazil's Net?" *New York Times*, March 30, pp. C1, 4.

———. 2008. "In Babel of Tongues, Suriname Seeks Itself." *New York Times*, March 23, p. 10.

———. 2011. "Brazil's Long Shadow Vexes Some Neighbors." *New York Times*, November 4, p. 1.

———. 2012a. "A Forest under Siege in Paraguay." *New York Times*, March 25, pp. 8, 10.

———. 2012b. "Where Daniel the Cuckhold and Zig Zag Clown Vie for Office." *New York Times*, September 17, p. 6.

———. 2012c. "Brazil Registers Anemic Growth, Surprising Ecoomists." *New York Times*, December 1, p. 11.

Rossini, Rosa Ester. 1995. "O retorno as origens ou o sonho de encontro com o eldorado japonês: O exemplo dos dekassequis do Brasil em direção ao Japão." In *Emigração e imigração no Brasil contemporânea*, edited by Neide Lopes Patarra, 104–10. Campinas: Programa Interinstitucional de Avaliação e Acompanhamento das Migrações Internacionais no Brasil.

Roth, Joshua Hotaka. 2002. *Brokered Homeland: Japanese Brazilian Migrants in Japan*. Ithaca, NY: Cornell University Press.

Rouse, Roger. 1991. "Mexican Migration and the Social Space of Postmodernism." *Diaspora* 1:8–24.

Rygiel, Kim. 2010. "Mobile Bodies, Risky Subjects and the Securitized Citizen: Citizenship as Biopolitics." Paper presented at the Geographies of Risk Conference, University of Illinois, Urbana-Champaign, September 23–24.

Ryssdal, Kai. 2008. "Brazil's Expats See Value in Going Home." *Marketplace*, April 1. http://www.marketplace.org/topics/world/brazils-expats-see-value-going-home.

Sá, Natalia Coimbra de. 2009. "Brazilian day em Nova York: Primeiras notas." In *ECUS: Cadernos de pesquisa*, edited by Leonardo Boccia, 145–63. Salvador: Universidade Federal da Bahia.

Sacchetti, Maria. 2009. "Snapshot of 2 Immigrant Groups." *Boston Globe*, October 15.

Salariômetro. 2010. www.salariometro.sp.gov.br/.

Salek, Sylvia. 2002. "Imigrantes brasileiros trocam os EUA pela Grã-Bretanha." BBC Brasil, November 28. http://www.bbc.co.uk/portuguese/noticias/2002/021127_brasileiross.shtml.

Sales, Teresa. 1995. "O trabalhador brasileiro no contexto das novas migrações internacionais." In *Emigração e imigração no Brasil contemporânea*, edited by Neide Lopes Patarra, 90–103. Campinas: Programa Interinstitucional de Avaliação e Acompanhamento das Migrações Internacionais no Brasil.

———. 1996. "Migrações de fronteira entre o Brasil e os países do mercosul." *Revista Brasileira de Estudos de População* 13, no. 1: 87–98.

———. 1998a. "A legitimidade da condição clandestina." *Travessia: Revista do Migrante* 30 (January–April): 13–16.

———. 1998b. "Constructing an Ethnic Identity: Brazilian Immigrants in Boston, Mass." *Migration World* 26, no. 5: 15–21.

———. 1999a. "Pensando a terceira idade da primeira geração de imigrantes brasileiros nos Estados Unidos." *Travessia: Revista do Migrante* 35 (September–December): 32–36.

———. 1999b. "Identitidade étnica entre imigrantes brasileiros na região de Boston, EUA." In *Cenas do Brasil migrante*, edited by Rosana Rocha Reis and Teresa Sales, 15–44. São Paulo: Boitempo.

———. 2003. *Brazilians Away from Home*. New York: Center for Migration Studies.

———. 2007. "Second Generation Brazilian Immigrants in the United States." In *The Other Latinos: Central and South Americans in the United States*, edited by José Luis Falconi and José Antonio Mazzotti, 195–211. David Rockefeller Center Series on Latin American Studies. Cambridge, MA: Harvard University Press.

Sales, Teresa, and Márcia Loureiro. 2008. "Adolescent and Second Generation Brazilian Immigrants in Massachusetts." In *Becoming Brazuca: Brazilian Immigration to the United States*, edited by Clémence Jouët-Pastré and Leticia Braga, 287–311. David Rockefeller Center Series on Latin American Studies. Cambridge, MA: Harvard University Press.

Salgado, Eduardo. 2001. "Eles fogem da bagunça." *Veja*, July 18, pp. 94–100.

Salomon, Gisela, and Jenny Barchfield. 2012. "Brazil's New Consumer Class Flocks to U.S. to Shop." *Washington Times*, March 11.

Sanchez, Casey. 2008. "Brazil Nuts." Southern Poverty Law Center, no. 129. http://www.splcenter.org/get-informed/intelligence-report/browse-all-issues /2008/spring/brazil-nuts.

Santiago, Silviano. 1994. *Stella Manhattan*. Translated by George Yúdice. Durham, NC: Duke University Press.

Santos, Camila. 2006. "From the Land of Samba, a Stew of Memories." *New York Times*, May 21, p. D6.

Santos, Fernanda. 2006. "A Brazilian Outpost in Westchester." *New York Times*, June 26, pp. B1, 4.

———. 2008a. "A Populist Threat Confronts the U.S. Catholic Church." *New York Times*, April 20, pp. 33, 36.

———. 2008b. "A Police Effort to Improve Relations Starts with Language." *New York Times*, April 24, p. B5.

Sasaki, Elisa Massae. 1995. "Dekasseguis: Trabalhadores nipo-brasileiros no Japão." *Travessia: Revista do Migrante* 21 (January–April): 20–22.

———. 1996. "Os dekasseguis retornados." *Revista Brasileira de Estudos de População* 13, no. 1: 99–100.

———. 2006. "A Imigração para o Japão." *Estudos Avançados* 20, no. 57: 99–118.

———. 2009. "Ser ou não ser japonês? A construção da identidade dos brasileiros descendentes de japoneses no contexto das migrações internacionais do Japão contemporâneo." PhD dissertation, Universidade Estadual de Campinas, Campinas, São Paulo.

———. 2010. "Depois de duas décadas de movimento migratório entre o Brasil e o Japão." Paper presented at the seminar 20 anos dos Brasileiros no Japão, Universidade das Nações Unidas, Tokyo, July 30.

Scheller, Fernando. 2008a. "Entidades buscam alternativa para quem volta sem dinheiro." *O Globo*, March 26.

———. 2008b. "A importância do dinheiro do exterior para 'Valadólares.'" *O Globo*, March 25.

———. 2008c. "Foram os americanos que começaram." *O Globo*, March 25.

Schemo, Diana Jean. 1998. "Strains Seen as Brazilians Tighten Belts." *New York Times*, January 5, p. C16.

Schreiber, Angela. 2009. "Cresce número de brasileiros voltando para o Brasil." *Comunidade News*, November 16.

Scudeler, Cristina. 1999. "Imigrantes valadarenses no mercado de trabalho dos EUA." In *Cenas do Brasil migrante*, edited by Rosana Rocha Reis and Teresa Sales, 193–232. São Paulo: Boitempo.

Seccombe, Mike. 2011. "More Islanders, a Little Older, More Diverse." *Vineyard Gazette*, May 20, pp. 1, 6.

Sekles, Flavia. 1997. "Jeitinho brasileiro em Nova Iorque." *Jornal do Brasil*, February 16, p. 18.

Semple, Kirk. 2012. "For Many Immigrants' Children, American Dream Lies Abroad." *New York Times*, April 16, pp. 1, 3.

Shenon, Philip. 1997. "Judge Denounces U.S. Visa Policies Based on Race and Looks." *New York Times*, January 23, pp. 1, 9.

———. 1998. "State Department Illegally Denying Visas, Judge Says." *New York Times*, January 23, p. 1.

Sheringham, Olivia. 2009. "Ethnic Identity and Integration among Brazilians in Gort, Ireland." *Irish Migration Studies in Latin America* 7, no. 1: 93–104.

———. 2010a. "A Transnational Space? Transnational Practices, Place-Based Identity and the Making of 'Home' among Brazilians in Gort, Ireland." *Portuguese Studies* 26, no. 1: 60–78.

———. 2010b. "Religion across Borders: The Role of the Church in the Experience of Brazilian Migrants in London." In *1º seminário de estudos sobre imigração brasileira na Europa*, edited by Flávio Carvalho, Maria Badet Souza, Manuella Callou, and Mar Rubiralta, 186–95. Barcelona: Universitat de Barcelona.

Shirley, Robert W. 1999. "Brazilians." In *Encyclopedia of Canada's Peoples*, edited by Paul Robert Magocsi, 273–82. Toronto: University of Toronto Press.

Silva, Henrique M. 2003. "A colonização teuto-brasiguaia no oriente paraguaio: Meio ambiente, economia e condicionamento cultural numa fronteira binacional." PhD dissertation, Universidade Estadual de Maringá, Paraná.

Silver, Jim. 2005. "Portugal Dumps Brazil TV for Home-Grown Soap Operas." *Bloomberg*, December 15. http://www.bloomberg.com/apps/news?pid=news archive&sid=aRpl2JgGjs3E&refer=latin_america.

Sims, Calvin. 1995. "The South American Art of Name-Calling." *New York Times*, July 30, p. E4.

Siqueira, Carlos Eduardo, and Tiago Jansen. 2008. "Updating Demographic, Geographic and Occupational Data on Brazilians in Massachusetts." In *Becoming Brazuca: Brazilian Immigration to the United States*, edited by Clémence Jouët-Pastré and Leticia Braga, 105–24. David Rockefeller Center Series on Latin American Studies. Cambridge, MA: Harvard University Press.

Siqueira, Sueli. 2007. "Emigrantes empreendedores: Sucesso e insucessos no retorno ao Brasil." Paper presented at the meeting of the Latin American Studies Association, Montreal, September 5–8.

———. 2008. "Emigrants from the Micro-Region of Governador Valdadares in the USA: Return and Investing Project." In *Becoming Brazuca: Brazilian Immigration to the United States*, edited by Clémence Jouët-Pastré and Leticia Braga, 175–93. David Rockefeller Center Series on Latin American Studies. Cambridge, MA: Harvard University Press.

———. 2009a. "The Crisis and Return of Brazilian Emigrants to the Birthplace." Paper presented at the meeting of the Latin American Studies Association, Rio de Janeiro, June 11–14.

———. 2009b. *Sonhos, sucesso e frustrações na emigração de retorno*. Belo Horizonte: Argumentum.

———. 2011. "Imigração e retorno na perspectiva de gênero." In *Gênero, sexo, amor e dinheiro: Mobilidades transnacionais envolvendo o Brasil*, edited by Adriana Piscitelli, Gláucia de Oliveira Assis, and José Miguel Nieto Olivar, 435–59. Campinas: Núcleo de Estudos de Gênero, Universidade Estadual de Campinas.

Siqueira, Sueli, Gláucia de Oliveira Assis, and Emerson César de Campos. 2010. "Of the Place for the Global: Configuration of Transnational Flows Between Brazil and the United States." Paper presented at the meeting of the Latin American Studies Association, Toronto, October 6–9.

Skorczeski, Laura Aldea. 2009. "Ethnic Place Making: Thirty Years of Brazilian Immigration to South Framingham, Massachusetts." MS thesis, Portland State University, Portland, OR.

Smith, Tony. 2003. "In Brazil, All May Not Be as Relaxed as It Seems." *New York Times*, May 20, p. C8.

Soares, Carla Andrea. 1997. "As emigrações de cirugiões dentistas para Portugal." MA thesis, Universidade Estadual de Campinas, Campinas, São Paulo.

Soares, Weber. 1995a. "Ser valaderense: A conquista de nova posição no espaço social e a "(re)territorialização na origem." *Travessia: Revista do Migrante* 21 (January–April): 23–27.

———. 1995b. "Emigrantes e investidores: Redefinando a dinamica imobiliária na economia valadarense." MA thesis, Instituto de Pequisa e Planejamento Urbano e Regional, Universidade Federal do Rio de Janeiro, Rio de Janeiro.

———. 1999. "Emigração e (i)mobilidade residencial: Momentos de ruptura na reprodução/continuidade de segregação social no espaço urbano." In *Cenas do Brasil migrante*, edited by Rosana Rocha Reis and Teresa Sales, 167–93. São Paulo: Boitempo.

———. 2002. "Da metáfora à substância: Redes sociais, redes migratórias e migração nacional e internacional em Valadares e Ipatinga." PhD dissertation, Centro de Desenvolvimento e Planejamento Regional, Universidade Federal de Minas Gerais, Belo Horizonte.

Soliani, André. 2004. "Brasil e Suriname fazem pacto de imigração." *Sindicto Mercosul*, December 22.

Sotero, Paulo. 2006. "Brasileiros se mobilizam nos EUA." *O Estado de São Paulo*, April 23, p. C1.

Souza, Ana. 2010. "Language Choices: Portraits of Children's Identity Negotiations in a Brazilian Portuguese Community Language School." In *Multilingual Spaces: Complementary Schools in Contemporary Britain*, edited by V. Lytra and P. Martin, 97–107. London: Multilingual Matters.

Souza (Galvão), Heloisa. 1992. "Brazilian Neighborhoods in Boston." *Brazilian Monthly*, July, pp. 1, 3.

———. 2002. "Brazilians in Boston: Before and after 9/11." Paper presented at the symposium What about the Other Latinos? Central and South Americans in the United States, David Rockefeller Center for Latin American Studies, Harvard University, Cambridge, MA, March 18–19.

Sperandio, Marcelo. 2012. "Entrava dólar, agora sai real." *Veja*, April 25, p. 112.

Sprandel, Marcia Anita. 2006. "Migração transfronteiriça na Venuzuela." *Estudos Avançados* 20, no. 57: 137–55.

Stellin, Susan. 2011. "A Long Wait Gets Longer." *New York Times*, August 23, p. B4.

Strategier, Valerie. 2006. "Made in Brazil, Imagining America: Brazilian Immigrants in New York City." MA thesis, Utrecht University, The Netherlands.

Streitfeld, David. 2011. "Affluent Buyers Reviving Market for Miami Homes." *New York Times*, July 26, p. 1.

Suarez, Ana Veciana. 2003. "Brazilian Community Growing Strong in Broward." *Miami Herald*, April 9, p. 1.

Suwwan, Leila. 2005a. "Embaixador em NY, Júlio César Gomes dos Santos diz que imigrantes brasileiros nos EUA não devem se 'misturar.'" *Folha de São Paulo*, October 20.

———. 2005b. "Cônsul em Nova York se desculpa por chamar hispânicos de 'cucarachos.'" *Folha de São Paulo*, October 21.

Swift, Mike. 2002. "A Worldly Place: Flood of Immigrants Brings International Flavor, Age-Old Problems to Danbury." *Hartford Courant*, January 13.

Tabuchi, Hiroko. 2009. "Goodbye, Honored Guests." *New York Times*, April 23, pp. B1, 10.

Taylor, Paul, Mark Hugo Lopez, Jessica Hunter, and Gabriel Velasco. 2012. "When Labels Don't Fit: Hispanics and Their Views of Identity." Pew Research Center, April 4. http://www.pewhispanic.org/2012/04/04/when-labels-dont-fit-hispanics-and-their-views-of-identity/.

Tedesco, João Carlos. 2008. "Redes étnicas/informais e institucionais: Controle imigratório de brasileiros para a Itália." Paper presented at the conference Fazendo Gênero 8—Corpo, Violência e Poder, Florianópolis, August 25-28.

Teixeira, Rafael Tassi. 2007. "Éramos bossa nova hoje somos *sin papeles*: Transnacionalismo, pertencimento e identidade nas representações dos migrantes latino-americanos e brasileiros na Espanha." *Cadernos de campo* 16:45-54.

Thompson, Ginger. 2004. "Trying to Stop Surge of Illegal Migrants, Mexican Authorities Meet Them at the Airport." *New York Times*, August 8, p. 12.

3News Company. 2007. "Minister Worried about Brazilian Workers in Queenstown." 3News, August 3. http://www.3news.co.nz/tabid/419/Default.aspx?ArticleID=31905

Torresan, Angela Maria de Souza. 1994. "Quem parte, quem fica: Uma etnografia sobre imigrantes brasileiros em Londres." MA thesis, Museu Nacional, Universidade Federal do Rio de Janeiro, Rio de Janeiro.

———. 2006. "Emoções fora do lugar: Negociando amizade em Lisboa." In *Um mar de identidades: A imigração brasileira em Portugal*, edited by Igor José de Renó Machado, 189-228. São Paulo: Editora da Universidade Federal de São Carlos.

———. 2007. "How Privileged Are They? Middle-Class Brazilian Immigrants in Lisbon." In *Going First Class? New Approaches to Privileged Travel and Movement*, edited by Vered Amit, 103-25. London: Berghahn.

———. 2012. "A Middle Class Besieged: Brazilians' Motives to Migrate." *Journal of Latin American and Caribbean Anthropology* 17, no. 1: 110-30.

Tosta, Antonio. 2004. "Latino, *eu*? The Paradoxical Interplay of Identity in *Brazuca* Literature." *Hispania* 87, no. 3: 576-85.

Tota, Antonio Pedro. 2009. *The Seduction of Brazil: The Americanization of Brazil during World War II*. Translated by Lorena B. Ellis. Austin: University of Texas Press.

Trebat, Thomas. 2011. "New Approaches to Development." Seminar at the Bildner Center-CUNY, New York.

Tsuda, Takeyuki. 2001. "Reality versus Representations: Ethnic Essentialization and Tradition in Japanese Media Images of Japanese Brazilian Return Migrants." Paper presented at the meeting of the American Anthropological Association, Washington, DC, November 28–December 2.

———. 2002. "Crossing Ethnic Boundaries: Nikkejin Return Migrants and the Ethnic Challenge of Japan's Newest Immigrant Minority." Paper presented at the meeting of the American Anthropological Association, New Orleans, November 20–24.

————. 2003. *Strangers in the Ethnic Homeland.* New York: Columbia University Press.

————. 2004. "No Place to Call Home." *Natural History,* April, pp. 50–55.

TV Globo. 2012a. "Brasileiros que moram no exterior podem sofrer da síndrome do regresso." TV Globo, March 14. http://globotv.globo.com/globo-news /jornal-globo-news/v/brasileiros-que-moram-no-exterior-podem-sofrer-da-sindrome-do-regresso/1856107/.

————. 2012b. "A volta dos brasileiros que moravam no exterior." TV Globo, April 17. http://globotv.globo.com/rede-globo/profissao-reporter/v/a-volta-dos-brasileiros-que-moravam-no-exterior-parte-1/1908007/.

U.S. Census Bureau. 2006. Standards for the Classification of Federal Data on Race and Ethnicity. Washington, DC. http://www.census.gov/population/socdemo /race/fr28au95.

U S. Department of Homeland Security. 2005. Immigration Monthly Statistical Report. Washington, DC.

Vásquez, Manuel A. 2009. "Beyond *Homo Anomicus*: Interpersonal Networks, Space and Religion among Brazilians in Broward County." In *A Place to Be: Brazilian, Guatemalan, and Mexican Immigrants in Florida's New Destinations,* edited by Phillip J. Wlliams, Timothy J. Steigenga, and Manuel A. Vásquez, 33–56. New Brunswick, NJ: Rutgers Univerity Press.

Vásquez, Manuel A., Lúcia Ribeiro, and José Claudio S. Alves. 2008. "Congregations as Spaces of Empowerment and Disempowerment among Brazilians in the New South." Paper presented at Brazilian-Americans in Georgia and Beyond: A Multi-Disciplnary Symposium, University of Georgia and Georgia State University, Athens and Atlanta, GA, April 25–26.

Veja. 1995. "Os preços muito loucos da era do real." *Veja,* July 19, pp. 18–24.

Wagner, Carlos. 1990. *Brasiguaios: Homens sem patria.* Petrópolis, Rio de Janeiro: Vozes.

Wehrfritz, George, and Hideko Takayama. 2000. "A New Open Door Policy?" *Newsweek,* June 5, pp. 26–31.

Weiden, Fernanda. 2011. "E se Lula criasse a secretaria da emigração?" *Estado do Emigrante,* May 5. http://www.estadodoemigrante.org/noticias/eselulacriassea secretariadaemigracao.

Weisman, Jonathan. 2012. "I.R.S. May Look Hard at Expats." *New York Times,* May 18, p. 20.

Whitaker, Bill. 2012. "Facebook Co-founder Renounces U.S. Citizenship, Draws Heat." *CBS This Morning,* May 14.

White, Cassandra. 2008. "Concepts of Class and Citizenship in Atlanta." Paper presented at the meeting of the Brazilian Studies Association, New Orleans, March 27–29.

Whitefield, Mimi. 2011. "Brazilians Making an Economic Mark." *Miami Herald,* February 14.

Wilson, John F., James Diego Hay, and Maxine L. Margolis. 1989. "The Bi-National Frontier of Eastern Paraguay." In *The Human Ecology of Tropical Land Settlement in Latin America*, edited by Debra A. Schumann and William L. Partridge, 199–237. Boulder, CO: Westview.

Wilson, Richard A. 1995. "Shifting Frontiers: Historical Transformations of Identities in Latin America." *Bulletin of Latin American Research* 14, no. 1: 1–8.

Wong, Bernard P. 1997. "Transnationalism and New Chinese Immigrant Families in the U.S." Paper presented at the meeting of the American Anthropological Association, Washington, DC, November 19–23.

Wooldridge, Frosty. 2006. "Mestizos Threaten Massachusetts." *National Vanguard*, March 2. http://www.solargeneral.com/mirrors/national-vanguard /www.nationalvanguard.org/story015a.html?id=8113.

Yamada, Mutsuo, ed. 2003. *Emigración latinoamericana: Comparación inter-regional entre América del Norte, Europa y Japón.* JCAS Symposium Series 19. Japan Center for Area Studies. Osaka: National Museum of Ethnology.

Yamanaka, Keiko. 1993. "New Immigration Policy and Unskilled Foreign Workers in Japan." *Pacific Affairs* 66:72–90.

———. 1996a. "Return Migration of Japanese-Brazilians to Japan: The Nikkeijin as Ethnic Minority and Political Construct." *Diaspora* 5, no. 1: 65–97.

———. 1996b. "Factory Workers and Convalescent Attendants: Japanese-Brazilian Migrant Women and Their Families in Japan." In *International Female Migration and Japan: Networking, Settlement and Human Rights*, 87–116. Tokyo: International Peace Research Institute.

———. 1997. "Return Migration of Japanese Brazilian Women: Household Strategies and the Search for the 'Homeland.'" In *Beyond Boundaries: Selected Papers on Refugeees and Immigrants*, vol. 5, edited by Diane Baxter and Ruth Krulfeld, 11–34. Arlington, VA: American Anthropological Association.

Zanin, Valter. 2010. "Inserção sócioprofissional dos imigrantes brasileiros e ítalo-brasileiros no mercado de trabalho na Itália: Estudo comparativo." In *1° seminário de estudos sobre imigração brasileira na Europa*, edited by Flávio Carvalho, Maria Badet Souza, Manuella Callou, and Mar Rubiralta, 215–20. Barcelona: Universitat de Barcelona.

Index

Note: *Italicized page numbers refer to tables.*